IN ONE NEWSPAPER

IN ONE NEWSPAPER
A Chronicle of Unforgettable Years

Ilya Ehrenburg
and
Konstantin Simonov

Translator
Anatol Kagan

SPHINX PRESS, INC.
NEW YORK

The Publisher wishes to thank Mr. Georgi Isachenko of Novosti Press for suggesting the publication of this book and for his assistance, which was essential for its successful completion.

D764
E733
1985

Copyright © 1985 Sphinx Press, Inc.

All rights reserved. No part of this book may be reproduced by any means, nor translated into a machine language without the written permission of the publisher.

Library of Congress Cataloging in Publication Data

Ehrenburg, Il, ia, 1891-1967.
   In one newspaper.

   Contains articles appearing in Krasnaia zvezda from 1941-1945.
   1. World War, 1939-1945—Soviet Union—Addresses, essays, lectures. 2. World War, 1949-1945—Campaigns—Eastern—Addresses, essays, lectures. 3. Soviet Union—History—German occupation, 1941-1944—Addresses, essays, lectures. I. Simonov, Konstantin Mikhaïlovich, 1915-   . II. Krasnaia zvezda. III. Title.
D764.E733   1983   940.53'47   83-12392

ISBN 0-8236-8655-8

Manufactured in the United States of America

IN ONE NEWSPAPER

Konstantin Simonov

Ilya Ehrenburg

CONTENTS

A Chronicle of Unforgettable Days
  L. Lazarev — xiii
TO THE READERS—*Konstantin Simonov* — 1
1941 (poem)—*Konstantin Simonov* — 9

THE WAR IN PHOTOGRAPHS

1941

1941 (poem)—*Ilya Ehrenburg* — 43
COVER UNITS—*Konstantin Simonov* — 45
COALITION OF FREEDOM—*Ilya Ehrenburg* — 51
JULY 28, 1941—*Ilya Ehrenburg* — 55
AT RUMANIAN SHORES—*Konstantin Simonov* — 61
OCTOBER 4, 1941—*Ilya Ehrenburg* — 67
OCTOBER 25, 1941—*Ilya Ehrenburg* — 73
TO THE CZECHOSLOVAKS—*Ilya Ehrenburg* — 79
NOVEMBER 6, 1941—*Ilya Ehrenburg* — 81
ON THE NIGHT OF THE ANNIVERSARY
  Konstantin Simonov — 85
PURSUER OF PURSUERS—*Konstantin Simonov* — 93
JUNE–DECEMBER—*Konstantin Simonov* — 99

CONTENTS

1942

1942 (poem)—*Ilya Ehrenburg*	113
MOZHAISK HAS BEEN RECAPTURED *Ilya Ehrenburg*	115
IN THE QUARRIES OF KERCH *Konstantin Simonov*	119
APRIL 20, 1942—*Ilya Ehrenburg*	139
ABOUT HATRED—*Ilya Ehrenburg*	143
THE ANNIVERSARY—*Konstantin Simonov*	151
A RUSSIAN HEART—*Konstantin Simonov*	161
ON PATRIOTISM—*Ilya Ehrenburg*	171
JULY 28, 1942—*Ilya Ehrenburg*	179
THE THIRD ANNIVERSARY—*Ilya Ehrenburg*	185
SOLDIER'S GLORY—*Konstantin Simonov*	191
DAYS AND NIGHTS—*Konstantin Simonov*	203
"RUSSIAN PLYWOOD"—*Konstantin Simonov*	215
LIGHT IN THE DUGOUT—*Ilya Ehrenburg*	225
DECEMBER NOTES—*Konstantin Simonov*	233

1943

1943 (poem)—*Konstantin Simonov*	247
January 14, 1943—*Ilya Ehrenburg*	249
IN THE WINTER OF 'FORTY-THREE *Konstantin Simonov*	255
DO AS I DO!—*Konstantin Simonov*	265
ON THE OLD SMOLENSK HIGHWAY *Konstantin Simonov*	281
THE FATE OF EUROPE—*Ilya Ehrenburg*	291
OBSTINATE EUROPE—*Ilya Ehrenburg*	301
IN THE DISTRICT OF PONYRY *Konstantin Simonov*	309
AUGUST 13, 1943—*Ilya Ehrenburg*	329
DRIVING OUT THE ENEMY—*Ilya Ehrenburg*	335
THE LABORERS OF VICTORY—*Ilya Ehrenburg*	343
THE NEW BROTHERHOOD—*Ilya Ehrenburg*	349
THE SOUL OF RUSSIA—*Ilya Ehrenburg*	353

CONTENTS

1944

1944 (poem)—*Ilya Ehrenburg*	367
FEBRUARY 21, 1944—*Ilya Ehrenburg*	369
DELAYED IN DELIVERY . . .—*Konstantin Simonov*	377
THE SIEGE OF TERNOPOL—*Konstantin Simonov*	383
JULY 23, 1944—*Ilya Ehrenburg*	395
AUGUST 10, 1944—*Ilya Ehrenburg*	401
EXTERMINATION CAMP—*Konstantin Simonov*	405
SERGEANT-MAJOR YERESHCHENKO *Konstantin Simonov*	431

1945

1945 (poem)—*Konstantin Simonov*	441
JANUARY 24, 1945—*Ilya Ehrenburg*	443
IN THE HIGH TATRA MOUNTAINS *Konstantin Simonov*	449
APRIL 27, 1945—*Ilya Ehrenburg*	479
JUNE 16, 1945—*Ilya Ehrenburg*	485
LESSONS FOR THE FUTURE—*Konstantin Simonov*	493

A CHRONICLE OF UNFORGETTABLE DAYS

In 1943, at the very height of the war, Ilya Ehrenburg remarked in an article entitled "The Role of the Writer:"

"Writers have brought their voices to the newspaper as a speaker would mount a rostrum; this is not their work desk, not their regular habitat. But neither is the dugout the regular habitat of the steelworker or the gardener. War uproots people and hearts. In peacetime the newspaper is a supplier of information, but in wartime the newspaper becomes the very air one breathes. The newspaper becomes a letter addressed to you personally, and people open the newspaper before they open a letter from a friend, for their fate is tied up with what is printed in the newspaper."

Such was the wartime newspaper—thanks largely to the writers who contributed to it. In those years the newspaper became the basic medium between the writer and the reader, and it was also the most influential catalyst of the literary process. Almost everything that has been created during the war by writers—epic and lyrical poems, plays and stories—saw the light of day in the newspaper column. Of course, the union of the writer and the newspaper was born of the newspaper's need for the writer's pen and the writer's word, but as this union became established and customary it could not help turning into a union with literature as well. Even the traditional newspaper genres whose purpose is to illuminate the current day's news—reportage and pieces on public affairs (and these, naturally, obtained the widest dissemination and were the ones most often referred to)—even these genres took on the quality and the virtues of belles lettres, including their permanence, if they were written by a gifted artist.

Much of what was hurriedly written in the wartime years for tomorrow's paper has preserved its vital strength today. There is nothing surprising in this if we recall that such major artists as Aleksei Tolstoy and Mikhail Sholokhov, Ilya Ehrenburg and Konstantin Simonov, Aleksandr Tvardovsky and Nikolai Tikhonov, Andrei Platonov and Vassili Grossman, Vsevolod Vishnevsky and Boris Gorbatov were among the permanent correspondents of wartime newspapers. These and many other talented writers worked at one time or another for the main Army newspaper *Red Star* which was popular among readers both at home and at the Front, due in no small measure to its becoming the most "literary" newspaper of that era.

Possibly more than one volume could be compiled from the feature stories and articles produced on *Red Star*'s pages. Unfortunately, one cannot contain the boundless, and so for this book we have selected the work of two authors only—Konstantin Simonov and Ilya Ehrenburg. However, this very limitation gives us the chance to present their creative work of the war years more fully, and to highlight the special qualities of each man's outstanding talent, revealed so brightly during that brief period.

What, then, determined our choice? There is something these two writers shared in common, despite the fact that they belonged to different generations and had different life experiences and a different aesthetic outlook. Their fellow-editor, the poet Aleksei Surkov, reminisces about this: "Ehrenburg was the oldest among us in respect to age and to literary and life experience, being over fifty at that time. But although we all worked whole-heartedly and selflessly, not one of us, except perhaps young Simonov, could equal this old 'newspaper wolf' in inexhaustible energy." In fact, none of the Soviet writers —Surkov did not place these two names together by accident—wrote as much during the war as Ehrenburg and Simonov, nor did any other writer appear in print as often as they did.

It is characteristic that when in one of his dispatches Ehrenburg devoted a paragraph to the work of *Red Star*, Simonov was the only war correspondent he named. "Three girls are deciphering telegrams from war correspondents: 'Crimea, Donbas, Murmansk: Enemy battalion destroyed . . . heavy losses inflicted.' The poet Simonov is the war correspondent. He has just returned from the Front. During the winter he had been to both Murmansk and Kerch, he has sailed in a submarine to the shores of Rumania, and had his face frostbitten in a plane." This was written in April 1942; more than three-and-a-half years of war still lay ahead, and Simonov would have to go out on assignments many more times to different parts of a Front that stretched from the Black Sea to the Barents Sea. I shall not enumerate the places he went to, for it would make too long a recital. Besides, there is no particular need for this, since the reader will get the picture from the Simonov feature stories selected for this edition.

What has been written by each of them—Simonov and Ehrenburg—is a fresco composed of feature stories and articles depicting the events of four long years of the cruel war against Fascism. The contributions of both writers supplement each other and, placed side by side, they present a stereoscopic view of the People's War.

Ehrenburg is chiefly a pamphleteer, his main genre is the article. Simonov's favorite genre is the feature story, his articles (very few) represent essentially a series of essay-sketches, linked together by war news or lyrical digressions. Ehrenburg rarely describes something for its own sake. For example, if he makes use of a landscape, then it will be as a rule in the capacity of a symbol. His own impressions and observations—and as a civilian he traveled repeatedly to the Front (it rarely happened that he traveled with Simonov, although they, or rather their writings, frequently "met" on the newspaper page)—form part of the artistic fabric on equal terms with actual letters, documents, quotations from newspapers, evidence of witnesses, testimony of prisoners-of-war, etc. A contrasting comparison, a sharply stressed transition from a particular detail which, however, strikes the imagination towards a generalization; from merciless irony to heartfelt tenderness; from angry invective to an inspiring call—this is what distinguishes Ehrenburg's style, this is how the lyrical stress, peculiar to his talent, reveals itself in his articles. I remind you that Ehrenburg is a poet.

Simonov is also a poet, but of a different mold—he always gravitated towards poems with a plot. In his feature stories he usually depicts what he saw with his own eyes, he shares what he experienced himself, or he tells the story of some person with whom the war had brought him together. There is always a narrative subject in his feature stories and they often resemble short stories. In his essays we find without fail a psychological portrait of the hero—say, an ordinary frontline soldier or officer—which reflects the conditions of life that have formed his character, or describes in detail the battle in which the hero has distinguished himself. Simonov's task is to reveal what used to be called the "spirit of the Army" in olden days—this is why his writing is built on a detailed description of what the soldier or officer had to endure, how he marched in the bone-penetrating cold or rain through impassable mud along the endless roads of the Front, how he pushed skidding vehicles and dragged along solidly stuck cannons; how he lit up the last pinch of shag mixed with crumbs, or chewed an accidentally preserved biscuit—how many a day there was nothing to eat or to smoke: either the Rear could not keep up with supplies due to the lack of passable roads, or the field kitchen and the master sergeant's car had been blown up somewhere on the way to the forward position; how he ran across an open space under mortar fire, with shells bursting ahead and behind him, feeling with his whole body that the next mortar shell would hit him, or how when overcoming that dull emptiness in his chest, he came up to meet machine-gun fire and the last assault on the enemy's trenches.

Brought together under one cover Ehrenburg's articles on public affairs and Simonov's feature stories seemed to call for a "montage," for they presented the war at two levels—the close-up and the overall aspect. They conducted the "shooting" in those fiery days from two different positions: one worked at close range, where all details of what was happening were precisely stated and which became diffused as one stepped a little further back; the other worked from a distance, where the strategic factors were clearly seen and the connection between events, impossible to discern from close range, were revealed. The reader will immediately see the mutually supplementary advantages of each of these levels of observation. Simonov tells of what was happening in the forward positions, conducting his reportage from trenches, a tank, a torpedo boat, an aircraft, a submarine. Ehrenburg lends his ear to the march of history, his attention is concentrated on the relationship between nations and governments, he is interested in the clash of political doctrines and moral principles.

A special place is occupied by those articles which Ehrenburg wrote for foreign publications (the reader will discover these articles without difficulty: they have no titles and we placed the date of writing at the head of the pieces); he usually wrote them late at night in his editorial office at the *Red Star*, when the work on the next issue of the newspaper was being completed. The manuscripts of these articles were discovered after Ehrenburg's death, and they received their first publication in Russian a few years ago in the book entitled, *Chronicle of Courage*. In these articles the writer strove to tell the foreign reader who had gleaned most of his information on life in the Soviet Union from frankly anti-Soviet publications or, in the best cases, from those which were fairly far removed from us in their views, about the truth about Russian history, about the many-centuries-old Russian culture, and about the building of Socialism and the Soviet way of life. Such accounts very often contained hidden or direct polemics directed toward those who depicted the Soviet Union as a barbarous country with Asiatic customs and an antedeluvian way of life, and the Soviet people as ignorant and downtrodden, deprived of initiative and self-respect. Almost the central place in Ehrenburg's articles of 1942 and 1943 is occupied by the question of the Second Front, the sorest problem in the relationship with the Allies: the author makes it clear to foreign readers in the most unambiguous manner that certain political and military leaders of Western nations were impeding and sabotaging the landing of armies on the French coast, that they were not discharging their duty as Allies, that their deliberate dilatoriness was delaying the rout of Hitlerite Germany and the liberation of the peoples of Europe from the Fascist yoke. Ehrenburg says plainly, without any diplomatic beating around the bush, that foreign propaganda often greatly exaggerated the military efforts of the Allies and the size of their supplies to the Soviet Union. He continually stresses that the Soviet people were carrying the main brunt of the struggle with Fascism, that the contribution of the Allies did not correspond to their abilities and could not in any way be compared with those sacrifices which the Soviet people were placing on the altar of victory over the common enemy.

Simonov's feature stories and Ehrenburg's articles on foreign and public affairs have been arranged in this book in a general time sequence corresponding to their dates of publication, which coincides with the respective times of writing, with one exception: Simonov's feature story, "In the High Tatra Mountains," written in February 1945, was printed in December, but its place in the book was determined by the date it was written. Two items which complete the book were written after victory—Ehrenburg's article of June 16, 1945, and Simonov's address at the United Nations meeting in San Francisco (incidentally, in the summer of 1946 Simonov and Ehrenburg traveled together to the United States); but these pieces dealt with some results of the recently terminated war, about its lasting lessons and the struggle with Fascist ideology, which must not cease after the smashing of Hitlerite Germany. It is this theme which makes this postwar material a legitimate finale to the publicist narrative of the Great Patriotic War.

Both writers—Konstantin Simonov as well as Ilya Ehrenburg—when later reprinting their newspaper correspondence of the war years—invariably indicated the respective dates of writing. It was not accidental that they accorded a special importance to this: their articles and feature stories reflected the events of a fast-flowing time, and in order to fully understand the problems dealt with therein and their principal motivation, it was necessary to know the respective time of writing. Such chronological structure reveals yet another quality of these contributions: brought together in one collection, they are perceived as an artistic chronicle, a chronicle of the Great Patriotic War—a chronicle of sorrow and courage, of severe trials and exalted bravery.

This is a chronicle of its own kind: it lacks the impassivity and calmness which is considered proper—as is customarily thought—for this kind of narrative; it was created by people who felt from the first to the last day of the war as soldiers, participants in a great and just battle with Fascism, people for whom words of truth were a weapon to strike down the enemy. This is how what they wrote was perceived by the readers at that time.

I would like to quote the words spoken by Simonov at the very end of the war, forty years ago—they helped to underscore the pathos of this book. Spiritual force—Konstantin Simonov wrote at that time—was possessed not only by the heroes who fought at the Front and to whom poems and feature articles, stories, and plays have been devoted, but that force was also possessed by the people of the arts who write these poems and tales, feature stories and articles: "They, too, did not bow down, they also fought, they were also strong in spirit;" "during the most difficult days the people in our profession, together with the Army, the Party, and the whole nation, had faith unanimously and unwaveringly in victory." These words, in full measure, relate to both authors of this book: Konstantin Simonov and Ilya Ehrenburg.

And there is something else that needs to be said . . .

In September of 1978, Konstantin Simonov wrote in his address to the readers of the first Russian edition of the book *In One Newspaper:*

"Of the two authors of this book who used to work in the *Red Star* newspaper, I am the only one alive today.

"So, as the only survivor, I must tell the others of the past."

In a year, Konstantin Simonov, too, passed away.

UNFORGETTABLE DAYS

This collection of the war-time feature stories and articles was the last one to be published in his lifetime. This book, for some particular reasons, was very dear to him. When he received the book, Simonov wrote a letter to the publishers expressing his gratitude for their idea of publishing, under one cover, the war-time essays and articles written by Ehrenburg and himself . . .

Since Simonov thought it his duty to dedicate a chapter of the book to Ilya Ehrenburg it is imperative, now that the American edition is about to be published, to tell you a few words about Simonov himself.

The significance of Konstantin Simonov's poems, essays, stories, and plays in the spiritual life of our people during the war is well known. They were on a par with the literary masterpieces that will always remain in the memory of his contemporaries. They have become as distinctive a feature of those hard times, as the voice of the Moscow Radio announcer, Yuri Levitan, who broadcast alarming communiques of the Sovinform-bureau and victorious orders, as a grave melody of the 'Sacred War' songs, or as the names of the famous battles and glorious chief commanders.

Later, during the post-war years, everything that Konstantin Simonov wrote—in verse, prose, for the theater, or the film—was related to the war. The Great Patriotic War was not only the main subject of his creative activity but also the very substance of his whole life; the subject of his constant and haunting thoughts. His most important creations were associated with these most difficult times that were full of people's sufferings; he tested the events of peace-time as well as many human qualities on the basis of his demanding experience as a soldier; he measured all these by the standards of far away 1941, the year that "is for ever cut" into the memory of several generations.

In the evening of his life, defining the life program

that he adhered to consistently and strictly, Simonov wrote to one of his correspondents:

"The social activity that I am engaged in, is directly related to my work as a writer and to my personal life experience. Several years ago I made my final choice when I decided, until my very last day, to use all of my remaining physical power, first of all, to write and tell the truth about the war, to the best of my abilities and understanding; secondly, as best as I can, to prevent lies from being said and written about the war; thirdly, to try to present the role of the rank and file who bore the main burden of the war on their shoulders in its true tragic light for posterity. And, finally, I regard it as my personal duty, whenever I come across instances of injustice, whether occurring today or having occurred in the past, toward any participants of the war, to do every thing I can to correct these wrongs, either myself or with the assistance of others.

"All of the above—the first, the second, the third and the fourth—are tied up in one knot. This is what I am busy with, and this is my life goal."

Indeed, his days and all his creative activity were filled with this goal for many years. Even when he thought of his approaching death, being engrossed in these sad thoughts, he always returned to his nation's great war.

As he requested in his will, his ashes were dispersed over the Bujnichisky field near Mogilev where, back in July of 1941, he saw our infantry men and artillery men meeting their death, making it impossible for the German tanks to pass through. It was a miracle he came out alive. And throughout his later years, he felt inseparable from those who met their death on the battle field, just as he might have done, those whose destiny failed to provide them with the post-war life. His ashes were finally mixed with those of the dead who gave their lives for their Motherland in 1941. He was reunited with them—for ever.

TO THE READERS

Of the two authors of this book who once worked together on the *Red Star* newspaper, only I am alive today. And I, as the one who stayed behind, must speak about the departed. If I were to try to sum up the main thing about Ilya Ehrenburg's wartime writings, then it is my deep conviction that he did and wrote more at that time than all the rest of us.

This thought is not just today's thought, and not just my thought. It was shared both by Ehrenburg's literary colleagues, and what is more important, by his readers, who also were fighting Fascism. At the height of the war I expressed the above thoughts in terms of that time on the pages of the newspaper, *Literature and Art*. Here it is, that small article, printed on May 6, 1944:

"I have been told by people who can be trusted that in one of the large partisan detachments a handwritten order to the troops contained the following item:

KONSTANTIN SIMONOV

After they have been read, all newspapers are to be used for making cigarettes, except Ehrenburg's articles.

"This is truly the shortest and most satisfying review for a writer's heart that I ever heard of.

"When one thinks about Ehrenburg, it is necessary to say about him simply, first of all, that he was adopted by our Army, and although this simile did not originate with me, I would like to repeat it, since it is exact to the nth degree. This is precisely what he was: adopted.

"Some time ago (I think it was early last year), a creative conference was held in the Writer's Union at which was discussed at great length the question of what the Soviet reader needed most during wartime—profound, extensive works, or the daily newspaper and magazine articles of writers who strove to give an immediate answer to what seemed to him the important questions of the day. Since the supporters of each theory were inclined, in the first place, to raise the question of 'either/or' to a high-principled level, they tended to make one forget the simple fact that nobody prohibited the writer from occupying himself simultaneously with both concerns; secondly, by emphasizing the profundity and extent of their works, they attempted to camouflage the fact that they worked slowly, badly, and unprofessionally; while others, asserting that superficial comments on events was all that people demanded from them, often pretended that they did not want to create anything profound and serious when, in fact, they quite simply did not know how to do it.

"The name of Ehrenburg was often used in that contrived discussion, although he had nothing to do with it. Moreover, all his wartime work speaks of the unsuitability of such a discussion. In fact, whenever there is talk about the profundity, seriousness, and importance of what the writer writes, I always want to ask the question: what is meant by profundity and importance; of what does it consist?

TO THE READERS

"The Tsar's cannon is, as of now, obviously still the largest cannon in Russia; however, does it follow therefrom that no weapon excels it in fire power? Must it be reckoned that the profundity and importance of a work is determined by its, so to speak, caliber, if by caliber one means the number of printed pages contained therein or the amount of time spent by the writer in creating that work? Should the stylistic complexity or the number of people or events described in a work be the basis of its profundity and importance?

"It seems to me that as the effectiveness of artillery is not determined by the impressiveness of its outward appearance, so the profundity of a work is determined not by the author's desire to write a profound and important work, but by the effect of that work upon its readers—by the depth of its influence on people's feelings, and the reflected depth of those feelings in people's souls after they have read it. Simple aesthetic delight, even of a very high quality, does not bear witness to the profundity of the writer's influence, but if people read and weep, read and laugh, read and despise, read and hate, and if these feelings aroused within quite different people of different upbringing, education, and cast of soul become general feelings, then that work will be profound and important, despite the fact that it is measured not by volumes but by two newspaper columns which took only an hour and a half to write and which were typed directly for that day's newspaper.

"It is self-evident that all that has been said above is directly relevant to Ehrenburg. I do not wish to be misunderstood: I am not concerned here with championing the newspaper page, the newspaper article, and the feuilleton as against the novel, the story, and the tale. It is just as axiomatic for me as for everyone else that all genres are good. But this rule is often incorrectly interpreted here, and when speaking about equality, it is always thought necessary to defend the novel, or the tale, or the story, while sometimes the newspaper feuilleton is just as entitled to aspire to that equality, and also needs to be defended.

"The best contributions among the articles Ehrenburg has written during the war for our newspapers are profound and important. I am convinced that they are more profound and important than many other tales and stories which were written during the war; in comparing and arguing on these grounds one must consider length. Here one can appeal only to the soul of the reader, and it would of course be only good fortune if we could read a novel which would produce such a profound and striking impression on the readers' souls as one hundred lines of Ehrenburg's article 'To Withstand,' or his article 'Kiev,' or his article 'Kill'—such a novel would then be considered a classical work.

"What do I want to say by this comparison? Only that Ehrenburg's best articles written during the Patriotic War are superb examples of Russian writing on public affairs and of the Russian pamphlet by the power of their influence and their true depth. There are writers with an inexhaustible inventive ability—they are good writers. There are writers with an inexhaustible heart—they are good writers. Ehrenburg is a writer with an inexhaustible heart. Yes, having read through hundreds of his pamphlets and articles, we can find not a few stylistic coincidences, paragraphs resembling one another, comparisons and assimilations to which we have already become accustomed from him. But the angry and, at the same time, kind heart of the writer is inexhaustible. It is inexhaustible in respect to what it wants and what it demands, to what it loves and what it hates.

"Last autumn I had to travel with Ehrenburg to the Central Front. An elderly, extremely 'civilian' man in a baggy brown overcoat, a civilian fur hat, and a cigar in

TO THE READERS

his mouth, he traveled in a mud-splashed Jeep along muddy Front-line roads riddled by shellholes in the zone adjoining the Front. He walked unhurriedly about the forward positions, slightly hunched, talking in a soft voice and not trying to conceal for one second the fact that he was profoundly 'civilian.' But this civilian was adopted by the Army as a warrior, and if an inquiry should be made among all those who fought at the Front in these days—everyone from a general to the last transport driver who jogged along the road in his horsedrawn gig—I am certain that not one person would be found among them who did not know or has not read Ehrenburg. Not everyone understood the references in his articles to the chimeras of Notre Dâme de Paris, or Ariadne's thread, or Proserpine, but everybody knew what love for one's people was, and everyone understood what hatred for the Hitlerites was. While the style of Ehrenburg's articles might not appeal to every soldier, their force reached everyone because no matter how much Ehrenburg wrote he was never stingy, he always shared his heart with the reader, and the reader always felt this. And when Ehrenburg wrote daily, especially during the grave days, his articles were looked forward to and read every day, his writings seemed monotonous only to critics and to people satiated with literature who looked for the repetitions in his epithets and metaphors; but the soldiers and the officers took these writings every day as spiritual food, and it was precisely every day that this spiritual food was needed by them. They loved their Motherland, they hated the Fascists, they went into battle, and this happened every day. And Ehrenburg's next article, invaluable for the soul, formed part of that day, it animated them, it armed them.

"Some day a book will be composed from the best of Ehrenburg's articles written during the war which will be studied in schools as an example of noble and passionate

KONSTANTIN SIMONOV

Russian writing on public affairs. May we all now, or many years from now, write our novels, tales, and stories in other genres which will tell about that war in a different manner, but with the same profundity.

"When a writer-colleague is rewarded for high merit in the service of the Motherland, it generates a feeling of pride for one's profession. When Ehrenburg was rewarded, one felt particularly good and joyful; a man had been rewarded who—I am convinced of this—had worked during the most bitter years of the war harder, more selflessly, and better than all of us. Honor and praise to him for that!"

Remembering those years today, there is nothing for me to add to what I said at the time . . .

Konstantin Simonov
September 1978

1941

That longest day of the year
With its cloudless skies
Brought with it for all of us
Four years of terrible misfortune.

Its heavy footprint
Pressed so many on the ground
That after twenty years,
    thirty years,
Those alive still cannot believe they are alive.

                                              K. Simonov
                                               1945

KONSTANTIN SIMONOV

These are the covers of just some of the wartime books by Konstantin Simonov and Ilya Ehrenburg. They wrote many more during those years: according to general acknowledgment, they were the most effective and the most active working war correspondents. While contributing continuously to *Red Star*, Simonov and Ehrenburg also had their writings printed in *Pravda*, *Izvestia*, and in many magazines, and they also wrote for foreign newspapers. Aside from poems, plays, and the tale "Days and Nights,"

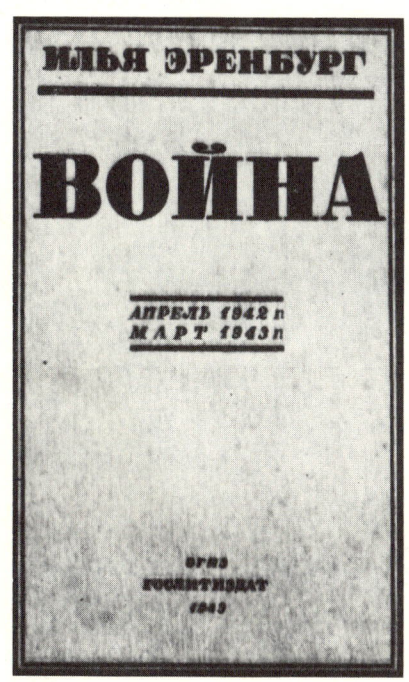
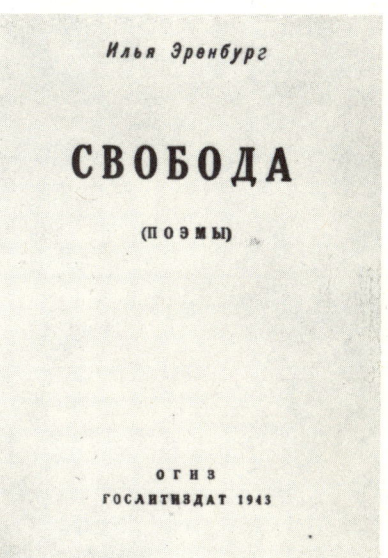

during the war Simonov brought out six collections of Front-line feature stories, correspondent's reports, and tales: and four books, including *From the Black to the Barents Sea, Yugoslav Notebook,* and *Letters from Czechoslovakia.* In recalling that time Ehrenburg said: "I never wrote so much." About 1,500 of his articles, notes, and feuilletons were published during the war. "Ehrenburg's pen," wrote Marshal I. Ch. Bagramian, "was truly more effective than an automatic."

БЛИЗИТСЯ ЧАС

Илья ЭРЕНБУРГ

Немецкий лазутчик

А. ЖДАНОВ

Совещание комсомольских работников фронта

Константин СИМОНОВ
Мы возвращаемся!
1. ТОВАРИЩ
2. ДОРОГА
3. ВОСПОМИНАНИЕ

Большой успех фильма о параде 7 ноября
Шестьсот тысяч зрителей

THE WAR IN PHOTOGRAPHS

One worked so hard and so long during those years that there was simply no time left for anything else—people who worked side by side in the same editorial office, like Simonov and Ehrenburg, met mostly in their newspaper columns. This is page three of the December 20, 1941, issue of *Red Star* at the time when the German-Fascist forces were routed from the environs of Moscow. Konstantin Simonov's cycle of poems, "We Are Coming Back!" and Ehrenburg's article, "The Hour Is Approaching," were printed side by side on the same page.

During the entire war their reportorial assignments brought them together at the Front only a few times. This is one such meeting in 1943, showing Ehrenburg introducing to Simonov his old friend from the Spanish Civil War, General Batov: "This is Fritz, whom I love very much." In Spain Batov was called by the pseudonym Fritz.

KONSTANTIN SIMONOV

When the war began the young poet Konstantin Simonov was only twenty-six years old. Within a few months after the publication of his poem, "Wait for Me," he became the bearer of one of the most celebrated literary names of the time. Simonov's Front-line experience is truly unique, for who else among the war correspondents was able to be in besieged Odessa and Feodosia just as they were liberated by a landing party; to be among the Yugoslav partisans, and beyond the Arctic Circle in the Finnish rear; to be in Stalingrad, and on the Kursk Arc; to observe the retreat of the Germans near Moscow and their desperate resistance in Silesia; to be present at the bloody battles during the first days in Belorussia and at the storming of Berlin. He has been in the hottest places of the war.

THE WAR IN PHOTOGRAPHS

"The less you risk the less you see—and the worse you write," thus Simonov formulated for himself one of the most important commandments of the Front-line journalist. But this is not all: a genuine war correspondent should be able to write under any conditions, wherever and however one had to. Nikolai Tikhonov told how Simonov worked during the war: "He can write during the march, in a jeep or truck, in the dugout between two battles, during an unexpected overnight stay, under a charred tree, writing down what he saw in a notebook." These two photographs may illustrate what Tikhonov says. The first shows the editor of *Red Star*, General Ortenburg, and Simonov (in the center) in the autumn of 1942 at Stalingrad during one of the Volga crossings. The second was taken at the Front in 1943.

KONSTANTIN SIMONOV

The popularity of Ehrenburg's articles could not be compared with anything else; it was unprecedented. His articles were the first thing people turned to in the newspaper; in the partisan detachments, where every piece of paper was used for smokes, only Ehrenburg's articles were saved; the men at the Front wrote letters to Ehrenburg about his articles. This photograph shows Ehrenburg among the fighters who took part in the rout of the Fascist aggressors near Moscow.

Love and hatred—without these emotions one could not bear the unimaginable tension of those grave days; love and hatred nourished the writer's word. Ehrenburg listens to accounts of the Fascist "New Order" and the enemy's atrocities from the inhabitants of a village liberated from the Hitlerite occupiers . . .

THE WAR IN PHOTOGRAPHS

This is how the war started during one short June night of 1941—peaceful towns jolted awake by the explosions of German bombs. . . . In the life of every person there are days which leave an indelible imprint on the memory, everybody has such unforgettable days of their own—but this day of June 22, 1941, is remembered by all of us. The war continued for four terrible, endless years. The cost was twenty million lives for victory, for peace on earth, for the freedom of our people and for the nations of Europe.

In the photographs included in this book the war appears as Simonov and Ehrenburg saw it, as it was imprinted on their feature stories and reports—it is thus that it lives on even now in the memory of many thousands of Front-line soldiers and officers. . . .

KONSTANTIN SIMONOV

Those who had occasion to live through this experience, who had to attack under machine-gun fire, to cut barbed-wire barriers under artillery bombardment, to land with an advance landing party on an ominously silent enemy shore, know the price of these fateful minutes when life and death are on equal terms. What intensity in the eyes of the gunner—he must not miss the mark, for the next enemy shell can hit him . . .

KONSTANTIN SIMONOV

On November 7, 1941, when the enemy was pressing hard against the approaches to our capital, the annual parade was held in Red Square to celebrate the anniversary of the Revolution. The parade was a challenge to Hitlerite Germany, a demonstration of our con-

viction that Moscow would not surrender under any circumstances, and a demonstration of our faith in victory. From the parade these soldiers went straight to the Front.

KONSTANTIN SIMONOV

Here in Leningrad everything was an exploit: any sort of effort was an achievement—walking the few blocks to reach one's place of work; hauling a bucket of water. . . . The sufferings that befell Leningraders could be endured only in the name of the Motherland. But the Motherland, too, did everything to lighten their fate—what would have become of them without the "Road of Life" across frozen Lake Ladoga?

THE WAR IN PHOTOGRAPHS

This city appears to be dead—it was bombed by hundreds of Fascist aircraft, it was crushed by large-caliber artillery, it was burned with flame throwers. Everything that could burn, burned here, every inch of ground is soaked with blood and hammered down with lethal metal. But such was the force of resistance of the city's defenders that the Germans could not capture Stalingrad. The people of Stalingrad stood to the last man, they fought for every building, every floor, every ruin, they fought while surrounded and cut off from their own; they fought without leaders or direction. . . .

Here it is, Hitler's "New Order:" mass shootings of peaceful inhabitants, orphaned children, villages burned to the ground. In Belorussia the Fascists annihilated every fifth inhabitant, six hundred villages shared the terrible fate of Khatyn—the executioners left behind them a burned and depopulated space after their "action."

THE WAR IN PHOTOGRAPHS

The Hitlerites sent hundreds of thousands of people from different countries to extermination camps that were monstrous death factories. Many volumes of documents with blood-chilling details have been published on this terrible chapter in the history of humankind—but here we shall confine ourselves to only one quotation from the testimony of Vaillant-Couturier, a prisoner of Oswiecim, at the session of the International Military Tribunal at Nuremberg: "Once, during the night," he said, "we were awakened by terrible screams, and on the next morning we found out from the people working in the *Sonderkommando* (a squad working at the gas chambers) that there had not been enough gas the previous day, so that children were thrown into the crematorium ovens to be burned alive." This is what Fascism is like.

KONSTANTIN SIMONOV

But the more brutally the Hitlerites behaved in the land they had seized, the deeper and stronger became the resistance to the invaders. Partisans' detachments, pursued by the executioners, exhausted by the "block system," grew and became strong. Young and old fled into the forest to join the partisans. "The battle-front with the Hitlerites," wrote the well-known Belorussian writer Vasil Bykov, "passed through every neighborhood, through every homestead, through the hearts and souls of the people. The all-national struggle meant that everyone was a warrior, with all the consequences implicit in that word. Everyone was a warrior independent of age and sex, without regard to whether the person carried weapons and shot at the invaders, or only planted potatoes and brought up children."

THE WAR IN PHOTOGRAPHS

It was not so simple a matter to transform the formidable German military equipment of tanks, guns, and automobiles into these gigantic scrap heaps. It required not only the bravery of soldiers and officers, but also superiority in aircraft, tanks, and artillery. And it was for this cause that people worked on the home front, depriving themselves of sleep or rest. Women and children began to appear at the lathes, replacing those who left for the Front. The factories which had been hurriedly evacuated to the east still lacked roofs, but the assembly of tanks and aircraft was already proceeding at full speed.

THE WAR IN PHOTOGRAPHS

The hour came when our aircraft began to completely dominate the air. And our fighters, assault planes, and bombers earned the highest appreciation, not from the flyers who had to fly them, but from the enemy who experienced their fighting power.

And the fiery arrows spewing from the Katyushas became the nightmare of the German infantry.

More and more German soldiers and officers had to take recourse in this eloquent gesture of surrender. And the further our Army proceeded west and the stronger its blows became, the more the enemy was compelled to finish the war in such a manner. Long columns of German prisoners-of-war stretched toward the east.

KONSTANTIN SIMONOV

But victories did not come easily, even with superiority in military equipment. Each small hill that was recaptured, each block, each inhabited place had to be paid for in blood. And someone in the advancing file would call out "Sister!" and a girl in a military tunic would crawl under fire to the wounded man in order to tend to him.

And yet war is not just death and blood, but also hard work, a tunic stiff with perspiration. Above: artillerymen straining to the utmost pull a gun through the swamp with their own strength, for no motor vehicle, no tractor will pass here . . .

THE WAR IN PHOTOGRAPHS

In one of his articles Ehrenburg called the sappers "the Laborers of Victory." He wrote: "October nights on the Dnieper are cold. The sappers stand in the icy water; they drive piles, they build trestles. They work for twelve hours on end. The medical orderlies carry away the wounded while the sappers work without stopping. They have not slept for six days. Before that they hauled logs for over two miles with their legs sinking into deep sand. The sapper knows that one cubic yard of wood supports a load of 660 lbs. on water, but who will work out what a sapper can stand, an ordinary person who, before the war, wrote papers or sowed oats? . . ."

KONSTANTIN SIMONOV

The war also evolved its own way of life. A long-expected letter from home—what a joy for the soldier! But everything here at the Front—both misfortune and joy—is equally shared, and a letter from one's family must be read to comrades.

The war went on for so long that eventually everything that could happen, happened. And there were occasionally moments of wonderful relaxation that are also unforgettable.

THE WAR IN PHOTOGRAPHS

No, not the 1,100 miles' distance on the map, but considerably more had to be covered by the soldier in order to get here to Berlin, because in the beginning, pressed by the enemy, he went east, not west, and because the road was not straight. And it was very hard. But throughout the four long years of the war—"from the bell to the bell"—as they said in the Army at that time, it was straight to Berlin that the Soviet soldier was marching; he marched in bitter cold and heat, through autumn slush and storms, under the whine of bullets and the crashing of shells, flattening himself against the ground during bombing and tank attacks. And all along the endless road, at every mile, there were the graves of his fallen comrades. And thus we came to Berlin; here, from where the war had come to us, we came here to finish with Fascism once and for all.

KONSTANTIN SIMONOV

The last battles for Berlin are being fought, the Reichs-Chancellery has been taken. The Reichstag is being stormed.

There he is, the victor over Hitlerite Germany, at the entrance to the Reichs Chancellery. We don't know the name of this soldier, we don't know where he joined the fighting, in what battles he had taken part, how many times he had been wounded, by what roads he had arrived in Berlin. But if it weren't he, then it was his comrades who had fought to the last bullet in the Brest Fortress in June, 1941, who had defended Moscow and Leningrad, Sevastopol and Stalingrad, who had liberated Warsaw and Budapest. And all this, so that he could arrive in Berlin as the victor.

KONSTANTIN SIMONOV

In autumn of 1941 the Hitlerite Command planned a victory parade in Moscow. Invitation cards had already been printed, and it was only necessary to fix the date. Some of those who were to take

THE WAR IN PHOTOGRAPHS

part in that victory parade saw Moscow later on—this was in July, 1944—when columns of German prisoners-of-war, many thousand-strong, were led through the streets of our capital.

KONSTANTIN SIMONOV

But those banners under which the Hitlerite troops had planned to march victoriously across Red Square were thrown

THE WAR IN PHOTOGRAPHS

down into the dust and hurled to the base of the Mausoleum during the Victory Parade in Moscow in 1945.

KONSTANTIN SIMONOV

He came back—alive, with victory. And how many tears she had shed during four unimaginably long years of the war, how she had waited and how she had dreaded the postman—what would he bring her: the "triangle" of a soldier's letter, or a death notice? And there is happiness—he has returned, the war is ended.

1941

They attacked furiously
Threatening with the cold of the grave,
But there is such a word as "withstand"
Even when it is not possible to withstand.
And there is a soul—it will endure everything.
And there is the earth—she is one,
Large, kind, angry,
And like blood, warm and salty.

         I. Ehrenburg

Konstantin Simonov

COVER UNITS

"Our cover units are going over to the counter-attack to delay the enemy until the arrival of our main forces."

We have repeatedly come across this modest, businesslike phrase in Informbureau war communiqués. But how much is hidden behind this phrase, what exploits, what iron tenacity stand behind the simple words—"to delay the enemy until the arrival of our main forces," is not clearly visualized by everyone. The military language is laconic. The order says to delay the enemy. But in our Army, to delay means to delay at all costs; to fight in our Army means to fight to the last drop of blood.

Cover units—the units which take upon themselves the enemy's first onslaught—are the first to experience his strategy and tactics, and the first to learn new methods of fighting him while on the move and during the battle. They delay the enemy, sometimes they commit errors which cost them dearly, and in correcting these mistakes they acquire a new fighting experience which will be utilized by the whole Army, today and tomorrow, to smash the enemy. This will be achieved by our Army which has concentrated and deployed itself while the cover units were gaining time for it—time—whose real value can only be grasped in war.

The Army has deployed itself, the cover forces have been transferred to the Army's rear for some dozen miles. But there is no clear boundary between Front and Rear in this war.

At night, when all is quiet, one can hear the distant cannonade of heavy guns. This is the artillery firing of our own corps. When darkness begins to fall, white reflections flash in the forest—dot, dash, dot, dash. These are German sabotage groups trying to communicate with each other or to give a sign to their aircraft. The lights go out quickly, for our reconnaissance has learned to work with precision; at the third dash the signaler had to raise his hands in surrender.

The cover units are replenished, the losses replaced. New artillery pieces and machine guns are brought up to replace those crippled in fierce battles. But if you should start talking with the commanders and soldiers of such a unit which has recently come out of the battle, you will rarely hear them talk about losses; the soldiers and commanders talk about battle experience, about the enemy's weak spots, about new tactics which they had worked out in the fighting and which they now are using against the enemy. And when they do talk about comrades who have perished, they reminisce about them not simply with regret, but they discuss and applaud their conduct in battle, their fighting experience which they passed on to others at the price of their lives.

The N-infantry regiment, together with the other regiments of the division, was alerted on June 22nd, and after

COVER UNITS

bringing itself into battle readiness, carried out a forty-six-mile march in twenty-one hours. Having changed over into motor trucks under enemy aircraft fire, the regiment arrived at dawn at the place of concentration.

Only a distance of a few miles separated the regiment from the approaching tank division of the enemy. After deploying itself with a rush, the regiment took up the defense line along the sloping bank of the Sh.- River. In order to give the regiment the chance to dig in, and the howitzer division time to occupy advantageous firing positions, the 2nd battalion was thrust forward. It was given the honorable task of receiving the first blow.

It is difficult to dislodge steadfast infantry which has managed to dig in and to consolidate itself, even if a tank division operates against one regiment. The Germans understood this no less than we did, and while our regiment was digging in, foreign bombers swooped down screaming every fifteen minutes over its head. But the enemy's calculations for panic and for slowing down the tempo of the defense works were frustrated. Hiding themselves, taking cover behind trees, lying down and rising again, the soldiers continued their work coolly and rapidly. There was no running about, no random shooting from rifles, everyone was occupied with his own business: the soldiers with theirs, the antiaircraft gunners with theirs.

And one must say that the antiaircraft gunners operated fairly successfully in the first battle. Quietly waiting for the second attack when the Nazi bombers would go over into a dive, the squad of large-calibre anti-aircraft machine guns fired rounds straight to the head at the enemy aircraft motors. One after another three bombers burst into flames, and breaking through the trees with a roar, crashed into the forest.

In the meantime, the 2nd battalion was already accepting the uneven battle. Our antitank guns fired pointblank at the enemy tanks. Retreating from line to line, our machine gunners attempted to separate the enemy infantry from their tanks, forcing it to lie down, not allowing it to raise its head. There—one tank caught fire, then a second, a fourth; the others were moving slower now than in the beginning, stopping to fire at our antitank guns and pulling after them their infantry, which was proceeding without much bravery under fire. In the meantime, the 2nd battalion, having carried out its task of delaying the enemy, gradually retreated to the left flank of the N-regiment.

By four o'clock fighting had flared up along the entire front of the regiment. According to the number of the attacking Nazi tanks, it could now be easily determined that a full mechanized enemy division was operating against us. Only a narrow river strip with a single bridge separated us from the enemy. Emerging on the bank, German tanks were drawing together towards the bridge, but fierce artillery fire did not allow them to approach the bridge itself. The German infantry which had gathered at the edge of the wood tried to reach the river bank by short rushes and to wade across it.

Several more enemy tanks caught fire. From our position it could be clearly seen how the German infantry behaved. It still tried to advance under machine-gun fire, although more slowly. But when their tanks lit up right and left, like black torches, the infantry lay down, and it was apparently difficult for their officers to prize it off the ground. Their faith in these steel engines with which victories had been so easily achieved until now, this faith, it turned out, had its reverse side. Their engines burned one after another. The German infantry was not used to this, it was scared, and it did not want to advance on its own. Let the tanks go first.

And the tanks moved again, and clustered again at the bridge, and again they caught fire. German artillery

COVER UNITS

now came to their assistance. After bringing up their tank-support artillery to the river, the Germans started to hunt down our antitank guns. With the combined efforts of their tanks and their artillery, half our guns were out of commission by evening.

But the Russian artillery is not famous for nothing. Our remaining guns detected the enemy's position and by nightfall destroyed eighteen enemy guns by accurate fire and set sixteen tanks alight. Our machine gunners, assisting the artillery, hit accurately at the observation slots of the tanks, blinding the enemy.

But the losses nevertheless were telling. Our fire was less frequent now, and making use of this, units of the German infantry crawled over the bank and began to wade across the river. On seeing this, the second company of our regiment came out from cover and launched a swift counterattack. Frightened of bayonet thrusts, the German infantry retreated hurriedly to the other bank.

It was dark by now, and a lull descended on the battlefield for a few minutes. But at exactly ten o'clock, presumably despairing of capturing our positions with a rush, the enemy moved up howitzer artillery and opened a hurricane of fire. The bursting of shells continued as a solid barrage of fire roared from the bank of the river into the depths of the forest and from the flanks to the center of our positions. It required iron tenacity to sit it out under this fire, keenly watching every move of the enemy. Under cover of the blistering barrage fire, German infantry began to cross the river and to gather on this bank.

At exactly twelve o'clock midnight, the Germans directed their artillery fire into the depth of our lines. Convinced that our units had been destroyed and demoralized by the two-hour-long hurricane of fire, they had finally decided to launch an attack. But at exactly the same moment the commander of the Russian regiment, having decided not to wait for the German attack, pulled together all his surviving fighters, and bringing them into action, led them into a counterattack with a shout of "Hurrah!"

The redoubtable Russian "Hurrah!" crashed quite suddenly on the German soldiers who were crossing the river. They rushed back in disorder, some wading, some swimming, in instinctive avoidance of a bayonet battle. Far from all of them managed to escape beyond the river, however, and many had to experience the thrust of the Russian bayonet. Thus finished that difficult day for N-regiment.

The German tank division had been held down for twelve hours. Up to thirty enemy tanks and eighteen guns had been taken out of commission. We, too, suffered serious losses. But despite our heavy losses, our fighters felt themselves victors that night. The smashed German tanks and guns, the annihilated German infantry—all this was only half the victory. The second part of the victory was the gain in time. Twelve hours of military fighting time! The soldiers knew that our main forces were being deployed back there, in the rear, making good use of these twelve hours they had gained for them in bloody battle.

Towards dawn the N-regiment left this forest, which was now riddled and torn up with shells that had been zeroed in accurately by the German artillery, and retreated to a new line of defense where the same kind of fierce and heroic battle was in store for it.

And in the Informbureau report there appeared in the morning the terse phrase: "In the course of the day gone by, our cover units stemmed the advance of the enemy until the arrival of our main forces."

July 5, 1941

Ilya Ehrenburg

COALITION OF FREEDOM

Plutarch assures us that Caesar conquered and enslaved a million people. What chance has he compared with Hitler! In all of history there has been no such greedy and ferocious slave-owner as Hitler—he has turned one hundred million souls into slaves.

Whom does he want to deceive by talking about the "Coalition of European Nations" against Russia? Dr. Goebbels? The young Stormtroopers, taught from the cradle on not to think? The Martians? There are no nations in the countries seized by Hitler. Hitler has abolished nations. There are slaves of various categories—the Dutch milk cows for Hitler, the Norwegians dry cod for Hitler, the Hungarians, Italians, Finns, and Rumanians die for Hitler.

Hitler assures us that a "Coalition of States" is marching against Russia. Perhaps he asked the Finns whether they wanted to die for "Great Germany"? Perhaps he inquired whether the Slovaks wished to shoot at their brothers, the Russians? No, he issued an order, and his hirelings—the cowardly and lascivious Mussolini, the ignorant Tito, the miserable fiddler Antonescu, the blockhead Riuty, did not dare to object.

I know Italy well. I know her people—peace-loving, kind-hearted, cheerful. The Italians never liked the Germans—they remember the age-old oppression. But the love of the Italians for Russia shows at every step. They remembered how during the earthquake of Messina, the Russian sailors rescued Italians. They talked of the heroism of the Russian fliers who rescued the Italian polar expedition. When Gorky used to arrive in Naples in Mussolini's time, students, fishermen, and longshoremen would come running to welcome the great writer. Who will believe that the Italians voluntarily went to war against the Soviet Union?

In Slovakia I saw streets named after Pushkin, Gogol, Tolstoy, Gorky. The Slovaks sing our songs, at concerts they perform our music from Mussorgsky to Shostakovich. Students devour Blok, Sholokhov, Tolstoy. The classic Slovak writer Kukuchin was brought up on Russian literature. The Germans and the Magyars suppressed Slovak culture. The pioneers of national culture, the "arousers," spread the light of Russian thought to every isolated farmhouse and cottage. Five years ago I attended a congress of Slovak writers. There were Leftists and Rightists, Catholics and Prostestants, and they all spoke with the greatest love for our country. During what nightmarish moment of insomnia did Hitler conceive the absurd idea of declaring that Slovakia was at war with Russia?

The cannibal is short of human flesh: Germans are not enough for him, he sends foreign people to be slaughtered. His "Coalition" consists of unfortunate Rumanians and Slovaks who are chased into the fire by Prussian lance-corporals.

There *is* a coalition—not of slaves, but of free nations.

COALITION OF FREEDOM

This is the coalition against Hitler.

The courage of London was the first victory of human dignity over Fascist barbarism. The huge splendid city was subjected to terrible bombardments night after night, week after week, month after month, but England remained at the time the only one who stood against Hitler—the French Fascists had betrayed their motherland, but England did not surrender. The historian will tell what the long winter nights meant for London. Residential buildings and museums were bombed to rubble. The vandals destroyed the historic House of Commons of the English Parliament. City blocks were set ablaze, but the British people quietly answered "No."

Once a delayed-action bomb fell in London. A workman seized it and carried it to the antiaircraft defense headquarters while his little son went ahead calling out to people to step aside. What tenacity! What a symbol of dignity and bravery! England was protected from the cannibals not only by the Channel, but it was protected by its will to resist; an attitude which is learned on the island from the cradle up is, "An Englishman will never be a slave."

Two Fronts? No, dozen of Fronts. The daredevil French are already fighting under the command of General de Gaulle. This is only the reconnaissance, only the advance detachment; soon the entire French nation will fling itself at the invader under the strains of the immortal "Marseillaise." And what of the Norwegians? And the Czechs? And the Poles? And the Serbs? The enslaved nations are awaiting the first defeat of the Hitlerite Army. The hour is near. The brotherly front of the three Great Powers—this is the force which will shatter Hitlerism, hated by all the world. With us, with our cause, is now allied the stubbornness of the British, the might of America, and the unparalleled courage of the Soviet people.

July 20, 1941

Ilya Ehrenburg

JULY 28, 1941

Moscow's idyllic surroundings—forests, a small river, meadows with bright flowers, the fragrance of pine resin and hay. No one would guess that this is the command post of an airfield. Bold fliers guard the Moscow sky.

It is quiet towards evening. Some airmen are asleep, others read the papers or lie about on the lawn. The hour for the night's work is approaching. The telephone rings; a group of bombers has been spotted above Vyazma. The pilots are at the ready. Powerful searchlights pierce the sky, their beams scour and rush about to seek out the invisible enemy. There he is! And immediately a Russian pursuit plane chases after him.

The aerial combat lasts twenty minutes. Bursts of machine gun fire can be heard. There are small fires in the sky. And suddenly there is a flame above the forest—it is a Junker coming down. The pursuit plane requests permission to land. Light flares up for a minute. The victor lands. All this seems simple and incomprehensible—the sharp vision and stubbornness of the pilots, their skill in not losing the enemy, in finding the airfield in pitch darkness, in landing when a white mist rising from the ground conceals everything. It would seem that these people have second sight.

And other pursuit planes are already up, they wait, search, and overtake the enemy. From the ground it is radioed: "To the right, more to the right." Two German bombers turn west after the first round of machine gun fire. An hour later we learn that one of them was shot down ninety miles from here.

In the east there is a magic picture—the barrage ring of long-range antiaircraft guns: Moscow is guarded not only from the air but from the ground. The shafts of searchlights pierce the blackness . . . this night, which recently seemed so quiet that one could hear the peaceful croaking of frogs, suddenly comes to stormy life—no one sleeps. In the subway, in the shelters, Muskovites wait for the all-clear while the battle rages above them and around them. Her people fight for Moscow, which has now become even dearer, even more precious to every Russian.

Talk about tension, about tiredness? These words can hardly express the heroism of the pilots. It is enough to say that some of them have taken off for the fifth time during the last twenty-four hours. They sleep in the dugout, snatching a scant hour of rest, and then they jump up, gulp a mouthful of cold tea, and run to their aircraft.

At the airfield I made the acquaintance of Lieutenant Konstantin Titenkov. He is thirty years old, the son of a locksmith, born in Yartsevo in the Smolensk province. He was keen on aviation as a youth, and became a pilot. During the last few days Titenkov brought down two of the German bombers which flew to Moscow.

JULY 28, 1941

He is a modest man; brave in the air, he is bashful and shy in conversation. He brings along his engineer, a Komi-Permiak, a member of a small nation. Titenkov says: "Without him I could not have brought down . . ." and he goes on to tell in a businesslike manner how he brought down the leading plane of the squadron which was on its way to Moscow. He attacked the Heinkel from the left; the young pilot, Bokach, flew on the right. The latter was excited, and he opened fire too soon. Titenkov says, "I came up to within 175 yards of him and began to spray him without haste . . ." This was the first battle in which Titenkov took part. "I've never seen such a big target before." Then the searchlights let the enemy slip away. But Titenkov still caught up with him. He killed the rear-gunner-radio-operator. The Heinkel had to turn left without reaching Moscow and drop its bombs in the forest. "I hit it hard in the right engine, coming very close to it. It was tossed upwards—I got into the slip-stream. The Heinkel should be on fire, but it still does not burn. I'm almost out of cartridges and shells, but then it came down—into the mist, into the small river below." A lieutenant-colonel, a captain, and a lieutenant were aboard the knocked-down aircraft. It was a picked crew whose documents included service records of London, Coventry, Crete, and a plan of Moscow.

Three days later Titenkov brought down a Junker. He chased it west for an hour. "After I killed the gunner," Titenkov says, "the Junker started to maneuver. It climbed into a cloud, but it was a small cloud the size of an egg which it butted into out of despair. I cut through the cloud, and the Junker goes into a dive. I followed it. I had started to reel when suddenly—a flame. The bomber started to slice through pine trees. It dropped its bombs on a meadow with cows. Finally it caught fire."

An arrogant German lieutenant-colonel was in the plane. He had many decorations, including a badge of distinction for the destruction of London. His face was the face of a degenerate. Morals?—to kill—it does not matter how, it does not matter whom, as long as it is to kill. And by contrast, Lieutenant Titenkov is modest and quiet. We talk about Leo Tolstoy and Dickens. Truly, two worlds collided in the black sky over Moscow, and one rejoices in the very meaning of "man," on seeing the skeleton of the Heinkel brought down by the son of the Smolensk locksmith, Kostya Titenkov . . .

Three-quarters of the German planes turn back after seeing the fiery ring of the antiaircraft fire, or hearing the first bursts from pursuit planes. The German pilots were much braver when they shot up defenseless refugees on the fields of the Île de France and the Touraine. The forests are alight—this is because the Hitlerites had dropped their cargo. I don't know whether they reported to their Command that their bombs had not been dropped on the Moscow Kremlin, but on forests and swamps instead. It seems to me that the German war communiqués are prepared not by military men but by Dr. Goebbels—one can feel his pen.

Yesterday the young pilot Vasilyev brought down a Junker. The burning aircraft could be seen from the airfield. The construction workers confirm that it fell "there—in the forest . . ." But the aircraft could not be found, and in our communiqué we reported eight and not nine German planes shot down. Vasilyev says, "It is a pity—until one finds it in the forest . . . As far as I'm concerned, I don't mind, but it's a pity that it does not say nine. For it would please everyone to read nine and not eight . . ."

In the afternoon girls from the village went out to gather berries and came upon the remains of a burnt-out German bomber. This was not the one Vasilyev brought down, but another one. It is not known who finished it off; it was not included in any communiqué. A silver cigarette case was found among the remains and in it a note

JULY 28, 1941

in German, "The third bombing of Crete." I don't know why the German pilot had stuck that paper into the cigarette case.

Again a telephone call. And again a pursuit plane takes off. And again there is a battle. And the stars grow pale. The white mist thickens. It is cold. Then a very large red sun comes up, the working night is finished. The pilots wash, sleep, listen to the voices of the birds in the field.

We return to Moscow. The chimneys smoke on the houses, and buses speed by on the streets. Bomb craters are being filled with asphalt. Moscow lives a hard but exalted life.

Konstantin Simonov

AT RUMANIAN SHORES

A small tugboat, puffing along ahead of us, opened the net which bars the entrance to the bay. Our submarine is leaving for a long cruise away from the Crimean coast. This is its seventh wartime crossing of the Black Sea. The commander of the vessel has three lengthy and arduous voyages behind him.

A number of dents and shot-holes can be seen on the body of the vessel, and the upper glass of the steering telegraph has been cracked by the splinter fragments of enemy shells. Now the submarine is leaving the bay once again, steering its course southwest to the distant Rumanian coast.

Shortly before midnight the experienced eyes of the signalman spots the hardly visible outline of a ship on the black horizon. Rockets flare up briefly in the sky above us. It's one of ours!—a Russian destroyer returning to base after a fiery raid on the Rumanian troops besieging Odessa.

On the stroke of midnight supper is served in the submarine. Everyone eats separately, each in his assigned compartment at his appointed battle station. There are several compartments, subdivided by impenetrable bulkheads with hermetically closing hatches. The vessel must be of great vitality; the men must be ready for any eventuality. The submariner's law is: in that second when a depth charge explodes near the vessel, tearing the lining of one of the compartments and allowing the water to pour into the opening, the men must not rush to the hatch and jump over into the next compartment to save their lives. They could wreck the whole vessel this way.

No, when the water pours in, the man on duty in the compartment will batten down the hatch from the inside, and the men will fight for their lives inside their hermetically sealed compartment. They will release the compressed air, endeavoring to stop the water, they will attempt to batten down the shot-hole, but if this does not succeed, they will quietly perish, saving the vessel with the price of their lives. This is the meaning of the compartments with the hermetically sealable hatches, this is the meaning of military honor and of the combat law of the submariners.

Days alternated with nights. In traveling across the sea the submarine used the periscope, surfacing only for a few hours during the night. Water, water without end, was the sight one saw through the periscope. Waves surging over the periscope concealed the horizon for a second under an impenetrable green band, and then once again the endless white combs of the waves loomed in one's field of vision. The sea was deserted.

Navigation Officer Bykov sits below in the tiny navigator's cabin, under a huge navigation map. The submarine must come out at the coast exactly on time at the

AT RUMANIAN SHORES

appointed place, and the navigation officer sits for days crouched over the map without straightening his back, but at long last, after having raised the periscope endless times, the commander gives the order to enter the long-awaited sentence into the logbook: "Coast ahead on course." The Rumanian coast. At present it is no more than a barely visible strip, but soon we shall come closer, much closer to it than would be dreamed of by the observers of the coastal batteries who are sitting in wait there, or by the German aircraft coursing overhead along the coast. The hands on the clock approach four; I see the Rumanian coast through the periscope. It seems to be quite close—precipitous mountain slopes, drifts of loose stones, small houses hanging onto rocks.

A new night begins. We rummage around in the harbor; from the bridge we can see lights appear, at times to the right, and then to the left. The sea is calm, there is silence.

We travel for hours at a great depth without benefit of periscope. It is stifling in the submarine, it is hard to breathe from want of habit. But these hours of deep submersion are, at the same time, rare hours of rest. It is quiet in the submarine, one tries to talk and to move as little as possible to conserve oxygen. Only here, under intense strain, locked in a narrow compartment, can one properly understand what discipline and friendship are. It is crowded, every inch is filled with a thousand instruments, everything is calculated to the last centimeter of space, it is impossible to make an unnecessary move.

The commander enters the mess room. He sits down and drinks coffee, gulping avidly. "Everything!" he says, speaking for the first time during the trip. "We've done everything we had to do, we're returning now." He shuts his eyes, dark from insomnia, and after several seconds he falls asleep right there at the table, his head leaning against the wall. The crew maneuver carefully in the narrow space and proceed quietly past him to their stations.

KONSTANTIN SIMONOV

Twenty-four hours later we are proceeding in the open sea and are beginning to draw further away from the Rumanian coast. It is dawn, but the coast is comparatively distant, and it is possible not to hurry with the submersion. Duty-Commander Velizhenko gazes intently at the horizon. He stares for a long time at one spot which is visible only to him, and then, turning suddenly to the commander, he says, "Outline of ship on the horizon!"

The commander raises the binoculars to his eyes for a second and raps out the order: "Immediate submersion!"

The guard, who is at the top, instantaneously slides down by hand along the ship's ladders. The submersion signal is sounded. When the commander, who is the last to leave the bridge, battens down the overhead hatch in his compartment, the vessel is almost submerged, the water comes up to the bridge. After a few dozen seconds only the black eye of the periscope remains above the water.

Inside, at the central post, the commander looks intently into the periscope. "Make a note in the logbook," he dictates. "A Rumanian ship . . ." And after a pause, he issues an order to the helmsman: "Course three hundred and five to port side!"

The submarine changes its course sharply. It is now proceeding straight towards the ship. But its outline in the periscope is seen more and more faintly as the speed of the ship turns out to be faster than the underwater speed of the submarine. A few more minutes and it will disappear from sight.

"Prepare for surfacing! Gun crew to the top!"

The submarine surfaces. Now the dot, moving away on the horizon, can be seen from the bridge through binoculars. The submarine increases speed, but the dot on the horizon begins to enlarge too slowly. Judging by its fast speed, it is apparently a Rumanian auxiliary military vessel. We shall not manage to catch up with it until it

AT RUMANIAN SHORES

reaches the very coast. The chase has lasted an hour and a half already; the body of the ship can be seen now, but the distance is still great.

"We shall strike from this distance," the commander decides.

The gun crew takes up positions at the gun. The senior mate issues the final instructions to the gunners and commands: "Fire away at the enemy vessel!" The heavy torpedo takes off with a roar. Twenty seconds later a column of water surges up at the starboard side of the Rumanian ship.

"Seven to port side! Fire!"

Again a torpedo. We wait twenty, thirty, fifty seconds, but no new column of water spurts up next to the ship, although the smoke plume above it deepens and darkens.

"Fire!" the senior mate commands for the third time.

But when the smoke from the third torpedo disperses, we see that the horizon is clear, there is nothing there. Twenty seconds later the column of water from the third torpedo surges up from the spot where, only a moment ago, there had been a vessel. There is no ship. Now the absence of a column of water after the second torpedo was fired becomes clear. We had had a direct hit with the second firing; a rare case in artillery practice.

The submarine continues to travel at full speed to the place where the ship sank. There is not a single piece of debris on the water, only a large flock of seagulls wheels at some distance above the quietened water. The commander sets the submarine back on its previous course. The observers watch the horizon particularly carefully because the vessel, when sinking, could have sent radio signals to German aircraft. Half an hour, one hour elapses, and at the beginning of the second hour Observer Kovalinsky, standing at his anti-aircraft machine gun, reports curtly: "Aircraft—a hundred sixty to port side!"

KONSTANTIN SIMONOV

Again there is an immediate submersion, while the hand of the depthfinder jumps rapidly from figure to figure: 5—10—15—20—25 meters. Everyone waits. Did the aircraft spot us or not? If it managed to do so, then depth charges will begin to explode now, not far from us. All is quiet underwater. Fifteen minutes, half an hour passes; it is as quiet as before. This means they did not spot us. We surface. It is dark, night has come. One more night and one more day of safe traveling and we will be at our home shores.

The fourth trip is concluded just as successfully as the three previous ones. Thus ends one more everyday event in the life of the crew, men who are modest, quiet, and formidable in battle, the men who fight with the enemy for our Russian Black Sea.

September 19, 1941

Ilya Ehrenburg

OCTOBER 4, 1941

The Germans talk about the start of a new military operation. Let us wait a few days. This is not the first time that Hitler has consoled his people with promises of an imminent dénouement.

Right now, instead of glancing over the Front-line with its enigmatic curves, I would like to take a look at our country. Fifteen weeks have passed since the invasion of our land, and we have gone through a great deal. Regions which once flourished have been turned into deserts. The cities cannot be recognized—they have been camouflaged. Friends cannot be recognized in their military uniform. Our resistance has amazed the world. The German newspapers must explain to their readers every day why the campaign against Moscow is not like other campaigns.

I have traveled a lot, I have seen the Front and the

ILYA EHRENBURG

Home Front. Every day I meet different people: I meet commanders and soldiers, scientists and workers, writers and members of collective farms, heroes and men in the street. I would like to talk dispassionately about the essence of our resistance, relinquishing anger and faith for an hour.

A hundred years ago the great Russian poet Tiutchev wrote: "Russia cannot be understood with the mind nor measured with an ordinary yardstick." The history of our people is full of obscurity for the foreigner. Once upon a time, in the depths of the dark forest, the Russian people erected cities and temples which were harmonious and bright, like those of ancient Greece. The sunny poetry of Pushkin was born in deep winter cold. The Russian intelligentsia burned brightest during the epoch of its rulers' dark fanaticism. Even at the beginning of this century our peasants still had fireplaces without chimneys in their cottages and burned wood splinters to provide light. But during that time Russia ruled the advanced minds of humanity: the world waited for what Tolstoy would say.

I know what the Russian nation is capable of; in 1919 I saw people push railway carriages with their bare hands because there were no locomotives; in 1932 I saw the Kuznetsk plant built in the wilds of the Siberian *taiga*. This war against poverty was a real war, with its own foxholes and heroes, its own deprivations and martyrs.

For our people this war is not a shout but a long, slow song. We suffered enormously simply to be able to change bast shoes for boots, we took so much pride in finally being able to provide electric lights for our villages. But the fateful hour struck and the war arose before the Russian people like a vague, atavistic apparition, with its darkness, its farewells at the stations, its sleeplessness, its Front-line trenches. But no privations can intimidate this nation.

The Russian people were never nationalistic. We are

OCTOBER 4, 1941

not presumptuous by nature. Here in this country the war has reached the consciousness of the people only as the defense of their land. This is how it was in the days of Napoleon, and this is how it is now.

Everybody's life has changed. Old women knit and groan while agreeing over yawns of fatigue that "It seems to be a demolition bomb . . ." They hobble along the street amid the thunder of antiaircraft guns; they are afraid of mice and drafts, but not of bombs. Children, while playing, put out incendiary bombs. When an air-raid alert interrupts a play in the theatre, people are indignant: they want to know what happened to the heroine—did she fall in love with the hero or not?

Many people spend the night in their factories, offices, or stores; some, because they work so desperately hard that it would be a sin to lose two hours in commuting; others because they guard goods and do not want to leave the lathe or the storeroom for a minute. Theirs is a strange bedroom: half sleeping quarters, half military encampment. But when you go to the theater you see that everybody has dressed up, and it isn't possible to recognize in the ballet enthusiast, delighted by toe dancing, the engineer who sleeps three hours out of twenty-four on a folding bed in the workshop.

The railroad workers couple up carriages during air raids, they load shells and drive trains through dark autumn nights under bomb attacks. When the bombs drop people swear, shake themselves, and go on with their work. Have a word with a railroad worker: he will grumble that his favorite cigarette brand is not available, that the nights are cold, that he does not like the music of the radio broadcasts. But he is a real hero. Yesterday he saved four trucks loaded with shells. Only a sorrowful sigh will indicate that he does not know where his family is, he is from Kiev . . .

What are partisans? They are ordinary Russian people. Their resistance is organic—this is how the earth defends itself. The enemies become bogged down in it. Each day people manage to cross the Front-line, they crawl across it inch by inch in order to tell us the position of an enemy battery or airfield. Very old men come in, they mutter dimly, "The German has planes there . . ." Children come in with tracings of enemy positions.

I saw an old woman. Her husband repeated the exploit of Ivan Susanin—he led a German detachment into a swamp, and then he summoned the partisans by whistling. The Germans shot the old man. His wife was telling about his death sadly but quietly, as one tells about an unavoidable misfortune.

General Yeremenko congratulated a soldier who fought his way out of an encirclement, shooting six Germans in doing so. The soldier said to him, "Comrade General, I had to get through, I had a dispatch for Comrade Lieutenant . . ." The crew of an antiaircraft battery is being celebrated for having brought down seventeen aircraft. The men ask, "If we could only sleep for a few hours, then we'll bring down the eighteenth." When a Red Army detachment enters a village the peasants bring out everything to the soldiers: lard, honey, sour cream. I wanted to pay a peasant woman for some eggs, but she refused. "I will not take it," she said. "Someone else somewhere will give food to my own . . ."

The Germans hoped to provoke a civil war in Russia. But all distinctions between Bolsheviks and non-Party people, between believers and Marxists, have been obliterated: some defend time, others defend space, but time and space—this is the Motherland, this is the earth, this is such-and-such height, such-and-such line, such-and-such inhabited place. They pray for the Red Army in old churches, the domes of which have been darkened so that they would not attract German pilots. Muftis and rabbis pray for the Red Army. To the old grandmothers in the

OCTOBER 4, 1941

village, Hitler is the AntiChrist. To the young Shortsy astronomer whose father believed in sorcery and gave his last sheep to the shaman, Hitler is the darkness.

Millions of people have just started to be alive. These days of trial were their first books, their first theatre, their first happiness. The thunder of an explosion echoes far around: the dam of the Dnieper Hydroelectric Station was deliberately blown up. They will give up everything if only not to be German slaves.

And new echelons march there in darkness. People dig for potatoes under machine gun fire. They perish, but they save a sack of flour. They perish, but they save a child. Old men march with rifles, they squint, they want to be snipers. Girls on high heels inquire with a matter-of-fact air how to throw Molotov cocktails. Soldiers at the Front study tactics during free moments. Poets at battle stations read poems to the soldiers between attacks. Military leaders from among the people are born in the darkness of the trenches. All words have become insipid; people trust only weapons. No one counts the victims, no one talks about privations. The people have become heroic, but the people as rank-and-file soldiers do not understand that they are heroes.

We know that the Germans have thrust deeply into our land. We know how to survive bad war communiqués, for we know that good communiqués are ahead. We do not amuse ourselves with illusions, we do not fight on stilts. The stories of the bravery of our people are modest, even drab. This is bad for literature—the exploit of the pilot who carries out a suicide dive is related as if it were a matter of catching fish. But this is good for victory; one cannot be a hero on festive days only, the nation for whom heroism is a weekday affair is the nation that will win.

Ilya Ehrenburg

OCTOBER 25, 1941

Quite recently I was traveling along the Mozhaisk Highway. A little blue-eyed girl tended geese along the roadside and sang an adult song about somebody else's love. In the distance the domes of Mozhaisk glistened dimly. The Germans are there now. Our guns talk there, they talk about the fury of a nation that is defending Moscow.

A few weeks ago I was writing in my room. Above me hung a landscape by Marke, a scene of Paris, the Seine. Moscow, golden and pink, could be seen through the window. This room no longer exists, the house it was in has been demolished. My correspondence did not get posted, and now it is out of date. I'm writing the new correspondence now in a new room. My typewriter stands on a box instead of a table.

A great misfortune has befallen the world. I knew

that it would long ago, back in August, 1939, when carefree, summery Paris suddenly began to buzz like a beehive turned upside down. Every nation, every person is destined to lose comfort, possessions, happiness in this misfortune. We have lost much, but we have kept one thing: hope.

In donning the soldier's greatcoat, a man leaves behind his warm, shaggy, complex life. All that concerned him yesterday becomes illusory. Had he really been pondering against which wall to place the divan, had he been collecting engravings or pipes? Russia is in a soldier's greatcoat now. She is rattling along on trucks, marching along roads, rumbling in carts, sleeping in trenches and in supply trucks. She does not feel sorry for anything.

The Dnieper Hydroelectric Station has been blown up, magnificent factories, bridges, dams have been blown up, enemy bombs have burned down Novgorod, they tear to pieces the wonderful palaces of Leningrad, they wound the tender heart of Moscow. Millions of people have been left without shelter. For the sake of the right to breathe we have renounced what was dearest to us—every one of us and all of us, the nation.

Long trainloads go east, filled with lathes and poets, children and archives, laboratories and actors, People's Commissariate and telescopes. In 1914 the French Government was in Bordeaux, and the Paris taxis rushed troops to gain the victory at the Marne. In November, 1936, the Government of Republican Spain left Madrid for Valencia. I lived through this hurried departure. But the Army retained Madrid at the time. It also held her later for two years under bombs and shells. In the end Madrid was not conquered by force, but by treason. Moscow has now turned into a military camp; she has been relieved of civic responsibility. She can defend herself as a fortress. She has been granted the lofty right to stake her life on survival. Therein lies the significance of recent events.

OCTOBER 25, 1941

I saw the defenders of Moscow. They fight well, so well that the ground becomes viscous when Moscow lies behind one; it is hard to retreat one step. The enemy strains all his strength to gain ground. During the last few days he threw in new divisions at Mozhaisk and Kalinin; troops from Brittany, from Holland. Every day Moscow beats off massive German air raids. Many buildings have been destroyed.

In the south the Germans are approaching Rostov. They dream of breaking through to the Caucasus. Hitler is in a hurry these sunny, late autumn days. And all is as silent as can be in Europe. Only the Czech heroes and fifty hostages of Nantes fell on the battlefield next to the defenders of Moscow.

I lived through the exodus from Paris. France's soul was leaving at that time. The despair of the French Army and the misfortune of tens of millions of refugees could have engendered resistance, they engendered instead indifference and Pétain's senile babble. Surely Hitler is not hoping to find a Laval in Russia? Foolish dream. We have malicious little old men, but we have no Pétains. And we have thieves, but we have no Laval. Russia, scared off the premises, Russia marching along the roads, is more formidable than a settled Russia. Our people's misfortune will turn on the enemy.

I do not want to embellish anything. The Russians never distinguished themselves with the accuracy and methodicalness of the Germans. But in their stern hour our people, who are rather reckless, rather happy-go-lucky, pull themselves together and become tempered.

For about a week I have been looking at different cities, stations, and roads. Our railroad men have proved themselves to be heroes: under enemy bombardment hundreds of trains carried away from the capital all that had to be carried away. The evacuated factories are already working beyond the Volga and in the Urals. The machines are being installed at night. The workers often sleep in freezing supply trucks and start the job after warming up at a bonfire. Young men study in dozens of airforce schools—after several months they will take the place of those who perished. New armies are being formed deep in the Rear.

The nation understood that this war was for a long time, that it could not be measured in months, that ahead lay years of trials. The nation grew gloomy, but it did not give in. It was ready to live in caves, ready for a nomadic existence, for the most terrible deprivations. The war is presently changing its nature: from a political clash and from battles whose outcome seemed to prophesy an early resolution of the conflict, it became a truly patriotic war, an epic of the people as long as life, it became the fate of a generation. For the first time it became clear to everyone that it was a case of the fate of Russia for many centuries to come. "We shall fight for a long time," said the soldiers leaving for the west, "a very long time." And our hope lies in these bitter words.

Russia cannot be occupied. This has not happened and will not happen—not only because it is far from Mozhaisk to Lake Baikal—Russia has always swallowed up her enemies. The Russian is generally good-natured and hospitable, but he can be angry. He can take revenge, and he endows revenge with a keenness of wit and even a businesslike spirit. We know that Hitlerites are being killed near Moscow, but we also know something else: they are being killed in Kiev, in Minsk, and in thousands of villages throughout Russia. There is no argument that General Guderian is good at maneuvering, but what about pacifying peasants from Novgorod to Melitopol? The German Army does not conquer anything; it only moves from town to town. It has tens, hundreds of Fronts.

Russia is a special country, it is hard to understand her on the Kaiserdamm or in the Wilhelmstrasse. Russia

OCTOBER 25, 1941

can forego everything. People here are accustomed to a rigorous life. Perhaps Magnitogorsk did look like a picture abroad; in reality its still mills constituted heavy warfare. We are not discouraged by failures. Since olden times our military leaders have learned and grown from failures. Since olden times our nation has been tempered by misfortune. Perhaps we shall correct our deficiencies, but we shall withstand and defend ourselves—not only the history of Russia, but also the defense of Moscow gives proof of this.

Sumner Welles wrote recently: "We help you very little." I would like to reply: "No. Perhaps you help yourselves very little."

And what about our personal fate? . . . Maybe the enemy will succeed in thrusting deeper into our land. We are prepared for this. We have ceased to live by a transitory count—from the morning to the evening communiqué. We have switched our breathing to a different rhythm. We are looking towards the long hard years ahead of us. The phrase, "Victory will be ours," was only a newspaper phrase four months ago. It has now changed to the rumble of Russian forests, to the howling of Russian snowstorms, to the voice of the Russian land.

Ilya Ehrenburg

TO THE CZECHOSLOVAKS

Friends—Czechoslovaks, this day was the day of your pride. Czechs rejoiced on the Vaclav Nameste and in thousands of villages. Czechs rejoiced beneath the landmarks of Bratislava, on the squares of St. Martin and Zhilina. This day has remained the day of your pride. But it has also become the day of your sorrow. Suffocating in bomb shelters, buried under debris, people learn what happiness the air is. Under Hitler you learned what happiness freedom is. You are proud people, and you cannot live without it.

On this day I want to embrace my friends. I shall not call out their names: the executioners will hear us. And all Czechoslovaks are now my friends. On this grave day I would like to spell out to you the simple words of hope: we shall meet in a free Prague, in the café, in the "Narodny Divadlo," on the wonderful streets of Mala Strana. We shall meet in Bratislava, on the Danube quay, "Under the Landmarks." We shall travel together to Tissovec and Detva. We shall sing songs about Janosec. We shall see the three-colored flag above Hradcany.

You are celebrating the festive Day of Independence above the fresh graves of the martyrs. But heroes are being tortured in the torture chambers. The statues of the Prague Bridge are crying. The square of the Hussite Tabor is draped in mourning. Moravian girls have removed their gaily colored attire. The forests of Ostrava are cursing Judas Tiso. But the holy blood will not dry. It burns, it turns into rivers, it awakens the sleepers, it eats away iron. Czechoslovakia's heroes have not perished in vain. Their death is a clarion call. Their graves are the first stones of independent Czechoslovakia.

The Russian nation bows before your courage. A salute is sounded above the mass graves: these are the guns of the defenders of Moscow saluting the heroes of Prague. For each Czech shot there are thousands of Germans killed near Moscow. We have lost much during these months: peace, comfort, belongings. Our cities are on fire, our people are dying, but we have defended honor. We shall also defend freedom—ours and yours.

November 4, 1941

Ilya Ehrenburg

NOVEMBER 6, 1941

    This year the festive day is clouded by ruins and graves. Previously, Moscow Radio used to broadcast a roll call of the cities on the seventh of November. Minsk and Vladivostok, Archangelk and Odessa vied with each other in telling about the festive columns passing through the decorated streets. Today Minsk is silent, Kiev is silent, Odessa is silent, Kharkov is silent. Only the tramp of German soldiers and the weeping of women can be heard among the ruins. Leningrad and Moscow celebrate the festive day on the battlefield with weapons in hand.
    Bright banners hung on this pediment last year. Today there is debris, broken bricks—a demolition bomb exploded here. Glass splinters ring underfoot. A year ago young people danced in this square, now they are fighting on the Mozhaisk Highway. Many of them have perished. There is pathos and tragedy on this twenty-fourth anniversary of the Revolution.

ILYA EHRENBURG

People of my generation had lived almost half their life before the October Revolution. Our life was as if split in two. The young ones did not know pre-revolutionary Russia. All that the Revolution brought with it, the wonderful or the harsh, was for them as natural as the air. They are dying for their lives, for something profoundly dear and natural. For them Revolution and Motherland are the same thing.

Now is not the time to look back. We feverishly await the war communiqués. We are tormented by the question: what happened at Tula? We do not feel like making historical appreciations. And yet, for one minute, on the eve of the seventh of November, one wishes to fall to thinking, to remember, to weigh up. There was much that was remarkable. But there were also not a few mistakes. Sometimes that which was excellently thought out was badly executed. But who would dare to deny that our Revolution was the greatest social movement of the century, that it changed an immense country, that it placed the globe into the hands of a shepherd and has welded together one hundred nationalities who had been at loggerheads with each other until then? Even people who severely condemn our system listen anxiously to the thunder of our batteries near Moscow—surely the fanatic from the Tyrol is not destined to destroy the Russian home and Russian thought?

We do not hide the truth from ourselves. Against us is Germany; a power which has conquered France within four weeks, a power which has seized ten States, a power which is successfully fighting in Norway and in Libya. Germany has thrown all her forces against us. She succeeded in occupying immense territories. We have lost great industrial centers, the Krivoy Rog iron ore territory, the Donbas coal area, the factories of Dniepropetrovsk and Kharkov. The factories of Leningrad and Moscow have fallen into the position of refugees. The country's economy has been shaken by the enemy invasion. Millions

NOVEMBER 6, 1941

upon millions of refugees who have been left without shelter have crowded into the already packed cities of the Rear. The life of the State and the life of every one of us has become arduous. I shall introduce a personal touch into this picture so that it should not sound journalistic: my books and the manuscripts I have been working on—all have perished. Many of my relatives and friends are no longer among the living. Others can also reiterate my words. Yes, we have lost much, very much. And yet we look ahead with faith. The wind blows out a match, and the wind fans a bonfire. Misfortune arouses Russian resistance.

Our faith is not blind. We know the steadfastness of the Russian people. The defense of Leningrad is an epic worthy of a great city. The nations of the whole world look with admiration at Moscow, and at no time did Moscow appear so bright as now—blacked-out, having fraternized with the night, mutilated by German bombs. I saw the reserves—wonderfully equipped and trained divisions. I saw the factories which had been evacuated from Moscow and which are already operating in their new locations. I saw the schools for pilots. I know what the industry of the Urals and of Siberia is like. Our fathers used to say: "There is still powder in the powder flask."

In Moscow a poster hangs on the facade of a building which has been half-destroyed by a bomb: "Long live the fighting alliance between the U.S.S.R. and Great Britain!" In a small town in the Rear on the former smithy where the Moscow aircraft factory is situated now, the wind sways banners inscribed: "Long live the United States of America!" This is for tomorrow's anniversary . . . I would like to say to my friends in England and in America: look intently into the night, listen to the sound of the battle. We have not shunned the fighting. We know that great nations are predestined to undergo great ordeals. Welcoming Britain and the United States on the day of our celebration, we give free rein to our heart: we welcome our friends. At the table, friends clink glasses. At war, friends fight side by side.

Konstantin Simonov

ON THE NIGHT OF THE ANNIVERSARY

On the evening of the sixth of November a small reconnaissance party was leaving for a mission deep in the enemy's rear. The head of the party briefed the participants in the small cramped room of the Command Staff.

"According to the latest information the Germans are carrying out a regrouping here, on the shore. You will land at night and check to see if their battery and cover forces are on the northern promontory, as before. If they're not there, then annihilate everything that they have built there, and if their forces are there, then annihilate them, too, along with their works." The head glanced over those present. "It will be necessary for you to spend this night from the sixth to the seventh of November in the enemy's rear. See to it that it should be a festive time for you and a sorry time for them."

KONSTANTIN SIMONOV

The reconnoiterers drew up in the yard, they were already invisible there in their white cloaks against the background of snow. On that anniversary night I, too, went with the detachment, with the head's permission, as a rank-and-file soldier.

The small launch was thrown about by the waves, now up and now down, while being flooded with water it nevertheless proceeded at full speed so as to lengthen the time of reconnaissance for the men after setting them down on the shore at the exact moment of the onset of complete darkness. Liuden, the commander of the detachment, a former cavalryman, a man with a merry soul, stared with hostility at the full moon rising above the horizon. "Here you are—this is dialectics," he remarked, pointing at the broad moonlight spreading over the waves. "What pleases you when you're young, saddens you in mature years. The moon—it's the fifth month now that it has been my personal enemy, but once upon a time—ah, what memories!"

The launch was already traveling alongside the enemy shore. A week ago I saw the Germans subject one of our motor boats to shrapnel fire. But now everything was quiet. Only in the distance, much further west, could there be seen brief flashes of the guns of the destroyer firing at the shore.

The ebb tide had begun. The launch ran afoul of a row of submerged stones and could not proceed any further. A tiny boat with the friendly name of *Little Ace* was lowered into the water, and a ship's ladder was put across to it from the launch. A second ship's ladder was lowered from the *Little Ace* straight into the water. It could not reach the coast, in any case. Then two Red Navy men from the crew of the launch jumped into the icy water without awaiting anyone's order, standing up to the waist in water so as to assist the disembarking reconnoiterers. The reconnoiterers had a march ahead of them, and in order to keep their feet dry the Red Navy men carried them carefully, like children, one by one, to the shore. This was a friendly service, executed in silence and without the expectation of receiving thanks; it was an expression of grateful soldierly friendship.

The waves were rolling in strongly, however, and many, including myself, had the bad luck to fill our boots with water, nor were we spared from taking a bath up to our waist. After we had assembled without a word on the shore, we set off inland, single file, toward the objective of our journey, which lay fifteen miles away over steep, snow-covered, and iced-over coastal rocks. The flaps of our water-soaked cloaks, which had iced over instantaneously and become warped, rattled and rustled when moving. We kneaded our cloaks on the move, reestablishing the silence which was precious to us.

Three men who had been on this mission before were at the head of the line. As they moved they looked attentively at every crack, every spot in the snow, searching for traces of enemy activity. But there were no such traces, only tiny footprints left by hares, and stripes resembling human traces where otters had tumbled along the slope into the water.

The rocks were piled up one on top of the other. From the distance it seemed each time that there was no way to get past them, but as we came closer we would find some crevice, some ledge, which permitted us to climb over them. The bare, almost precipitous slopes where the snow had covered the rock with an even layer were the worst. Blown on by the wind, that layer was hard as a stone and desperately slippery. One wrong move would suffice for a man to drop down a good ten yards, slipping along the incline.

Liuden, who was directly ahead of me, slipped and immediately dropped far down the slope. The reconnoiterer Khrabrin, who rushed to his assistance, could not get a grip either and dropped another five yards further down the slope. When at last they had both clambered up again, someone remarked in a whisper, "This is really a Suvorov crossing." The commander, who was limping after the fall but who had not lost heart, turned around. "I forbid this word," he said.

"Why?"

"Because it is necessary to achieve Suvorov-type results before talking about a Suvorov crossing."

A brief halt was granted at last. The men lay down in the snow in the shelter of a huge rock. Someone looked at his watch—it was exactly twelve o'clock midnight.

The seventh of November . . . Yes, the seventh, and someone began to reminisce in whispers how he had spent that night last year at his home in the Dniepropetrovsk region.

Far in the distance the opposite shore could be seen through the white mist. Very far away the headlights of a motorcar flashed up like a blue spark, which immediately went out. "Ours are driving over there," someone said. And at that moment it was very important for us to know that over there, on our shore, our people, our very own, were driving our motorcars.

Our ice-covered capes rendered us a good turn now, for they stood upright, sheltering us from the penetrating wind while we rested. When it was time to move forward again we had no sooner started than Kovalev, who was in the lead, came upon a communication line. This thin wire connected the German forward positions with the command staff. Placing a stone underneath it, he cut the wire with a dagger, and after cutting off a few feet he trampled the ends into the snow. Let them find it now! This operation was repeated again three or four times along the next mile.

It was not far now; the ridge of high stony mounds descended to the sharp promontory which projected into

ON THE NIGHT OF THE ANNIVERSARY

the water. We split up into three groups and crawled along, bypassing the mounds on three sides and gradually climbing them. The night was moonless now, but bright with the Aurora Borealis playing from edge to edge of the horizon. And yet the men crawling within thirty paces along the snow appeared merely as snowed-filled rock ledges, and even the dark patches of our boots and submachine guns did not betray us. Here on this stony ground they appeared as lumps of rock jutting out from underneath the snow.

We climbed higher and higher along the slope. If the Germans were here they would have seen us by now in this bright night, but everything was quiet. When we finally crawled up to the first trenches all signs indicated that they had been abandoned a day or two ago. Lanterns and lamps hung in the trenches, unburned wood lay in the stoves which were made of brick. Several buildings which seemed to be for storage rose on the rock closer to the promontory. All doors were tightly closed. Someone suggested we "break them open with a grenade." But Liuden, wanting to avoid unnecessary noise, forbade this. His assistant, Inzartsev, with the aid of several soldiers, broke down the doors with rifle butts within fifteen minutes.

The rooms were indeed storerooms: bran, flour, loaves of baked bread, wrapped together with bran in transparent paper with German markings, were piled up inside. Sacks of coffee, chicory, egg-powder, large woven bottles with spirits had been dumped nearby. In general, the stores were half full. A mutilated mountain cannon had been abandoned, under cover, not far from the storage supplies. An abandoned German gun—this was understandable, but abandoned German stores with provisions—this was remarkable. No, the Germans had not cleared out for good. They were apparently only changing their units, and today or tomorrow a new company would arrive at this deserted sector of the Front. These provisions, carried up here by great effort on the one winding path, must have been left specifically for the new company.

Yes, of course, this is how it was. I suddenly recalled the German captain we had recently captured. I had seen him three days ago during questioning at Staff Headquarters. He had sat there, dirty, shabby, in a worn greatcoat and soiled underwear; we had been feeding him our nourishing rations for one day already and yet as soon as the interrogator bent over the report he stealthily pulled out of his pocket the sugar which had been given to him as reserve and avidly gnawed at it. Upon catching my gaze he began to hurry, shamefacedly—as an officer of the German Army he was embarrassed—and yet he gnawed at that sugar, his stomach was full now but the feeling of chronic hunger was too strong for him. I involuntarily remembered that scene when I saw the storerooms of German provisions. Of course, they will come back here. If they had left for good they would have scraped up everything, from the last handful of flour to the last grain of coffee.

Liuden ordered the radio operator to call the launch, which was marking time somewhere far out to sea. The dots and dashes of our radio began to rap, barely audible in the deep silence, as the decision was made to burn the stores. When the launch, following our call, came up to the coast, everything was ready for starting the fire. The reconnoiterers climbed into the launch one after another, and after the boarding was accomplished the four of us who were the last to remain on the coast poured petrol over the boards and boxes which were piled up in a pyramid in the middle of the storeroom and set them alight.

Running down to the coast, leaping from one rock to another, we glimpsed the still hardly noticeable dull red tongues of flame penetrating through the cracks of the

ON THE NIGHT OF THE ANNIVERSARY

doors. It was still dark, but it was getting near dawn as the launch took off silently from the coast. We traveled for half an hour along the stormy bay when the stores finally lit up fully. Unexpectedly for us the fire assumed impressive proportions, sending a huge column of fire above the coast. Now it dropped, now it rose high as something inside kept on exploding with great force. Apparently, apart from provisions, the Germans also kept ammunition somewhere in the basements. Well, so much the better; they would remember this festive night for a longer time.

We sailed towards our shores.

The sun had already risen when, after disembarking from the launch, we made our way through the city, frozen but cheerful. The night of the anniversary was coming to an end, but we had celebrated it well, there was now something to commemorate it with. Near the entrances to the buildings our own red flags, with the hammer and sickle, familiar to us from childhood, swayed in the wind.

November 23, 1941

Konstantin Simonov

PURSUER OF PURSUERS

In the course of his thirty-some years this quiet man had passed through many, perhaps too many, professions. And each profession had left its stamp on him. He was a waif who became a herdsman, then a glassblower; then he joined the army, the air force; there, he also tried many professions, he was a reconnoiterer, an aerial bomber, and then finally, he became a pursuit pilot. He had walked and flown pretty much about the world, and those 4,500 flights which he had completed before the war were now of great service to him. He had become accustomed to flying under all conditions and in every situation, and he had acquired the knack of remembering forever a locality once he had flown over it.

And thus, pursuit-plane pilot Senior Lieutenant Kovalenko found himself here in the Extreme North. There was no time to look around and become accustomed to things. Air combat began on the very first day. It was necessary to fly and to fly well.

"During the first days there were more of them than of us. There was nothing left for us to do but to fly and to fight better than they," remarks Kovalenko, remembering his first aerial combats in the North.

The air is rigorous in this rigorous country. Very rarely was it possible to keep to a straight course in flight. Seeking out the enemy, creeping up on him, it was necessary to fly close to the ground through winding mountain gorges. Playing hide-and-seek, avoiding ambushes, keeping alert every second—all this is the North, whose strict rules he, Kovalenko, must make work for him and against the enemy.

Reference points—these could only be called that conditionally. Hundreds of identical rocks, buried in snow, went past the wing; they resembled one another like two drops of water, and a sharp and accustomed eye was needed to distinguish among them that unique rock which had to serve as a reference point in this particular square.

And this was not easy to achieve. It was not for nothing that the commander of the German bombers, Lieutenant Schuppius, who was given the assignment to fly from Stettin to Kirkenes, landed within sixteen miles of Kandalaksha instead. Kovalenko remembers this event with a smile—he can still see before him the surprised grimace of the German when he was told where he was.

It is both hard and easy to talk to Kovalenko. It is easy, because everything he says is precise, well-thought-out, and verified. He speaks slowly, as if the picture of aerial combat about which he is talking is being reconstructed from beginning to end before his eyes. And if he forgets something, even a small point, he pauses and does not continue until he has remembered that small point.

But it is hard to talk to him because he talks too sparingly about himself. No, this is not superfluous modesty, although this man is really modest, and his commander names a much higher number of aircraft he has brought down than he names himself. And yet this is not a case of modesty. In talking about his aerial combats there lies more than modesty in Kovalenko, there is a point of view which compels him to tell the story precisely this way, and not differently. This is a distinctive trait of Soviet pilots, their tactical doctrine of aerial combat. The number of aircraft he has brought down is not as important to Kovalenko as the general outcome of the combat, the combat result of the whole group he has led in the air.

"In our squadron there are many young pilots, and we make them understand from the very first day the meaning of gain in combat, how much more important the general result of combat is than the personal one," says Kovalenko. And it is not accidental that when you ask him to talk about the most successful aerial battles, he does not talk about those battles in which he had brought down the largest number of planes, but about those battles which, in his opinion, were noteworthy from the point of view of mutual gain and tactical cooperation.

"One day, Semenenko and I," he recalls, "ploughed into the thick of a squadron of Messerschmitts. I shot up one German, but saw at the same time that a Messerschmitt was sitting on Semenenko's tail. Then I dropped my German and went to Semenenko's aid. His German, who did not expect this, was quickly knocked down, and having got rid of him, Semenenko and I together managed to catch up and finish off my German whom I had dropped a minute earlier."

The next day the same story repeated itself, but in reverse order. Kovalenko was attacking a Messerschmitt, but no sooner had he managed to knock it down than two more appeared from behind. On seeing this, Semenenko got onto their tail, knocked one down and forced the other to detour sideways. Then Kovalenko, with his tail protected by his friend, dealt with the Messerschmitt which he had been attacking in the first place.

Kovalenko tells how knowledge of the locality and the determination to continue the fight under any conditions help them to conduct it in mountain clefts, maneuvering between the rocks, descending at times to the very ground. "I can now remember an incident," he says, smiling, "when we, the pursuit-plane pilots, bombed German positions with the help of the Germans. Yes, yes, we bombed them.

"It was a day when the clouds were pushing in all around, it was snowing, and the mountain tops were concealed. We flew in a formation of seven about our own positions, on the way to attack, when we suddenly noticed a bomb explosion below us on the ground. Bombs usually drop from above, so we immediately looked upwards to see where it was dropping from. A whole squadron of bombers and pursuit planes was flying above us. In the first attack Safonov and I knocked down one bomber each. Turning and attacking them in sections, we chased them back to the German positions. One more bomber caught fire. Then, in a desperate attempt to catch us, the other German bombers started to drop bombs on their own position. I became a bit heated and found myself in such a crowd of Germans that it was difficult to fire, there was nothing to do but to worry about how not to collide and how to disentangle oneself. Incidentally, it was not any easier for the Germans, either; they surrounded me so tightly from all sides that they could not even fire at me. In the end I was able to find an opening and dived through the gap back to my side. That time we carried out, as they say, a double assignment—we bombed the Germans with their own hands.

"But somehow I love pursuit planes more and more, I like to bring them down more than the bombers. I love the 'Mister Hundred and Ten,' it's a good aircraft in the sense that it's big and there's plenty of it to hit. And then, it has greater firepower, it's not so scared to go into battle. And this is precisely what our kind needs. I always take the first blow head-on; I fly to meet the enemy head-on. He won't stand for this and at the very last moment he'll turn sideways so that the tail gunner can strike at me with the tail machine gun. But while he turns I fall upon the gunner from behind, execute a half-roll, and fire at the gunner—and that's when I usually bring him down," Kovalenko concludes in a matter-of-fact manner.

He narrates all this without a smile, with the calmness and the attention to technical detail of the professional, of a master in his own trade. And you believe him, you believe that he really "loves" the "Hundred and Tenth Mister"—which is how he familiarly refers to the Messerschmitt 110—he loves it because it is a powerful aircraft and because it flies head-on more often than "Mister Hundred and Nine."

He sits on the step of the dugout, thoughtfully tamping down the snow with his boot, a thickset, small man with clear eyes and a muted voice. Presently he is in "readiness No. 1," with his helmet and parachute. But it is not only now, but also after he removes all that gear and seats himself at his place at the table that he is just as smart, self-possessed, and alert. It seems that wherever he was he would always be internally in "readiness No. 1."

"Kovalenko?" the commander of the unit asks. "Well, Kovalenko is a good pilot. He has knocked down about ten aircraft in slightly over a month."

"He said seven," I said.

"Ah, seven! Let it be seven, if he wants it that way. By the way, almost all planes knocked down by him are pursuit planes. That's what he's called here—pursuer of pursuers."

And, on hearing this nickname I again involuntarily recall the heavy strong figure of Kovalenko, his low voice

KONSTANTIN SIMONOV

which, for sure, is redoubtable and imperious at certain times, and his quiet phrase sounds in my ears: "I love the 'Mister Hundred and Ten,' it's a good aircraft, it has great firepower and it's not too scared to fly head on towards me . . ."

December 11, 1941

Konstantin Simonov

JUNE—DECEMBER

1. This happened on the 24th of June. The train which for some reason was made up of suburban carriages, pulled out from the darkened platform of the Belorussian station. The only light was from blue lanterns. One was not yet used to them. The train was going to Minsk, and it carried mostly commanders who were returning from leave to their units. The war had been going on for three days, and they were all hurrying there to the west.

A tank corps colonel was sitting next to me, a short, greying man with the Order of Lenin on his tunic. His son was traveling with him; I can't remember but I think he was called Misha. The father had received permission from the People's Commissariat of Defense to take his sixteen-year-old boy to the Front as a volunteer. They looked like each other, father and son—both small, thick-set, with stubborn chins and grey, steady eyes.

KONSTANTIN SIMONOV

The train did not go beyond Borisov. Ahead were the Germans, wrecked tracks, and utter uncertainty.

Several thousand commanders and Red Army men who were returning to their units had assembled in the forest near Borisov, on the bank of the Beresina. The above units were engaged in fighting on the Front, but between them and us were the Germans who had suddenly broken through to Borisov.

Low-flying German aircraft passed in wave after wave above our heads. They bombed and shot at us from sunrise to sunset while artillery thundered ahead of us. All the officers were from different units, no one knew anyone else and no one knew what was happening around us. And yet, a man turned up who welded all those men together and put everyone in his required place. The small colonel who was traveling with me in the train turned out to be the heart and soul of the men who were assembled in the forest near Borisov. He was the first here to speak the words: "Take up the defense line!" He was the first to gather the senior commanders around him to make a count of weapons and to break up the men into companies and platoons, so that the men began to feel like an army.

With him in charge, suddenly some guns were found, a number of machine guns, and men were sent back to Borisov for amunition. We dug trenches and slit-trenches, we selected positions for ourselves and lay down with our rifles in preparedness for defense. There were the most diverse people here from all walks of life; to my left there lay a captain of artillery and a military lawyer, to my right two civilian lads who were truck drivers.

I shall never forget the colonel's son. The boy did everything that it lay within his strength to do. Without taking the carbine from his shoulder, he ran around carrying out assignments, delivering food and water, bringing cartridges and, in any rare free seconds, casting delighted sidelong glances at his father. The boy was

JUNE—DECEMBER

pleased that he was fighting and proud that it was his father who, in this difficult minute, proved to be the most determined of all the grown-up, military-clad men who were there.

He was right. He could be proud of his father. The colonel behaved as if nothing had happened, as if under his command were not the most diverse people who had never set eyes on each other before, but a cadre regiment which he had been commanding for at least three years. He issued orders in a quiet, low-pitched voice. A slight metallic note was audible in this voice, however, and everyone submitted to him. His name was mentioned aloud in my presence several times, I remembered it then but I forgot it later on.

The next day I parted from the colonel and never saw him again.

In November on the Karelia Front on the Rybachy Peninsula we finally received greatly delayed newspapers from the center. I can't remember in which of these there was printed on the first page a photograph with the caption: "The Commander of the 1st Guards' Motorized Infantry Division, Hero of the Soviet Union, Colonel Lizyukov, is receiving the Guards' banner." On the photograph, in front of the formation, stood a colonel dressed for winter with a banner in his hands. Small, thick-set, with a stubborn chin . . . I recognized him at once—yes, of course, it was the colonel whom I had seen in the forest near Borisov in June. And then I recalled the name which I had heard at the time, but had later fogotten—Colonel Lizyukov. For some reason I wanted to see his son next to him on the photograph, just as they were back in June . . .

These things came back to me with particular vividness now during these December days when, on traveling along so many roads leading to the west, I saw the traces of the German retreat. For now, during these days when we have been learning to be victorious we may finally allow ourselves to remember what was too painful to remember before. One can now bear to remember the first perilous June and July days, the first cruel reverses and lessons, the bloody roads along which we retreated and along which we are now returning. And now one can pronounce, with a feeling of pride and gratitude, the names of the men who were the soul of our forces at the time, the sight of whom during the gravest days of this past summer made one believe that this will come to an end some day, that we shall be victorious one day and will return without fail. We did not know when this would happen, but the sight of these men made us know that it would be so without fail.

When Russia was devastated by the Tartar invasion, when her cities were burned, downed in their own blood, the people recorded in songs these unforgettable pages of blackest sorrow and misfortune. And side by side with this in the chronicles of every region—those of Novgorod, Suzdal, Vladimir, and Ryazan—the story of the Ryazan hero, Evpaty Kolovrat, has been preserved. On returning to his village after a campaign and finding it burned down to the ground, Evpaty gathered a small band of warriors and took off after the countless Tartar invaders. When he caught up with the Tartars, Evpaty slew a huge number of them and died a hero's death when he and his entire band perished in the uneven battle. The Tartar invasion passed into history and the battle of Kulikovskaya was fought and won, but the name of Evpaty Kolovrat, the people's hero from the first sorrowful days of the Tartar yoke, has been preserved in the people's memory, together with the name of Dmitri Donskoy. The memory of Evpaty has been preserved because in those hard and bloody times his exploit was not only an adornment, a matter of pride, but it was also a token of victory.

Times and enemies change—I do not want to make any historical comparisons—but the people's heart does

JUNE—DECEMBER

not change. It remains as brave and enduring as ever in ordeals, and it has a retentive memory for those who, during these ordeals, were more pure of heart and firm of spirit than anyone else.

And this is how it will be now. The names of the victors will not obscure in the people's memory the names of the heroes of the battles of June, July, and August, 1941. I can well remember how, during the days of the gravest reverses we, the people who had to tell the nation about what was going on at the Front, were searching and in most cases found, those whose stories inspired faith in victory: these were the Bolsheviks of the Army, the soldiers with Bolshevik training; during the most difficult days they took the whole brunt of the struggle onto their shoulders.

Middle of June. From the east bank of the Dnieper a solitary wooden bridge has been constructed to the west bank. There was not a single cannon on it, not a single anti-aircraft machine gun. We crossed to the west bank to the regiment defending Mohilev. A heavy, bloody battle took place on that day. The regiment knocked out forty German tanks, but it, too, bled profusely. In the evening we spoke with the commander of the regiment, Colonel Kutiepov. He was a very tall, skinny, slightly awkward man who had served in the Army for many years and still had the air of having put on a military uniform only yesterday. On his hairy, unshaven and tired, deathly tired, face, there suddenly appeared during the most critical moments a sudden soft, childlike smile.

We told him about the bridge. There was not a single anti-aircraft machine gun there, and if the Germans should destroy the bridge by bombing, he and his regiment would be cut off here beyond the Dnieper. "Well, so what?" Kutiepov suddenly gave his childlike smile. "Well, so what?" he repeated gently and softly as if talking about something quite ordinary. "Let them bomb. We've decided that if the others retreat, we shall stay here and die, the whole regiment has decided this. We've already talked about it."

I can still remember Kutiepov standing at his command post, and a messenger running up to him. "Comrade Colonel, there are still thirty tanks on the right flank," he says, out of breath.

"What? Where are there still tanks?" One of the commanders standing nearby who had only heard the word "tanks," but who had not heard how many, directed his question to the colonel. "Tanks? Yes, there are some three, mangy tanks on the right flank," Kutiepov said, smiling.

I remember his worried eyes and his smile. Worried eyes—because on his right flank there were thirty tanks and it was necessary to take measures. And the smile, because the commander will now proceed to the left flank, and it will be better for him to think that there were not thirty, but three tanks on the right flank. I don't know, perhaps this was not correct from a military point of view, but having looked at the hero during that minute I began to believe that we would be victorious without fail. Without fail, for it cannot be otherwise.

2. How the Front-line roads have changed! I shall never forget the Minsk Highway crowded with refugees, filled with lines of them without end. They went as they were, as they had jumped out of bed, carrying small bundles of food in their hands, bundles so small that one could not discern what they were, but which sustained them during the five, ten, fifteen days that they were on the road while German aircraft screeched overhead above the highway. Today the German planes do not fly like this. They don't dare, and they cannot. But in those days they flew low, as if they wanted to crush you with their wheels while they bombed and fired at the road. Not able to withstand their devastating onslaught, the refugees withdrew from the blood-spattered asphalt into the depths

JUNE—DECEMBER

of the forest from whose shelter they continued to follow the road along both its sides, a hundred paces in from it. By the second day the Germans had caught on to this; now their aircraft did not fly directly above the road but some distance away at the side of it, within a hundred yards of it, and dropped their bombs in a straight line there where, according to their calculations, the people who had left the road were making their way.

I can remember the villages where they asked us, "You won't let the Germans come here, will you?" and they looked intently into our eyes. They asked, "Tell us, perhaps we should leave here right away? What do you think?" and again they looked intently into our eyes.

And it seemed to be easier to die than to answer this question.

I was unable to think about this before, for it was very hard to do so, but I do think about it now, because I have passed back and forth toward the west along many of those same roads along which we were retreating east some months ago. Refugees move along these roads again, but they are different people now. They're not going away, they're coming back. Only in days of trials will one understand what the power of the native land is, how it draws people back to the native places they have had to flee. They do not wait for or seek safety, they follow immediately on our army's heels. They go at a time when danger has not yet passed, when the fires haven't yet gone out, when the firing of guns has not yet fallen silent. They don't want to lose a single day. They must be home today, in the evening, following on the heels of the soldiers who arrived there this morning.

There is a war on now, and military men are supposed to know more than anyone else; they must answer all questions, they dare not be "I don't know's." The people who move along the roads like to ask questions, they would like to know much, very much, and they want answers today, now. They asked questions in June, and they're asking questions in December. But how these questions have changed! I remember how it was when we were passing through Shklov in July. The refugees who were going along the road were worried about every motor vehicle that they met. If the motor vehicles passed westward toward them, they'd stop and ask, "Perhaps one should not leave, perhaps there will be no Germans here?" they ask. Hope is shining in their eyes.

But again, if military motor vehicles pass eastward, then the refugees accompany them with sad looks; they urge on the horses, they hurry. They ask, where should they go?—as far as Roslavl—or further?

December. The same roads again. And in Odoyev we are surrounded by people who have just returned here. They ask us, when will Mtsensk be taken? When will Belev be taken? Their relatives have remained there, and they believe that if their relatives are still alive, they will soon see them again. They believe that Belev will be taken without fail, they are only interested in how soon it will be. Yes, we say; soon. We also believe this. Then they start asking about Kaluga, about Orel, about other towns. "When?" they repeat, and look at the Red Army men with unwavering faith. And under this gaze our cavalry men involuntarily spur on the horses and hurry at a trot to the gate leading west from the town.

3. In November, at the Staff Headquarters of our Extreme Northern Army when the Aurora Borealis was playing across half the sky, an officer of the Special Department who had come out with me for a smoke and a breath of frigid air, turned to me as if suddenly remembering something and said joyfully, "You know, you'll have some interesting material. We've captured three German officers."

"Of what rank?" I asked.

"I still don't know."

"Are they still with the division?"
"No."
"With the regiment?"
"No. You see . . ." my interlocutor faltered, "you see, the thing is that they're not here yet, these prisoners-of-war, they're still there in the German rear. They were captured nearly a hundred miles away in the rear, between the Staff of the Corps and the Staff of the Division. Fifteen of our frontier guards went there and took them. They sent a message over the radio that they're bringing in three officers and will cross the Front with the prisoners in two or three days. So you and I will have to wait a little."

I remembered about this incident now because it was not simply a matter of the audacity of a small band of courageous men, it was a matter of assurance, which grew stronger from month to month in the army. In July, Germans were still not taken prisoner at a hundred miles from the Front-lines. In November we began to capture them. Moreover, this began to be considered a commonplace occurrence, so that one was not even particularly astonished about it. Three days later I saw these three German officers. They were brought in wearing felt boots which had been thoughtfully requisitioned specially for this purpose. They were clad in felt boots not out of unnecessary softheartedness, but out of sound calculation—that it would be easier to bring them in. They looked very miserable and disconcerted, these three officers of the famous Crete Mountaineer Brigade. They were still not accustomed to be captured in this manner. They were told that not only they, but others of their colleagues should become accustomed to this fairly soon. They kept quiet when told this. Their silence was not a matter of showing off—as it used to be before—but simply because they had nothing to say, because they were robbed of their will and were spiritually bankrupt.

How these soldiers of the "invincible" army had

changed within six months! In July it was not clear who among them was brave and who was a coward. All their human qualities were hidden behind arrogance—the common, general impudence of aggressors. Finding that as prisoners they were not being beaten or shot, they posed as courageous men. They calculated that the war would be over within two weeks, and that hence this captivity was for them no more than an enforced rest, and that we were treating them humanely only out of fear, fear of their subsequent revenge.

This has changed now. Some of them tremble and cry and breathlessly spill all that they know; others are sullenly silent, locking themselves up in their despair. In their days of defeat the army of impudent fellows has changed. This of course is natural for an army which is used to easy victories and which is now subjected to defeats for the first time.

The Germans are retreating. They fight, but they retreat. They snap at us, but they run.

An operational map lies in front of the general. I saw many such maps during the war, but how changed is its face! You remember the July maps, the August maps, the October maps with the large blue arrows and the red semi-circles on them? Today the map looks different. The Germans are retreating. The red arrows now reach west further and further from Moscow and cut deeper and deeper into the blue lines of the enemy. They break them up and disconnect them. The blue semi-circles become smaller and smaller, they break up more and more often into regiments, battalions, companies.

I see the map on which the operational situation has been entered. Our troops have cut an eighty-five-mile wedge into the retreating German divisions. Whole German regiments still roam about in the rear, every day the roads are cut by small groups of sub-machine gunners, but our divisions advance, they have faith that they will encircle the enemy and will annihilate him. For a moment I try to imagine this picture in July or in August. Yes, if we had had a look at this picture then it would have seemed to us that not the Germans, but ourselves were surrounded in this sector! At the same time, the encircler came to be in some degree the encircled—this is an old truth, but it was not only a matter of who had how many regiments and divisions, but who was the attacker, and who considered himself the encircler, and who considered himself the encircled.

A much more important thing occurred than the capturing of ten or twelve inhabited places: a giant, magnificent break occurred in the psychology of our troops, in the psychology of the Russian soldiers. Our Army has learned to be victorious. Now—even when its regiments find themselves in difficult situations, when the military scales are ready to tip, they feel themselves to be victors, they continue to attack, to beat off the enemy.

And the same break, only in a reverse direction, occurred on the German side. They feel themselves surrounded, they retreat, they uninterruptedly attempt to straighten the line of the Front, they are afraid of even a small group of men who have entered their rear and who have a firm faith in victory.

The Russian colonel receives a report that a company of German sub-machine gunners has appeared in his rear. "So what?" he says. "Some of ours will come up from the back and wipe them out, but our business is forward, forward." And, dismissing all thought of that German company in his rear, he gives the order for further attack.

The enemy must be crushed. All our men know this, they know this, and what is more important, they know this with all their hearts. They pursue the aggressors, and they will surround and hunt them down along the roads, and where there are no roads, along snow-covered fields where motor vehicles cannot pass, where one's feet sink in and it is devilishly hard to walk, but if you go forward you gain some unprecedented strength, a second wind. We will force our will upon them, we will become masters of the situation. The enemy will come out of the encirclement through burned villages, through impassable forests, they will freeze to death there in their hundreds where today they freeze in their dozens. They will be killed not only with sub-machine guns and artillery pieces, but they will be killed along the way with stakes and pitchforks by women and old men—this is how other invaders were killed in 1812.

They must not count on mercy. We have learned how to be victorious, but we have acquired this science at too high and too cruel a price to spare the enemy.

Let them know and remember that the words of our Supreme Commander in Chief—"a war of extermination"—is not just a battle slogan for the rank-and-file Red Army man. These are not only great words, they are also a dead enemy lying in the snow, one dead enemy and another, and yet as many dead enemies as there is strength and life in us to kill.

December 31, 1941

1942

What did he die for? He will not answer you.
And if you hear him, you will think—the wind.
For the dense grass to be greener here,
For you crying and, therefore, alive,
For the sad rustling of the tree,
For a vague Russian charm,
For the earth having four corners,
And how much we walked and the places we walked.
There could possibly be one, more brilliant, more elegant,
    richer,
But there is none like him for whom you weep.

                                              I. Ehrenburg

Ilya Ehrenburg

MOZHAISK HAS BEEN RECAPTURED

In front of me is a German map retrieved from an abandoned motor car. On this map there are two arrows directed into the heart of Russia—Moscow. One arrow pierces Odintsovo, the other Golitsyno. This is a November map of the so-called Mozhaisk Sector.

We have recaptured Mozhaisk. Everyone expected it, yet for us it seems to be an unexpected joy. The name of the ancient town has become a symbol for the Muscovites: "The Germans are still in Mozhaisk." Tanks went against Moscow from Mozhaisk. For the Germans Mozhaisk was the last small station before Red Square; the Germans celebrated the victory beforehand at Mozhaisk. Today the Muscovites will say with relief: "They are no longer in Mozhaisk."

People's faces and staff maps have changed. There is Lieutenant General Govorov looking at the map. The red arrows are bursting out toward the west. The last scene of the great battle for Moscow was played to the finish at Mozhaisk. Steadfast soldiers, courageous commanders, tank men and artillerists, pilots and cavalry men took part in this battle. The alert and quiet eye of the People's Commissar for Defense watched every detail of the gigantic battle.

In front of me is one of the participants in the battle for Moscow: General Govorov. A good Russian face, large, as if molded features, a deep intent gaze. One can sense tranquility appropriate to strength, a controlled passion, a natural and simple courage. For a quarter of a century now General Govorov has been engaged in the lofty work of an artillerist. He beat the Germans in 1916, he beat the interventionists, he pierced the Mannerheim Line.

Artillery is of old the pride of Russian weapons. The artillerists of the Red Army have inherited glorious traditions. Soviet artillery maintained its superiority during the gravest days. In every artilleryman there is a magnificent mental sobriety, a feeling of measure, a passion verified by mathematics. How unlike the hysteria of a German hit-and-run attack, the crash of sub-machine guns, the thunder of motorcycles, the comedian speeches of Hitler, the drunken snouts of the SS men! Perhaps this is why General Govorov, an artilleryman from head to toe, appears to me a personification of quiet Russian repulse.

The general tells about the courage of the artillerists who defended Moscow in October. It happened that they were left on their own . . . They did not let the Germans pass. Now the artillery has gone over to the attack: "We have to gnaw through the enemy's defense. The artillery takes part in all phases of the battle. It must destroy the nucleus of resistance, isolate it from other centers. Then destroy the second nucleus, then the third. The saturation with automatic weapons allows for limitless suppression of weapon emplacements. Drive them underground? No, wipe them out. The artillery cannot be guided only by the

MOZHAISK HAS BEEN RECAPTURED

demand of the infantry now. The artillery conducts the combat . . ."

The telephone does not fall silent at Staff Headquarters. It rings all night. The general does not sleep. His heavy, leaden eyes are glued to the map. He speaks into the receiver: "No. To the right. The 'Tongue'* has testified that they are retreating along the left flank . . ." Then the general puts on his greatcoat and strides like a great bear over the snow, he checks on everything, brings some things to a stop, urges others to hurry, he is modest and brave, a good manager and a good soldier.

On the tenth of January the German front was broken in the Mozhaisk Sector. Our banner now flies over Mozhaisk. Here the Germans had huge stores of equipment, all of it intended for Moscow. Much of it will actually get to Moscow—such things as German tractors, German guns, German motor vehicles . . .

Burned buildings. Poisoned wells. Not only the roadsides, but even the corpses of the Fritzes have been mined as the Germans try to delay the Red Army by barbarous destruction. Vain efforts! The water in the wells is subjected to analysis. A mine-detector exists to deal with the mines. And buildings? . . . Well, the soldiers have been used to forests for a long time, it is more peaceful outside of the inhabited places.

The soldiers march over the snow. The signalers lay wires. The guns thunder. A broad straight road leads west from Mozhaisk. We have completed only the first part of the march. It is a long road. From here to the extreme cape of Europe, to the "world's end"—Finisterre—is the kingdom of death. This is a difficult road. But the snow creaks obediently, the soldiers step with assurance, the long path will be traversed.

January 21, 1942.

*A German prisoner who gives information to the Russians.

Konstantin Simonov

IN THE QUARRIES OF KERCH

"I, the undersigned—a member of the Partisan Detachment named after Lenin, of the Stalin District of the City of Kerch—declare solemnly that my hand and my heart will not falter in the exercise of the sacred duty before the Motherland in the fight with the Hitlerite bandit horde.

"I swear to take cruel and merciless revenge on the enemy for our desecrated land, for the cities and villages burned to the ground, for the torturing of the population and for the mockery of my people.

"I swear that no torture will break my spirit, that I shall never betray the secrets of the detachment nor the secrets of my Motherland, and if I should repudiate my oath and solemn promise, then let my fate be that of general contempt and hatred, and the measure of revenge should be my physical extermination and contempt for my family and descendants."

KONSTANTIN SIMONOV

Sixty men signed that oath of allegiance, sixty Kerch workers, stonemasons, foundry workers, fishermen, Party members and unattached who had decided during the days of the German occupation to remain in their native city and to continue, at whatever cost, the struggle against the enemy.

The oath of allegiance had been written by Nikolai Ilyich Bantysh—the chief of staff of the partisan detachment, a hereditary fisherman, a stocky, quiet man who from his childhood had been taught by the sea not to be surprised by anything and not to retreat before anything. The men signed the oath of allegiance at night, after assembling in a cramped room of the District Committee of the Party. Fighting was already taking place near Kerch itself. The wounded were being moved through the city to embarkation points, and the sound of the cannonade, which was coming nearer, could be heard throughout the entire night.

Kerch is famous for its quarries. Near the city, at the Kamysh-Burunsky port, the rocks are dug up from endless labyrinths of subterranean corridors with dozens of entrances and exits and narrow black galleries. It was in these old and new quarries near the village of Adzhimushkay where the partisans decided to make their fortress.

Our forces were still in the city, but the Germans were already sending in their spies; traitors who had waited a long time for this moment were lifting their heads; it was necessary to be on the alert, and the detachment was being formed in strict secrecy. During the day the men worked as always in factories and at their trades, but at night they went beneath the rocks, going deep into the stony corridors where they constructed their fortress. Night after night they carried there food, cartridges, rifles, hand machine guns, grenades, "bat" lanterns, candles, matches —everything that could be of use to them during the forthcoming days. One could not forget anything because later it would be impossible to leave, one would be cut off from the whole world, locked up in these quarries, and one could not count on anybody's assistance for a long time.

Everything was brought in during the night. The detachment had not a single motor-car driver, but the engineer Ivanov who had passed a test for the "Prepared for Labor and Defense" badge, 2nd class, some time ago, had an amateur license. No stranger could be entrusted with transport, so Ivanov was forced to do the driving. This was a real torture: the motor car did everything it wanted with the novice driver. It either stopped unexpectedly or went again just as unexpectedly for him, but one way or another Ivanov could state to the Chief of Staff by the end of the week that he had transported everything he had been ordered to. "Everything in the world," he said, panting.

But one more complication emerged. It was necessary to store water for some three or four months, and it was decided to construct stone basins for this purpose inside the most distant galleries and to cement those in. Since there were no specialists in cement work among the partisans, Bantysh called for three old workers, three well-known masters, and trusting in their workers' honor, he let them into the secret of the detachment and obtained from them a signature in respect to guarding the secret.

The old men worked underground for two days. On the third day the basins were completed and were filled with water. But the caves were like this: put out the light and you are doomed; even though you may have been born there within that cave, if that light was put out for a minute—you are doomed. And along these corridors which were illuminated by the uneven light of lanterns, people walked for many miles night after night stooped under the load of sacks filled with equipment and food.

The Chief of Staff ran a tight ship: he entered into a

ledger everything that was delivered beneath the rocks, trying not to forget or omit anything vital. But at the same time this sleepless man, who appeared to be tireless, managed to keep a personal diary as well.

"2nd November. Today was my first partisan night. I spent it in the rocks, stationing sentries and arranging rosters. No Germans yet, but one must get accustomed to this new habitat."

This was the first entry in his diary. The following day and night were taken up by the final selection of men, and by the morning of November 4th sixty persons—fifty-five men and five women—had assembled beneath the rock in their fortress, which they had created by their own hands.

"4th November. Came out into the light for the first time," Bantysh wrote in his diary. "Was home in the evening at my mother's, took leave of her. Told her that I shall stay here. I have a Nagant revolver, I said, in case anything happens—six shots for the Germans, and the seventh for me. Well, mother cried, of course."

On the 7th of November the Germans came quite close. Voytenko—one of the members of the detachment—went up to see what was going on. Like everyone else, he carried no documents whatsoever, only a Nagant revolver, tucked against his chest. At night he was stopped by patrols of our retreating units. They began to ask who he was and where he came from, but he could not produce any documents, nor had he the right to make known that he was a partisan or to give the whereabouts of his detachment. He was held for two days under the threat of being shot; the situation seemed hopeless. He was saved through pure luck—some people turned up who recognized him. On the third day he came back to the detachment, where they had already begun to worry; surely he had not got scared, surely he had not left the detachment? He came back hale and hearty except that

IN THE QUARRIES OF KERCH

they had taken the Nagant revolver from him during the arrest and then, for some reason, had not returned it, which served as grounds for friendly banter: he had not even started partisan action yet but had already been disarmed. "Oh, what a partisan you are!" he was told.

These days and nights were spent in making the last, strenuous preparations. Some of the internal passages and openings which were too wide were blocked up with stones. The galleries were partitioned off with stone walls from behind which, if necessary, one could fire under cover.

"10th November. We detained a deserter in the quarry. I saw the hopeless situation of a man who had condemned himself to death, and for the first time in my life I signed a man's death warrant."

This was the entry which the Chief of Staff made in his diary. Actually, the full story was a grave and complicated one, in which a cruel but necessary decision had to be made. A certain Rutkovsky had deserted from the Red Army during the last days of a fierce battle. At first he had managed to reach the upper quarries, and later, driven by fear and having decided to hide even deeper in the mine, he had crawled down through to the lower quarries where he had stumbled into a partisan sentry. The partisans took him to the Chief of Staff, who received him in a wide, angular gallery under a kerosene lamp, seated at a table knocked together from boards. The deserter stood surrounded by partisans; he was visibly scared. When they asked him where he was from he said that he was from Kerch and that his name was Rudenko. He was searched, and it turned out that he was not Rudenko, but Rutkovsky, that he was not from Kerch, but from Dzhankoy, and that he wanted to wait a while and then make his way from here over to Dzhankoy, which had been occupied a long time ago by the Germans. Cornered, he shook and swore that he did not want to commit anything evil, that he was simply scared. He wanted to prove that he was not an enemy, that he was nothing more than a coward. But a coward was an enemy now.

What should be done with this man? To keep him here meant that he had to be guarded, which meant spending on him the efforts of people who were needed in the fight against the enemy. To let him go meant running the risk that he would disclose the secret of the detachment. A brief trial was held and he was condemned to death. The verdict was carried out in one of the remote galleries.

Fighting was already taking place overhead. The echo of the firing and the thunder of nearby bombing resounded dully in the caves, and the men on sentry duty at the secret exits could see the reflection of nearby flames. Bantysh was so busy with final preparations that he did not even have time to enter the particulars into his diary. His entries on these days are brief and spare:

"11th November. I watched my native town burning. I have lived in it all my life.

"12th November. Kerch is still burning. Mayorov came and said at the Staff conference that the Akmonaysky quarries have been smashed up by the Germans and that all who were there had perished. A grave silence ensued. Now, more than ever, do we need nerves and courage.

"13th November. How the mare rang."

That entry is just an aid to memory. Among the grim experiences of those first, difficult days, there were also funny, everyday incidents—the above entry is concerned with one of these. A signal system had been laid on to all thoroughfares and sentry posts in the caves, but in those days horses, who used to bring water to the workers, still remained under the rocks. A mare who was walking along a corridor in the darkness became entangled with her hooves in the signal system and raised the alarm throughout all the quarries. From that time on a saying was coined

IN THE QUARRIES OF KERCH

during the long days of the siege—every time someone caused a false alarm it was said: "Ah! How the mare rang!"

The Chief of Battle Supplies, the old mechanic Perepelitsa, who had been a partisan in these same quarries back in 1919, was engaged in setting up a mechanical workshop. Pushing his steel-rimmed glasses onto his nose, he rummaged for days on end constructing some artful contrivances from whatever was at hand.

On November 14th it was reported from the control post that Zhabkin—one of the three old men who had constructed the cement basins for the water—had shown up at the entrance to the quarry and moreover, that he had not come alone but had brought five Red Fleet sailors with him. Zhabkin was taken to Staff Headquarters where he explained that the Red Fleet sailors were staying at his apartment, and when the Germans came close, the sailors, who had been unable to get back to their unit, had asked the old man if there were any partisans hereabouts and how they could reach them. The old man, having decided in the simplicity of his soul that while a vow was a vow, good lads should not perish, took them with him to the quarry. The Chief of Staff quietly produced the oath of allegiance and showed it to the old man. The old man was silent; what could he say?

The Chief of Staff took out the Nagant pistol; he did not shoot, but merely threatened old man Zhabkin in order to impress on him not to act with such simple-heartedness in the future. Then a representative of the sailors was called in, and it was agreed that the sailors would undertake a last attempt to get through to their unit, and if they should fail, that they would then be accepted into the detachment. As it turned out, the sailors succeeded in breaking through to their unit the next day.

This was on the 14th, and on the 15th of November Bantysh wrote only three words in his diary: "Zoya, Zoya, Zoya." He was lonely, he was thinking of his wife and visualizing the coming great days of their reunion, which seemed so far away—and, who knows if it would ever happen? The siege had begun. The Germans were everywhere now, they had surrounded the quarries. But no matter how busy he was or what his mood might be, Bantysh considered it his duty to keep his diary regularly.

"16th November. Have blocked the passages, lit the fuses, and blown up some of the exits. Now it will be hard to get through to us. Saw some Germans, live ones, at a distance of thirty meters, through an opening in the rock. Was seized by a terrible feeling. In the evening the Germans shot the first four men in Adzhimushkay. We held a Party meeting during the night. Anger boiled. Wanted to cry for anger. Thought about mother and sister.

"17th November. Held alert at 2:20. Went off well. All at their stations. Perepelitsa, seeing that I keep a diary and records, rigged up the lamp in such a way that it would hang above the table. Then he went to sleep, and when he woke up he said loudly to the boys that he'd had a dream in which the Chief of Staff had given him one hundred grams of alcohol for suspending the lamp about the table, and he said that whenever he had a dream it always came true without fail. But I told him that this time the dream would not come true, although I thanked him for the lamp. Reconnaissance reported marauding by Fascists. Want to fight, seems we are slow, but endurance is needed, and again endurance. It is necessary to conserve strength and strike when this can be done with the greatest benefit.

"18th November. One a.m. Wife's birthday. The boys drank Zoya's health, celebrating with me. Light can be seen behind the wall and conversations heard. Here among the rocks every finger tap carried for three hundred meters. Everybody lying down. Cherkez looks at the historical revolutionary calendar. German cart can be heard passing overhead. Took out wife's photograph. Voytenko

IN THE QUARRIES OF KERCH

congratulates me, looks at photograph and says, 'Well, Zoya Nikolayevna, we are drinking your health. Zoya Nikolayevna, keep well!'

"19th November. Made rounds of all the rock faces together with Golikov. Everything is in order, all are at their stations.

"20th November. Put right all the telephone sets. Set up telephones at main posts and laid wires to Staff Hdq. Everything is done properly, like in a fortress. Found a German leaflet to partisans, thrown into hole."

The twentieth of November was the last relatively peaceful day. On the twenty-first the Germans penetrated into the upper quarries and began to drive out the people sheltering in the outer corridors. And on the twenty-second, continuing to penetrate deeper, they reached our posts. We could hear their soldiers dismantling the galleries which had been blocked with stones. The Germans were afraid of the dark. Clearing away the stones, they fired downwards into blind empty space with tracer bullets. But everyone kept quiet down there. The order had been given not to answer the shots before time. At night the partisans came up to the outer passages, laid demolition charges there, and when the Germans came to work the next morning, all the demolition charges exploded. Shouts and moans could be heard in the galleries. The Germans were removing the killed and wounded all day. On the second day a voice could be heard through the dismantled opening: "Russians, surrender! The Germans will not shoot!" The partisan on guard duty smashed the lamp with his first shot, and when the Germans found themselves in darkness, another demolition bomb was exploded. Everything thundered and shook in the stores.

Thus the siege began. The Staff was called together on the twenty-first, and on the chance that the Germans might possibly have been able to discover the approximate whereabouts of the detachment, it was resolved to reduce the distribution of tobacco and matches. One-and-a-half months of intensive daily war began from this day on. The enemy soldiers started to round up the population and to make them seal up some of the passages with cement; other passages which could not easily be sealed were blocked with stones with the aid of explosives. The Germans wanted to bury the detachment in the quarries. And it must be said that they would have succeeded in this if the population, who knew every gap here, had helped them. But the Adzhimushkay peasants, who had been forcibly driven together to work under the threat of bayonets, worked only where they had been ordered to. No threats could force them to tell the Germans where there were still other passages and how to achieve the complete sealing off of the quarries. And without this knowledge, all the labors of the Germans would be in vain. A whole regiment of German infantry was concentrated around the quarry; at every exit there were posted heavy round-the-clock patrols. But it was frightening for them to climb down inside the quarries. It was particularly frightening since, according to German information which it was not in our interests to deny, there were not a mere sixty partisans, but up to two thousand of us hiding in the quarries.

On the twenty-fourth of November two bold spirits —a German officer and soldier, penetrated into the interior corridors. Our eyes were kept glued on them and they were permitted to walk around a little. They walked around with a burning torch, waved their hands about, and being afraid of the dark, they talked particularly loudly. The echo of the shots attracted the German guard to this gallery, and it was not possible to take away the bodies of those killed. The Germans kept part of the rock on which the bodies were lying under fire through an upper gallery and lit them up with torches, but they did not succeed in removing their dead, for at each attempt

IN THE QUARRIES OF KERCH

the partisans fired into the darkness. Then, in despair, the Germans blew up a corner of the upper gallery and buried the bodies of the soldier and the officer under the collapsed stone.

It became harder all the time to go out on a reconnaissance. The sound of a slight tapping could be heard for two hundred meters. Light penetrated through cracks. One night partisan Victor Yudin, endeavoring to go out on reconnaissance, made an opening to the outside in one of the upper corridors. But on emerging waist-high from the ground he discovered that he had made the opening at the feet of a German sentry. The German became confused at his unexpected appearance and instead of striking Yudin with his bayonet he simply placed it against Yudin's back, obviously counting on the latter to surrender. After scratching his back against the bayonet, Yudin slipped down into the earth again and disappeared from view.

Noise could be heard above the rock during all these days. The Germans were afraid of sorties, and fearful of patroling in an open place, so they constructed fortified points with gunports at the top of the rock projection. They thought the partisans were vast in number, but the partisans were short of people. A guard had to be mounted in each of the endless galleries. Anything unexpected could mean the doom of the whole detachment, and the men were on duty for days on end, sleeping for only two to three hours.

But war is war and life is life. Living underground as a way of life soon established itself. It was predicated on absolute darkness, which did not allow one to make a judgment about either time or space beyond the perimeter of the two or three feet lit up by a lamp. A large marine clock and a calendar were under the strict supervision of the Chief of Staff. He personally watched over each one. They were extraordinarily important, for here where there was no difference between day and night, it would have been easy to mix up dates and days. In the evening of every day the Chief of Staff turned over a calendar leaf, and three specially appointed men checked to see whether he had turned it or not. It became clear later on, after the partisans emerged into daylight, that the calendar had been kept faultlessly all during that time, and only the marine clock was two hours fast. There were meals twice a day. At first there was bread, but the stores were terribly damp, everything flowered and stewed under there, and by the second week the partisans were eating doughnuts which were baked by the domestic method.

Water was distributed once a day after breakfast. Everyone received his two glasses of water a day and could do with it whatever he liked. Anna Rodionovna, as she was called, was in charge of water rationing. She distributed the water in strict accordance with the rules, for every gram was accounted for. The water which was issued to the kitchen for cooking was more difficult to control. On one occasion the women displayed kindness of heart by giving someone some extra water. But pity was out of place. Bantysh called the women in to see him and said: "It is like this—I shall not say much, but the next time I catch anyone doling out extra water I'll take her to the farthest gallery and shoot her without a word. There is no court here, no attorney, no defense lawyer, so keep this in mind."

This offense was not repeated again.

Water was a difficult problem, but here and there in the corridors rare drops of cold, clean water dropped from the stalactites. Everyone procured himself a small can and suspended it in order to catch such a drop. This one tried in one corridor, the other in another corridor. Thus each one collected twenty, or if he were lucky, sometimes thirty or forty grams of water during a day. Once two partisans went to a distant gallery where they had hung water cans, but before they could collect them their candle suddenly went out. They wandered for many hours in total darkness unable to find an exit, and were finally found only by the efforts of the entire detachment, who ended up frozen and weary from the search.

One fine day Chief of Provisions Voytenko decided to give a treat to the whole detachment by preparing a Russian salad. But the menu had to be approved every day by none other than the Chief of Staff. When Voytenko came to him and asked for permission to prepare a Russian salad, Bantysh, who immediately liked that idea, agreed in the enthusiasm of the moment. But as soon as he had dismissed the Chief of Provisions he suddenly remembered that the beetroots and potatoes for the salad must be cooked in their skins, which meant that the water would be lost. He immediately went to Voytenko. "Your Russian salad is canceled, Comrade Voytenko," he said harshly.

"Why?"

"And where, if I may ask, will you put the water from the potatoes and beetroots?"

"From the potatoes? The water from the potatoes will go into the soup."

"And the water from the beetroot?"

To this Voytenko could find no answer, he was stumped and the Russian salad was prohibited. However, the partisans who were free from duty and who had been enticed by this gastronomic idea kept on calling all day on the Chief of Staff in an attempt to soften his unbending character. Towards evening he gave in at last and issued them half a bucket of water.

Snow fell during the first days of December, it came in through the external openings and piled up in drifts in the passages of the upper quarries. Inside the quarries it was muddy and damp, the walls were black and slippery from mold, and it was difficult to express how urgent everybody's desire, especially the women's, was to have a wash. A whole delegation came to the Chief of Staff and to the Commissar, Cherkez, requesting permission "to go to steal snow from the Germans." Permission was granted. During the night snow was brought in buckets into one of the corridors where it was melted, and everybody in turn was allowed a shampoo.

An old partisan, the Chief of Intelligence, pulled the Chief of Staff away from his work and dragged him into a home-made bathhouse, repeating all the time, "Come, come, son, I am old enough to be your father, I shall give you a dressing down, although you are Chief of Staff," and he washed the latter's hair with his own hands.

The Chief of Staff continued to keep a diary.

"5th December. Held a meeting, celebrated the Day of the Constitution.

"7th December. Was on reconnaissance in the upper gallery. Everything as usual.

"8th December. Germans are filling in and blocking up the upper passages. A Russian was with them today—a traitor. Could not identify him. But a clue from the voice—a frequent expression he used was "the flies are eating him." Never mind, we shall find out who he is.

"9th December. Installed a telephone at the second side post.

"10th December. From morning on we heard violent bombing and antiaircraft fire. Apparently, our side worries them. At 12:30 Germans blocked up the round pit. Three loud explosions. Again one exit less. At 19:40 Kochubey went on reconnaissance along the lower passage.

"11th December. Nothing unusual. Waiting for Kochubey.

"12th December. The Germans raging again and putting down ammonal for explosion. At 16:12 dull explosion. One more passage blocked. Waiting for Kochubey. Still not returned.

"13th December. Kochubey returned at 14:40. So much joy!"

IN THE QUARRIES OF KERCH

"So much joy"—this is the single entry in the diary about this event, but the reconnaissance which Kochubey carried out deserves a fuller story.

Kochubey left for the reconnaissance on the tenth of December. During the day he climbed out to the starting position beyond the edge of the rock and lay there until nighttime. During the night he proceeded to the outskirts of the city, to Kolonka, after making his way past the German patrols, and at midnight he quietly knocked at the window of his house. His wife let him in; he was soaking wet and as black as an apparition from the next world. Having found out in the course of twenty-four hours everything that could be found out, and everything that was known in town, he returned on the evening of the twelfth. But in the darkness, and being pursued by the Germans, he turned by mistake into the wrong gallery, instead of the one from which there was a descent and a passage down, he found himself in another one which was tightly blocked with stone. There was no road back. For the rest of the day and throughout the night and morning he dismantled the wall with his bare hands, tearing his nails and skin to make a narrow opening for himself. On the thirteenth, bleeding and broken down, he did not so much climb through as literally drop down to his people.

One can easily imagine with what impatience people who were hermetically cut off from the world were waiting for him. He reported that Moscow and Leningrad were surrounded, according to German information; that the Germans in the Crimea have been promised leave after the capture of Sevastopol, and that this meant that neither Moscow nor Leningrad nor Sevastopol had been taken. This was a great joy. But the best thing was that the people were telling how leaflets had been dropped from Soviet planes to the population promising that we in the Crimea shall all celebrate victory together. Kochubey was allowed to go to sleep then, and life continued on in its own way. In the evening of the same day Bantysh entered in his diary:

"13th December. 20:30 hours. Ordered to have Stepanenko shot for falling asleep for the second time while on duty. Zaychenko took him to be shot but on the way he stopped and gave him five minutes' time, saying: "I'm telling you as an old man, go and ask the detachment again for pardon, perhaps they will forgive you, and if not, then nothing can be done." Stepanenko came back, and we forgave him this time.

"14th December. Mayorov, Golikov, and I went around corridors to check on the possibility of gas entering here, since according to Kochubey's information, the Germans were preparing an attempt to poison us with gas. We lit torches along corridors and checked on the movement of smoke. Result bad. It pulls down all the time, directly at us. During the night meeting of the Komsomol we expelled Stepanenko for sleeping on duty.

"15th December. Zaychenko reported that noise was heard above, apparently the Germans decided to drill rock from above. Ordered gas masks issued and stones prepared for placing under ceiling when it was drilled right through, so that it would not be noticed that the drill had gone through, and they would continue drilling. 11:00 hours. Germans attempted again to come through underneath rock. Repulsed after exchange of fire. Killed one, wounded another.

"16th December. Everything normal. Went on reconnaissance.

"17th December. Bombing heard at 12:30. Artillery fire at 13 hours. Yudin overheard conversation of passersby through upper hole: "How will this battle end?" Went around part of old rocks with Golikov and Yoytenko, shot rockets along corridors there—checked and saw smoke from there also pulling toward us.

IN THE QUARRIES OF KERCH

"18th December. Germans carried out nine more explosions. At the opening which Yudin had cut, there is a whole guard. Germans threw down leaflets demanding surrender.

"19th December. We can hear how heavily our side is bombing the Germans.

"22nd December. 20 hours. We all ate pie and drank the health of Comrade Stalin. Germans everywhere overhead, no possibility of getting out on top."

During the night of the 21st, when entering the events of the day into his diary, Bantysh remembered Stalin's birthday. He woke Anna Rodionovna and asked her to bake a large festive pie for the whole detachment for that occasion.

"And out of what?" she asked. "Most likely it has to be a sweet pie?"

"Out of sheep's milk cheese," said the resourceful Chief of Staff. "Take the sheep's milk cheese, soak it properly, sprinkle sugar over it, and we will have such a festive cheesecake, it will be a beauty."

"23rd December. Germans continue to block shafts. Two strong explosions today. Bombing at night. Our side is bombing the Germans. Up to ten raids during the night. Artillery bombardment taking place, apparently, across gulf from Chushka spit. Zinchenko wanted to climb outside without order to see what was happening. Put him under arrest for five hours for breach of discipline. At night a red glow is visible through cracks of upper galleries. The Port is burning.

"24th December. Heavy bombing all the time. Germans endeavor to break through to main entry. Retreat after exchange of fire. Shooting again with submachine guns at cracks all day. Heard fifteen heavy explosions in the evening. This is no longer in our pit but somewhere above. Each of us thinks to himself that perhaps it is a landing party, but do not say so to each other in meantime while waiting, afraid to believe it.

"26th December. Unceasing rumble of artillery fire above. Noskov and Buzhenko went on reconnaissance into upper galleries where they ran into Germans and killed two. Germans retreated, heavy exchange of fire began. Upper posts reported at 18 hours that German guard had begun withdrawing from main passages. Conference of Staff at 20 hours."

The twenty-sixth of December—this day would be remembered all their lives by everyone who had spent one-and-a-half months under the rock. They went into the rocks in order to fight, and if necessary to die, but no one wanted to die.

For one-and-a-half months the Germans kept more than an infantry regiment around the quarries. For one-and-a-half months they spent thousands of kilograms of ammonal in order to seal the quarry. For one-and-a-half months they feared every day that these subterranean Russian forces would break out of the quarries to the top and into the city. But—and this was the main thing—for one-and-a-half months everybody in Kerch, which had been sacked and drenched in blood, knew that not everything had been taken by the Fascists, they knew that they had not succeeded in subduing everybody, that there still was in the midst of Kerch another force and another power which, day and night, was fighting the Fascists and destroying them.

It is hard to appreciate what that knowledge meant to people who lived in an occupied, strangled city. And if the partisans had achieved only this, they would have had done their job. But they were dreaming of something greater. They wanted to strangle with their own hands the German guards who had kept them in a mousetrap for one-and-a-half months; having managed to stay alive, they now wanted to see the entry of the Soviet troops into Kerch and to help them recapture the city. Thus the Staff assembled on the twenty-sixth of December at eight

IN THE QUARRIES OF KERCH

o'clock in the evening to make plans for coming out and beginning an open fight. They still did not know how the battle was evolving; all they knew was that our troops had landed and were conducting the battle somewhere. They were accustomed to discipline, and the Staff conference was businesslike and ordinary; the detachments were broken up into combat groups, scouts were appointed. And only their voices were muffled from excitement, from the restrained desire to get out more rapidly, to see their own people and to see real daylight once again—and even, let it be said, the nocturnal light, the moonlight.

During the morning of the twenty-seventh the first scouts reached the upper galleries across those which had been blocked by explosions and came out into the light. It was a bright day, the sun was shining on the cold white snow lying all around, and for the first minutes the light was unbearable. Their eyes hurt so much that the men cried, and it was difficult for them to take aim, they had to wipe off tears all the time. The Germans were retreating, and the partisans dragged machine guns up from the caves and opened fire on them. But on this day there were still major German units coming through and the mountain was still surrounded, and although they engaged in battle the whole day the partisans still did not succeed in breaking out of the quarries into the open. But on the twenty-eighth they continued to break out stubbornly from morning on. They occupied the passages, one after the other, and came still closer to the road running through Adzhimushkay. Their first victim was a German radio crew which had broken off from its column. The partisans destroyed the radio station and wiped out everybody who was near it. The last German posts guarding the approaches to the mountain were retreating from it, and on December 29th at three p.m. the partisans attacked a large convoy, set six motor vehicles on fire, seized several dozen carts and the staff documents of a German infantry regiment, and killed eighty-five soldiers who attempted to defend the convoy.

From this hour on the partisan detachment straddled the road which led to Adzhimushkay, and the Germans had to retreat by making a detour along country roads, suffering losses from rifle and machine-gun fire. By nightfall, after breaking into the village of Adzhimushkay the partisans liberated fourteen hostages who were to be executed the next day. The partisans would have achieved even more if their eyes had not been sore from one-and-a-half months of darkness and if they were not nearly blinded by the sun and snow.

"One believes and one does not believe, and one does not know—is it you or not?" Bantysh wrote in his diary on that day. "There is air to breathe all around, and you can stand up to full height! We carried the banner of our partisan detachment outside and flew it from the highest rock."

And on the morning of December thirtieth when Kerch was occupied by a Soviet landing party and there were only a few hours left before the meeting with regular Soviet units, the following typewritten noticed appeared in the streets of Adzhimushkay village:

Notice:
The present Staff of the Partisan Detachment named after Lenin announces that as of this day the power in the Stalin District has passed into its hands.
The Staff of the Detachment.

The epic story, which started with the solemn oath of allegiance, ended with this tersely worded notice that was nevertheless suffused with restrained force.

March 1942

Ilya Ehrenburg

APRIL 20, 1942

I saw a German tank painted green. Our forces disabled it in the beginning of April when snow was still covering the ground, and the German tank reminded one of a dandy who had changed his clothes too soon. It was not dandyism, however, but necessity, which had driven Hitler's spring tanks and spring divisions into the cold. But now the snow has gone and the roads have begun to flow. They are covered with branches, you drive and bob up and down as if the motorcar were galloping. The season of bad roads has slowed up military operations for several weeks. The attacks of our units continue somewhere—in Karelia, in the district of Staraya Russa, on the Bryansk Front—but these are separate operations. A menacing calm has taken over before the May battles begin, but the last ice floes are now floating down the Desna and the Dnieper, and in the fields one sees smashed German motor vehicles, corpses of men and horses, helmets, unexploded shells—with the melting of the snow a gloomy picture of the war spring has been revealed.

Never has spring been talked about so much as this year. Hitler used to cast a spell with that word—"spring." He wanted to inspire the German people. Spring has come now, and two armies are getting ready for battle. In the meantime Hitler begins to look back feverishly. What confuses him? Tommy's high-quality demolition bombs? The campaign in America and in England for a Second Front? The growing rebellion of the enslaved nations? One way or another Hitler began the spring with a campaign—to Vichy. He did not have to use up much fuel for that—merely a few tanks for the trips of Laval and Abetz. The British radio broadcasts claim that von Rundstedt has migrated from the Ukraine to Paris. But this is only the journey of a general. On the way von Rundstedt was to meet the German echelons: Hitler continues to transfer divisions from France, Belgium, and Norway to Russia. Apparently neither the Royal Air Force, nor the articles in the American press, nor the anger of the weaponless French have had an effect on German strategy.

Before the spring battles begin Hitler wants to inspire his soldiers who have suffered a defeat this winter. He launches rumors about the new "colossal" German armament. He spreads foolish reports about the weakness of the Red Army. The soldiers of the Sixteenth Army will hardly be rejoicing, having heard over the radio from Berlin that there are now only sexagenarians and sixteen-year-olds in the Russian regiments.

Now is not the time to talk about our reserves. The summer battles will tell the story. I visited one of the reserve units and saw young, sturdy soldiers who were well-trained and well-equipped. The mood in the reserve units was excellent: everybody understands that the enemy is still very strong, but everybody also understands

APRIL 20, 1942

that the enemy will be beaten. During last summer people remembered Paris, Dunkirk, Crete; now they remember Kalinin, Kaluga, Mozhaisk, Rostov. Hatred toward the aggressors inspires the reservists. Last summer Germany appeared to the Russian peasant as a State, and Fascism could still be taken for a journalistic term. Now Fascism has become a reality—incinerated peasant huts, bodies of children, the sorrow of a nation of people. Between New York and The Philippines there are not only thousands of miles, between them there is peace; the Siberian feels that at Smolensk he is defending his land and his children.

Our factories worked well this winter. It is not worth reminding anyone under what hard conditions this work took place. Millions of evacuees proved themselves to be heroes. We have tanks. We have planes. Our friends often ask, "How did the American pursuit planes prove themselves? And the British tanks?" It is easy to understand the feeling of the American worker or the English sailor who would like to check whether their labor has not been spent in vain. I shall answer at once: not in vain. I have seen German bombers brought down by American pursuit planes. I have seen Russian villages in whose liberation English Matilda's participated. But the truth is dearer than everything, and one must tell only the truth to friends: we have a Front not just of a hundred miles, and along our immense Front the English and American pursuit planes and tanks are only separate incidents. It is sufficient to remember that all of Europe's factories are working for Hitler. And Hitler does not collect planes, Hitler does not save his tanks—his planes and tanks are not in France, not in Norway, they are not even in Libya—they are in front of us and above us.

Everyone here talks about the Second Front—women and soldiers, commanders and workers talk about it in trains and in trenches, in cities and in villages. We do not condemn, nor do we argue, we simply want to understand. We have read the statistics of the monthly production of the American aircraft factories, and we smile; we are proud of our friends. And immediately the thought springs to mind: what will be the destiny of these planes?

We speak of the Second Front as of the destiny of our friends. We know that we are now fighting alone against the common enemy. It has been 300 days now that the war has been devastating our fields; 300 nights that the sirens have been piercing our nights. We have taken on all sacrifices. We do not play poker, we fight. The fate of Leningrad, her mutilated palaces, her slaughtered children—this is the symbol of Russian courage and Russian preparedness for sacrifice. On the eve of spring we talk about the Second Front as about military wisdom and as about human morality. Like a mother whose children are all at the Front, looks at another whose children are at home . . .

Ilya Ehrenburg

ABOUT HATRED

Unappeasable dark spite ignites the heart of Fascism. This is the spite of the Ruhr magnates who in the Twenties of this century became frightened of the morning dawn, of the maturity of nations, and of the idea of justice. This is the spite of Krupp, of Voegler, of the owners of Fiat and of Schneider who have called in a band of adventurers and unscrupulous killers for assistance. This is the spite of the Prussian barons, of the Andalusian earls, the Rumanian boyars and the Hungarian counts, the untalented and feeble-minded epigones of a once-splendid world who look on countries as hunting grounds with hounds, and at the peasants who collect acorns on the lord's land as game. This is the spite of the little, ignorant, petty bourgeois, who is revolted by the complexity of culture, by the boldness of thought, and by progress. This is the spite of failures, of provincial Caesars, backwoods Napoleons who are thirsting to enter history, even if by the back door. This is the spite of the renegades who strive to defile everything that they had once loved. This is the spite of old age, soullessness, and death.

The Italian Fascists, coming out onto the stage, dressing themselves up in black shirts, have established the cult of the she-wolf and have adopted from the wolf pack the call "Alala." The Spanish Falangists have introduced the ritual of "betrothal with death," carrying their banners to cemeteries, holding processions with naked hunchbacks, God's fools, and gravediggers—processions resembling the nightmarish visions of the great Goya. The French Cagoulards put on blind capes taken from the Middle Ages born out of plague epidemics. The German SS men wear skull and crossbones on their sleeves. Goering has revived the executioner in a frock coat with an axe. Himmler has transferred into his torture chambers the torture instruments kept in the Nuremberg Museum. Even the Fascist window-dressing bears witness to black, desperate spite.

Fascism is a monumental attempt to halt the course of history. It has resurrected certain rituals and delusions of the Middle Ages, but the people of the Middle Ages did not live only by these rituals and delusions; within them there burned a genuine faith; they created wonderful cathedrals, remarkable epic poems; with their labor, their ecstasy, even with their ignorance they prepared for the age of the Renaissance. The Fascists must not be compared with the people of the Middle Ages. They live in a different epoch. They attempted to abandon the concept of time; this explains their sterility. Of course, Italy's grapes still continued to yield wine even under Mussolini; of course Germany's factories continued to function even under Hitler. But the Fascists did not create anything. They only mobilized contemporary technology for the struggle against the spirit of our time. They turned all achievements of civilization towards destruction.

ABOUT HATRED

Italy was justly considered the land of the arts. Fascism did not give birth to any artists; Fascism killed artists. Can the Italian people be proud of the conquest of Abyssinia, which was subsequently lost, proud of the use of mustard gas against unarmed herdsmen, proud of the destruction of Málaga, of the shootings in Greece and the gallows in the Ukraine? Did the spirit of Leonardo da Vinci, Dante, Petrarch, Leopardi, Garibaldi express itself in these crimes? When reading the illiterate and dull books of Rosenberg, the articles of Goebbels and Streicher, can we find therein a shadow of German genius, the lucidity of Goethe, the complexity of Hegel, the love of freedom of the Romantics? The destruction of hundreds of cities, Europe turned into a desert—such is the creative activity of Fascism. Countries cleared of people and the human head cleared of thought—this is Hitler's ideal.

It is not surprising that Fascism is attracting the dregs of humanity, people with a slovenly biography, sadists, mental freaks, traitors. The untalented painter Hitler, the untalented novelist Goebbels, the untalented dramatist Mussolini—is it not striking that at the head of Fascist States there are people who dreamed of artistic laurels and were denounced as mountebanks? Fascism attracts all renegades. Judas hanged himself out of sorrow. The Fascist Judases prefer to hang others. Mussolini appeased his spite by the killing of former comrades—socialists. In France Hitler found two followers, two apostates—Laval and Doriot. Sexual perversion and, in the first place, sadism have become a stronghold of Fascism. The morphine addict Goering, the lecher Goebbels, the sadist Himmler, "Doctor" Ley, the specialist in seducing those under age, degenerates about whose whereabouts directors of prisons and hospitals should be arguing, found themselves in ministerial positions.

Spite is a petty and mean feeling. In life we are justly ashamed of expressing spite. The untalented poet hides his resentment of his more gifted confrères. A greedy man will try not to make an ideology out of his fear for his buried money. An old man, envious of someone else's youth, will grumble, but will still fall silent. The Fascists made a religion of spite. There is no room for human brotherhood in Fascism. The German Fascist despises the Italian Fascist, and the Rumanian Fascist dreams of how to strangle the Hungarian Fascist. There is no room for justice in Fascism: for the German peasant the war means the grave or, in the best case, it means crutches; for *Reichsmarshal* Goering the war means huge profits which he transfers abroad without shame. In Fascism there is no place for right: the whim of an epileptic Hitler has been substituted for all laws in Germany. For century after century Humanity has endeavored to perfect man's defense against arbitrary rule; but in 1942 the executioner Himmler tortures French scientists and Norwegian artists, Czech workers and Polish agriculturists. International law, criminal law, civil law are all replaced by the morbid stupidity of any SS man. There is no place for creative thought in Fascism: books are replaced by pogromist brochures, universities are closed or converted to special courses for hangmen; Europe, only recently searching, bringing to fruition inquiries as complex as the convolutions of the human brain, has become a uniform desert under the heel of Fascism.

Spite drives every soldier of Fascism. After losing a battle they subsequently hang women and torture children. After entering someone else's house and not finding anything to loot, the Fascist soldier kills the housewife. One German lance corporal wrote in his diary that torture "cheers and even excites" him. In Hitler's speeches there is no love for the German people, his speeches breathe one thing: spite. Even Hitler's voice resembles the hoarse bark of a hyena. Hitler endeavors to warm the hearts of the German soldiers with spite: burn, rob, kill! He sends

ABOUT HATRED

out his divisions into faraway lands like poison-tipped arrows. And what could guide a native of Bavaria or Westphalia who has been sent to kill Ukrainian and Russian children except senseless, blind spite?

The Russian nation has come through a great and difficult time; its path to happiness and perfection has not been covered with roses. But even during the hardest years of his history, the Russian shielded himself from dark spite. Russian patriotism was nourished not on contempt for other nations, but on love for its own. The Russian soldier felt sorry for the prisoner of war and never harmed those without weapons. Russian literature of the nineteenth century gained a hold on the conscience of all progressive mankind; there is no European writer who has not been learning humaneness from the Russian novel. Our national, political, and social struggles—from the Decembrists to Zoya Kosmodemyanskaya—has shaken the world by its unselfishness, selflessness, and nobility of spirit.

The feeling of spite does not entice us even now. The idea of vengeance does not satisfy our outraged reason. We do not speak of spite but of hatred; not of revenge but of justice. These are not shadings of words—these are entirely different feelings. Hatred, as love, is inherent to pure and warm hearts. We hate Fascism because we love people, children, the earth, trees, horses, laughter, books, the warmth of a friend's hand, because we love life. The stronger the love of life is within us, the firmer is our hatred.

In the newspaper one comes across the expression "the enemy's infantry." To us the Hitlerites are not simply enemies; to us the Hitlerites are not people, to us they are murderers, executioners, moral freaks, cruel fanatics, and we therefore hate them. In the beginning of this unusual war many of us did not understand who was trampling our soil. People who were too trusting or too distrustful believed that Hitler's Army was the army of a hostile but cultured State, that it consisted of educated officers and disciplined soldiers. The naive ones thought that there were people marching against us, but against us marched monsters who had selected the skull as their emblem, young and shameless robbers, vandals who were thirsting to destroy everything in their path. Several times that spring the war communiqués reported attacks by drunken German soldiers. But the Hitlerites came to us drunk not only with schnapps, but drunk with the blood of Poles, Frenchmen, Serbs, with the blood of old men, young girls, and infants-in-arms. And they brought death with them to our land. I do not speak of the death of soldiers: there is no war without victims. I speak of the gallows on which Russian girls swing, of the terrible ditch near Kerch where the children of Russians, Tartars, and Jews are buried. I speak of how the Hitlerites finish off our wounded and burn down our peasants' homes. Now everybody knows about this: from the defenders of Sevastopol to the women members of the Siberian collective farms. Each crime of the Germans has fanned our hatred. All Soviet people finally understood that this was no ordinary war, that opposite us was not an ordinary army, that the argument was not about territory or money but about the right to live, the right to speak one's own language, to nurse one's own children, the right to be a human being.

We do not dream of vengeance: can vengeance quench our indignation? For the Soviet people will never become like the Fascists, they will not torture children and torment the wounded. We seek something else: only justice can soften our pain. Nobody will resurrect the children of Kerch, nobody will erase from our memory what has been experienced. We have decided to annihilate the Fascists: justice demands this. Our understanding of the brotherhood of man, of kindness, of humaneness, demands this. We know that people of different tongues,

ABOUT HATRED

different customs, different faiths, can get along together on earth. If we have decided to annihilate the Fascists then it is because there is no room on earth for both Fascists and for people—either the Fascists will wipe out mankind, or people will annihilate the Fascists. We know that death cannot defeat life, and we are therefore convinced that we shall annihilate the Fascists.

For us the German soldier with a rifle in his hand is not a human being, but a Fascist. We hate him. We hate every one of them for everything they have wrought together. We hate the fair or the dark-haired Fritz, because for us he is a small Hitler, the defiler of the land, the one who is responsible for the sorrow of children; because for us he is a Fascist. If a German soldier will drop his weapon and surrender, we shall not lay a finger on him—he will live. Perhaps a future Germany will reeducate him, will make a toiler and a man out of a dumb killer, but let the German pedagogues think about this. We have something else to think about; we think of our land, our toil, our families. We have learned to hate because we know how to love.

Recently on the Northwestern Front seven soldiers under the command of Lieutenant Dementyev defended a small hill. The Germans counterattacked with large forces. Forty bombers, the fire of guns and mortars were thrown against eight brave men. The heroes perished, but the slopes of the hill became covered with German bodies. More than three hundred Fascists died storming a hillock against eight heroes. Lieutenant Dementyev and seven soldiers—I don't know their names—gave their lives for their friends, their relatives, their home and for our common home—for immortal Russia. They wiped out hundreds of Fascists; thereby they saved the lives of many honest people. An old Serbian peasant woman could say a prayer for Lieutenant Dementyev and the seven soldiers, and far away beyond the ocean people will say, "May they be forever remembered!" During the last minutes the eight heroes were inspired by a great, indestructible love like the golden dawn, and the holy hatred came like the blood-red sunset over their faces inspired by the battle. He who loves strongly, hates strongly. Red banner of regiments and divisions, onward to the field of battle, you carry the blood of sacrificial love, you carry our anger and our hatred, you carry our vow! Russia shall live, the Fascists shall not live!

May 5, 1942

Konstantin Simonov

THE ANNIVERSARY

The snowstorm subsided by morning. Maybe tomorrow it will hide the sky and the mountains again behind a white shroud, but now it has cleared up.

A May day behind the Arctic Circle. The rocky maritime tundra is heaped up with snow, the mountains rise on all sides like a cluster of high white hats, and only their very tops, blown bare by the wind, stick out like small, round black keels. Here and there giant grey-green boulders are piled up as if glued onto the steep slopes. They are overgrown with Iceland moss. The Iceland moss, resembling silver which has turned green, crops up in small islands from underneath the snow. Reindeer chew the moss, inclining their branchy heads. The Nenets drivers who had arrived earlier from Yamal, stand next to the light sledges sucking on their pipes. They have brown faces with high cheekbones and the imperturbable tranquility of people who have lived all their lives in the North.

KONSTANTIN SIMONOV

The troops are moving ahead, the Staff is moving to an advance position, and the basic necessities of the Staff are loaded onto sledges: telephones, tents, light iron stoves. There are many places here where a motor car cannot pass and where horses sink into the snow up to their chests. But the reindeer with sledges can go everywhere, transporting provisions and cartridges and carrying the wounded to the rear.

We have just traveled eighty miles along the road which has been cut through the mountains toward the west after many days of labor by the field engineers. The road has been cleared and the snow which is banked up on the slopes on either side towers like a solid wall. Its banks are so high that the tall hospital buses travel along the road invisible from the side.

But now the road turns left and only footpaths lead up to the mountain, to the artillerists' observation posts. Their black-and-white camouflaged gun barrels project from the low shrubs at the side of the road; the black thread of the telephone line crawls from here to the summits of the rocks. We proceed for nearly ten miles along this thread, clambering higher and higher along the rocks. Ahead is the Resets Mountain—the aim of our trek. Until recently German mountaineer troops had been entrenched here, but they were thrown down from the ridge and our observers have clambered up the Resets Mountain. A low wall, resembling an eagle's nest stuck to the rock, has been put together out of boulders on a stone platform open to the four winds. In height this nest comes up to a man's chest, and from its two sides rise the two-horned eyepieces of the stereoscopic telescope.

At the observation post there are at present, aside from the duty commander, the telephonist, and the scout, two other persons: Lieutenant Colonel Rycklis, the commander of the regiment, and a German lance corporal. Yes, a German lance corporal, the Austrian Franz Maier

THE ANNIVERSARY

in a blue-grey greatcoat powdered over with snow, with a silvered metal edelweiss flower on the sleeve. The edelweiss flower signifies that Franz Maier is a soldier of the 6th Austrian Mountaineer Division which, in its time, became famous for the capture of Crete and is now counting its days in the tundra beyond the Arctic Circle.

The Russian lieutenant colonel unfolds a map which flaps in the wind, and the German lance corporal passes his finger over it for a long time, then both of them walk up to the stereoscopic telescope. Maier focuses it with the habitual movement of an artillerist, and having caught some point which is scarcely visible from here, he points it out to the lieutenant colonel. The lieutenant colonel nods; yesterday's observations coincide with the testimony of the prisoner-of-war. Maier is taken away from the observation post to the dugout behind the slope of the mountain.

Following with his gaze the stooped figure of the Austrian as he disappears below, the torn flaps of his greatcoat flapping in the wind, the lieutenant colonel tells us his brief story: Franz Maier is an artillerist-observer. He became lost this morning making his way to his observation post and was captured by our scouts. He surrendered, did not attempt to fight, and having been taken prisoner, did not lie and claim that he was a deserter.

He is not a deserter, he is simply a soldier who had been endlessly frozen and was tired of the war, in addition to being an Austrian, a man to whose motherland Hitler has brought nothing except slavery and sorrow. He had come to the point where he was waiting with equanimity for the bullet which would cut short his life. When he was surrounded he did not grab his carbine with his frozen fingers. He simply waited in silence; he did not care; there was death one way or another. He thought that he would be killed in captivity. This is what they write in their soldiers' paper, *Wacht im Norden*, this is what the officers said, this is what he thought himself, knowing what they did, by General Dietl's orders, when they captured Russians.

He was disarmed and led away. He was not shot, he was warmed at an iron stove in a Russian soldier's tent and given some Russian bread. Then they started talking to him. They did not beat him, as Sergeant Major Griml did to the Russian prisoners, they did not throw him face down into the snow, as Sergeant Major Krause would, nor did they tie him to a post, like Captain Oberhaus would. The warmth of the tent, the mug of tea, a piece of bread and human conversation were small things, but these small things suddenly gave Franz Maier a shock, due to the contrast between what he expected from captivity and those cruel customs, introduced to his corps by General Dietl—the "Mountaineers' death," as the soldiers had dubbed him among themselves. The Russians who talked with Franz Maier did not promise him anything, but he suddenly felt by the tone of their words and the expression on their faces that he would not be killed here, and that they would not mock him.

Something very light, which had been forgotten, crushed by fear and drill, awoke in him. At this moment fear did not play a part in his decision. He simply suddenly felt the wish to somehow repay the people who treated him in a human manner. Excited, he told the interpreter that he would like to explain everything that he knew. Excited, he poked with his finger at the German map which they had found on him, and it was only at the observation post, suddenly becoming relaxed, that he got hold of the stereoscopic telescope with the firm movement of a man who has decided to go to the end. This was the story of Franz Maier, told to us by Lieutenant Colonel Ryklis.

It was eleven o'clock at night but the approaching polar day had hopelessly mixed up all concepts of day

THE ANNIVERSARY

and night for the past two weeks. It does not get dark during the night hours, the sky only turns more leaden and the distant mountain ranges more blue, but every rock and hollow can be seen in a radius of several miles from the observation post. The frosty mountain air shortened distances, everything appeared to be nearby, and the German fortifications which our units were storming were actually not quite so far away. Turning the stereoscopic telescope we could see the stony excrescences of the German pillboxes on the crest of the rocks and the thin lines of stakes with barbed wire.

An hour of lull had set in now after lengthy fighting. The lieutenant colonel, who was getting ready to descend after a duty of twenty-six hours, inspected the landscape lying ahead with a thrifty master's eye. It seemed that even now this landscape was accurately subdivided in his eyes into squares, exactly as on the map which lay in his artillerist's map case. Beyond the stony hills, in the hollows, were the German batteries which he was fighting. Some of these had been smashed, others had been silenced. The day had been successful. That morning on a distant height which resembled a saddle by its shape, the battery of Senior Lieutenant Vinokurov had surprised a battalion of German mountaineers who were concentrated for an attack. The grey spots of wrecked and deserted blockhouses could be seen on the neighboring height.

There were only two colors in the landscape—white and grey—and it was difficult to distinguish the fortifications and dugouts from the huge stones which looked as though they'd been strewn over the slopes by a giant. But the lieutenant colonel, having focused the stereoscopic telescope accurately at some distant point, suggested that we look at it. "You see three spots?"

"Yes."

"These are camouflaged dugouts. We discovered them this morning, but there is no lively movement there as yet. I decided to leave them until tomorrow. Tomorrow we shall catch them."

The lieutenant colonel spoke of these dugouts with the tone of a careful manager, leaving them for tomorrow, in reserve, fully convinced that they would not get away from him.

It was quiet now. From time to time only the firing of one of our batteries harassing the German supply route to the Front could be heard. Through binoculars one could see horses and men moving along the road in Indian file. A brief puff of smoke—and a horse and a man fell down, the others scattered. A few minutes of silence, and again a methodical shot and a puff of smoke somewhere further along, behind the invisible curve of the road.

Partly slipping, partly rolling down, we reached the base of the mountain where Lieutenant Colonel Ryklis' tent stood. An aide and two telephones is all that he brought with him to this advance position on leaving the regiment's Staff Headquarters. The tent swayed in the sharp gusts of wind. A box which served as a small campaign table, a small iron stove, and two heaps of cut branches instead of beds completed the furnishings for the temporary quarters of the commander of the regiment.

Yefim Samsonovich Ryklis was warming his frozen feet at the fire. I had met him half-a-year earlier on another sector of the same Karelian Front. He had advanced from major to lieutenant colonel since then, the Order of the Red Banner had appeared on his tunic, but he was unchanged in all other respects. The same dark Southern eyes and Southern excitability, and in his conversation the same love for his long-range guns which were dear to his heart, the same ability to talk about them as of something animate, the same suddenly sad undertone in his voice when the conversation turned to his family. An old artilleryman, a master and patriot of his cause, the lieutenant colonel had traveled a harsh military road in twenty years.

THE ANNIVERSARY

A Jewish boy from Moldavia who spoke Russian badly, he had joined the Red Army and had been enrolled in one of our first artillery schools. In the beginning the going was tough for him; apart from everything else, it was necessary to learn the language. But he was stubborn, and within two years he had mastered Russian perfectly. Then, after graduation, there came one year after another of garrison service in artillery regiments. The places of service and the garrisons changed, and with every transfer he moved further and further east. His first son was born in Perm, the second in Chelyabinsk, the daughter in Buryat, Mongolia. In the family she was thus called a Buryatka. The soldier's family led a nomadic existence with him.

Ryklis spent five years on the Far Eastern border in the Barkhan among the remote forests of the Trans-Balkal Region. This tough Far Eastern training completed the artilleryman's education. By the time Ryklis arrived in the Extreme North he was prepared for all trials and eventualities. He met the war on the Rybachy Peninsula. Incredible snowstorms, wild winds, complete isolation from the whole world—it was under such conditions that the war began for him. In a critical moment Ryklis' batteries did not allow the Germans to burst into Rybachy. He was decorated, transferred here, and he continued fighting here with the same passionate love for his job.

Men at the observation post, frozen still from the north wind, changed and went to get warm, but the lieutenant colonel sat for hours behind the stereoscopic telescope as if possessed and gave commands in a hoarse voice to his batteries. Today, for the first time in the last three days he thought it permissible for himself to get warm and go to sleep. He lay down on the waterproof cape-tent spread over the branches, but he was not sleepy. He suddenly started to remember how, three days ago, under conditions of snowstorms and the absence of roads his artillerymen brought ammunition up here. First the motor vehicles became stuck, then the tractors. Then they began to transport the shells in pack loads, but soon the horses, exhausted, became stuck in the snowdrifts. But the guns had to keep firing, whatever thd cost, so the men began to carry the shells—one heavy shell to a man. Thus, for days they went on, one behind another, mile after mile in inclement weather. It was hard, almost unbearable, but the guns kept on firing.

Snow blew in from the flap of the tent as it was lifted; the messenger, a cheerful, tow-headed lad with the girlish name of Marusich, climbed into the tent. He brought a sack of provisions for the lieutenant colonel from six miles away. Ryklis opened a can of preserved food with a knife, and after pouring some vodka into two "artillerist's goblets"—shellcaps—he said thoughtfully, "This is my twentieth anniversary. Well, it's even good that it occurred here. The day before yesterday it was exactly twenty years since I've been in the Army, but there was no time to celebrate and no one to celebrate with. And today, even postdating it, we can still celebrate it. Well, and now if I can sleep, then I'll sleep."

He lay down and closed his eyes, but after a second he remembered something and opened them again. "There is one battery here that I have an old account to settle with. It has transmigrated from that place where I was before, it was called target Number Seven at that time, now it has been renamed target Number Fifteen. The old enemies travel after me. Never mind, I shall get even with it here." He turned to his side and immediately fell asleep like a man who had not rested his head for a long time.

The next day I happened to witness how the lieutenant colonel got even with his old enemy. We had been sitting in the observation post for three hours now. Night was falling according to the clock, but to the eye it was as light as before. The lieutenant colonel was adjusting

THE ANNIVERSARY

the fire from the batteries. At times the Germans fell silent, at times they returned the fire. They were striking at the line of defense, and suddenly a high explosive shell burst above the very summit of the rock within two hundred paces of the observation post. A small round cloud of smoke, visible from a long distance, congealed in the air. The Germans were obviously attempting to register the observation post. Several grenades followed the high-explosive shell.

The lieutenant colonel listened to the distant claps of the shots. "This is the fifteenth," he said with assurance, "but it has only moved somewhere to the left and closer." He rapidly made several corrections in the previous data, abruptly passing orders to the telephonist, and began to search among the many rocks for his old invisible foe. Our salvoes followed upon the German shells.

Ryklis, making new corrections, was apparently coming closer to the German battery. But the Germans, having found the range, struck more accurately. Several shells exploded within forty paces of the lieutenant colonel, splinters screamed above the stone wall. Ryklis did not pay the least attention to this. He was busy, very busy. He had no time. He had discovered his old enemy and was creeping up on him. He gave out orders more and more swiftly, the salvoes of our guns followed each other more and more frequently. The excitement of this artillery duel burned on the faces of all those at the observation post. In this cruel and obvious struggle it was necessary to reach the Germans before they reached us. The next German shell burst in front of our very wall.

The lieutenant colonel sucked in air with his nose. There was a smell everywhere of smoke and powder. He looked intently into the stereoscopic telescope for a long time, and then, after making the last corrections, he ordered his men to fire another salvo. The battery thundered behind us. Ryklis pulled on his gloves and buttoned up his map-case with the movement of a man who has completed his job and is about to leave. We looked at him with a silent question.

"We've got it now," he said with assurance. "That was its last shot. We can go to get warm. But, if you like, we can wait."

We waited another fifteen minutes. The Germans were silent. Apparently, the lieutenant colonel was right. In honor of his soldier's anniversary he was victorious today in yet another duel.

May 13, 1942

Konstantin Simonov

A RUSSIAN HEART

Captain Pozdnyakov was being buried in the morning. His comrades placed fir branches around the coffin which lay on the crosscountry vehicle, and accompanied him on his last journey. The pilots who were off duty and all those who had been with him in the last battle walked behind the coffin. His friend and deputy Alyosha Khlobystov was there, he walked as he used to fly—without a helmet on his curly head—his expression gloomy and his eyes downcast. A brass band brought from the town played a funeral march, and when the coffin was lowered into the grave the airmen were dry-eyed, but they could not utter a sound.

Standing above the grave, after following the deceased for the last time with his gaze, Khlobystov looked around at everyone with his dry eyes which were dark from fatigue and sleeplessness and said that he, Aleksey

Khlobystov, friend and deputy of the one who had perished, would take vengeance. Then a triple salute was fired from the rifles, and the general threw the first handful of earth into the grave.

An hour later Khlobystov was on duty at his aircraft. These were northern spring days when the sun came close to the horizon, but did not set below it. The pilots were on duty for twenty-four hours a day, sitting in their hunchbacked, droning pursuit planes. There was almost no time to sleep. But even in these few hours which were allotted for sleep, Khlobystov could not go to sleep. He lay motionless on his cot and silently, without a break, gazed at the vacant cot beside him.

While on duty he sat in the cabin of his plane glancing around absentmindedly. Looking at his neighboring aircraft, he suddenly recalled the first plane he had ever seen at close range. It was near Moscow, where a U-2 had unexpectedly appeared on the construction site of their factory. The plane was old and shabby, but Khlobystov, then still a boy, had experienced a strange shivering sensation and a desire to climb immediately into that cabin, grab something there with his hands—what, he did not clearly know—and to take off. Yes, he already had the same character then; he loved to act out his desires at once. Six months later he was training in the aeroclub. He smiled as he remembered his old teachers and chiefs. He was lucky; they were all real lads. And the last one was like that, too—Captain Pozdryakov.

A revenge account! Yes, this is how he had put it at the graveside: a revenge account for Pozdynakov! He would make it a long one, he could do it now; he was no longer that immature youngster who had brought down his first Junker on the first of July and had become so excited that he had run a temperature and had to be taken straight from the aircraft to the medical section. Together with his comrades he had brought down twenty-two

A RUSSIAN HEART

planes, and six on his own—this was, after all, no joking matter! When he climbs out of the aircraft after combat his back and chest hurt from strain, but he is not excited. He is cool and quiet now. When he climbs into his green machine it becomes an extension of his body, its guns strike ahead like a straight blow of the fist. Yes, if he were not flying now, if it were not for this machine, he would have completely eaten his heart out from sorrow. A good machine! One cannot live without such a machine—for him to live without it would be the same as not breathing.

In autumn when, after bringing down his fourth aircraft, he had slammed into the forest and, lopping off the tops of pine trees had crashed to the ground. Afterwards, when he lay in the hospital with a ruptured thorax, it had seemed to him that it was painful to breathe, not because his chest had been smashed, but because of the hospital air: because he could not get into the machine, rise up and up, high above the clouds, and take a deep breath. The doctors said that it was not like this, but he knew that he was right and that they were not. And one evening when he was visited and was asked: "Khlobystov, do you want to fly a new machine?" he silently closed his eyes in affirmation, since he was afraid to answer aloud: the cough was choking him and he was afraid that he would have a coughing fit right then and would be told he would have to stay longer in the hospital. Then he regained his breath and said, "I want to."

He had been brought to the hospital swathed in bandages and dressings, without helmet and overalls, and when he was released and had put on his overalls, he was seized by shivering for the second time in his life—the same shivering sensation he had experienced when he had seen the old U-2 on the factory site. A month later he was flying the new machine—exactly like the one in which he was sitting now, with its short, sturdy control surfaces and sharp nose like that of a spike.

KONSTANTIN SIMONOV

The sun came out of the clouds and licked the left control surface with a yellow tongue. He turned left and involuntarily recalled what that surface had been like when he had returned to the aerodrome after the ramming. Two thirds of it had remained, and torn shreds were sticking out where it had been cut. At that time the boys had asked him over the radio on the return journey, "How are you doing?" He had replied, "Not too bad." What else could he say? And he was really still flying, he was amazed himself that his plane was still flying.

. . . The tour of duty was nearing its end. Several men approached his aircraft. A political instructor from their airforce paper whom he knew—a good lad but a tormentor (you eternally had to tell him something) —introduced two correspondents to Khlobystov. Khlobystov was not pleased and was not even particularly trying to hide it. It is better to be silent and to think about the future than to recall the past. But the correspondents were either cunning or simply our lads: they did not question him on what height he commenced the pursuit, etc., but simply began to chatter about this or that, and what's more, one of them turned out to be a fellow countrymen from Ryazan, from the same places he used to crawl around as a little boy.

His tour of duty was over and they all went together to the dugout. And when the conversation in the dugout turned inevitably to that day on which all this had happened and after which his photographs had been published in all the newspapers, he again pricked up his ears and again, once more, for the nth time, he recounted in a dry and brief manner the circumstances of the combat.

But they did not leave him in peace. No, they knew all this themselves, they did not ask him to tell them about this, they only wanted him to recall, if he could, how he had felt at the time, what had been in his heart.

He planted his elbows on the table and lowered his head into his hands. Really, what had he felt at the time?

A RUSSIAN HEART

The day had been disturbing and he had been very tired. Yes, of course, he had been very tired that day. First he had flown out on reconnaissance together with Pozdynakov, then once again on a low-flying attack, then his aircraft had been refueled. He had stood next to it and he had wanted very much to have an hour of sleep, but he had to take off again. He could hear how the petrol was flowing bubbling into the tank. He could tell by the sound that it was nearly full. Five more minutes and he would have to take off again.

The commissar of the unit came up and handed him his Party ticket right there while he was on duty at his aircraft. And precisely because everything was so simple; that only he and the commissar were present and the aircraft stood nearby and the petrol was bubbling and he was about to take off presently—all this had appeared to him very solemn. He had become a little agitated, and with a voice which was a little more toneless than usual had said that he would be a Bolshevik, not in words but in deed, and he had thought to himself: not only on the ground, but also in the air. And just at that second a rocket had flown up and he was unable to say anything more, but then there was most likely no need for it.

And they had gone out on the low-flying attack: Pozdnyakov, himself, and four lads, still very young with only two or three combats to their credit. He could remember very well his first feeling when they saw twenty-eight German planes, the feeling that danger was threatening to overwhelm Murmansk. But the fact that there were twenty-eight of them had already become a secondary feeling. It was not frightening, but serious, very serious.

"Look how many are coming at us," he said over the radio to Pozdnyakov and heard the latter's voice in the earphones: "Look after the youngsters. I'm going to attack." The next minute they were in combat.

One Messerschmitt was shot in the first attack, Khlobystov thought in that minute that now there were twenty-seven of them. Then there was no time to think, for he was most of all concerned about the youngsters and about covering their tails by turning and dodging.

A two-seater Messerschmitt appeared underneath him. Taking advantage of his superiority in altitude Khlobystov went after him. He could clearly see the head of the German gunner and the fan of tracer bullets flying past. The distance was diminishing. The gunner dropped his head and fell silent. They were flying above the very edge of a forest, a mound lay ahead. And in that precise second at the sight of the mountain—when the habitual urge to pull the steering knob towards himself and take the aircraft up took hold of him—precisely in that second he decided to ram. To go upwards would have meant to let the German go.

He looked back for some fractions of a second to see that three more Germans were flying behind him. And, suddenly, because the first German was flying so close that he could clearly see the black cross on his tail, and because the distance was so precise and tangible, he thought clearly and coolly that he would be presently slightly back and to the right of the tail and that he would then raise the left control surface and hit the tail with its end.

This was an irrevocable desire multiplied by the speed of the obedient machine. The impact was violent and brief. The German crashed into the mound, but Khlobystov went upwards. And that his left wing was now shorter than the right because its end had been cut off, seemed strange on sight. He immediately noticed that the whole surface turned slightly upwards. In that second he heard the voice of his commander for the last time.

"Got one!" said the earphones with the somewhat toneless and triumphant voice of Pozdnyakov. But the airplane was no longer so obedient, it no longer seemed an extension of his arms and legs.

Our planes arranged themselves in a circle. The Germans, who had scattered after the ramming, recovered and went into the attack on a head-on course. Khlobystov saw Pozdnyakov go into a head-on attack on the German ace. Later, on the ground, when recalling this he understood that Pozdnyakov had decided to bring down the German commander and to disperse their unit's formation, cost what it may; if necessary at the cost of his own life. But in that second Khlobystov had no time to think about anything, for both pursuit planes came together at a frightful speed, the German did not want to veer off, and both planes collided and they collapsed as they crashed into each other with their wings. In the next moment he felt himself to be the commander: Pozdnyakov existed no more, there was no more Pozdnyakov and there never would be, and he, Khlobystov, had to finish the battle himself.

"I'm assuming command," he said over the radio with dried lips. "I'm going into the attack, cover my tail." He could immediately see the two Germans going for him. His fuel was running out, there were still many German planes, and behind his back were the four young pilots whose commander he had become.

This time, having decided to ram, he no longer believed he would come out alive. He had only one thought: that he would presently hit, the Germans would scatter, and the lads would get out of their encirclement. And again these thoughts were replaced by one-tenth-of-a-second's cold calculation. He took a sure aim, and when the German on the right veered off, he hit the wing of the one on the left with his own shattered wing. There was a violent blow, he lost control, and was pulled down behind the German who fell to earth in three long, spiralling loops. But just in that second when he was being pulled downwards and was instinctively struggling against it, he felt more than he understood that the aircraft was still sound and that he could pull it out. And when he lifted his head and found himself alive, the words which he later said at Pozdnyakov's graveside, flashed into his mind for the first time—"a revenge account."

The aircraft was listing and losing height, he no longer steered, but dragged it along. The men who came running when he landed; the fragment of the wing; the commissar who pressed him in his arms—all these things were getting mixed up in his head, obscured by the feeling of terrible human tiredness.

Khlobystov sat at the table leaning his head on his hand in the same manner and gazed attentively at those sitting beside him as he recalled what had been in his heart in those minutes. There had been much in his heart.

The door of the dugout opened. One of the pilots on duty entered, apparently a new one, and asked whether there was a vacant cot. Khlobystov was silent for a minute, and then pointed with a slow movement of his hand to the cot next to his. "There it is," he said, and after some more silence, he added: "Quite vacant."

. . . One polar night we were flying away from the North. "Is Khlobystov on duty today?" we asked.

"No," the commissar said. "He isn't here. He's in hospital. He undertook a third ramming yesterday and after bringing down the German, he bailed out with his parachute. He was unlucky yesterday; he was immediately wounded by a gunner in his arm and leg, and feeling that he wouldn't be able to fight for a long time, he undertook the ramming."

"Couldn't he have just dropped out of combat?"

"I don't know," the commissar said, "I don't know. Soon he'll recover, then we'll ask him. He will possibly say that he could not. He has such character: usually he can't stand it if a live enemy gets away from him."

A RUSSIAN HEART

I remembered Khlobystov's face in the cabin of the aircraft, the unruly shock of hair without a helmet, the bold, boyish, light eyes. And I understood that he was one of those people who sometimes make a mistake, sometimes take risks without need, but who have a heart that you will find nowhere except in Russia—the cheerful and indomitable Russian heart.

May 21, 1942

Ilya Ehrenburg

ON PATRIOTISM

It is not easy to grow a fruit tree: it requires much toil and care. But a thistle is not demanding. Hitler, in creating his "Hitler Youth," pandered to the lowest human instincts. He did not educate—he trained, he urged. The attitude towards the world of a German formed by Hitler cannot be called patriotism. Patriotism means love for one's country, for one's people, and like every great love, patriotism expands consciousness. A true patriot loves the whole world. One cannot, after discovering the greatness of one's own native land, come to hate the universe. People without love are bad patriots. But the pseudopatriotism of the Fascists rests on contempt for other nations, it narrows down the world to the limits of one language, one type of people, one color.

Long ago, before the First World War, while I was a youth I went to Germany where I gazed with admiration at the wonders of German technology. One day I stopped at a small out-of-town restaurant. It was Sunday. Some Germans sat in the outside pavilion; they had taken off their jackets, and with lifted beer steins they sang something as they rose from their seats. I listened, the words of the song were: "Germany is above all." In that same minute I understood that in spite of the tidiness of the Berlin streets, in spite of all the achievements of German polygraphy and mechanics, Germany was not "above all"; that in her self-assertiveness there were contained terribly low levels of the human spirit.

Hitler has found a suitable soil for his "race theory." He suggested with ease to young Germans (the sons of those who sang in the pavilion) that they, and only they, were people, while those around them were "the lower races," "sub-humans." It was flattering to the shop assistant in the cigar store to feel a "superman," to climb up on stilts and contemptuously look at the world from there. What is Paris?—Magdeburg is better. What is Oxford University?—Prussian barracks are more respectable. What about Leo Tolstoy?—Hans Ewers, the writer of pornographic novels, is much more absorbing.

The Hitlerites despise the French, calling them "negroid," and asserting that the French are mongrels. For tactical considerations the Hitlerites flatter the Moslems, but in Spain they indignantly wave off the Andalusians, and the word "Moor" sounds like an insult on the lips of a German: the Germans accuse the Andalusians of an "admixture of Arab blood." The alliance with Japan does not prevent the Germans from demonstrating their contempt for the "Mongol race."

In appreciation of the culture of the Slavic nations the Hitlerites set out from the general assertion that the "Slavs are the lowest race." The University of Prague is the oldest university in Europe. This does not prevent the German Fascists from stating that the "Czechs are savages." The music of the Polish Chopin is the "clucking of a stupid hen" to a Hitlerite journal. Hitler (a profoundly ignorant man and incapable of reading a book of one hundred pages) says that Leo Tolstoy is a "Russian cur."

The "race theory" pretends to be a science: the Germans like technical terminology. In Germany a charlatan who thought up a "theory" by means of which he could gain a million dollars in the game of roulette endeavors to adorn his computations with references to higher mathematics. The German nation, like other European nations, grew out of a centuries-old mixture of different tribes, in particular, of Central European Slavs who once populated a large part of Prussia. In the books published by the Hitlerites one can see photographs of the "best representatives of the Northern Germanic race." However, neither the ugly Hitler nor the lame Goebbels nor the fat Goering in any way resemble the "exemplary Germans."

Everybody knows that the Hitlerites destroy the national culture of other nations. But it is necessary to remark that they have lopped off and degraded the national culture of the German people as well. The poetry of Heine illuminated millions of hearts, its romantic irony was the salt in a country trained for unleavened bread. The Hitlerites found that Heine's skull was of an indeterminate type, and the new generation of Germany does not even know the poet's name. Thus Hitler, who has annexed the Polish Poznan and the French Lorraine to the "Reich," has divorced the Germans from a source of German poetry.

Having confined the meaning of national culture within the frame of one language, or by the relative definition of "race," Hitler has contributed towards a state of national cultural wilderness in Germany. The expulsion from the universities of scientists headed by Einstein who had exerted an immense influence on the development of German science, has had a sharp effect on the lowering of the cultural level of the country. Why did Germany have to part with many of her foremost minds? Because, in accordance with the "race theory," they did not turn out to be pure-blooded Germans.

Science has been replaced by pseudoscience. The new professors, for the most part ignorant people, have thought up "pure Aryan physics" or "strictly German mathematics." The Fascist professor Erwin Heck declared: "Mathematics is an expression of the Northern Aryan spirit, and of its will to dominate the world."

The Hitlerites have removed from the museums the works of modern French painting and have thereby placed blinkers on the eyes of young German painters. German literature knew of no great classical novel; it was, as it were, absorbed by poetry: Goethe, Schiller, Heine, Rilke. The German writers of the twentieth century learned from foreign language novels: Dickens' *The Old Curiosity Shop*, Hugo's *Les Miserables*, Balzac's *Père Goriot*, Tolstoy's *War and Peace*. What teachers have been left to the writers of contemporary Germany? Graphomaniac Goebbels . . .

Soviet patriotism is a natural continuation of Russian patriotism. Disdain towards other nations has always been alien to the Russians. Peter was not degraded by learning to be a shipwright in Holland. This did not stop him from becoming Peter "the Great." The young Russian patriots who fought against Napoleon found the still-warm ashes of the French Revolution in Paris.

Pushkin's genius, so organically Russian, so much attached by its roots to Russian history, to Russian nature and Russian speech, was at the same time a genius of all mankind. Pushkin passionately loved Shakespeare, Chenier, Byron, Michiewicz. As students Herzen and Belinsky avidly read Hegel. Italy's painting was not only a revelation for the Russian painter Ivanov, but also for his friend, the great Gogol. Mechnikov studied with Pasteur, as many Western scientists studied with Mechnikov. The

ON PATRIOTISM

experience of the workers' movement of France, Germany, and England helped the Russian spark to become a flame.

The Russian nation learned from other European nations and it taught its teachers in return. The Russian novel transformed the whole of world literature: the creative path of any French or German writer cannot be visualized outside of Tolstoy and Dostoyevsky. Russian music has spread to the most distant corners of the world. Every student at Cambridge and the Sorbonne knows the names of Mendeleyev, Lobachevsky, and Pavlov. There has been no event in recent history which has so transformed the path and face of humanity as has the Russian Revolution.

In its darkest hours the Russian nation did not despair over the fate of its Motherland, it loved her dearly, and defended her courageously—without spite towards other nations, without cheap conceit, without arrogant but essentially slavish shouts of "we are above all"!

Our Soviet Motherland did not fall to us easily; we paid for her with the blood of our best and the fierce toil of a whole generation. How much virgin soil had to be ploughed, how much wasteland built up, how much sluggishness and superstition had to be overcome! We did not close our eyes to our difficulties; we know that many trees bear fruit fifty years after they have been planted.

We did not expect miracles, but we had faith in the human will. And the country was changing before our eyes. As children rejoice over a new dress, thus we rejoiced over everything—over tomatoes at Arkhangelskoye and over the staging of *Hamlet* in a collective farm theater. We saw how our cities were growing. But most of all we rejoiced over the growth of man. It is easy to educate ten thousand selected ones at the expense of others, to counterpose an enlightened aristocracy to the ignorance of many millions. We wanted something else: light for everybody. We were the pioneers, and the path of progress is not a highway with milestones—it has to be carved through virgin forests. The light was before us and at times we lost our way, but we invariably came out on the right path. Soviet patriotism is illuminated by a great inner joy, our nation is justly proud of its historical mission. Soviet patriotism is at the same time simple and organic, like the attachment of the bird to the air, of the fish to the water: we love that element outside of which we cannot live.

Every Russian writer selflessly loves the Russian langauge. But did that love prevent writers from understanding the beauty and strength of other languages? We know what part has been played by the Caucasus in Russian poetry—from Pushkin and Lermontov to Mayakovsky. A Fascist hates a person whose hair is a different color and who talks in a different language. We rejoice at the diversity of the world; we are proud of the diversity of our Motherland.

During the days of grave trials the nationalities of our Motherland have demonstrated what genuine kinship is. The news of the first child killed in Belorussia awakened the Siberian villages. Russians and Ukrainians, Armenians and Georgians, Jews and Uzbeks—all the nationalities of our country are fighting in order to liberate the captive Soviet cities. The sons of the Ukraine display miracles of courage in distant Karelia, and Trans-Baikal divisions fight for dear Ukraine. The elder brother in the Soviet family, the Russian people, achieved the respect of other nationalities, not by self-assertion but by selflessness: it went ahead, it goes ahead of the others along the path where a man is met not only with flowers, but also with bullets. This is why the Russian people and the Russian language are surrounded by such respect. We said in peaceful times: this is the language of Pushkin and the language of Lenin. We shall say now: this is the language of battle.

ON PATRIOTISM

If we say "Russia," we do not mark out thereby this or that nationality. The word "Russia" is not the name of a State now, but something profoundly internal, linking us with our history, the Second Patriotic War with the First Napoleonic War of 1812, the young Red Army man with Suvorov, the cradles of the children with the graves of our ancestors. Mayakovsky wrote, "I would have liked to live and die in Paris if there had not been such a place as Moscow." The love for Paris did not make him forsake his native Moscow, but the love of Moscow helped him to love and to appreciate Paris. Our patriotism helps us to love other, distant nations, it helps us to understand foreign cultures.

We do not transfer our hatred of Fascism to races, to nations, to language. No crimes of Hitler will make me forget the modest house in Weimar where Goethe lived and worked. I love the Italian people, and when conversing with captured Italian soldiers I am pleased every time: Fascism in Italy has been unable to penetrate into the heart of the people; it has remained a disease of the epidermis, a disgusting eczema. And I'm sorry that that pathetic comedian Mussolini speaks the same language spoken by Petrarch and Garibaldi.

We know that the social system of a nation is not accidental. It is not accidental that a new chapter in the history of mankind opened on an autumn night in Petrograd. Nations proceed on the path of progress in a caravan and not in a throng. Honor and glory to that nation which was the first to enter that path!

It is not accidental that the Fascist armies suffered their first defeat on Russian, on Soviet soil, at ancient Tver-Kalinin and at youthful Stalinogorsk. This is why the word "Moscow" allows the tortured nations of Europe—the French and the Czechs, the Serbs and the Poles—to lift up their heads. When we call the Red Army a liberator we think, in the first place, of our captive cities, of the

ILYA EHRENBURG

Ukraine and Belorussia, of ancient Novgorod and Pskov. But millions of people at the other end of Europe, worn out by suffering, watch every step of the Red Army. The names of the heroes, soldiers, and commanders of the Red Army are repeated by the fishermen of Britany as well as by the shepherds of Greece.

The Hitlerites wanted to conquer the whole world, and in that war Germany lost its face and its soul—Germany lost Germany. We entered the fight in order to defend our home, our land, and in this just war we have gained the love and recognition of all the nations of the world. Such is the force, such is the magic of genuine patriotism.

July 14, 1942

Ilya Ehrenburg

July 28, 1942

The captured German lieutenant pilot had repeatedly bombed English cities from his Junker-88. In June, 1941, when his aircraft was brought down by British antiaircraft artillery, his rubber raft was punctured by a splinter and sank within minutes, but the German pilot managed to hold on for twenty-one hours in his life jacket until he was picked up by a fishing schooner. He was sent to the Eastern Front in June, 1942, and had been recently taken prisoner.

The captured pilot talks respectfully about the British pursuit planes: "The Spitfires are a terrible weapon and the German bombers have been ordered to avoid combat with them." The German pilot does not like the British: "I will say it directly that the Germans, and particularly we, the pilots, have some inner hatred for the British." The prisoner is a typical German of the new breed: dull, smug, cruel, and cowardly. Hatred from such a person can only please the British. The prisoner continues: "Over our way nobody takes the talks about the Second Front seriously. Not because the Second Front is no danger for Germany; on the contrary, it is very dangerous, but because nobody believes any longer that the British really want to help their ally."

One can, of course, be completely indifferent to the reasonings of a German pilot. However, recent events indicate that the German Command is reasoning the same as this prisoner-of-war: the transfer of German divisions from France to Russia is continuing. Recently I saw prisoners-of-war from the 323rd Infantry Division. They were young Germans who only recently were drinking calvados in a café in the city of Cannes. The 337th Infantry Division was brought in from Moulin, the 25th Division from the outskirts of Paris. The presence of three new divisions which have also been transferred from France has been observed on the Don, namely the 315th, 326th, and 709th Infantry Divisions. Thus Hitler has lately transferred two tank and fifteen infantry divisions from France.

During April the captured Germans spoke apprehensively about the possibility of a second Front. Letters from Germany which were written in the spring are full of anxious questions. "Surely we will not have to fight on two fronts?" "What will happen if the British should land, and the Americans with them? Could 1918 not somehow happen again? . . ." Now the Germans have relaxed. A letter was found on the body of Chief Lieutenant Richard Ullrich from his "Kommerzrat" brother: "The British thought that they would paralyze our forces by newspaper ballyhoo, but the Fuehrer knows how to take risks. If we can occupy the Caucasus before autumn, and consolidate ourselves on the Volga, the British will fare badly . . ."

Hitler's game is clear: he wants to beat his opponents one after another, in turn. He is still the same—from Mu-

JULY 28, 1942

nich to Rostov. Is it possible that some of his opponents have stayed the same?

Moscow is now the Rear. It is far from Moscow to the Northern Caucasus. Moscow realizes now the whole seriousness of the situation, nobody will reproach her for unconcern. The Germans have concentrated all their forces on the Southern Front. Having captured Rostov, they are endeavoring to exploit their advantage. They have forced the crossing of the Don in the Zimlyanskaya district. They threaten Stalingrad, the Kuban, and the Caucasus. The Germans enjoy superiority in tanks, aircraft, and artillery on the Southern Front.

It will be of interest to the British, who compare the struggle in Egypt with the battle on the Don, to find out that the Germans have concentrated more than twenty tank divisions on that sector of the Front. It will also be of interest to them to find out that Hitler is transferring his Air Force from Egypt to the Don. Here are the latest data: The 2nd and 3rd Group of the Pursuit Squadron, and the 2nd Group of the 77th Bomber Squadron, have arrived at the Don. Hitler's vassals render immense assistance to him. There are Italians, Hungarians, Rumanians, and Slovaks here. Even Finns have been turning up. While in America the Finns find an audience to whom they say that Finland is conducting a war of liberation, "defending her boundaries," the 722nd Finnish Infantry Brigade fights at the Don endeavoring to break through to Stalingrad. Evidently Finland's borders run either along the Don or the Volga . . . Casanova wrote once: "Nothing is easier than to deceive the one who in his heart is thirsting to be deceived."

"But where is the Second Front?" the Red Army soldiers ask. They can see one thing in front of them: German divisions, transferred from France. In the middle of June I wrote in the newspaper *Pravda*, welcoming the British: "We are awaiting the Second Front, as one waits for a good comrade at the Front-line—it is more cheerful to be fighting side by side." Now I should say that the soldiers are waiting for the Second Front in silence and concentration. They still smile when they read German leaflets. What does Goebbels write about to our soldiers? Well, about one thing only—"The Allies will deceive you." The soldiers still reply, "The British and the Americans will show the Fritzes . . ." but with every day their voices become more subdued and more serious.

The British say now that they do not want to undertake anything rash; they need to calculate and weigh up everything. This is laudable. I would like to assist our friends in the calculating and weighing up. According to the testimony of senior captured German officers, according to documents seized in German Command Staffs, one can determine what forces Hitler has left along the Belgian and Dutch coasts. In Belgium there are two infantry divisions. In France there are six infantry and three tank divisions of fighting efficiency. The infantry divisions are the 15th, 17th, 106th, 231st, and two others whose numbers I was unable to check. The tank divisions are the 6th, 7th, and 10th, all greatly worn out from last year's fighting on the Eastern Front. Altogether, Hitler brought out of France sixteen divisions of fighting efficiency, but left only nine such divisions there. The other units, which are in France, are security or police units, intended for the suppression of the population and not equipped with either artillery or mortars.

In weighing up and calculating one must think of these figures. The idea of a Second Front by two powerful nations—Great Britain and the U.S.A.—is called into question by many in the face of nine German divisions! Of course, even nine divisions are a force, but unfortunately there is no war without sacrifices. It is hardly necessary to insist on the gravity of the sacrifices which our country took upon herself. The German losses at the Don are ex-

JULY 28, 1942

ceptionally great, but our losses are also serious. They are felt in every Russian city, every Russian village. I ask British mothers to consider how Russian mothers who have lost their sons feel in reading the news about the transfer of the German divisions from France to the Eastern Front. It is not necessary to be a psychologist in order to understand this.

August was a grim month for all the Allies. It remains for us to remind them that one cannot gain everything without losing anything. In weighing up and calculating everything, the British and the Americans must not forget one factor, one which is perhaps hard to determine, but which is rather important for the outcome of the war—the Russian heart.

Ilya Ehrenburg

THE THIRD ANNIVERSARY

Three years ago Germany raved. Germans in new grey-green uniforms marched along the streets of German cities while the raving Fuehrer was promising imminent victory. "War"—the word inebriated the German people; the war appeared to them as a picnic, a shopping excursion for French trifles and English tobacco. They thought that they would be the only ones fighting. According to Hitler's idea there was only one thing left for the enemies: to capitulate. The Germans wanted to win the war with drums, with Hitler's speeches, with military parades. This was a psychological attack on humanity.

Historians will call the years preceding the Second World War the years of shame. The Germans staged a rehearsal for the conquest of the world in ill-fated Spain, the use of demolition bombs was tested on Madrid; the strategy of bluff was tested on Europe. According to their scenario, Hitler's hoarse bark was to scare the world. Timid ones said at the time, "He still does not touch us. Why should we get into the fray?" In the language of diplomacy this was called "non-interference." When German warships calmly smashed the defenseless Spanish city of Almeria, the shadow of the swastika loomed over Europe.

In a contemporary German novel the hero says, "If they cannot be talked into compliance, women are raped." A good dinner was prepared in Munich, soldiers marched resoundingly along the streets, and the Allies were handed a sheet of blank paper. Rape was not necessary; Hitler carelessly pocketed Czechoslovakia. This was the general rehearsal. Before even a year had passed the Germans began the war.

Hitler's soldiers burst into Poland. What could the defenders of Modlin and Westerplatte do? The whole of Germany's military machine came down on them. Poland's allies waited. "Non-interference" was, of course, militarized, it was dressed into a general's uniform and called strategy. Inactivity was now covered up by military secrecy. It was talked about as if it were a cunning plan. Poland was being bled white, but the French Army sat behind the Maginot Line and waited. The newspapers assured the world that the Army was waiting for the building up of aircraft, for the arrival of a contingent of British divisions, for spring. In reality, France was not waiting for anything, she was simply consoling herself with the respite. After becoming disengaged, the German divisions moved West. Spring came, but it did not at all turn out to be the spring about which the future collaborators of Abetz had been writing.

In the forest of Compiègne Hitler trod with his boots on a prostrate France. Great Britain withdrew to her island. The Germans celebrated the first anniversary of the war joyfully; it seemed to them that victory was imminent.

THE THIRD ANNIVERSARY

It is true that London responded with silence to the German overtures for peace, it is true that there were also widows on that first anniversary, but they became lost among the happy wives boasting about French perfume. The German newspapers said to the widows: "There is no victory without sacrifices." And the Germans believed that the soldiers who had perished in Flanders were Germany's last sacrifices. These were her first sacrifices. Germany was trying on the ball dress for the parade; nobody told her that the ball gown would have to be altered into a shroud.

The Germans celebrated the second anniversary of the war differently. They were still reveling in victories, but some Germans already understood that one cannot make one real victory out of one hundred victories. Many German women were already consoling themselves with "trophies:" not French perfumes (they no longer cared for perfumes), but good Lithuanian *polendvitsa*. But the number of widows had increased, and their silence often drowned the predatory squeal of the women unwrapping the parcels with "trophies." The newspapers wrote that the Germans would occupy all of Russia by Christmas, and that there would be peace then, a "real German peace." But the soldiers were already sending bitter letters home from Russia: "Here there is a real war . . ."

What happened during the second year of the war? The Germans had seized the Balkans. They had enslaved several more countries. They had destroyed several more English cities. But London remained deaf to peace overtures as before. Hess, upon landing in England, said cheerfully, "Let us shake hands." To his surprise he was not even offered a hand; the blood of London was on Hess's hands. Munich has not yet turned into a memory, but it has ceased to be real, it has become the spiritual underground of Europe.

Upon attacking Russia Germany experienced a repulse for the first time. In vain did the German generals gaze intently into the wide open spaces, awaiting truce envoys with bread and salt. Instead bottles with incendiary liquid struck German tanks, and peasant women of Byelorussia set fire to the huts in which German transport drivers were sleeping. The Germans advanced, but they paid dearly for every step. The historian will note that Lutsk cost the Germans more than Paris, and that it was easier to seize the whole of the Balkans than one Smolensk.

Germany is presently celebrating the third anniversary of the war. "We are in Pyatigorsk!" howls Goebbels. From Berlin to Pyatigorsk it is, of course, far, but it's much further from Pyatigorsk to victory! Achieving an advance of thousands of miles has not brought the Germans any closer to victory.

The third year was a cruel year for Germany. In November the Germans expected to see little white flags of capitulation in Russia. Snow covered the ground, but it did not bring Moscow's capitulation, it brought the Red Army attack. The oafs who were used to marching forward ran skipping along from Yelets and Kalinin. Troop trains carrying out their wounded and frostbitten ran back to Germany. Cold and fear made Germany shiver. The German divisions were thinning out, the German cities were becoming deserted.

Hitler had done everything to recoup himself. He extracted dozens of new divisions from his vassals. He removed German workers from their jobs, replacing them with alien slaves. He ransacked Germany, collecting all the juveniles and all the old men, and he launched an offensive in the South. He still gained a few victories; he still conquered a series of cities, but victory was even further away from Hitler. Now he no longer spoke of the "imminent peace," he spoke of a new winter campaign, and in August the Germans trembled; they sensed a new December.

THE THIRD ANNIVERSARY

"Our Cologne now looks like Rotterdam," writes a German soldier. Germany begins to understand what war is. She had thought of killing others, but now the others began to kill Germans. It was as if Russia's resistance had transformed the world's climate. The spirit of attack in the British and American nations is like a deep undercurrent demanding an outlet; a storm is brewing under the swell. Three years ago the men at Munich were called wise men, a year ago they were considered careful, at present they are called timid. Soon they will be pronounced deserters.

The nations subdued by Hitler expect a dénouement. Paris has become impassable for the Germans, like the mountains of Croatia, like the forests of Poland. The conquered nations are demanding German blood. The world's conscience demands German blood. Every living person in Europe and America, every city, every tree demands an offensive now. Millions of Frenchmen had to answer at the Maas and the Loire for non-interference in the fate of neighboring Spain. And now a shepherd from distant Uruguay demands interference: he knows that there are battles fought in the Caucasus not only for Soviet oil, but also for the future of mankind.

"How shall we celebrate the fourth anniversary?" ponders a melancholic writer in the German newspaper *Frankfurter Zeitung*. These insolent fellows have become more modest: during the first anniversary they did not rack their brains about the future. They drank French champagne and cut up the map of Europe. Now they ask: what will the fourth anniversary of the war be like?

Russian courage has opened the world's eyes. After Compiègne even the brave have become embarrassed, and after the German rout near Moscow even the extremely cautious began to get ready for the offensive. Enough of the Germans destroying and plundering Europe, enough of the German executioners converting groves into gallows and cities into cemeteries; the day of reckoning is approaching.

ILYA EHRENBURG

The witnesses will be sworn in. Paris will say, "Germany, do you remember the road of the refugees, the women who had been shot, do you remember the execution of the hostages?" The Norwegians will publish the lists of those shot, and Greece will say with a muffled voice, "The Germans have smothered my people with starvation." Britain will rap out curtly, "Can you remember Coventry?" Belgrade will arise from the ashes and will ask, "Can you remember?" Holland will remind them of Rotterdam, and Poland of Warsaw. "Lidice," will say the Czechs.

Long will be the Russian list—from the palaces of Leningrad to the rustic cottages of the Ukraine, from the pit at Kerch to Istra. A simple Russian peasant woman from the village of Lomovy Gorki will come up to the Judge's table and say, "The village was burnt down, everyone, young and old alike were shot. Senya Mikhailov was shot, he was ten years old, and the baby Anna Teplyakova, she was three months old." We shall ask, "Germany, do you remember Russia's torment?" This will be Germany's fourth anniversary.

August 27, 1942

Konstantin Simonov

SOLDIER'S GLORY

At night there is a red glow around Stalingrad. And during the day smoke rises from the steppe: black columns from exploding mines, a thin haze from the field kitchens and the rather bitter smoke from soldiers' tobacco. In the blue sky, which is unusually clear for September, pursuit planes trace white feathery trails, while the earth is furrowed by trenches, and the embankments of the mass graves rise next to the small mounds of the dugouts.

Nameless hillocks, cornfields, and glades overgrown with wormwood have become places which cannot be surrendered, for which one fights and dies, often without knowing the name of the village on the left or of the brook flowing on the right, but in the firm knowledge that Stalingrad lies around the bend and that it must be defended. Here one is faced with holding out for the price of one's life, for the price of one's death, for the price of no matter what. Today we're still holding on, we're not winning as yet, the glory of the divisions and armies, the glory of all Russian arms has not been born yet on these fields. But the glory of the soldier, the soldier's glory, is born every day and every night, now here and now there, and the courage of a man always remains courage and glory remains glory no matter how hard things were for the Army and the nation.

Semyon Shkolenko and I are sitting together on the dry earth of the steppes and a wind just as dry as the soil is blowing on his calm sunburnt face and his bleached light-brown hair. I asked him how it was.

"How it was?" he repeats thoughtfully, and glances far into the distance, remembering. And suddenly, as if wishing to tell me that his exploit was not born yesterday but a long time ago, that it had been thought out by the whole of his life, he begins without haste, remembering that life.

"Father was called Frol, he fought here too, near Tsaritsyn—at that time Stalingrad was still called Tsaritsyn—and he also died here in battle. He was a miner, like me. The mine is probably flooded with water now, or perhaps it has been blown up, who knows? Issayevskaya Mine No. Two—I passed the whole grade there underground—I was a sledgedriver and a hewer and a mine master, I went underground long ago, when I was still a kid, in nineteen hundred and twenty-four. How many years have gone by since then? Really, eighteen years already? Though today is my birthday, I have just hit thirty; this means that it's correct—eighteen years. Today the commissar and I drank a small glass, he treated me to it. I had a drink and remembered my wife and son, Yury Senyonovich. I haven't seen him yet, he was born to me on March twenty-seventh."

Shkolenko becomes immersed in thought and repeats again: "Yury Semyonovich." And one can feel by the serious way in which he called his son by his name and patronymic that he is proud of having a son, a continuator of his mining family. And one can feel in the way Shkolenko talks about his family, the mine, of his whole rigorous life of toil, that his soldier's glory cannot be called accidental. And when he begins to talk about his exploit, he also talks about it unhurriedly, deliberately, and calmly.

It was early in the morning. Koshelev, the battalion commander, called Semyon Shkolenko up to him and explained as usual without many wasted words: "We must get a 'tongue'" (an identification prisoner).

"I will," Shkolenko said. He returned to his trench, checked his sub-machine gun, attached three discs to his belt and prepared five grenades—two ordinary ones and three anti-tank grenades—and put them in his pouch. Then he looked around, and after some thought took a small piece of copper wire he had stored in his soldier's bag and hid it in his pocket.

His way led along the bank. He set out without hurry and with the proper caution. Everything was quiet. Shkolenko increased his pace, and in order to take a short cut he started to cross the small hollow on a straight line through small shrubs. A burst of machine gun fire resounded, the bullets flew past somewhere close. Shkolenko lay down and remained lying motionless for a minute.

He was displeased with himself. That machine gun burst—one could do without it. All he needed to do was to go through thick shrubs, but he had wanted to save half a minute, and now it was necessary to lose ten by going around. He got up and bending low ran over to the thicket. Within half an hour he had passed first one gully, then another. Immediately past this gully there stood three sheds and a house. Shkolenko lay down and began to crawl flat against the ground. After a few minutes he crawled up to the first shed and looked inside. It was dark in the shed and smelled of dampness, and on its earth floor some fowls and a sucking pig were poking about. Shkolenko noticed a small shallow trench near the wall and a hole cut out to the height of two logs. Next to the small trench there lay a packet of German cigarettes, half full. The Germans were somewhere nearby: this was now beyond doubt. The next shed was empty; near the third, by the haystack, lay two Red Army men, their rifles lying next to them. The blood was still fresh.

Shkolenko tried to reconstruct in his mind a picture of what had occurred: well, yes, they had come out from there, they probably had walked upright without hiding and the German had fired from the sub-machine gun somewhere from the other side. Shkolenko was gripped by vexation over this careless death. "Had they been with me I would not have allowed them to proceed like that," he thought, but there was no time to think further, it was necessary to find the German.

In the hollow which was overgrown with vines, he came upon a small path. The ground had not dried yet after the rain which had fallen in the morning, and footprints going into the forest could be seen clearly on the path. A hundred meters further on Shkolenko saw a pair of German boots and a rifle. He wondered why they had been dropped here, and to be on the safe side he thrust the rifle into the shrub. The new footprints led into the forest. Shkolenko had scarcely crawled fifty yards when he heard a mortar shot. The mortar fired, with small pauses in between, ten times in succession.

There were thickets ahead. Shkolenko crawled to the left through them until he spied a pit with weeds growing around it. In the clearing between the clumps of weeds he saw a mortar standing quite close by within the pit, and a few paces further on a hand machine gun. A German stood at the mortar, while six others sat around in a circle and ate out of mess tins.

SOLDIER'S GLORY

Shkolenko raised his sub-machine gun to fire a burst at them, but then he reasonably changed his decision. He might not have killed all of them with one burst, and then he would have been in for an uneven struggle. Slowly, moving without haste, he began to prepare the anti-tank grenade for combat. He selected the anti-tank one because the distance was not great and it could strike in a more concentrated manner. He did not hurry. There was no need to hurry, the target was evident. He set his left hand firmly against the ground, grabbing the earth in such a way that his hand would not slip, and lifting himself up, he threw the grenade. It dropped right in the middle of the Germans. When he saw, after the explosion, that six of them were lying motionless and that the one at the mortar continued standing there, gazing in surprise at the mortar barrel which had been mutilated by a grenade splinter, Shkolenko sprang up, and coming up to the German indicated by a sign, without taking his eyes off him, that he was to unbutton his ammunition belt and throw it on the ground. The German's hands were shaking, he took a long time to unbutton the belt and throw it away far from himself. Then Shkolenko, pushing the German in front of him, approached the machine gun. The machine gun had been discharged, and Shkolenko indicated to the German with a sign to load the machine gun on his shoulders. The German obediently bent down and lifted the machine gun. Now his hands were engaged. In spite of the seriousness of the situation, Shkolenko smiled. He found it amusing that the German had to carry the machine gun to the Russians with his own hands.

And thus they went back—the German in front with the machine gun loaded on his shoulders, Shkolenko behind him. The German proceeded slowly, stumbling; he did not resist but apparently had not lost hope of meeting someone who would release him, and he was dragging out the time. Shkolenko, who had done everything before without haste, was now hurrying. The feeling of loneliness and the fear that at any minute he could be shot in the back from any bush was not alien to him. Now he wanted to return more rapidly, and he impatiently pushed the German along.

Shkolenko reached the command post shortly after midday. The commander of the regiment sat there beside Captain Koshelev, and Shkolenko pushed the machine-gun-laden German forward carelessly, for the last time, and said, "There." And only afterwards did he formally report his arrival. The commander of the regiment pressed his hand, looked him over from head to foot, and then after firmly pressing his hand once again he went over to the side and began talking privately with the battalion commander. Their conversation continued for about a minute while Shkolenko silently waited.

"Good," the regimental commander said to him. "You have carried out his assignment," he nodded toward Captain Koshelev, "now carry out mine. You must find out where their remaining mortars are located."

"I will," Shkolenko said briefly, then added, "Am I to go alone?"

"Alone," said Koshelev.

"Well, never mind." Shkolenko shouldered his submachine gun.

"First have a rest," said the regimental commander, "then you will go."

Shkolenko went over to the signallers' section, took a spoon from his boot, and after settling down with his mess tin, began to eat *shchi* (cabbage soup). He was tired, and was pleased that he had been granted a respite. After finishing the *shchi*, he rolled a cigarette. He hadn't smoked all morning, and smoking was pleasant, especially when he had a feeling he would not have time to smoke again until night. Then he sat down and rewound his foot cloths. His feet hurt, and he rested for about half an hour, and then he got up, shouldered his sub-machine gun, and without adding any more grenades to his supply, he took off in the same direction he had taken that morning.

This time he took a course to the right of the village and closer to the river, hiding in the bushes growing along the side of the road. He heard the first shot from a mortar at five hundred yards. He had to crawl along a long hollow, making his way through a thick nut grove which scratched his hands and face. The mortar shells went toward Shkolenko and flew further on. He stopped for a minute, visualizing in his mind the trajectory of the flight, and established by sound the direction from which the firing originated. After the gully within the nut grove he had to get over a hillock, beyond which a densely wooded hollow began. By the time he had crawled along the hollow for another two hundred yards, the firing had ceased. The last shot was quite near.

Suddenly a German pulled himself up to his full height not far from Shkolenko. The latter kept quiet and remained lying down for some ten minutes. After the German had disappeared Shkolenko crawled through a thicket of low trees to a large shrub. All three mortars which stood in the gully could be clearly seen from behind the shrub. Shkolenko lay down flat and took out a piece of paper on which he had decided beforehand to trace for purposes of accuracy the exact position of the mortars. But the very second he had made that decision seven Germans who were standing at their mortars came up to each other and they all sat down near the mortar closest to Shkolenko, about eight or nine yards away from him. Only one was further away; he was telephoning while lying on the edge of his trench, and was apparently unable to get through. The fact that the Germans had come up so close to him and that they were all, except one, sitting together, induced Shkolenko to take a bold step.

His assignment was to note and to sketch the mortar's position, then to report to headquarters, and then the artillery would hit these mortars; in the meantime, however, the Germans were all sitting together and he had grenades at hand. The decision originated instantaneously, possibly because he had already been lucky today in exactly the same situation. One way or another he decided to tackle the Germans himself.

Still lying down he produced the two anti-tank grenades, then he took from his pocket the little copper wire he had put aside and tied it around the grenades. All he had to do now was to throw them. Once again Shkolenko leaned with his hand firmly pressed against the ground, took a deep breath, and threw the grenades. But the grenades were heavy—he was throwing two at once, and he was tired from this morning's foray—after all, this was his second reconnaissance of the day, and so when he threw them they fell half a yard short of the Germans. He managed to see this as he lay down flat on the ground, but in the next second he was hit, not violently, on the shoulder, and on grabbing his shoulder while still lying down he felt blood on his fingers.

He jumped up to full height then, holding his submachine gun at the ready, but the explosion had been very violent and the Germans lay dead like the last time, but this time no one remained standing up, everyone was lying down. Then the one who had stayed near the telephone moved a little. Shkolenko approached him and touched him with his foot. The German turned over, raised his arms while lying on the ground and began to talk, but Shkolenko in his excitement could not understand what he said.

The telephone lay on the ground next to the German. Since he couldn't count on being able to remove it Shkolenko kicked it several times with his boot and smashed it. Then he looked around wondering what to do with the mortars. Suddenly there was a violent rustling in the shrubs some twenty paces from him. Pressing the sub-machine gun to his stomach, Shkolenko fired a long, fan-shaped burst in that direction, but instead of the Germans he saw Satarov, a soldier of the 2nd battalion whom he knew well, and who had been taken prisoner by the Germans several days ago, jump out of the bushes. Satarov stood there, unshaven, bare-footed, dressed only in his drawers, and in a voice not his own he shouted back over his shoulder, "Ours, ours have come!" Sixteen more men came out of the bushes behind him. All were just as half-naked, unshaven, and terrible-looking as Satarov. Three of them were covered with blood, and one had to be carried.

"Was that you who was shooting?" Satarov asked.

"Yes," Shkolenko nodded.

"You wounded them," Satarov said, pointing to the blood-soaked men. "And where are all the others?"

"I'm on my own," Shkolenko said. "And what are you doing here?"

"We've been digging a grave for ourselves," Satarov said. "Two sub-machine gunners guarded us. When they heard the explosion they ran. But does this mean you are alone?"

"Alone," Shkolenko replied, and glanced at the mortars. No time could be wasted—that was the first thing he thought of at that moment. And the result of this thought was an immediate decision. "Quickly, take the mortars," he said. "What are you wasting time for? We'll go to our people now."

Several men got hold of the mortars and loaded them on their shoulders, the others led the wounded. Shkolenko was in an even greater hurry to go back now than he had been the first time; he still could not collect himself after his success. It seemed to him that any minute now the whole of his success would come to nothing if the time were drawn out. He brought up the rear of his little party, every now and then stopping to listen intently and to turn around with his sub-machine gun and scan the bushes. He walked behind those he had released from captivity and saw the bleeding bodies of the wounded. "It's good that I did not kill them," he thought. "But who would know them, I thought they were Germans." He repeated this aloud to Satarov who was walking next to him.

"I didn't know. I thought they were Germans."

"Of course," Satarov answered simply. "How otherwise?"

The captured German, the one who lay near the phone, walked between the liberated Red Army men, limping on one foot and holding his badly hurt head. He walked pressing his head with his hands and at times moaned, looking around with terror at the half-naked, blood-soaked men marching along next to him. Five minutes ago they had been digging their own graves; he was afraid of them as one is afraid of revived dead men. He was more frightened of them, it would seem, than of Shkolenko himself.

They reached the battalion after one-and-a-half hours. Shkolenko gave his report, and after listening to the captain's thanks, he stepped back five paces and lay down on the ground, face downward. Tiredness overwhelmed him immediately. He stared at the blades of grass growing up around him and it seemed strange that all this had happened and had come to an end, but that he was still alive and the grass was still growing around him, and that everything was the same as it had been in the morning.

The sun sets behind the steppe now; it is red and dusty, and the instantaneous southern darkness begins to crawl up from all sides. Shkolenko looks around for a long time at the steppe in its evening guise, and a bitter expression appears on his face.

"What are you looking at?" I ask him.

SOLDIER'S GLORY

"I look at how far the German has pushed us; he has pushed us a great distance."

But once upon a time the word "Borodino" was only known in the Mozhaisk district, it, too, was only a local word. But in one, single day it became a national word.

September 11, 1942

Konstantin Simonov

DAYS AND NIGHTS

Anyone who has been here will never forget it. When, many years later we begin to think about it and our lips pronounce the word "war," Stalingrad will arise before our eyes, the flashes of rockets and the glow of fires, and the heavy endless thunder of bombing will again resound in our ears. We shall again experience the suffocating smell of burning, we shall hear the dry rumble of roofing iron which has been burned right through.

The Germans besiege Stalingrad. But if one speaks of Stalingrad here, one does not mean by this word the center of the city, not Lenin Street nor even its outskirts—under this name one understands the whole, huge, thirty-seven-mile-long strip along the Volga, the whole city with its suburbs, factory sites, and workers' settlements. What we have are many settlements comprising one city which has girded the whole bend of the

Volga. But this city is no longer as we saw it from the Volga steamer. It has no white buildings climbing the mountain in a merry throng, no little landing piers on the Volga, no quays with rows of baths, kiosks, and small buildings running along the river. At present this city is smoke-filled and grey and the fire dances about it and the soot whirls day and night. This is a soldier-city, scorched in battle, with strongholds of self-made bastions built from the stones of its heroic ruins.

And the Volga at Stalingrad is not that Volga which we have seen some time ago, with deep and calm waters, with wide sunny beaches, with strings of speeding steamers, whole streets of pine rafts and caravans of barges. Its quays are dug up with shell holes, bombs fall into its water raising heavy columns of water. Ferries and small boats go back and forth across the Volga to the besieged city. The sound of armor clankings above the river, and the blood-soaked bandages of the wounded are reflected above the dark water.

Now here, now there, buildings burst into flame in the city, at night a constant glow spans the horizon. The din of bombing and of artillery cannonade reverberates day and night over the shuddering earth. There have been no safe places in the city for a long time, but during the days of the siege one became accustomed to the absence of safety. There are always fires in the city and many streets do not exist anymore. The women and children who have remained in the city seek shelter in basements, or they dig caves in the ravines descending to the Volga. The Germans have been storming the city for a month now, for one month they have tried to take possession of it at any cost. Wreckage from shot-down bombers lie scattered in the streets, anti-aircraft shells burst in the air, but the bombing does not stop for even an hour. The besiegers want to make a hell out of this city.

Yes, it is difficult to live here, the sky burns overhead

DAYS AND NIGHTS

and the earth shudders underfoot. The scorched bodies of women and children bombed by the Fascists on one of the steamers lie on the riverside Volga sand, clamoring for revenge. It is difficult to live here, but more than that: it is impossible to live here in inaction. But to live fighting—yes, that is possible here, this is how one must live here, and this is how we shall live, defending this city amidst fire, smoke, and blood. And if death is above our heads, then glory is next to us: she has become our sister amidst the ruins of dwellings and the weeping of orphaned children.

It is evening. We are on the outskirts of Stalingrad. The battlefield extends in front of us, a vista of smoking hills and burning streets. Darkness comes rapidly, as always in the South. Everything becomes shrouded with a bluish-black haze, which is ripped open by the fiery arrows of the Guard's mortar batteries. White German signal rockets fly up into the sky in a huge circle, marking the line of the Front. Darkness does not interrupt the battle. There is heavy thunder: German bombers have again plastered the city behind us with bombs. The rumble of the aircraft which flew overhead one minute ago from west to east can now be heard from east to west. Our planes flew westwards. Now they have suspended a net of yellow luminous "lamps" above the German positions, and the explosions of bombs cover the ground the lamps have lit up.

There is a quarter of an hour of relative silence—relative, because all the time a dull cannonade continues to be heard in the north and in the south, and there is always the dry crackle of sub-machine guns ahead of us. But here in Stalingrad this respite is called silence, since there has been no other silence here for a long time, and after all—something must be called silence! During moments like these of comparative rest you remember all the scenes which took place in front of you during these days and nights, the faces of the people, now tired, now excited, their sleepless, furious eyes.

We crossed the Volga in the evening. The patches of fires were already reddening against the black evening sky. The self-propelled ferry on which we were crossing was overloaded: it contained five motor vehicles filled with ammunition, a company of Red Army men and several young women from the medical ambulance battalion. The ferry traveled under cover of smoke screens, but the crossing still seemed very long. Next to me at the rail of the ferry sat a twenty-year-old Ukrainian girl, a military surgeon's assistant, with the surname of Shchepenya, and the quaint first name of Victoria. She was crossing to Stalingrad for the fourth or fifth time.

The usual regulations regarding the evacuation of wounded had been changed here under siege conditions. There was no place to locate medical institutions in this burning city: surgeons' assistants and ambulance girls, after collecting the wounded, drove them straight from the Front-line to the river, loaded them on boats and ferries, and after transferring them to the other side, returned for new wounded who were waiting for their aid. Victoria and my companion, the editor of the *Red Star*, happened to be compatriots. During the crossing they both vied with each other in remembering Dniepropetrovsk, their native city, and it could be felt that in their hearts they had not surrendered it to the Germans and would never surrender it, that this city, no matter what happened, is and always will be their city.

The ferry was already approaching the Stalingrad shore.

"Yet it is always a little frightening to come over here," Victoria said suddenly. "I have been wounded twice already, once seriously, but I kept on believing I would not die, because I have not lived yet at all, have not seen life at all—so how could I die?" In that moment her eyes were large and sad, and I understood that this was the truth: it is very frightening to have been wounded twice already at twenty years of age, to have been fighting for fifteen months, and to come here to Stalingrad for the fifth time. There is still so much ahead—the whole of life, love, perhaps even the first kiss, who knows! And there is night, continuous thunder, a burning city ahead, and a twenty-year-old girl is going there for the fifth time. But it is necessary to go, even though it is frightening. And fifteen minutes from now she will pass among the burning buildings and somewhere, on one of the streets of the outskirts, among the ruins and the buzz of shell splinters, she will collect the wounded and drive them back, and will bring them across the river, and then she will return here again for the sixth time.

Here comes the pier, a steep rise uphill, and this terrible smell of scorched buildings. The sky is black, but the skeletons of the buildings are even blacker. Their mutilated cornices and half-demolished walls thrust up into the sky, and when the distant flare-up of a bomb turns the sky red for a minute the ruins of the buildings appear to be the merlons of a fortress. Yes, and it is a fortress. The Command Staff works in one of the dungeons. Here, under the ground, there is the usual hurly-burly of Staff Headquarters activities. Girl telegraphers, pale from lack of sleep, tap out their dots and dashes, and communications officers, covered with dust and powdered over as if by snow from falling plaster, go past with hasty steps. The only encouraging thing is that in their reports there are no longer numbered elevations, hills, and lines of defense featured, but names of streets, suburbs, settlements, and sometimes even buildings.

The Command Staff and the Communications Center are concealed deep under the ground. This is the brain of the defense, and it must not be subjected to accidents. The people are tired, all have heavy sleepless eyes and leaden faces. I try to light a cigarette but the matches go out immediately, one after another—here, in the dungeon there is little oxygen.

It is night. We are driving, almost gropingly, in a broken-down staff *gazik* (a car with a gas-producer) to one of the command posts. Among a row of smashed and burnt buildings there is one which is intact. Creaking carts, loaded with bread, drive rumbling out of the gates: there is a bakery in this building which has remained whole. The city lives, it lives—come what may. The carts drive creaking along the streets and suddenly they stop when somewhere at the next corner ahead there is a blinding flash of an exploding mortar shell.

It is morning. Overhead is the even blue square of the sky. The Brigade Staff has settled down in one of the unfinished factory buildings. The street running north towards the Germans is exposed in its length to mortar fire. And there, where once maybe a militiaman stood, indicating where one could and could not cross the street, there now stands a sub-machine gunner under cover of wall fragments, indicating the spot where the street slopes down, and where one can cross unseen by the Germans without revealing the location of the Command Staff. One hour ago a sub-machine gunner was killed here. Now a new one stands here and, as before, "regulates the traffic" on his dangerous post.

It is already quite light. Today is a sunny day, the time is approaching midday. We are sitting in an observation post on soft plush chairs because the observation post is situated on the fifth floor in the well-furnished apartment of an engineer. Pots planted with flowers have been removed from the window sills and stand on the floor; in their place a stereoscopic telescope has been fastened on the window sill. The telescope is for the purpose of more distant observations, since the so-called Front-line positions can be seen from here with the naked eye: there

DAYS AND NIGHTS

German motor cars go along the outer buildings of the settlement, there a motor cyclist rushed by, there some Germans go on foot. Several bursts of our mortar shells. One motor car stops in the middle of the road; the other one, racing about, presses close to the buildings of the settlement. Immediately there is a responding howl above our heads as German mortar shells hit the neighboring building.

I move away from the window to the table standing in the middle of the room. On it there are some dried-up flowers in a small vase: books, and several students' copy books. On one of them the word "Composition" has been accurately traced out within ruled lines in a child's handwriting. Yes, as in so many other buildings, here life in this apartment has been cut short. But it must continue, and it will continue because it is precisely for this that our soldiers fight and die here among the ruins and fires.

One more day, one more night. The streets of the city are even more deserted, but its heart still beats. We drive up to the gates of a factory. The workers—home guards in overcoats and leather jackets, girded with leather belts, looking like the Red Guards of 1918, carefully check our documents. And now we sit in one of the underground rooms. All who have stayed to guard the territory of the factory and its workshops—the director, those on duty, the firemen, and the workers of the self-defense—all are at their posts.

There are no ordinary inhabitants left in the city—only defenders are left in it. And whatever may happen, no matter how many lathes had been transported away with the factories, a workshop always remains a workshop, and the old workers who had given the best part of their lives to the factory guard to the end these workshops in which the windows have been knocked out and where it still smells of smoke from the just-extinguished fires.

"We have not yet marked everything here," the director nods at the board with a plan of the works' territory in which the innumerable hits by bombs and shells have been accurately marked with set squares and small circles. He begins to tell how several days ago German tanks had broken through the defense and had rushed toward the factory. It was necessary before nightfall to somehow help the soldiers block the breakthrough. The director called the chief of the repair shop to him and ordered the release of those few tanks which were almost ready. The men who knew how to repair the tanks with their own hands, knew how in this risky minute to get into these tanks and become tank drivers.

Several tank crews were formed right here in the factory grounds from among the members of the People's Volunteer Corps—from workers and examiners; they got into the tanks and thundering across the empty yard, drove through the factory gates straight into battle. They were the first who happened to be in the path of the advancing Germans who had broken through at a stone bridge which crossed a small river. They and the Germans were separated by a huge ravine which the tanks could only cross by way of the stone bridge, and it was precisely on that bridge that the tanks from the factory met the German tank column.

An artillery duel ensued. In the meantime the German submachine gunners began to get across the ravine. During these hours the factory brought out against the German infantry its own men from the works—following the tanks there appeared two detachments of the People's Volunteer Corps. The Chief of Militia Kostyuchenko, and Panchenko, a department head of the Mechanical Institute, were in command of one of these detachments: the other was under the command of Popov, the foreman of the instrument workshop, and the old steel foundryman, Krivulin. Fighting broke out on the precipitous slopes of the ravine, often going over into hand-to-hand fighting.

DAYS AND NIGHTS

Old workers of the factory perished in these close engagements: Kondratyev, Ivanov, Volodin, Simonov, Momotov, Fomin, and others whose names are now remembered at the factory.

The outskirts of the factory settlement underwent a transformation. Barricades appeared in the streets leading to the ravine. Everything was thrown into the fray: boiler iron, armor plates, bodies of dismembered tanks. Wives brought cartridges to husbands as in the Civil War, and girls went straight from the workshops to the Front-lines, and after bandaging the wounded, pulled them back into the Rear. . . . Many perished on that day, but the worker-members of the People's Volunteer Corps and the soldiers delayed the Germans until night when new Russian units came up to the place of the breakthrough.

The factory yards are deserted. The wind whistles through the smashed windows. And when a mortar shell explodes nearby, glass débris pours onto the asphalt from all directions. But the factory fights in the same way as the whole city is fighting. And if one can get accustomed to bombs, to mines, to bullets, to danger generally, then it means that one has got accustomed to it here—accustomed as nowhere else.

We drive over the bridge across one of the city's ravines. I shall never forget this scene. The ravine extends far to the left and right, and it teems with life like an anthill; it is all dug up into caves, with whole streets dug out in it. The caves are covered with singed boards and rags—the women dragged everything here with which to cover their fledglings from rain and wind. It is hard to express in words how bitter it is to see—instead of streets and crossings, instead of the noisy city—the rows of these sad human nests.

The outskirts again—the so-called Front ones—débris of buildings which have been wiped off the face of the earth, low hills pitted with mortar shells. Suddenly we meet a man here, one of the four to whom the newspapers had been devoting whole editorials a month ago. At that time they had burned fifteen German tanks, these four anti-tank riflemen: Aleksandr Belikov, Petr Samoylov, Ivan Oleynikov, and this one, Petr Boloto who suddenly appeared before us now. Yet, actually, why suddenly? A man like him would be found precisely here, in Stalingrad, it is precisely people like him who defend the city today. And it is precisely because the city has such defenders that it has been holding out for a whole month now among ruins, fire, and blood.

Petr Boloto has a strong, thickset body, an open face with cunningly screwed-up eyes. Recalling the battle in which they knocked out fifteen tanks, he suddenly smiles and says: "When the first tank was driving toward me I thought—by God, the end of the world has come. But then the tank came closer and caught fire, and then it was its end, and not mine. And by the way, you know, during this battle I rolled about five cigarettes and smoked them to the end. Well, perhaps not to the end—I shall not lie—but I still rolled five cigarettes. It's like this in battle: you put the rifle aside and light up, if time permits. One may smoke in battle, one is only not allowed to miss. Otherwise, if you miss you may not be able to light up again—this is how things are . . ."

Peter Boloto smiles with the calm smile of a man who is sure of the correctness of his view of a soldier's life in which one may sometimes have a rest and a smoke, but in which one is not allowed to miss.

Different people defend Stalingrad, but many, very many, possess this same broad, sure smile of Petr Boloto, and they possess calm, firm soldier's hands which do not miss. And this is why the city fights, fights even when it appears almost impossible to fight, now in one, now in another place.

The quay—more correctly, what is left of it—skeletons

DAYS AND NIGHTS

of burnt-out motor cars, débris of barges swept up onto the bank, small houses which have sunk to one side while remaining intact. A hot midday. The sun has been clouded by dense smoke. Today the Germans have again been bombing the city since morning. One can see planes go into dives one after another. The whole sky is full of bursting anti-aircraft shells, it looks like the spotted, grey-blue skin of some animal. Pursuit planes circle with a whine as fighting proceeds overhead without a minute's break. The city has decided to defend itself at any price, and if this price is high and the exploits of people are cruel and their suffering unheard of, then nothing can be done about it: the struggle is to the finish.

The water of the Volga, lapping gently, washes up a scorched beam at our feet. A drowned woman lies on it, clasping it with singed, crooked fingers. I do not know whence the waves have carried her. Perhaps she is one of those who perished on the steamer, perhaps one of those who perished during the fire on the wharves. Her face is distorted, apparently the suffering before death was incredible. This was done by the enemy, he did it before our eyes. And let him not ask for mercy from one of those who saw this. We shall not spare him after Stalingrad.

September 24, 1942

Konstantin Simonov

"RUSSIAN PLYWOOD"

Here in the south at Stalingrad the Germans call them "Russian Plywood." At first, having thought up this name, the Germans took a belittling attitude toward "Russian Plywood." Really, what sort of wooden aircraft was this with control surfaces made of canvas? What sort of speed is sixty to ninety miles an hour? What sort of motor sound is it that resembles a motorcycle traveling on a bad road? And, finally, what sort of strange idea is it to bomb German troops and to attempt to disturb their peace by means of such antiquated contraptions?

This is how it was the first time that the first improvised night bombers visited the German positions. The pilots had no experience in night flying; they were very often caught in anti-aircraft fire, they had no rockets to light up the Germans, and they threw small bombs with their hands, having piled them beforehand into the cabin next to themselves. Sometimes, owing to lack of bombs, they threw hand grenades.

It was then that the planes were christened "Russian Plywood." But the Russians are stubborn people, and if a good thought enters their heads, they will sooner or later carry it into practice with a truly Russian sweep. Yes, the plane is glued together out of canvas and plywood, but for this reason it is light, and it can land anywhere and take off from anywhere in complete darkness. Yes, its speed is sixty to ninety miles per hour, but at this speed it can bomb at night with an accuracy undreamed of by any dive bomber. Yes, the sound of the motor really resembles that of a motorcycle, but if this motorcycle rumble is hanging overhead all night and is accompanied by the uninterrupted dropping of small- and medium-sized demolition bombs, then this sound gradually becomes threatening.

In autumn the Russian pilots trained for night flying, in winter they received new machines—just as light, constructed as before from plywood, but with a few simple improvements, and by the beginning of spring the nightly Russian Plywood bomber regiments began to bring down on the enemy's head hundreds of tons of bombs, and the term "Russian Plywood" immediately changed in its meaning; before the Germans pronounced it with sarcasm, now they say it with hatred.

As soon as it gets dark and the white rays of the rockets fly up into the sky along the Front line, picking it out, a continuous bustle and rumble begins in the air above the German positions. Searchlights scan the sky, German anti-aircraft guns fire into space as if aiming at a penny, multi-colored bursts of machine gun tracer bullets come together from all sides on the sound, but the aerial motorcycles continue to travel along the invisible road as if nothing were happening, and after suspending the green lamps of illuminating rockets now here, now

"RUSSIAN PLYWOOD"

there, they drop long rows of small bombs into the ravines onto German troops, and on the roads along which the German columns travel, and on the buildings in which the command staffs are situated. The Germans cannot spend a single night peacefully on any sector of the Frontline positions: the bombs drop down all night long.

After lengthy adjustments the German antiaircraft gunners established a new system of forestalling techniques which allowed for the speed of the "Russian Plywood" planes and then began to fire at them more accurately than before. But the pilots did not become confused, they simply adopted a new bombing method: climbing as high as possible, to 6,000 or 7,500 feet, and taking aim at the object of their bombing, they glided absolutely noiselessly from that height down to 1,200 or 1,000 feet, and there in complete darkness they dropped their load straight on the heads of the unsuspecting Germans. It almost became a rule that the anti-aircraft fire started after the dropping of the first series of bombs.

It was precisely then that the first fantastic hints that the Russians now had some strange aircraft, either with noiseless motors or without motors altogether, began to appear in the letters the German soldiers sent home. The officers did not write about it in their letters, and they attempted to convince the soldiers that the Russians had no engineless aircraft, but soldiers are stubborn, for it was on their own heads that Russian bombs suddenly dropped from the calm southern sky, and thus the legend persisted about the engineless aircraft.

In autumn there is a bitter wormwood scent in the steppe, and a cold wind blows in from the lower reaches of the Volga. There are almost no stars visible in the black sky which is covered by clouds: it is so black, dull, and impenetrable that were it not for the grass, wet at night from the dew, one would think he was somewhere underground in a dugout. Only to the left, on the horizon, can one see a broad red reflection stretching over many miles. Stalingrad burns there.

We walk across a flying field. Absolutely invisible planes drone somewhere quite close: a moment ago that drone could be heard on the ground, and now it has taken off into the air and is going higher and higher obliquely above our heads. Following guideposts visible to him only, my companion leads me to the command post. In the distance some ten or twelve miles away a searchlight flares up suddenly and goes out again after signaling with its beam in our direction.

"Ours are coming back. They're going to the take-off. He gives them the direction," explains my companion.

Finally we pull ourselves through a small door curtained by two cape-tents. A room has been arranged inside a haystack. Two tables standing in the form of the letter "T"—as if these were not tables but a take-off sign. The commander and the commissar of the U-2 regiment are seated at the "Bat" lantern. This is the busiest quarter-of-an-hour: the crews arrive one after the other and take off into the air again. Inside the haystack there is a scent of hay and of night freshness. The lantern casts a red reflection on the tired or excited faces of the reporting commanders, pilots, and navigators. As they begin to report they pull their helmets off their heads so as to hear better after the deafening motorcycle clatter of the engine.

Today the U-2 regiment has bombed the air base near Stalingrad which the Germans had burst into a few days ago. Major German units have established themselves at that base, and it has already been subjected to fierce bombardment for several nights. Many of those who are bombing this air base today had previously lived and trained there, and for this reason the assignments are particularly accurate today.

"Where did you strike at just now?" the commander of the regiment asks Captain Ovodov, a tall pilot who has just returned from an assignment.

"RUSSIAN PLYWOOD"

"At the third complex," the pilot said.

"Is that where you stayed?"

"No, I roomed in the fourth."

"You will fly there now and light a bigger fire. You will go first so that the others can see better. And where has Polikushkin been?" the commander asks after a pause.

"He's still flying, cheering up the Germans!"

"Does he chatter well in the air?"

"Very well indeed."

The commander is interested in what is happening along the line of the Front.

"How is the flying going?" he asks.

"They're fighting all night." The pilot bends over the map. "There's a fire here, and here, and here, and over here."

"Here?" the commander asks again, and becomes thoughtful. "Yes," he says, as if shaking off some thoughts from himself, "all in all, my house is either occupied, or it has already burned down. All right, take off! Are you frozen?"

"Frozen," the pilot answers, turning around on reaching the door. "A little frozen."

"Well, what of it, this is the month of September, after all," the commander says. "That's normal."

The arrivals and reports follow one after another almost without interruption. The time between touchdown and the new take-off on the airfield is very limited: it has to take place within ten and even five minutes. As soon as an aircraft touches down a truck with bombs drives up to it, the bombs are loaded onto the plane with the speed of lightning, and in the time that it takes the crew to make a report and receive a new assignment the aircraft is ready again for take-off. The reports are very brief for this reason.

"Raid one hour, thirty-five minutes. Height seven hundred and sixty meters. Bombs twenty-eight pieces at twenty kilograms. Assignment carried out."

Finally the last plane takes off into the air. Tiurin, the commissar of the regiment, exchanges glances with the commander.

"I don't like it," he says, "that they're all coming back together. The interval time is very close, they could crash into one another."

"Well, what of it?" the commander replies. "They rush back, they hurry so as to manage to fly six times before it gets light. Never mind, they won't crash into one another."

Every night they spend seven-and-a-half to nine hours in the air. Every night they go out on five to six sorties. Every night one small Russian Plywood plane drops one-and-a-half tons of bombs. At times it does not lag behind a large bomber, and sometimes it even outstrips it.

"Six times every day, including Sunday. We rarely have a day off," the commander says, "especially in summer. Except when there is an incredible fog, then we have a day off, and even then we sit around and wait in the hopes it will lift during the night. At first when we learned to fly we took one hundred kilograms of bombs with us, then one hundred and fifty to two hundred; now the usual norm is two hundred to two hundred and fifty. Everybody has become accustomed to it. One-and-a-half tons per night."

The tent cape, curtaining the door, swayed again. The Chief of Staff returned from the flying field.

"Well, major, how are they touching down out there?"

"The wind has become stronger. Last time they slightly overshot the lantern with the wind."

"Never mind, we'll have to adjust the signals for the return flight."

A pause ensues in the work of the command post. All the planes have taken off, the first one will not return

"RUSSIAN PLYWOOD"

for an hour. Taking advantage of the breathing spell, the commander tells me some details of the U-2 regiment's work. At the time the regiment was formed as a bomber unit and began to train for night flying, half the men in it turned out to be from military schools and half from the school of the "Osoaviakhim." At first some of the pilots who had just graduated from military school and had counted on becoming pursuit pilots turned up their noses when they were appointed to the U-2 regiment. But this passed quickly, and by the second month of combat activity they had all without exception become patriots of their job; they came to love it and to discover its own peculiar romantic quality.

It is self-evident that one cannot completely follow through on the analogy, but just as the sub-machine gun cannot always replace the old "threeliner" gun in the hands of an experienced sniper, thus the old, slow-moving, U-2's, which at times appeared antiquated, proved to be irreplaceable on their own terms. It was simply a matter of extracting from this machine everything that was possible, and its disadvantages, such as its slow speed, could be used to advantage in certain circumstances, and turned against the enemy. No modern night bomber can be given such assignments as are given the U-2 here where the Front line runs from building to building, from settlement to settlement, in zigzags, wedges, and tongues. They are given assignments to bomb a building, a definite building, not to the left nor to the right, but precisely this one which has been occupied by the Germans. They are given an assignment to bomb the German half of a district while its other half is in our hands. And with their slow speed, with their ideal aiming ability for bombing, they carry out the assignment, and as if suspended accurately above a particular building they bomb precisely that building without any mistakes and without being led into errors. They drop their bombs there where the German bombers do not risk going for fear of dropping their bombload on the heads of their own troops.

The pilots have become accustomed to their machines and have come to love them for their accuracy in bomb dropping, for their reliability, for the simplicity of their take-off and touchdown, for the fact that these machines of theirs, which looked so weak, were so slow in speed and so imperfect, turned out in reality to be a formidable weapon. They fly in any weather, three times during the night, they fly everywhere ordered, and they know that their own infantry, there on the ground, does not have such tender feelings toward any other aircraft as it has towards them. Flying so low that it seems they could catch you with their wheels, they are called by the infantry, depending on the landscape, either "foresters," or "corn cobs," or "truck farmers," but how much approval and even tenderness there is in these ironic names!

During this time the pilots had completed many hundreds of hours of flying, and every one to one-and-a-half hours of these represent 200 to 250 kilograms of bombs dropped on the heads of the aggressors. They have flown so much in that time that they have all, without exception, become highly experienced night fliers. They take off and touch down in absolute darkness; the Germans could not manage in any way to bomb the airfield since the only lighting they have is the blinking light of two small hand torches to indicate the direction of the runway. There is a joke in the regiment that they will soon be so well-trained that they could make the aircraft touch down guided by a lighted cigarette. And one must say that this is not so far from the truth.

Today is a red-letter day in the regiment—the pilots and navigators received rewards for their combat activity. Modest people who worked hundreds of nights as unskilled workmen, this morning, according to a soldiers' custom, punctured their comrades' tunics with a penknife

"RUSSIAN PLYWOOD"

and screwed on decorations. Almost all navigators and pilots took off today with decorations on their chests. A little while ago before dawn they have already gone out on their sixth sortie. This is the last sortie, and now they no longer hurry so much in reporting to the commander, they joke now, and rub their eyes, which are red from wind and lack of sleep, they huddle themselves up against the sharp morning chill. One of them who has just bombed a German airfield, jokes, "I burnt all their aircraft, and the mechanics went off crying."

"Why crying?" the commander asks, smiling.

"Even though they're Germans they're still sorry for their planes, that's why they're crying."

"I noticed that the Germans had a mortar shooting there," says another. "Tomorrow, as soon as I fly, I'll definitely knock it out."

"Well, that depends on the assignment you'll get," the commander says. "It'll be knocked out even without you from below."

"But I'll do it in passing, along the way. For I can see better from above." An absolute determination can be felt in the words of the pilot to still "knock out" the mortar.

"I struck at the road," reports a third, "at a column. Dispersed them."

"One sub-machine gunner dispersed as a result of the bombing," the navigator jokes good-naturedly, standing behind his pilot's back.

The last one of those who have returned complains that the whole sky became overcast with clouds in the middle of the night: "Now, during the first sortie there was moonlight. The results could be seen clearly."

"Well, did you get straight into the garret window, where the Germans had their laundry hanging?" joked the commissar. "What?"

"Yes, for sure, Comrade Commissar," the pilot replies with humor, "because we saw how they jumped out the window without underwear."

KONSTANTIN SIMONOV

Gradually all the crews have assembled at the command post. Now they will take a rest. The night—their work-day—is over. Dawn is breaking, it is time for sleep.

We come outside to the airfield with the commissar. It is still dark, but in the east, at the edge of the steppe, one can see the thin line of the dawn. Left, right — everywhere—invisible planes are taxiing to the parking areas. Pilots who came out for a smoke, stand at the sides of their planes, chatting; the little red lights of the cigarettes glimmer. The men talked in a tired, good-natured fashion. After a hazardous, hard night they would like to have a heart-to-heart talk, to stretch, to suddenly remember home, their people, to forget until evening that the same hard and hazardous thing will begin again today at nightfall.

Some day when the history of this war is written I hope the historian remembers among its unnoticed heroes the laborers of aviation, the modest men who knew how to transform the term "Russian Plywood" from a condescending appellation into a terrifying one.

October 9, 1942

Ilya Ehrenburg

LIGHT IN THE DUGOUT

When on a June morning the first shots startled the larks, they sounded like a dissonance. Nothing around corresponded to these sounds: the peaceful villages, and the slowly ripening ears of wheat, the children in the border town, and the human heart which still continued beating peacefully. How our country has changed! These are bright autumn days. The birch trees around the dugouts seem to be bleeding profusely. The sinister diversity of colors in the fallen leaves is akin to the war, and many trees are mutilated by mortar shell splinters. Iron has eaten out craters. In place of the village houses, there are only chimneys left standing. And even the faces are not the same; it appears as if the war has molded them anew. There was a softness in them like in the Russian landscape which can be easily glorified but which is so difficult to depict—limitless, lyrical, barely outlined. So too were the people, but now the faces are hewn from stone. In the eyes of weatherbeaten, sunburnt soldiers who have experienced enemy fire there is sternness, confidence.

Sometimes at night when the first green rockets cut across the sky, when the daytime cannonade falls silent and the nighttime cannonade has not as yet asserted its rights, the Front-line soldier dimly remembers the past. For a minute it seems to him that somewhere in the rear the life which used to be his life still goes on. He can see Moscow bathed in light. In the windows, under the lamps, people dine, laugh, read absorbing novels, children do their homework, young girls doll themselves up, for there is dancing tonight—are there not fireworks in the Park of Culture? And then the Front-line soldier remembers in a flash: war! The war is in Moscow also: the streets are black, the windows of the buildings are like eyes gone blind. Girls are busy gathering wood, musicians have become sappers or mortar gunmen, children have been evacuated to the Urals. A searchlight pierces the black sky. If you could fly above the land as in a fairy tale you would see the war everywhere. You would see cities burned down by the Germans, you would see factories in cottages, factories which have traveled thousands of miles. You will see girls who studied literature or played the piano who now fiercely cast shells. Gaze into the eyes of one of them in the half-dark, cold workshop, and you'll see something familiar in those eyes; she also fights. You will see women from Leningrad in Uzbekistan, you'll see children from the Poltava region in Siberia. You'll hear an old mother sighing, "There have been no letters for two months . . ." You'll hear a three-year-old child ask while rubbing his sleepy eyes with a small fist, "Where's daddy?" You will see much sorrow and much stubbornness. Not only the Front but the whole country fights. It diverts part of the night from sleep, it diverts a piece of bread from its mouth, it does not have a good time and is not in clover, it lives

LIGHT IN THE DUGOUT

with clenched teeth as you do in the dugouts, covered by the night, having dug yourself into the earth. It fights like you.

We have lost a great deal, and there is no person who is unaffected by these losses. A great misfortune is always diffident. A young woman who in times gone by used to complain about minor disorders is silent now. As she silently bandages the wounded, the soldiers whom she tends know one thing: she must not be asked about her husband. We have lost many wonderful, self-sacrificing, clever, and honest people. These losses are more bitter than anything else; they cannot be replaced. We shall rebuild the destroyed cities, they will be better than the previous ones. But the loss of that inspired youth who has not built anything yet—either a house, or his nest, but who it would seem could build a whole city—is irreplaceable.

We have lost wonderful dams and factories into which we have sunk our hearts. We have lost the ancient monuments of Novgorod. These relics of Russia, these stones, as if warm from the love of generations, have stood for centuries. Time itself had spared them, but the blasphemous hands of the Germans have destroyed them.

It was not easy for us to make our life. Often we lacked both skill and time; nevertheless this rough, unpolished life was our own. It resembled the draft of a beautiful poem which was all mottled with corrections. The dark past became tangled in our feet. We often swung like a pendulum from self-intoxication to self-deprecation. We were the first scouts of mankind, we cut a path, we went through the dark forest. While we built day nurseries, bad news carried across from the West; there they were building those bombers which in one night kill hundreds of children. The animal breath of Fascism was reaching us and we were telling our wives: "You will have to wear your same old dress again this winter, we have to build pursuit planes." We knew that children needed toys as birds need wings, but how can children play when there are Hitlerites living on earth? We made few toys, we made tanks instead. Cursed Fascism intervened into our lives ten years before the war, and yet we built cities, schools, rest homes, theaters.

A woman gives birth in pain. A fruit tree grows slowly. A quarter century is half a human life, but a quarter century is a short period for history. On the eve of the war we saw the first fruit in our gardens. Then the Germans fell upon us. Within one hour the SS men annihilated buildings, villages, cities which had taken us years to build while we deprived ourselves of other things, the way a mother goes short of everything for the sake of her child. We know how much we have lost. The Germans know it, too; they have seen our soldiers animated by such hatred, such fury that tanks retreated before them.

We often think about our losses. We can now speak about what we have acquired in this war. A mother does not notice how her child grows; all of a sudden he has grown up, but for the mother he is still a little boy. Our nation has grown unspeakably during sixteen months. It is not possible sometimes to recognize a young friend who has returned from the Front. It has been said that one must think in peace and quiet, and it seemed that young men grew up in decorous auditoriums, in libraries, or in small student rooms among a mountain of manuscripts. Dark dugouts do not resemble a university, and it is noisy at the Front, noisy and restless, but who will say now what people at the Front-line think about? They think tensely, stubbornly, feverishly. They think about the present and the past. They think about why yesterday's operation did not succeed, and they think about the many things they should have been taught in high school that would help them now. They think about the future, about that wonderful life which the victors will build.

LIGHT IN THE DUGOUT

People grow up miraculously during the war, like the forest in the fairy tale. They live side by side with death, they are acquainted with it as with a neighbor, and they have become wise. They have overcome fear, and this lifts up a man, gives him assurance, an inner gaiety and strength. There are no intermediate shades in the war or pale colors, everything is taken through to the end—the great and the despicable, the black and the white. The war is a great test for nations and people. Much is rethought, reviewed, reevaluated, in war.

A quarter of a century ago we placed the word "comrade" at the base of our life. The word implies an obligation. It is easy to say it, it is hard to respond to it. In the term "citizen" there is precision and dryness—it is a mathematical reference regarding the sum of rights and duties, while the word "comrade" requires enthusiasm of the soul. It has revealed itself in its whole depth to millions upon millions for the first time at the Front. It has become concrete, warm, viscous like blood.

In the war we see the strength of human friendship to the fullest extent. How many exploits has this remarkable feeling generated! There is a dear friend beside you, in the same battery, in the same platoon. Should he get killed you will not forget him, and you will not forgive the enemy. Before the war the name "friend" was easily given, but a friend was also easily forgotten. No longer so after combat. Before the war one used to say, "Friends are those who eat a pound of salt together." But what is salt next to blood? What are years compared with one night at Stalingrad? Observe the joy with which the soldier returns to his unit; he has returned home. He inquires about every comrade, about every friend.

The friendship of nations was our State principle, it has now become the feeling of each separate person. In one company there are Russians and Kazakhs and Ukrainians and Belorussians and Georgians. We have found that while speaking different languages we feel the same thing, we think of the same thing. Siberians are moved when hearing the wonderful Ukrainian songs, and the tale of the white nights of Arkhangelsk touches the heart of a black-eyed son of Armenia. At first we were unified by history, then by the high principle of equality, now we are unified by nights in the trenches, and there is no stronger cement.

Whatever is easily obtained is not valued. It is only now that our attachment to the Motherland has become firm, serious, insuperable. People sacrifice what is most dear for the sake of the Motherland. They were patriots before, but now they have given thought to their feelings, and these feelings have become more profound. Before they were seeking for an external explanation for their love. In the past they had at times an attitude of unjustified scorn or unjustified admiration for things foreign. Now they know that you do not love the Motherland for this or for that, but for being the Motherland. Thus a modest tree becomes more beautiful than all the groves of Paradise. One can see one's shortcomings; one will not stop loving the Motherland for this; one will only wish to improve oneself, to raise oneself up along with the country.

In war history revealed itself to us, and the pages of books came to life; the heroes of the past went from the textbooks into the dugouts. Who has not experienced the "Year Twelve" as a familiar and understandable tale? Which member of the Komsomol is not revolted by the ruins of the Novgorod Kremlin? We found that our new State was not built in an empty place. The steadfastness of Leningrad delights us, its sufferings demand revenge. We saw the work of Peter who had built a wonderful city. We understand that without Peter there would have been no Pushkin, and that without Petersburg there would have been no Putilov workers who, on a dark autumn night, opened the path to a new era.

LIGHT IN THE DUGOUT

Having run up against the barbarism of Fascism we felt all the things valuable and great that were acquired by the nationalities of Russia a quarter-century ago. Here, the son of a herdsman read Hegel. How must he look at the German "philosopher" who has transformed philosophy into a guide to animal husbandry? With what disgust do we listen to the stories of the German prisoners-of-war who tell us that they have "socialism" there, and that they have adapted Poles and Frenchmen for work instead of horses!

We value the heroism of the Spanish people, but it was difficult for many of us to understand that a half-illiterate Spanish peasant was more cultured than a Berlin professor. Now everybody understands this. We saw Hitlerites who keep diaries who have typewriters and gramophones at home, who by external appearance resemble civilized Europeans, and who would offend the moral feelings of any inhabitant of the Sandwich Islands. We will no longer be deceived by outward signs of culture. Now we know that what is important is not only the quantity and the external quality of printed words, but also the content of what is printed; that the cities of Germany with their clean streets, their well-equipped hospitals, their spacious schools, are the sanctuaries of a crude and disgusting barbarism. Of course, we do not deny the importance of material culture, but we have seen now that without spiritual wealth, such culture rapidly deteriorates into savagery.

The maturity of every Front-line soldier has made us strong. We have lost large areas. The second summer has brought us much sorrow. And yet we can say that we are stronger now than on the 22nd of June, 1941—stronger in our consciousness, mind, and heart. When we used to sing, "If there is a war tomorrow," there were many things we did not understand. We have cleansed ourselves of unconcern, of self-delusion, of bigotry. We have not achieved victory as yet, but we are preparing ourselves for it.

We think at times how hard it will be to heal the wounds, to rebuild the destroyed cities, to reestablish peaceful life. These are thoughts about what is lost. Let us remember about what has been acquired and tell ourselves that the man who will return from the Front is worth ten prewar men. People will work and live differently. In the war we have acquired initiative, discipline, and inner freedom.

The first morning after victory will be beautiful. We shall find out that a mother has slept peacefully. The postman will again become a part of life. A wife will embrace the hero. The air raid sirens will fall silent. In the evening bright lanterns will light up in Gorky Street and on the Nevski. Our flag will be unfurled over long-suffering Kiev. Perhaps it will be raining or snowing on that day, but we shall see the sun and the blue sky. Russia, who was the first to stop the aggressors with her head raised high, strong but peaceful, proud but not arrogant, will remove the rifle from her shoulder and will say, "Now—to live."

November 10, 1942

Konstantin Simonov

DECEMBER NOTES

A German tank stands in a cold, snowbound field within a few miles of Khimki. Built in Bremen, it has crawled a long way and has come to an eternal halt here. Generally speaking, perhaps scrap iron should be utilized, but maybe it is good that this tank remains standing on the exact spot it has reached. This tank was closest of all to Moscow. Closest of them all! Perhaps, after the war is over, a wooden or stone barrier will be formed around it, and it will stand there as a spectacle for excursionists; it will be a reminder of how close the Germans came to Moscow in 1941, that memorable year for Russia.

One day the Moscow region will be crossed by a black zigzag-shaped line marking out from the south, west, and north the points reached by the German Army on the fifth of December of last year. The borders will be reestablished, the spaces of free Russian lands will extend for many hundreds of miles west from Moscow, but this black line will remind us of the aggression, of the mortal danger which was successfully overcome by a superhuman effort of will, mind, and heart—everything in which a Russian is rich.

If you travel now from Moscow to Rzhev, passing the former Volokolamsk sector, the first thing that will catch the eye along the road will be the dead town of Istra. It has been burned to the ground. In order to call it a town again it will be necessary to build it from top to bottom. This is how close the Germans came up to Moscow! Here they walked along these devastated streets, here they excavated dugouts and trenches, attempting to linger on at whatever cost. The Germans were here—the Germans, may they be cursed! The same Germans, none of whom would dare today to approach this Istra any closer than 125 miles.

Heavy-duty Front-line roads run towards the west through the forests, roads patiently knocked together out of logs—log against log, decking against decking. It was precisely along these roads, after detraining from the carriages at the last station, that the reserve divisions of the Moscow Front—men to whom Moscow entrusted its fate at the most critical moment, rushed into battle here a year ago. It was here that these men fought, died, or came back wounded, with faces darkened from fatigue and sometimes pale from loss of blood. It was here that they pursued and routed the enemy.

Names of the villages, of those which have remained and of those which disappeared long ago while only burdock and wormwood have grown in their place—villages which were the Front and have become the Rear—flash past along the roads. There is the village of Petrovskoye, not far from Pogoreloye Gorodishche—the place of fierce fighting in August of this year. A bloody battle took place here four months ago. Today it is necessary to drive on

DECEMBER NOTES

for one, two, and three hours in one's motor car to arrive at a habitable village.

Long-suffering Russian land! You will be healing your wounds, it will take your sons—carpenters, stove-setters, concrete-mixers—a long time to recreate with their golden hands what has been destroyed. And yet, despite the fact that the land which has been retaken from the Germans is almost deserted and sad in its nakedness, it is particularly dear to the heart; and the thought that this land which has been won back at such a high price could again fall into the hands of the Germans, is particularly unacceptable. This shall never be!

Here we are, finally, on the battlefield. The smoke haze has lifted today, and from the observation post one can see not only our and the German shell bursts but the whole bloody horizon. Red glows flare up in places before nightfall on account of which the moon, which has risen, cannot be seen. The fir trees stand at the edge of the forest looking as if they had been carefully drawn in, and as if the red fiery background of the sunset has been purposefully placed behind them.

It is cold. High in the frosty sky pursuit planes trace trails resembling feathery clouds. The weather during the last few days has been constantly foggy and snowy. During the rare hours when it is clear, as is the case now, both our and German aircraft appear instantaneously above the battlefield. There, low above our heads, our attack planes have flown past, above them pursuit planes have rapidly streaked across the sky.

And there comes the response. A flock of Junkers which had entered our Rear in the first place approaches the forward positions from the east. One after the other the planes begin to go into power dives. Defending anti-aircraft fire covers all voices of the battle. A fiery curtain of shells and tracer bullets flies up in the air overhead. Yes, German gentlemen, this is not June and not July of the previous year when you flew at low level over these roads of the Western Front and shot refugees from a height of a hundred feet. These are not the first days of the war for you, when you boasted in your newspapers that you were on the verge of crushing the Red infantry under your wheels. A wall of anti-aircraft fire stands above the field of battle, and if the planes still go into power dives and drop bombs, then there is not even a trace of the previous impunity. Here alone, within the area which can be seen in its entirety from one hill—here alone the anti-aircraft gunners have buried in the ground thirteen German aircraft in the course of three days of fighting.

In Leo Tolstoy's tale "The Raid," one officer says that he is brave who conducts himself as one should. In other words, Tolstoy elucidates, he is brave who is afraid only of what one should be afraid of, and not of what one should not be afraid of. These are wise words, and they are always applicable to our warriors. Even in the first months of the war we had many men, as many as at present, who were bold and despised death. I saw commanders who, in order to encourage to others, stood upright under bombing when all the others around were endeavoring to press themselves against the ground. I saw men who came out face to face against tanks with only a grenade. We had all this from the very beginning. But bravery, that calm bravery of which Tolstoy speaks, this bravery as a mass phenomenon sprang up only during the ordeals of war. To conduct oneself in war as one should means that at the very first opportunity you must dig a small hole for yourself, a cleft, a small trench, for you know that the Germans will bomb, but after having dug such a small trench you can lie in it quietly during the bombing and attend to your business without fear of German bombs.

Bravery is closely linked to the art of conducting war. The art of digging a trench in such a manner that even a

DECEMBER NOTES

tank which has run over you could do you no harm, the art of the antitank rifleman who is confident that he will set fire to the tank from a distance of 200 to 100 yards; the art of the commander who behind his front line has established an antitank defense nuclei with antitank riflemen and artillerists sitting in ambush—it is all this added together which creates that mass bravery which springs up in an army, the bravery of experienced warriors who know the capabilities of the enemy weapons and the strength of their own.

It is no secret how terrible was the avalanche of German technology which crashed down on us. This technology still remains formidable now, and it would be, of course, naive to believe that the fear of a man against an advancing tank could ever disappear. But in the heart of a man against whom mortal danger is advancing there are ever two kinds of feelings toward it; to run, to get away from that death; or to kill it himself. And thus, between these two feelings which always struggle in the heart of the soldier, within the combination of these two feelings, the second one—to slay death himself—predominates more and more with every month of the war. And this is mass bravery, the bravery of an army tempered in battle.

We enter the observation post of General Mukhin at the very moment when it is reported to him that twenty-four German tanks were approaching a neighboring village we have recently taken: one tank has been hit, but the others are moving forward. After listening to this report the commander calmly gives orders to fire at the tanks from all available artillery, and issues a few additional orders regarding artillery support. And that is all. In the next minute he passes on to a different question, but if there had not been a small hill in front of the observation post, the approaching German tanks could have been seen with the naked eye.

The calmness of the division commander is not the

ostentatious calmness of a man who only wants to inspire bravery in the hearts of subordinates, but the inner calmness of a man who is confident that the danger will be overcome. I am convinced that the same commander would not have been as calm fifteen months ago when confronted with the same report about advancing tanks. Perhaps he would have had the same calm appearance, but he would not have been calm internally. And I do not want at all to say that he would not have been just as brave then, but he would not have had the confidence he now has in his soldiers' lack of fear of the tanks, in the existence of anti-tank defense areas at the back of his troops, and in the use of the weapons which could be used against tanks in a manner as necessary and as ruthless as it has to be.

During these days the division broke through the German fortified district. On the evening of November 22nd, as in every corner of Russia, the Soviet Information Bureau's report on our troops' offensive at Stalingrad was recorded at the division staff headquarters. Typists and copyists worked all night, and in the morning of November 23rd the text of the report was read to battalions and companies. Meetings were held where possible; where this was not possible, soldiers met in groups in the trenches, the dugouts, and the communication passages. Everyone talked and exchanged thoughts.

The division was also getting ready for the offensive. Here, too, the men longed to overrun the Germans and were getting ready for this. And although the day of the offensive had not yet been designated, the awareness of something great and solemn which always exists before an offensive was all-pervasive, making the men feel something great was expected from them. The news about Stalingrad came to them as an inspiration, and they were seized by impatience.

When troops stay at one place for a long time and

DECEMBER NOTES

take up defense positions, a wartime style involuntarily sets in to the degree in which the men get used to relative safety. No matter how well the attack has been organized and how thoroughly the artillery has wiped out the German weapons emplacements, one still has to advance the last hundred or so yards with his chest exposed to machine-gun fire. A man who is prepared to come out into the attack knows that in the hour or two before this formidable cannonade is over and he can go forward, anything could happen. If one speaks about the high morale of the soldiers, it does not at all mean that they try to forget the threatening, mortal danger. No, they remember it, and yet they go. And if they were offered a choice between quietly sitting in the defense position or attacking, they would always choose attack.

In this lies the secret of the Russian soldier's soul, the secret of the education of the Army. When our soldier sees a map of his Motherland, a major part of which is at present torn away, he will never, under any circumstances, during even the gravest days—during the days of bitter retreat—reconcile himself to this, that this is how it will be. When he retreats he says that this is only for the time being; when he sits in the defense position he knows that this is only for the time being; when he attacks and retakes a village from the Germans he says to himself: this is for the time being—one now, tomorrow the next village. And he is prepared to sacrifice his life for retaking that next village. An army that has preserved, nurtured, and confirmed within itself such a spirit during the days of unprecedented trials—such an army will win!

The suitable moment had arrived by the time the report on Stalingrad was read in the trenches, and the men were saying that we should now go over as soon as possible to the offensive. They were saying, "When do we go? It's time!" These were real, great words. They were saying, "We shall fight like the Stalingraders!" and poking a finger at an old map of European Russia hanging in the dugout they said, "Here's where we're closest to the border."

The morning was grey and foggy. During the night a snowstorm had started and it was now increasing in intensity. At 7:40 a.m. precisely, our artillery began to strike at the German positions. Howitzer shells flew above the heads of our soldiers making a sound like that of water pouring from a narrow bottleneck. Several artillery regiments fired simultaneously, causing a solid wall of black smoke to blanket the German side of the river. Snowflakes flew in, forming a diagonal white net against the background of this smoke. Our artillery fired for an hour and forty minutes. Its thunder was deafening, and the men who were primed for rushing into the attack knew that everything possible was being done now so that they would encounter as few as possible live German machine guns along their path, and so that they would come through these last, hardest, two hundred yards with the least losses when they had to scramble up the precipitous bank on the German side.

Our artillery still continued firing when our tanks and our infantry approached the base of the precipitous bank. They came up as close as possible—as close as they could be brought up without interrupting our artillery fire. Then the fire dropped and the infantrymen found themselves face to face with the Germans. They climbed upwards along the steep, iced-over, mined inclines. The remaining German machine guns doused them with fire from above, and the German mortars showered them with shells, and yet, after twenty minutes, the soldiers of Major Lunegov broke into the German trenches. They came out on top, on the plain, and the attack rolled on further, to the half-burned trees visible on the horizon, to the bluish hills of the second line of the German defense.

The snowstorm lasted all that day, all through the

DECEMBER NOTES

night, and all the following day, bogging down the German self-propelled guns, motor vehicles, and machine guns under heavy snowfalls. Their snowbound, mutilated, now impotent weapons stuck out along the road edges, and our tanks went over German corpses which were strewn along the roads. The sight of a crushed human body does not present anything cheerful in itself, but here on the battlefield a German crushed by a tank is only another dead German. And perhaps it is even good that during the first days of the offensive the corpses of the enemies are strewn about the edges of the roads, in the trenches, on the field—there, where death overtook them—and the advancing reinforcements go past them and count: one more, two more, again one more. That is how it should be! Yes, we killed them here—here on the narrow bit of ground between the bank and the abandoned village, the German Army has become reduced by another five hundred men. Another five hundred Germans have been turned into dead, iced-over dolls on our soil.

The offensive continues. Today the Germans threw themselves several times into counterattacks within the area of this division. Here they drew up their tanks and self-propelled guns and brought up reinforcements from the rear. Fierce fighting is taking place along the whole horizon, and while the sun is already setting there are no signs as yet that the fighting will begin to abate towards nighttime.

War is cruel, but men are rapidly tempered in its fire and become men of great boldness, of big heart, and a big mind. Half a year ago ambulance-man Guba, a forty-five-year-old member of a collective farm, a fearless man who had already carried over a hundred wounded from the battlefield, was accepted as a candidate for Party membership in the division. Finding himself alone with Guba, the commissar asked him whether he had written to his wife to say that he had been admitted to the Party.

"To whom, to Aksinya?" Guba said. "No."

"Why not?" the commissar said.

"No," Guba repeated, and smiled shyly at his thoughts.

"But why not, really?"

"Can't be done, she'll laugh."

"Why would she laugh?" the commissar wondered.

"But why wouldn't she? She'll say, 'How is it, you old grumbler, that you've lived forty-five years in this world and have suddenly hit upon this'?"

Guba was embarrassed by the unexpected change in his character brought about by his feelings at being in the war. He thought it strange even himself how much he had changed, and it seemed to him that his wife Aksinya would not understand the changes which had occurred in his soul during the war, and would laugh at him. However, the commissar talked Guba into writing a letter to his wife and in that letter he added a line himself to say that Guba had carried one hundred wounded men from the battlefield, and that he had two orders of the Red Star on his chest. And in their distant village his wife understood everything that had happened to her husband. She, too, was feeling the war over there; she, too, lived by the war and much had also happened within her soul. She replied to him with a warm, proud letter which Guba reread several times in astonishment. His wife had changed the same way he had. She had grown up in the same way, she understood all this thoughts, all his actions, and they appeared to her neither strange nor funny.

Guba became an ambulance instructor, a Party member. The no-longer-young collective farm member who went to war with his habits, weaknesses, and prejudices became an experienced and talented soldier. All the spiritual forces which lay concealed in him exerted themselves and permitted him to achieve that which he had never considered possible for him to achieve even in his boldest thoughts. In the cast of mind of such a man as Guba, as

DECEMBER NOTES

in hundreds of thousands of other soldiers like him in the great army, there is installed the symbol of that strength which still grows, stubborn, unbending, with each day of this bloody war, in spite of all losses and unprecedented sufferings.

December 5, 1942

1943

When you enter your town
And the women meet you
Lifting the children high
Above whitened hair;

Even if you were a hero,
Do not be proud—on that day
No thanks have you earned
From them, but only forgiveness.

You have only paid back the terrible debt,
Which you owed from that year
When your retreating regiment
Sent them into a year of exile.

K. Simonov

Ilya Ehrenburg

JANUARY 14, 1943

It is amusing to listen to the German radio these days. Even the voices of the announcers—the hearty Hans Fritsche and the impudent Lord Haw Haw, and Doctor Frank, the specialist in intimidating the French—reveal embarrassment. These gentlemen have become philosophers. The earth does not interest them anymore. Three months ago they used to glibly spout the names of Cossack villages and tiny hamlets in the Caucasus and Central Asia. Now they talk coldly about "the space between the Don and the Caucasus." They suggest the Germans take up history instead of geography. They touchingly recall last winter: how hard it was for Germany then! And they promise that, after the winter, spring will come without fail. But the winters do not resemble one another.

General Zhukov said to me, speaking about the defeat of the Germans near Moscow: "The German Army has been corrupted by the ease of success." A year has gone by since then, and we have learned much. It should be assumed that our enemies have also learned a great deal. A year ago they could claim unexpectedness: the character of the Russian repulse was new to them at the time; they did not know the conditions of a winter campaign in Russia, and finally, there was an early and unusually fierce winter last year. Hitler could blame Nature. Not so now. The Germans know now that it rains in the Caucasus, and that there are snowstorms on the Don. The Germans say themselves that "the weather does not favor the attackers." It is true that the German correspondents sometimes grumble about thirty or even forty degrees below zero, but this refers not to the data of the thermometer, but to the inner state of those who are in retreat.

The Russian offensive, which started at the end of November, is not only not weakening, it is developing. Now we can see the fruit of the November and December fighting. The encirclement of the German Army Group at Stalingrad determined the character of the winter campaign. It is not surprising that the Germans tried, cost what it may, to save those encircled; within the ring are not only men, but also equipment for twenty-two divisions. Every day our forces compress the ring and take prisoners. The encircled divisions are in agony.

Some foreign observers write that the Germans are retreating in the Caucasus for fear of being cut off. In the meantime, the Germans are offering stubborn resistance in the Caucasus, and they retreat only after desperate fighting. The best refutation of the Germans' "voluntary retreat" are the pyjamas that the German Staff officers were caught in during an attack by our cavalry men on one of the Caucasian resorts. The Germans are driven back for twelve to fifteen miles a day under difficult conditions of mountain warfare. Only recently they were near Vladikavkaz. Now (January 13th) our units are not far

JANUARY 14, 1943

from Stavropol. The Germans are also fighting back desperately at the Don. The fighting in the direction of Salsk bears an exceptionally stubborn character. Here Hitler is not only defending his booty—the Kuban—but also the German divisions which are between the Caucasus and the Don. However, our units continue to advance.

Rome reported yesterday: "The attacks of the Russians on Mineralnye Vody have been beaten back," but in the meantime, Mineralnye Vody is already in the rear of our units. Berlin talks about Velikiye Luki being "liberated from Russian encirclement," but in the meantime a Soviet newspaper is already being published in Velikiye Luki. Never before have the Germans lied as they are doing now. This tells about the spiritual condition of Germany.

The Germans are trying to explain to themselves where the Russians get their soldiers from, where they get their tanks from, and they get themselves all tangled up in explanations. For they have, after all, annihilated the Red Army on paper, but now this so-called "annihilated army" is driving them back West. The Germans were already getting settlers ready for the Don, colonizers for Kislovodsk; they have accurately divided the bear's skin. They must not accuse fate now: the settlers have been resettled under the ground and the colonizers populate the prisoner-of-war camps.

Where do the Russians get their soldiers? Apparently the Germans forget that Russia is big, that Siberia fights for the Ukraine, that there are not only Caucasians, but also men from the Ural mountains who drive the Germans from the Caucasus, that Uzbeks and Kirghiz fight at the Don. Or, perhaps Hitler thought that the Uzbeks and Kirghiz would fight for the triumph of the German race? Where do the Russians get their soldiers? This is the same as asking where does Russia get its people? There are no miracles.

Experienced soldiers are fighting the Germans who have already fought them last year, soldiers who have been annihilated on paper but who are alive in reality, who have carried out a retreat and have at last reached the days of reckoning. But new soldiers also fight Hitler: Russia has not been sparing and will not be sparing with sacrifices. We fight, and we fight in earnest. Where do we get our tanks? I saw factories which had sprung up almost overnight on an empty site. I saw women and juveniles who work better than experienced workers had worked before the war. All that is needed is the will to win. One can possess a wonderful skill, and mark time; one can possess hundreds of divisions and wait. There are no miracles. And if you wish you can dub a miracle that moral fire which allowed Russia to fight on her own against Hitler and his vassals, and after losing the Ukraine, the Don basin, and the Kuban, to assemble the weapons, to feed her armies, and not only to defend herself, but to pursue the enemy.

We had no combat experience in 1941, we learned to fight by fighting. In the Informbureau reports we find the names of generals whose units distinguished themselves in recent operations. I met some of these generals on different fronts. Military talent, like the talent of a painter, matures with the resistance of materials. General Rokossovsky recognized the difficulties of the fighting for Sukhinichi after the winter offensive on Istra. He also experienced Hitler's summer offensive. Victory is not molded from clay, it is hewn out of stone. General Yeremenko experienced Smolensk as well as Bryansk and the defense of Stalingrad. This is how this winter's operations were prepared in Russian minds and hearts. I knew General Rodimtsev as a major, I saw dozens of excellent colonels, lieutenant colonels, and majors who mastered the complexity of military art in the war. While Hitler was assuring the world and himself that the Red Army was

JANUARY 14, 1943

about to be finished, it was being born as a great creative force.

We shall not busy ourselves, like Hitler, in wiping out the German Army on paper. The enemy is still strong, he is still in possession of immense territories. His army is still not shaken. The Germans have a strong forehead, but the defeats of these weeks could be decisive if our offensive sounds like a battle signal to our Allies.

In summer during the most critical days, I wrote in *Red Star*, addressing myself to the commanders of the Red Army, "What is needed for victory? Some will say material resources, others will say live forces, still others will say good weapons. All these things are necessary for victory, but what is most important for victory is time; not to lose an hour. Every commander must be aware of time as if there was a huge clock-face in front of him. In this lies the miracle of coordination, in this is the guarantee of victory."

The recent military operations have shown that the Red Army has achieved coordination. But did the forces of the anti-Hitler coalition achieve coordination? Did all of them understand the meaning of time? Clocks can lull you to sleep, clocks can also waken.

At present the Germans are recalling last winter. It is necessary to deepen their memories. Why should we not remind them of 1918? This, by the way, is an anniversary: 1918 was a quarter-century age. An invisible hand chalks up "1918" on the walls of Paris and Prague. With what pleasure shall we write that date on the battlefields with the blood of the Fascists! 1943 might become 1918. What is required for this is what they talked about so much last summer: a Second Front. Europe is waiting for it. The world is waiting for it.

Konstantin Simonov

IN THE WINTER OF 'FORTY-THREE

1. Years from now, on looking through the tattered notebooks of the war period, it will be difficult to remember precisely the relationship between the names, denominations, and dates entered among the half-obliterated pencil lines. But the main thing will remain evergreen—not so much in the memory, but in the heart. As an eternal companion there will forever remain inside one the feeling with which we fought this war, that knowledge of the soul of the nation which will never be as clear as at present, because it is precisely during these grave and terrible years that this soul has opened up before our eyes to its full breadth and strength.

I had occasion recently to travel through the Caucasus, the Kuban, the Rostov district, and in my rucksack are leaflets of almost all the newspapers published by the German Command in Pyatigorsk and Armavir, in Maikop and Ust-Labinskaya, in Krasnodar, and Rostov. Before the war, Nazi professors and men of letters liked to philosophize on the subject of the enigmatic soul of the Russian people. It is hard to understand a foreign nation, it is especially hard if one hates it. They did not understand the soul of the Russian people—either before the war or during the course of it. But while making the transition during the war from philosophizing to killing they felt instinctively the force and insuperability of that soul, and the witness to this feeling are their newspaper leaflets which are now lying before me. They are dated August, 1943, when the Germans burst into Krasnodar; September, 1943, when they took Nalchik; October, 1943, when they were climbing to the passes of the Caucasian mountain range. It seemed that military fortune was kind to the Germans. But in every newspaper, on every page, side by side with the victorious communiqués, there sounded the same irritated, strident, hysterical note: "The Reds will not return," "the Reds will no longer return," "the Reds will never return—you understand, they will not return, you must, you are obliged to understand that they will not return under any circumstance."

The Fascists repeated this from issue to issue, from one day to another, confirming it with figures, calculations, comparisons. This was the main thing they wanted to convince everybody of who lived in the regions they conquered. Our people did not utter a word, they kept silent and knew that it was not so, and the more evident the German successes became, the more impressive their figures and calculations became, the more this silence and unbelief became frightening and incomprehensible to the Germans. They could enslave part of the earth but they could not enslave the soul of the people. The people knew that the Germans were not there for good, they knew that they were there for the time being. Perhaps only in the case of one in a thousand was that faith based on the

IN THE WINTER OF 'FORTY-THREE

knowledge of the real state of affairs, for the others could judge the position at the Front only from German newspapers, German radio, and German rumors. But the Russian heart, the faith in one's people, prompted one to feel that the Germans were there only for the time being, and not for good. One died with that conviction, along with bitterness not only about the Germans seizing one's city or village, but because one would not have the chance to see the day when the German would be driven out.

The same feeling dominated the hearts of the people who had remained in the German rear, and of the people who were leaving along with our retreating army. I cannot remember a single inhabitant of Odessa, or Kharkov, or Kalinin who did not speak about the day when they would return to their home town. I cannot remember a person who did not believe that we would return there from whence we came. People often doubted their personal destiny: will I return, will I live until then?—but they never doubted the destiny of their own nation, of their native town. For them victory was beyond doubt. It was precisely this unshakable faith in victory which was the outstanding trait in the spiritual make-up of the Soviet person which made it possible for him to suffer the most crushing disappointments and the most unbearable burdens.

2. One night recently during a wet snowstorm, while driving across the zone near the Front, we encountered soldiers of the First Railroad Brigade at a destroyed bridge. They worked furiously, having thrown off their greatcoats and quilted jackets in a frenzy in spite of the cold. Last summer and autumn they had proceeded along the whole painful path from west to east, from the Kiev region to the Caucasus, wrecking the railroad and blowing up the bridges behind them. For them a particularly somber feeling was connected with the retreat. They were the last to leave, and they blew up, blew up, blew up behind them everything that in the past had been built before their

eyes. They blew up bridges and railroads in order to hinder the enemy from moving ahead. An almost unbearable load had accumulated in their hearts during these months of retreat, which they counted not so much in days but in miles of blown-up tracks and bridge spans flying up to the sky. Now they were following the Army from east to west, and were rebuilding the blown-up bridges. They worked with the fury of people who are very pressed for time, who are desperately pressed for time, not only because this was required by the Army, but because it was emotionally necessary for themselves.

They told me about an incident which had taken place at the Darkokh bridge. Perhaps, if one were to look at it prosaically, then this incident takes on overtones of poetic symbolism. This is the story:

In the autumn we were retreating from Darkokh. Lieutenant Kholodov was left behind as the last one to blow up the Darkokh bridge. After the bridge was mined, Kholodov waited until some twenty German sub-machine gunners had reached the center of the bridge and then he lit the fuse. The Germans noticed Kholodov at the last second and they dashed forward across the bridge and killed him with a sub-machine gun burst. In that same second the bridge flew up into the air, killing the German sub-machine gunners. As Kholodov fell he grabbed his rifle in his hands, but then an avalanche of collapsing stone and earth buried him right there near the bridge, spreading a large, sepulchral mound over him by the force of the explosion. Time went by. During the winter when we went over to the offensive and once again reached that other bank of the river, the guardsmen of the Railroad Brigade who had begun to rebuild the bridge saw this stone hill; and from it they noticed the rusty point of a bayonet projecting from the midst of earth and stones. "Here is Kholodov," they said, impelled by some instinctive feeling, and they began to tear apart the frozen earth.

IN THE WINTER OF 'FORTY-THREE

Underneath they found Kholodov; he was not lying down, but was standing underneath the earth, holding his rifle clenched in his hands with the bayonet pointing upwards. He had stood under the earth for one-and-a-half months like a dead sentry, as if expecting his comrades' return to this bridge—as they will sooner or later return to all the blown-up bridges across the Don, and across the Dnieper, and across the Bug, and across the Dniester.

3. The year one thousand nine hundred and forty-three . . . On the night of New Year's Eve the snowbound command post of the division was situated in one of the passes over the Caucasian mountain range. A Front-line artists' brigade had just arrived there; they had an accordion with them. All night the accordionist played Russian and Ukrainian songs—"Viyut vitri," "Luchinushka," and dance tunes, and all night the telephone rang incessantly. The commander of the division would make a sign with his hand, the accordion would stop, directions would be given over the telephone—and then the music would continue again. Suddenly there was one more telephone call. "Comrade Colonel," a distant voice spoke into the telephone, "permit us to make a request. You have an accordion playing songs there; it carries over to us, although faintly, so don't let them hang up the receiver over your way, as the whole line would like so much to listen in."

The receiver was not hung up, and throughout the night of New Year's Eve in the dugout on the snowbound pass communications men listened over telephone receivers to echoes of songs coming from afar, men from Moscow, Kiev, Siberia, and Novgorod, listened in. They remembered their native places, the music was interrupted by commands, and the year 'forty-two was going over into 'forty-three, the new year which on that night everyone had already linked with the word "victory." Now the passes are deserted, the troops have descended from the mountains, and those who on New Year's Eve heard the music between the snowy pinnacles of the Caucasus, are fighting on the Taman, at Taganrog, in the Donbas.

It was winter, it was arid, and strong winds blew on the naked steppe where only lonely *charbarni*—herdsmen's shelters—provided here and there not the possibility of getting warm, but only of hiding from the wind in a place where a haystack was a desired shelter, and a burrow in the snow appeared almost like a house. The infantry, with faces darkened by frost and wind, and with reddened hands, marched one hundred, two hundred, three hundred miles. The army rearguards lagged behind the infantry which was moving ahead. The men marched without time out to eat, they chewed dried crusts on the move and had the chance only perhaps every other day to gulp down a mess tin of hot soup. The words "The Motherland is calling" can only be understood after tramping all these endless miles. If a monument were to be erected to the greatest force in the world—the force of the soul of the people—then an infantryman with a cap pulled down over his eyes, a kitbag, and a rifle behind his back should be sculptured on that monument.

In snowdrifts where no motor vehicle could move, the artillerymen of Major Rogan dragged their guns for a dozen miles with their bare hands. Rotmistrov's tank men did not climb out of their iron boxes for several days during the winter cold; devilish patience was needed to drag the heavy tanks across the rivers of the Zymla, the Kuberla, the Sal, and the Manych. A new technical term originated—"ice accumulation." To accumulate ice meant to lay logs and straw upon them, dousing them with water, putting down another layer of logs and straw and again dousing them with water, until all this wood would stand the weight of a KV tank crawling across the river. The men went barefoot through half-frozen swamps and marshes to bypass the Germans, carrying their felt boots in their hands so that later, after reaching firm ground,

IN THE WINTER OF 'FORTY-THREE

they could advance faster in their dry boots against the German.

The Army endured unheard-of burdens during these winter months; all of them endured, from privates to generals. And if I can tell about Sergeant Starchevoy, who went from Stalingrad to Rostov with rifle and kit bag through what cannot even be dreamed about by man, then I can tell the story of the general who commanded the regiment in which Sergeant Starchevoy served. About the general, whose old wounds had opened, and who, suffering pain and torment in a soldier's way, nevertheless went forward with his army and during brief halts, shutting his eyes against the pain, issued orders over the telephone in his usual, even voice and reassured the men going with him, who were tired but happy over the victory.

4. Recently, an expression born in this war became widespread among the German soldiers which, literally translated into Russian, means "a shot for the Fatherland." The meaning of this winged sentence is essentially much more terrible and sad for the Germans than the next bad communiqué from the Fuehrer's headquarters. "A shot for the Fatherland" means sustaining a serious wound, after which the German soldier is sent back to Germany in the hope of never again returning to the Eastern Front. Previously the Germans had dreamed of parcels from home, now they dream of "a shot for the Fatherland." Times have changed.

When I read in German letters the sentence "a shot for the Fatherland," I recall by contrast the story of attack aircraft pilot Victor Shakhov—a story whose ending I do not know, but whose beginning is remarkable.

Shakhov flew dozens of low-flying attacks. And each time it was an open question—to live or to die—and each time he resolved it in his favor, until one day when his aircraft caught fire deep in the German rear. Shakhov bailed out by parachute and crossed over the Front-lines. It was winter, he had to walk for a long time almost barefoot, and his feet became frostbitten. When Shakhov finally arrived at his own lines his feet could no longer be saved; in spite of all the doctors' efforts both his feet had to be amputated. He stayed for a long time in hospital until some good artificial limbs were made for him with whose aid he could still walk, although not as before. It would seem that all that was left for him to do was to go back home to the small town on the Oka where his relatives lived. But Shakhov succeeded in being returned to his regiment. He was given a job at the regimental Staff Headquarters, and every day he watched with envious eyes as his comrades took off for low-flying attacks.

Several months went by. Shakhov often visited the airfield where he would climb into the cabin of an attack plane and spend a long time there. Finally he submitted a request to the commander of the regiment stating that he was able to fly again; he had checked everything and was certain the artificial limbs would not be a hindrance. At first the commander of the regiment did not even want to listen to him. Shakhov kept insisting and producing evidence; he persisted like one possessed in trying to gain the right to fly, since it was a matter of his life's happiness. And this happiness lay only in continuing to fight personally as long as the war lasted. The force of his stubbornness was such that the commander of the regiment finally agreed to submit a report to the division commander in support of Shakhov's request. At first the division commander, like the commander of the regiment, did not even want to hear about it, but in Shakhov's desire there was that Russian strength of spirit, that determination to go through to the end, which could not be denied. In the end, the commander of the division supported Shakhov's request before the Staff of the Army.

I don't know whether Shakhov has been given per-

IN THE WINTER OF 'FORTY-THREE

mission to fly or not, but when I think about it, about the fact that we shall without doubt be victorious, I remember Shakhov.

5. At the crossings of Front line roads there are posts with new small signs projecting in various directions. Sometimes there are so many small signs that they look like a fan. To Armavir, to Kropotkin, to Tikhoretskaya, to Krasnodar, to Kushchevskaya, to Novo-Kubanskaya — roads, radiating in the form of a large star go to places which were until only recently occupied by the Germans, and a cut-down post with Gothic lettering on it lies beside it like a fallen soldier.

I recall a September day last year when we disembarked from the aircraft, after touching down near Stalingrad on the steppe beyond the Volga where, in the distance, the salt lake known only from geography books was showing white, while the waterless steppe, which appeared like the end of the world, stretched all around as far as the eye could see. It was not possible to fly any further, and we had to travel to Stalingrad by motorcar, and later, by water. Perhaps I had not had as painful a feeling throughout the whole war as I had on that day. How far the enemy had penetrated!—this was the feeling that weighed on the heart of everyone who was there.

We regained our peace of mind only on the next day in one of the battalions defending the northern outskirts of Stalingrad. There, all the thought and emotional strength of the men were directed towards one, it would seem, small but in reality great task—to defend the small village of Rynok against the Germans. This was the task of life. And no matter how the general course of the battle turned out; here, along a front of one mile the battalion wanted, at whatever cost, to achieve victory, and they were achieving it—in a soldierly, Russian way, without sophistry. They did not deliberate as to what the small village of Rynok meant compared with the Germans coming up to the Volga. To them the small village of Rynok meant life, and it was right here that they wanted to be victorious. And on the scale of the Front which, after all, consisted precisely of such small villages, hills, city blocks, river crossings—in each such place men, by being victorious, forged the general victory.

This force of spirit does not consist only in the readiness at any hour to give away one's life for the Motherland, it also consists in not losing one's presence of mind in the face of the enemy within the general life-and-death situation; in not allowing oneself to believe in German superiority, but to believe that one is cleverer, stronger, and more experienced. A great quality of the soul of the Russian soldier and officer is faith in his own strength. One paid in blood for mistakes, one learned from failures; one acquired experience from battles, but in spite of everything our commander never allowed faith in his strength and ability or his pride in his uniform to be shaken.

The battle of Stalingrad, in which all the stubbornness of our nation revealed itself with particular emphasis, educated a whole galaxy of commanders and generals. We learned much, so that what seemed to be an achievement yesterday seemed insufficient today. When the commander of the regiment which attacks a town reports to the commander of the division that he is "squeezing the Germans," the commander of the division shouts into the telephone with a hoarse voice which is the result of a chill: "Don't squeeze them, take them!" This is not a mere phrase, this is a new stage of the war when the commanders believe that what was a success a year ago is now no longer sufficient.

We not only have a presentiment about victory now, we are beginning to feel it, for in addition to a great and brave soul, our nation has strong soldiers' hands which know how to fight and how to gain victory.

February 27, 1943

Konstantin Simonov

DO AS I DO!

The fighting flared up today with renewed force, and the walls of this hut shake about every five minutes from the thunder of distant bombing. The Germans are bombing road crossings both to the right and to the left of the village.

But the tank men will not go into battle until tomorrow; today they are resting after the tank raid. Before me sits a man of average height, with a young, but already tired face which, aside from his will, reflects inhuman ordeals, sleepless nights, familiarity with ever-present death—everything that has been the constant companion of our people for twenty months now from the first day of the war. When in talking to me he tries to gesticulate in the Southern manner, he sometimes suddenly grimaces with pain because he has been wounded in both arms—the hands of one arm and the elbow of the other. Somehow he is still able to move the fingers of the right hand, but the left arm hangs powerless in a sling. Nevertheless he says that tomorrow he will go into combat, as if both arms are obliged to heal overnight without fail. An orderly sits on a stool some distance away, and threading cotton into a needle awkwardly with the wrong hand, male fashion, sews on shoulder straps to the greasy, grey tank tunic of his lieutenant.

Lieutenant Chistyakov is the same age I am. He was born twenty-seven years ago in the same year, he lived for a long time in the same city on the Volga; we studied at neighboring schools and walked the same streets—he is my fellow townsman, and it seems to me that, had I not taken part in the tank raid with him, had I not experienced everything that he had experienced, I could still clearly imagine everything that he had experienced during that time.

As is the way with people who can remember the war from the very beginning, we do remember it from the June days of 1941; we remember now this Front, now another, now the cities from which we withdrew and to which we have already returned, and from which we shall never again withdraw. But Chistyakov remembers, above all, the last three days. He has not had enough sleep since then, he still has dark rings under his eyes, a tired face, and injured hands in bandages after these three days.

Three days in a tank . . . A deep-thrusting tank raid by an advanced detachment—that very same move that the Germans had loved so much in the beginning of the war whereby, it must be confessed, they often threw us into confusion—a tactic which now, in the days of the Russian offensive, decides victory so often and throws into confusion not us, but the Germans from whom we have learned a thing or two. We have learned them so well that there are now three hundred miles on a straight line between me and Stalingrad where, back in September, I had sat in a dugout on the very banks of the Volga.

DO AS I DO!

The raid began in the morning. Chistyakov's tank was unloaded near a small town which had been captured during the night. He had in his group ten squat, solid T-34 machines, beloved by the tank men and the infantry, or "Thirty-fours," as they call them in the Army. Four crews had already been in combat, six still had their first battle ahead of them; they had it ahead of them to fight for the first time the way tank men have to fight—to be merciless to the enemy, merciless to themselves, and to come through and win or to stop and die, since either one or the other usually happens to tank men.

The commander of the brigade, Major Ovcharov—who was also the same age as Chistyakov and I, and who had been in the recent past a philologist and was at present a veteran—gave Chistyakov a route to follow and an order which, as often happens during an offensive, did not distinguish itself by verbosity: to chase the Germans and not to fall back an inch from them.

"Not to lose touch," Ovcharov said to Chistyakov, "you understand that the main thing is not to lose touch so that they can't catch their breath."

Chistyakov set the task before his crews and then gave them the manful command of the tank men which leaves no room for wavering: "Do as I do!" For while radio communication is, of course, indispensable, the example set by the commander who breaks out to the front of his crew is at times something no radio can replace.

The tanks began to roll then, and we drove for about six miles over the sodden road, throwing up fragments of ice and big splashes of water before we finally caught up with our first Germans—some four hundred men. They were proceeding along the road in a column, and when the tanks appeared from behind the hillock, the field resounded with disorderly shooting from rifles and big bursts from machine guns. The Germans ran to the right and the left from the road over to the field where they lay down and squatted. Some fired, others simply fell down flat, clasping their heads with their hands, and waited for death to crush them or go past them. Chistyakov did not fire during that moment which separated the tanks from the Germans. The tanks raced past for that half-mile in silence, and it was only when they cut into the fleeing German soldiers that Chistyakov began to fire from the machine gun. He had been through too many burned cities and incinerated villages, he had seen too many tortured people who had lost everything in the world, he had seen too many gallows and prison walls with executed prisoners lying about—he had seen too much Russian sorrow to think now, as he was crushing his enemies with the caterpillar tracks of his tank, of love of man, or of pity or mercy. He was carrying out his orders as a soldier; he was killing Germans. Neither did he feel sorry for them, even simply as human beings; this feeling had vanished from his heart back in July and August of 1941; back then, when the Germans had captured Smolensk and had trampled the fields of the Ukraine, was a time when real, complete revenge did not appear as close as it was today.

Everything thundered inside the tank, the engine roared, the machine gun clattered, and nothing could be heard apart from these sounds; in the thick glass of the panoramic viewfinder one could see only soundlessly firing, soundlessly falling, soundlessly shouting Germans. Five minutes later those who remained alive raised their hands. After throwing their rifles and machine guns on the ground they approached the tanks, which had stopped, and the terror in their eyes could be seen even through the dull glass.

Upon Chistyakov's order five sub-machine gunners climbed down from the tanks, and after methodically lining up the prisoners, marched them back along the road going east. Before giving the order to proceed further,

DO AS I DO!

Chistyakov lifted the hatch cover of his tank and gazed after the prisoners. They marched as a grey crowd, their shoulders mechanically stooped, having lost their usual bearing, and the color of their grey greatcoats merged with the color of the road and the color of the dirty, trampled-over snow. He gazed at them for a few seconds, then turned, gave the order, and the tanks went onward toward the west.

At first a level field stretched to the left and to the right of the road, then the field went over into a slope, and here, as they were coming down from a hillock the tanks came under artillery fire. A self-propelled German gun was firing from some six hundred yards away. A bluish mist which had not lifted since morning lay in the hollow, and Chistyakov could only see the flashes of the guns, firing one after the other. He fired two or three times in that direction with fragmentation bombs and then steered the tank at full speed directly at the gun. During this minute he was convinced that he would not be killed, but that he would kill. He wanted to reach the gun at all costs and to squash it with the tank's caterpillar tracks or to fire at it pointblank from twenty, thirty yards, and then still run into it and run it over, feeling how the tank would crawl with its weight over squashed German iron. He fired several times while still on the move, and when the tank came up close to the outskirts of the village, there where the gun stood near a stone fence, Chistyakov saw that the gun crew had been killed by one of the shells. But he could not hold back anymore and ran over this gun before bursting into the streets of the village.

He was the first to burst into the village, half a minute earlier than the rest of his tanks, and while firing he turned first to the left and then to the right, dispersing German infantry in all directions. Beyond the village the road again went up a hill. The hill was steep, and Chistyakov could clearly see how German trucks were slowly, with effort, skidding and crawling uphill on the dirty road followed by the infantry which was climbing uphill helter-skelter behind the motor vehicles. After speeding over a small bridge Chistyakov bypassed the motor vehicles from the left, climbed up the hill ahead of them, and having ascended the crest of the hill, felt himself to be master of the situation. He opened fire at the German infantry from his cannons and the machine gun. The motor vehicles were also very close. They began to rush about, and in attempting to turn back on the steep, slippery road, they skidded and stopped. Chistyakov did not shoot at them. He felt that the first excitement of the battle had subsided in him. The motor vehicles could not get away in any case, and as much as he wanted to crash down on them from above, to crush them, and grind them into the ground, he did not do this, for a dozen trucks in a condition of repair are an incomparably better trophy than a dozen pancakes of wood and metal splinters pressed into the ground.

The other tanks moved along the village streets. Near the outskirts the sub-machine gunners dismounted and began rounding up German soldiers in the farmsteads. Now Chistyakov opened the hatch and heard shots and the confused hubbub, so joyous to the soldier's heart, of the Germans—those self-same Germans who once used to drive around so arrogantly and so presumptuously on these roads in these same black motor vehicles which had seemed so invulnerable.

Half an hour later ten of Chistyakov's tanks advanced along the road to the next village. There they found that a German infantry defense line stretched along the crest of the hills. On the command of "Do as I do!" all ten tanks climbed the hill and after bursting through to level ground, began to crush the infantry. The Germans started to raise their hands. Chistyakov opened the hatch and climbed up in order to command the firing to stop. In that second—or rather, in that tenth of a second—he noticed that a German officer who was standing quite close to the tank held a revolver in one of his raised hands. Chistyakov instantly moved aside and the bullet whistled past his ear. He let the hatch cover drop and with a machine-gun burst cut down the officer. Then he again opened the hatch. The German soldiers were now surrendering. While waiting for the remaining sub-machine gunners to arrive, the tanks cruised around the Germans with their hatches open. When the sub-machine gunners finally arrived Chistyakov ordered another ten men to stay behind for convoy duty of the prisoners while the others got into their tanks and moved on to the next village.

Chistyakov again pulled away from the others and was the first to drive into the village. He rushed right through it, squashing a staff car on the way, and on the central square he came under violent artillery fire, first from one side, then from all four sides. Several shells hit the turret without piercing its armor. Chistyakov swung around and, firing on the move, scooted back to his tanks along the edge of the village. His machine gun which was paired with the cannon did not function: its barrel had been knocked off by one of the shells. The commander of the brigade met Chistyakov on the outskirts, and seeing that he was returning from the village asked him what was going on there.

"Oh, nothing special, Comrade Major," Chistyakov said. "Four guns are firing."

"Where from?" the major asked.

Chistyakov indicated the four points he had roughly located. Six of his tanks bypassed the village, while he along with three others burst into the village straight along the street. The four guns were crushed, one after the other, but there was a din in the turret, and it seemed to Chistyakov that his head was bursting as if it had been hit several times with a heavy hammer. During these last minutes three more shells had scored direct hits on the turret of his tank without piercing it, and although the tank had scarcely been damaged, a heavy leaden headache pressed on one's eyes and ears that seemed as if it would never go away.

The German sub-machine gunners ran out of the village in all directions and hid inside of haystacks, and the tanks drove up in turns now to one, now to another huge haystack and set them alight with fragmentation bombs. The German sub-machine gunners darted out of the burning haystacks and again scattered over the field where they were shot down by machine guns, and it seemed to Chistyakov that this battle had finished well for his tank. His turret gunner, so as not to unnecessarily burn down one of the haystacks, looked out of the turret to see whether there were Germans in it. In that second a German sub-machine gunner sitting in the haystack fired a long burst, and the turret gunner fell down dead, hanging over the rim of the turret. Chistyakov pulled him inside and closed the hatch, ordering the radio operator to take the turret gunner's place, and coming right up to the haystack, they set it alight and mercilessly shot down all the German sub-machine gunners who scurried out of it.

Carried away by the pursuit Chistyakov drove up the hill in his tank, and then, after going over the top he drove up to the cemetery fence where an anti-tank gun scored several hits in a row. One direct hit made a deep dent in the turret, another tore off a piece of armor. Chistyakov aimed his cannon and smashed the antitank gun with a successful shot which struck it directly under the wheels. The Russian sub-machine gunners guarding the tanks made the rounds of the village streets, capturing German soldiers who had still remained hidden here and there, while the tank men, on Chistyakov's order, were refueling their machines from the gasoline tankers which had just caught up with the tanks. The field kitchen had also ar-

DO AS I DO!

rived on the heels of the gasoline tankers, and sweaty and deafened tank men climbed out of their machines, and crowding around the field kitchen, hurriedly ate some hot soup. Before serving the soup the cook dispensed the guards' rations from a large can, filling their water bottles and mugs. While fuel was poured through hoses into the tanks the men had a quiet smoke break for the first time in twenty-four hours, and exchanged terse remarks about the battle which had just come to an end.

Chistyakov looked at his watch and noticed with surprise that exactly twenty-four hours had passed. The sky was already beginning to lighten but he felt no tiredness, not even drowsiness—only the importunate headache continued to torment him. After the smoke break the men got into the tanks and continued along the route. A small frozen river wound its way between hillocks before a large village. A forced crossing began during which the ice was broken by the tanks' caterpillar tracks. As they approached the village they were fired upon from the outskirts by German guns.

The task of breaking the ice and crossing the river delayed the tanks, and here Chistyakov suffered his first loss: Tsysayev's tank, which was following him, was set alight twenty yards away from him. Now there were only nine tanks left. They crawled across the river and went straight up the hill. A barn which stood at the top of the hill could be clearly seen from below, it was from here that the German anti-tank battery was firing. As one, all the tanks concentrated their bombardment on that barn until it caught fire, then shells began to explode inside, and then the battery fell silent. Fifty more infantrymen were taken prisoner here, and again several sub-machine gunners were detached to escort the column of prisoners back to the Russian lines.

It was now full daylight. The inhabitants came crowding out into the streets of the village. Chistyakov opened the hatch and drove through the village waving to the people who lined both sides of the streets. His tank men drove behind him with their hatches open too, waving, nodding, and saying some words which could not be heard over the rumble of the caterpillar tracks. Dirty and covered in grease, Chistyakov climbed out of his tank into the middle of the street and several little girls who were crowding around began to embrace him and to kiss his unshaved, grease-smeared cheeks. Old women brought lumps of steaming cooked meat and homemade bread. The few remaining cows were hurriedly milked in nearby barns, outside of their regular timetable, and fresh milk was brought to the tanks.

The gasoline tanks arrived half an hour later, and after the tanks refueled again they moved on, without rest, to the next village. A chain of high hills, strongly fortified by the Germans, stretched straight in front of the tanks, barring them from the village. Chistyakov retraced his tracks for half a mile, turned into a deep hollow, and deviating sideways along it for some four miles he bypassed the hills and entered the town with his tanks from the other side. He stopped his machine near a small cottage at the crossroads; the roads here had not been driven on and were buried under the snow. For a long time no one came out of the cottage, and then a tall, white-haired old woman looked out from the door. She hooded her eyes with her hand and gazed for a long time at the tanks as if she could not believe that ours could turn up here, out of the blue, and then all of a sudden, throwing up her hands, she ran up to Chistyakov's tank, hurled herself against its armor-plated side, and reaching up for his hands she cried, "Sonny! Sonny!"

She repeated this word about ten times, and then after she had calmed down she explained how best to drive to the next village by means of a bypass, and it seemed to Chistyakov that he need only say the word and

DO AS I DO!

the old woman would climb into the tank with the submachine gunners and would accompany him into battle.

It had begun to darken, and it was nightfall before the tanks entered, by roundabout ways, the road leading into the next village. They stopped there at the intersection; it was necessary to refuel again, and they had to wait for the gasoline tankers which had dropped behind somewhere. Snow began to fall, and soon a heavy snowstorm was under way. The snow was burying the tanks, and when the men climbed out of the turrets to breathe some fresh air the snow immediately covered their helmets and their flushed, sweaty faces with a mantle of white. It was only here, during this involuntary stop, that Chistyakov began to feel how tired he was. He did not feel it immediately; at first he noticed that the turret gunner on the neighboring tank was asleep standing up, leaning against the open hatch cover in a position which was so uncomfortable that only a deathly tired man could sleep like that. Chistyakov suddenly felt that he, too, could go to sleep like that at any second, if he were only to shut his eyes. But he ordered his men to sleep in turns, for they could not even consider sleeping at the same time. For an hour and a half the men took turns sleeping under the curtain of falling snow, some staying below in the tank, some sleeping in the turret while others stood guard and watched the road. After an hour and a half the fuel arrived, and the tanks began rolling again. Several miles later the tanks burst into the streets of the village in the dead of night. They were now far in the vanguard, and the German garrison, which did not suspect anything, was sound asleep inside the houses. The retreat was taking place, and all the streets were blocked by motor vehicles clustered near the houses. Chistyakov counted up to one hundred and fifty cars and trucks. In order to clear a path he had to crush some two dozen vehicles—although it was a shame to lose them that way.

KONSTANTIN SIMONOV

All this time a Lieutenant Khlopov, the commander of another tank company which had been put out of action, had been riding in Chistyakov's tank, along with the sub-machine gunners. He did not want to remain in the rear, and when his tank was set alight he had asked to be taken into Chistyakov's tank and to continue the chase after the Germans, even if only with a sub-machine gun in his hand. At this village he was killed on the spot, shot through the chest in the street-fighting when, along with several other soldiers, he was freeing Russian prisoners-of-war who had been locked in a barn. When our compatriots poured out into the street, their condition was so terrible that it was only by great effort that Chistyakov was able to restrain his tank men and sub-machine gunners from dealing in kind with the captured Germans.

By daybreak the battle in the village came to an end. The inhabitants, accompanied by this or that sub-machine gunner, made a search through every hut and barn to rout out the remaining Germans. An old man at whose house a German commandant had been staying, came and said that weapons and documents, a greatcoat, boots, and a cap had been left behind in his house since the commandant had fled dressed only in his underwear. Thus it remained unknown whether the commandant had succeeded in running away or whether he was killed, for among the corpses lying about in the street, a good half were in the same state of undress as the commandant. And the outfit he left behind was really fully intact, beginning with the cap and the boots and finishing with the documents secreted in various pockets of the uniform.

It had been freezing, but this was a bright sunny day, and here in the village the tank men had a bite to eat for the third time during all that period. To be sure, the kitchen had fallen hopelessly behind, but aside from the hospitality which the inhabitants vied with each other in offering, the tank men also took advantage of conquered trophies; they warmed themselves with German brandy and ate some chocolate, and more from curiosity than for pleasure they drew a few times on strong-smelling German cigars, and then they remounted their tanks and moved on again.

It was already after midday by the time the next village was liberated. It, too, was filled with retreating German infantry, but here the Germans, having heard the thunder of the tanks from a distance and seeing that they could not in any case manage to disperse as usual, hid themselves instead inside the cottages and farm houses. Chistyakov felt it an unbearable pity to have to fire at these humble Russian cottages in which the local inhabitants were locked inside with the Germans. It was necessary to sacrifice them, and while the tanks stood at the outskirts of the village guarding the entrances and exits, the sub-machine gunners by force cleared out one house after another of the Germans without advance artillery preparation. It was here that Chistyakov, who had opened the hatch and had stood up in order to see better, was wounded in the right hand. He let the lid of the hatch fall shut behind him and without leaving the tank, dragged himself to the first-aid box and hastily bandaged his fingers.

There now remained as the main obstacle on the way to the town which was the final point of this operation, a strip of fortified hills where the Germans had obviously decided to make a final, desperate stand. Deploying themselves in a large semicircle, the tanks moved towards the hills. On Chistyakov's orders three tanks burst into a small village situated at the base of the hills, and there to their surprise, they captured two high-powered guns which the Germans had not managed to remove in time and with which they had only yesterday bombarded the Front-line, which was at a great distance from here.

The hills were attacked late in the evening. They were

girdled by a veritable fireworks of gunfire. The Germans shot from rifles and large-caliber machine guns and from artillery pieces; intermittent colored chains of machine gun bursts stretched like dots and dashes, and long-range shells or, as the tank men call them, "pig iron," flew past whistling like fiery ingots. But the tanks, along with the sub-machine gunners who followed them, climbed up the hills. The hills were heavily iced over, and after getting half-way up their steep inclines, the tanks slid down backwards. It was necessary to climb up again, overcoming the ice-covered ground by climbing diagonally across the profile of the hills. The crew of Rodionov's tank, which had broken through ahead, perished in the very first minutes. A German gun had been aimed at it pointblank. The tank went straight for the gun, but was blown up in the minefield surrounding the gun within ten yards of reaching it. The driver had been driving the tank at such a speed, however, that although it was disabled and had a dead crew inside; it rushed ten yards ahead by the force of inertia and crashed into the gun, crushing it.

The crew of Salmanov's tank was blown up by mines after the tank had climbed up the hill, then Bobkov's tank burned up. Before that Chistyakov himself had crushed a gun. He was literally deafened by the fierce firing from all sides. There were five more direct hits on his machine, with one of the armor-piercing shells actually becoming stuck in the double facing of the turret, but his tank continued to go. Six crews managed to climb to the top of the hills, and after crushing and shooting up a dozen guns and large-caliber machine guns, moved on toward the town after crossing the ridge.

The night was dark, and since the approaches to the town had not been reconnoitered the tanks stopped to wait for dawn while the scouts moved on ahead. But the tank of young Lieutenant Yermokhin, who was taking part in the fighting for the third day only and who had not managed to receive the order to wait until dawn, raced rashly into the streets of the town and wandered around in it all night. Chistyakov could not go to sleep in spite of his terrible tiredness. He could hear the tank traveling along the street with a growl and firing, and then when he heard its engines suddenly stall, his heart was wrung, he was afraid that everything was finished with Yermokhin. But the tank began to growl again, and once again firing from its cannons and machine guns could be heard, and the tank men who had gathered into groups and were listening intently said, "He's alive!"

By morning the minefield had been reconnoitered and a safe path found through it, and the tank men burst into town with the morning mist. Lt. Yermokhin, who had a smashed cannon, stood in one of the streets on the outskirts and fired furiously from his machine gun. Everything was finished after one hour: Chistyakov's tanks and other tanks which had approached the town somewhat later, combed right through the town. Chistyakov climbed out of his tank and leaned against the wall of a building, and for a minute it seemed to him that he would fall down—that's how tired he was. He had been wounded for a second time during this last attack; this time it was his left arm; the arm hung helplessly down from the elbow, it was cut by a splinter a little below the elbow and blood streamed along the torn tunic and down the numb fingers which could not feel anything. He could not even bandage his arm by himself, and his driver, after turning up his sleeve, tied a tourniquet on it for the time being in an attempt to stop the bleeding until the arrival of a nurse or doctor. He removed Chistyakov's wristwatch which, by a miracle, was still intact, and placed it nearby on a wall projection. Chistyakov gazed mechanically at the watch; according to it the time was seven a.m.—exactly as it was three days ago when the tanks had gone into battle. Three days—four tanks had been left by the wayside, but six had nevertheless got there—they had got there whatever the cost.

And in spite of tiredness and giddiness Chistyakov suddenly felt a surge of that happiness which occurs only after a hard-won victory, when your tank, knocked about by shells, steaming, tired, and seeming to breathe heavily, stands next to you with its machine gun smashed and its turret damaged, with fragments of trucks stuck in the caterpillar tracks and its armor full of scratches and splashes of blood. But still it had got there—by Jove—it had got there where it had to get to, and victory is victory no matter how much blood has been spilt or how much tiredness and suffering it has cost.

March 9, 1943

Konstantin Simonov

ON THE OLD SMOLENSK HIGHWAY

When I think about the Motherland I always remember the Smolensk region, its roads, its white birches, its small villages on low hillocks, and although I was born far from there, it is precisely these places which seem to be the closest and dearest to my heart. This must be because my involvement in the war began precisely here, on these roads, and the greatest sorrow in life—which is sorrow over the loss of one's native land—caught up with me here in the Smolensk region. It was here that I traveled through villages and knew that the Germans would pass over their dusty streets in an hour's time. It was here that, on turning back, I saw fields ripe with corn and I knew that we would no longer reap them. It was here that, on leaving the motor car in order to have a drink of water at a well, I could not find within me the strength to look into the eyes of the peasants, because in their stricken eyes was the unspoken question: "Are you really leaving?" And I could not say anything in reply, aside from a bitter and sorrowful, "Yes." I knew that the alien power would enter here tomorrow, and that tomorrow neither I nor anyone else would be able in any way to help these women who were crowding around our motor car in the street.

I remember the village cemeteries with a particular pain which still lives in me without relenting for a moment. In the Smolensk region these cemeteries are usually somewhere quite close to a small village, on a hillock under old, wide-spreading trees. The small village is tiny, made up of some twenty to thirty small peasant cottages, but the cemetery is large. Many, many of the old crosses have turned dark from the wind. And when you look at such a village cemetery you can feel how many generations have been laid down here into their graves, into their own soil, next to their grandfathers and great-grandfathers' cottages, and you can feel what kind of village it is, what kind of Russian soil it is, how impossible it is to take it away from us—as impossible as tearing out one's heart and still being able to live. I speak for myself, but I know that the same feeling was experienced by everyone who was retreating along the Smolensk roads almost two years ago. And I know more: in the depths of the soul of each of us there was harbored faith in our return. We did not believe that we could die without returning here, without passing these places again.

Wherever I have been since then, I always carry in my field bag among the maps I need of one or another sector of the Front, one particular map which seemed to be useless. This is not a General Staff map—it is an old school map of the Smolensk region which I bought during the second week of the war in one of the small towns near the Front. By October, 1941, we had left the Smolensk region, and it had become useless—but I put this map in my field bag, and there it is, tattered, frayed, and torn in

ON THE OLD SMOLENSK HIGHWAY

the folds, lying before me. How many times in the course of a year and a half did I take it out and spread it out in front of me the same way and look at its green surface, at the black hairlines of the roads, the blue threads of the rivers, and I would see not a map but these roads and rivers and the foliage of the forests and the yellow of the fields. I would shut my eyes and try to imagine traveling again through the villages which we had left behind us, to picture how the women who once took leave of us in tears would smile at meeting us, how an old man would come out of the gate and, shading his eyes and screwing them up, would look at our machines coming in from the east.

And now this map has become necessary, necessary at last. I took it out of a remote compartment of the field bag, glued up its folds, and getting into the motor car I triumphantly spread it out on my knees. But how can one express in words the sorrow which grips the heart when one returns to the places one loves so much that one could cry, and which have changed so much that it is hard to believe; can the soil, the forest, the field, the road—all that which opens up before one's eyes, change that much?

Topography is a precise and cold science, and the paper on which the map has been printed is only soulless paper and the lines traced on it will not change. But if the map had changed as much as the land has changed it would be difficult to read it now. The thaw had eaten deeply into the snow, there was water on the roads, and the sky had turned blue almost like a summer sky. Spring remains spring, and sunlight remains sunlight, and the saddest landscapes are somehow more cheerful when they are warmed by the sun and slaked with March rains. We drive through a disfigured, bombed, and burnt-down world; where there had once been villages there are now only chimney stacks left standing, their dead, blackened arms raised in a cry for retribution. We drive through land disfigured by explosions of mines, through endless fields scarred by craters as if by smallpox, along roads which have almost ceased to be roads, since the Germans in retreating have hacked them to pieces like a live human body and have blown up all the bridges. We drive through chopped-down birch forests—and although a telegraph pole is only a pole, I am seized by a feeling of anger and pain when I see that the Germans have made all these temporary poles from freshly cut-down young birches, and as if it were not enough to chop down one small birch, they braced it on three sides with three more, and they had also built fences from these small birches to put around car-parking areas, around mined fields and soldiers' latrines. One feels that if they could have cut down all the forests here in Smolensk they would have done it in the same way as they have burned down all the houses and disfigured all the roads.

The lands of the Smolensk region have become a desert. Every now and then one can meet a stooped old woman on the road pulling a sleigh on which two bundles lay, from one of which the copper lid of a samovar projects—all that was left from a home, from the goods and chattels of a life, such as it once was.

We drive through one village after another, and those who have remained alive, those who have not been dragged away into distant slavery, stand in the midst of deserted homesteads and at the ruins of peasant cottages. And even the people's attitudes are somehow the same; speechless amazement, arms folded on the chest, heads hung low, a gaze seeking for at least traces of that which once had been here. In pits covered over with scorched boards there are children who cry and laugh, and who are too young yet to understand the tragedy of all that has happened, while a five-year-old girl standing next to an old woman looked with an unchildlike, sad, knowing gaze at the bodies of three men and two women lying near the wall of the shed. These people are not from here—they had been brought here from the neighboring village, and then when they became an encumbrance to the Germans they were shot right here, at the wall of the shed. The little girl looks at them, and it seems to me that many years from now when she has become an adult and this war lives only in her memory, the expression of the same unchildlike astonishment will remain in her gaze.

At the entry to what was once the town of Vyazma, two people stand in the midst of smoldering ruins which look the same as thousands of other smoldering ruins—an old man and an old woman. From a pit covered with straw one can hear the cries of the child of their son who has gone to war. The old woman bakes millet cookies on a small iron stove which stands directly on the ground. The old man tells us how he placed a sheet of plywood with the inscription, "Mines here" near the road because he saw the Germans lay them before they left. He is a man of seventy years of age, an old railway worker who, for fifty years of his life has worked here in Vyazma; he talks slowly without hurrying while rough-hewing a scorched log which he intends to secure above the entrance to the pit where the child cries so as to construct some semblance of a roof. He rough-hews the log without haste, but suddenly, unable to bear it any longer, he furiously drives the axe into it with all his might, blow after blow: "Well, I shall cover the pit so that the kid will be warm, and then I'll leave for the Army. I'll do it, I can't live here. Let the old woman look after the kid. I'll leave to fight the Germans, may they rot in hell . . ." And he swears rudely, obscenely, with boundless, unbearable hatred. And the old woman stands opposite him making little, senile nods with her head. The little grandchild bawls in the pit. And chimneys, chimneys, chimneys endless scorched chimneys tower all around. And further ahead, between these chimneys, one can see the bell towers of the Vyazma churches, with blue gaps showing the sky and fantastic fragments of blown-up buildings. The air all around is filled with the smell of burning, and the snow is blackened as if those who remain alive have strewn their land with ashes as a sign of mourning.

During last winter our troops had come close to Vyazma. The partisan detachments had begun to raise their heads, and its inhabitants had started to cross the Front during the night, and German soldiers were being killed in the streets, and it seemed that liberation was not far away—but it did not come about at that time, it did not succeed. . . . And now, two weeks ago, sensing that this town would not remain long in their hands, the Fascists remembered last winter and they destroyed this quiet, ancient town, dealing with it in a manner in which perhaps, until now—even they had not dealt with any other town. They vindictively blew up one street after another, one building after another, until they had blown up everything—from the first to the last. And now we stand on the outskirts of the town and we can see right through to the snow-covered fields stretching beyond the other side of the town—the whole town can be seen through, for it does not exist anymore, it has ceased to be a town.

We drive over what, before, were the streets of Vyazma. My eyes seek the house where, in the summer of 1941, we spent the night two or three times between trips to the Front, but I cannot find either it, or even its ruins, for it is impossible to fathom out anything within this expanse of smoldering ruins.

The wet spring road runs from Vyazma westward to the Front. On a hill immediately beyond the town stretches a huge German cemetery. Thousands of black crosses, accurately spaced out in rows and divided into sectors, stretch for many hundreds of yards. The Germans are buried in date order: the accuracy of the gravediggers allows us to find out how many of them we have killed

ON THE OLD SMOLENSK HIGHWAY

on what date. There is a whole avenue on which Knights of the Iron Cross have been buried, and on each cross there is one and the same date: Died 1/27/42. Paul Schilling - 1/27/42, Hermann Schumacher - 1/27/42, Johan Schutz, Anton Radick, Hans Eller, Max Hermann, Heinrich Lautenjot, Jost Schultz, all died on 1/27/42. And the following row is dated 2/12/42. Then 1943. And further come those of March, quite recent ones, the soil is fresh and the crosses have just been hammered into it. These here were killed at the time when those who were still alive began to burn down the buildings and streets of Vyazma.

The road runs further westward. It is soggy, tractors crawl along it with difficulty, dragging guns behind them, and the Russian infantry marches with the unhurried pace of veterans. I do not know when, but this infantry will reach the frontier some time and will cross it. In the gait of the soldiers, in their faces and in the glances which they cast about them at their scorched land there is something which says they will reach it, they will reach it without fail. The spring sun warms one's back. The infantrymen march on sullenly, more silently than usual, wiping the sweat from their tired faces.

There is the next village out of Vyazma, there is the ravine in which lie the still unburied women and old men who were killed only yesterday. One of the women lies there with her head thrown back, convulsively clutching a dead child to her breast. A platoon of field engineers stops above the ravine: initially the first two come up, then the rest begin to press closer. A middle-aged field engineer with a ginger moustache gazes for a long time into the ravine at the dead woman with the child. Then, without addressing anyone in particular as he adjusted his rifle on his shoulder, he says in a voice thickened by a cold, "They didn't even spare the little kid." And after a long pause he repeats it: "They didn't even spare the kid." He does not add anything to these words, neither swear words nor shouts of indignation, nothing. But behind his words one senses the weighty decision which he has just arrived at—not to spare them—not to spare those who did not spare others.

A very old man on crutches comes out of a half-demolished peasant cottage to meet the field engineers. He watches them as they spread out in all directions from the road with their mine detectors, and then he says in his cracked old man's voice, "Don't look here, sons. They didn't lay any mines here. They laid them over there." Leaning heavily on his crutches he takes some twenty paces and then raising one crutch points with it sideways. "That's where they laid them. And they laid them here, too—and over there . . ."

One more village. The Germans have just left here. All the survivors have assembled in two peasant cottages that were spared by the general fire. A woman, still not old, with white hair, sits on a wooden trunk and cries silently, without sobbing, propping up her head with her arms. She had not got the strength to say anything, but the daughter of the woman next door—a snubnosed sixteen-year-old who, an hour ago, had come running home from the forest where the people from the neighboring villages have been hiding—takes us aside and in a childlike manner, hastily, breathlessly, begins to tell us what happened:

"She cries because she has a son who was killed. Sasha Ivanov was her son. He was killed two days ago. They attacked the Germans, and the Germans killed him and three other boys. From this village—Sasha, and from Filin—Ananka and Vaska—and another one from the town, from Vyazma." Hurriedly as before, but simply and artlessly, she tells how the four lads (the eldest was seventeen) found out that the Germans intended to drive the women and children they had taken from the villages, through the forest. "The lads had among them one semi-sub-machine gun, a rifle, and two Nagant revolvers. They decided to lay an ambush in the forest and either rescue the children from the Germans or die. They laid the ambush and attacked the Germans, killing one and wounding another, but three of them also died in this uneven fight, and the fourth, whose legs were smashed, was captured by the Germans. They dragged him along the road as far as the village and then they shot him there. That was all." The snub-nosed girl cannot contain herself any longer, she sobs and adds with a quavering voice, "Of course, they had only Nagant revolvers, and Nagant revolvers do not shoot far. But the Germans had machine guns. So they killed them. And this is Shashka's mother. She keeps on crying."

The creak of sleighs which have driven up can be heard outside the window. The woman gets up from the trunk, straightens up, and with a quiet, firm gait, without lowering her head or wiping the tears from her face, comes out into the street. She takes the reins from the hands of the boy who has arrived, seats herself just as erectly in the sleigh, and the sleigh moves off amidst general silence.

"Her Sashka still lies out there on the road," the girl says. "Now she has driven away. She wishes to bury him."

The sleigh travels slowly along the country road in the midst of mined fields, shell craters, and knocked-down poles. The horse is driven by the woman sitting erect in the sleigh with a stern, as if petrified, face. This peasant woman from near Vyazma, driving off to find the body of her son, she resembles Russia herself, burying her dead sons amidst obscure snows, with her head bare.

The roads run westward. Troops move along them, and naked spring forests run up the hills and come down from them. And the snow melts, freeing at last the liberated earth from its bluish shroud. And such sorrow grips the heart, such grief over the people who perished on this sad earth that it seems that this sorrow—profound, ineradicable, insatiable—will one day lift like an avenging hand above the killers who are now retreating, pressed by us even further along the snow-covered roads running westward. And in my ears there still ring the words of the field engineer: "They didn't even spare the little kid," and I can still see his stony face in that moment when he spoke those words.

March 17, 1943

Ilya Ehrenburg

THE FATE OF EUROPE

Recently I had occasion to visit the Gzhatsk district which has been liberated from the Germans. The word "desert" can hardly express the spectacle of the cataclysm which arises before your eyes as soon as you get to the places the Germans had been occupying for seventeen months. The Gzhatsk district had been prosperous and happy. Milk from pampered Swiss cows was supplied from there to Moscow, skillful tailors and garment workers came from there to the capital. The old interlaced with the new in the quaint manner of our country. In Gzhatsk beside the ancient Kazan Cathedral and the small wooden houses there towered the spacious, light-filled buildings of the school, the club, and the hospital. In Gzhatsk there were small muddy lanes and byways, and there were youngsters who dreamed about flying into the stratosphere. But now, instead of the town there is only an ugly conglomeration of iron bars, scorched stone, and broken brick. Gzhatsk appears on the map, it has a meaning for the heart, but it no longer exists on earth. The Vandals of our century have annihilated the town in accordance with the latest technological achievements. They blew up day nurseries and churches with tolite. Bursting into peoples' houses, they broke the window glass, poured fuel over the walls, and rejoiced at the "Bengal lights,"—Gzhatsk was burning. Half the villages in the district have been burned, only those villages survived from which the Germans were pulling out in a hurry under pressure from the Red Army. Few people still remain here; the Germans have deported 6,000 Russians from Gzhatsk to Germany. Visions of dark antiquity, of the beginning of human history, arise. In vaid did mothers attempt to hide their children from the German slave-traders. Mothers buried young boys under snow—and they froze to death; mothers covered girls with hay, but the Germans pierced the haystacks with bayonets. Twelve- and thirteen-year-old youngsters were driven along the streets by rifle butts; these were the Germans driving the children into slavery. At times whole families, whole villages were driven out. The district was becoming depopulated as hunger, typhoid, diphtheria, and the torture chambers of the Gestapo did their job. But possibly more frightening than physical extermination was the moral suppression of human dignity. When one comes into a town liberated from the Germans one is frightened not only by the ruins and the corpses, one is also frightened by human eyes which looked as if they had been burnt out. People talk in whispers, they start at the sound of footsteps, and flinch back from a shadow. I saw this in Gzhatsk in March. I saw it in Kursk in February. In the beginning of the war the newspapers talked about what Fascism had in store for the world. Now we can see what Fascism has brought to the regions the Germans have seized. The word "death"

THE FATE OF EUROPE

is too much a part of life; it is out-of-place here where it is better to say: non-existence, gap. The old peasant woman was right when she said to me sadly that the Germans were "worse than death."

When one looks westward one sees terrible pictures—somewhere far away there is another Kursk, another Gzhatsk. At first they are called by names which are close to us—Minsk or Chernigov. Then the names change; these smoldering ruins were once the French town of Arras, these executed people were carried out of the Czech town of Tabor. The French call the far-western district of Brittany—the European cape turned towards the New World—"Finisterre," the "End of the Land." From Gzhatsk to Brest to Finisterre, there is the same night, the same desolation, the same picture of mockery, killing, and barbarism. The "End of the Land" has become the end of the great European night.

We passionately love our land, our roots, our history. We are proud of our "Slavonic Ancient Greece"—the Ancient Kievian Russia, the harmony of St. Sophia, the tears of Yaroslavna, the classical clarity of Andrei Rubliov, the civic freedom of Novgorod, the war exploits of Alexander Nevsky and Dmitri Donskoy. But we have never separated our culture from the European, we are linked with it not by wires, not by rails, but by blood vessels, by convolutions of the brain. We were both diligent students and teachers of Europe. Only an ignoramus can conceive of Russia as a child admitted two hundred years ago to the school of culture. The legacy of Ancient Greece, this cradle of European consciousness, came to us not through the Rome of conquerors and law-givers, but through the Byzantium of philosophers and thinkers. It is sufficient to compare the painting of Andrei Rubliov with the masters of the early Renaissance—Cimabue and Giotto—in order to see how much closer to the spirit of Ancient Greece, to its clarity and gaiety, was the old Russian art. When

ILYA EHRENBURG

Russia in the nineteenth century staggered the world by peaks of thought and word, this was not birth but maturity. Who would say what agitated Pushkin more—the poems of Byron or the tales of the nanny Arina? During the last century the advanced minds of Russia shared the passions of Europe, her hopes, her sorrows. They introduced Russian passion, truthfulness, humaneness, into the European consciousness. In the "fury" of Belinsky, in the selflessness of Chernyshevsky, in the heroism of the Russian revolutionaries are visible not only the gifts of the West, the heritage of humanism, and the French Revolution, in them is also felt that search for truth which was the historic path of Russian culture. This is why Tolstoy, Dostoyevsky and Chekhov, Tschaikovsky and Mussorgsky have enriched any cultured European, have deepened and broadened the very meaning of Europe. This is why Lenin remains an example of Russia's genius of statesmanship and the peak of all European thought, as well as that of all mankind.

We understand the misfortune of France not only because we have Gzhatsk, Kharkov, and Minsk, but also because the fate of European culture is infinitely dear to us. We remember that the Decembrists were inspired by the "Declaration of the Rights of the Citizen," that Turgenev was a friend of the best writers of France. We do not look at the tragedy of Europe from the sidelines.

For one thousand days the Germans have been trampling down the countries of Europe which they have conquered. I repeat: for one thousand days. The recently flourishing multiform continent has become a terrible place. Death is monotonous. It is sufficient to see Voronezh, Vyazma, and Istra to get an idea of what has happened in a multitude of European towns. The Germans and their henchmen cannot restore what has been destroyed; all their forces are directed toward further destruction. Thus the Spanish town of Guernica is still a

THE FATE OF EUROPE

heap of ashes, the streets of Almería are dust. General Franco could not manage to rebuild Barcelona or Madrid within five years. The Spaniards cannot devote themselves to their affairs, they are forced to serve the German commissariat and to die for Berlin at Leningrad. The ruins of Rotterdam are a twin to the ruins of Belgrade. The North of France, which resembled a stone anthill, where the streets of one town became the streets of another, has become a stone desert. The towns along the Atlantic Coast have been turned into splinters and have been burned down.

What has become of the people? One woman in Gzhatsk whose four children were driven away by the Germans, who then burned down her house, told me, "A house—that will come again with time, but without one's children, one cannot live . . ." The Germans have not only trespassed on the ancient stones of Europe, they have trampled over her body, her youth, her children. The people have been deprived of the most elementary right: to live in their own country. The French underground newspaper *Voix du Nord* reports that professors of Kiev University and women students of Kharkov and Minsk do convict work in Lille and Valenciennes. And French engineers and workers, brought by the Germans from Paris, pine away in the military workshops in the town of Zaporozhye. Hitler trades with slaves. Thus he sent Poles for forest work to Finland, and Slovenes for farm work in Poland. People from the Alsace are sent to the Ukraine to build roads for the Germans. Belgian pastmasters of lace work dig earth in Lithuania. Round-ups take place in the streets of French towns; the Germans hunt for the able-bodied and drive them to work in the East. Every day tens of thousands of prisoners are deported from France. The weeping of the Gzhatsk mothers resounds like an echo in Lyons, only it is not an echo, it is the weeping of the mothers of Lyons.

ILYA EHRENBURG

"Our times can only be compared with the years of plague and pestilence during the Middle Ages," writes the *Journal de Genève*. Once upon a time a French king said, "I would like each of my subjects to have a chicken in the pot." In the Gzhatsk district there were 37,000 fowls before the arrival of the Germans. There are 110 left. . . . Recently I read a detailed article in a German economic journal on the disappearance of eggs in Europe. Some "Herr Doktor" was discussing the question of the place which eggs occupied in international trade, and he concluded melancholically, "It will be necessary to find new export articles for Denmark, France, the Protectorate." "Export articles" have been found: slaves. But it must be noted that in discussing the question of the disappearance of eggs in Europe, the German "scientist" did not note one of them: soldiers—fowl-eaters.

The French have already eaten all the stocks of their seed-turnips, they have eaten the crows, they have eaten the sparrows. In the South people eat grass, calling it "Laval's lettuce," in the North people eat acorns and crushed bark. In Greece, people crazed by hunger, chew hedges. Shadows wander in the streets of Athens; these are scientists and workers, artists, and artisans. They are not hired for work; they haven't the strength to lift a spade. They beg for alms, and the German soldiers kick them like dogs. And there are no more dogs: they have been eaten.

Terrible diseases mow down those whom the slave-owners have left in their own countries. The Germans have brought infection with them, like plague rats. In once well-fed, red-cheeked Holland, the land of Van Houten cocoa, 17,000 cases of tuberculosis were noted during the first nine months of 1942. In France, according to the data of the controlled newspaper *Sept Jours* there are one million people affected by an acute form of T.B. The number of those suffering from syphilis has grown twelve times, of those suffering from skin diseases—thirty times. There is no soap, there is no medicine; there is no bread. One third of the population has perished from hunger and epidemics. Diphtheria has made the rounds of Poland and Czechoslovakia; there are no inoculations, and mortality among the children reaches 60 per cent.

Even worse is the life of Europeans who have been uprooted by the Germans. Half-a-million French slaves have already died in Germany, two million are expecting death. "We live in a terrible barracks among excrement and lice. We are fed on a soup made from potato peels. We are beaten on the back with clubs," reports a Frenchman who escaped from Germany (*Le Document*, March 1943). Recently the German newspaper *Danziger Vorposten* announced that two Serbs were given a prison term for a "barbarous act"; they had eaten a kitten belonging to a woman resident of Danzig.

Europe has been filled with homeless children. A correspondent of *National Zeitung* writes that in France he had come across "crowds of children who had turned wild: they would run away screaming at the approach of a human." In the Salpetrière Hospital in Paris there are 286 girls within the ages of nine to fourteen who suffer from syphilis. In Marseilles, two boys have been arrested, one eight years old, the other eleven years old, charged with a series of murders. In Servia homeless children roam in groups of twenty to thirty. In Greece cases of cannibalism have been noted among homeless children.

Is it necessary to speak about cultural decline into savagery? Schools and universities have either been closed down or turned into breeding grounds of Hitlerite ignorance. In the newspaper *Marseillaise* there is a description of a lecture by a "professor" at the Collège de France; "He described at length that a chin which was not clearly outlined, and a wavy outline in the oval of the face, bear testimony to racial impurity." This takes place in the same lecture theaters where the mathematician Poincarré, the chemist Perrin, and the physicist Langevin had lectured. The newspaper *Dépêche de Toulouse* remarks with sadness, "Among the youths who have passed their final examinations, unprecedented illiteracy has been noted." The book stock of the Czech libraries dropped by 70 per cent after the Hitlerite "purges." I managed to see some books published in France during the German occupation. I shall not talk about ideas: even the books devoted to Philosophy are full of the cattle-breeding pathos which is obligatory in the "New Europe," I speak about something else: these books have been written by savages. Every schoolboy used to be able to express his thoughts clearly. In France at present even "writers" do not know how to say what they want to say. One thousand days is not a short term. One can learn much in one thousand days, one can also forget much.

The institution of hostages, the sight of executions and tortures deform the souls of those who are weak. Children see gallows. Juveniles are told: "If you betray your father, you will get a tin of conserves and a bottle of wine, if you hide your father we shall take you to the Gestapo where they know how to drive pins under your nails." Terror deforms people. Some become cowards. Some become pathologically cruel. The standard of behavior disappears, the foundation of every form of community life becomes shaken, Europe becomes prone to infection, to collapse of tissues, to anarchy.

Europe does not want to die. The French and Yugoslav partisans fight while bleeding. There are still many cells which have not been affected by disease. The red corpuscles fight against anemia. The heritage of the ages, the brilliant European past is resisting the brown plague. Europe can be saved. But time is impatient. It is naive to believe that the nations who have held out for a thousand days will also hold out for another thousand. This spring

THE FATE OF EUROPE

a stern word is sounded to all defenders of life and culture, to all nations fighting against Fascist death: time!

No one doubts about the final victory of the anti-Hitler coalition. Stalingrad was a brilliant beginning. The Red Army and the country supporting it have demonstrated strength of spirit and resolution. We know that, together with the Allies, we shall deal the final blow to the Hitlerite war machine. But Sleeping Beauty must be liberated from the predicament of becoming a dead beauty—I speak of Europe imprisoned by Fascism. It is not enough to be victorious, it is necessary to preserve those natural forces which will allow the winegrowers of Burgundy to plane vines, the fishermen of Norway to cast their nets again, the stonemasons of Europe to rebuild the cities, and the scientists to carry to the young generation the half-extinguished torch of knowledge. Bitter will be the victory if neither doctors nor painters nor winegrowers nor electricians will be left in France!

I saw villages which had survived in the Smolensk, Orel, and Kursk regions: the Germans had not managed to burn them down. The Red Army has saved many treasures from destruction, it has saved millions of people from physical and moral death. The armies of the anti-Hitlerite coalition can save Europe, her people, her culture, her soul. There are things dear to all enemies of Fascism: the scientists of Oxford and Leningrad know what the Sorbonne and the Pasteur Institute are, Londoners love Czapek's plays, but there is no Czapek without a live and free Prague; and without a live and free France the Americans will never see the paintings of Matisse and Marquet. No matter how this or that statesman-thinker will conceive of the future of the European States, it can only rest on culture, on standards of living together, on human dignity. One can construct buildings of the most diverse styles out of stone, but in the desert there is no stone, in the desert there is sand, and one cannot build anything out of sand.

ILYA EHRENBURG

Never has spring caused old Europe so much torment. The spring of 1943 rises before Europe not only as a change of season, as a tide of cosmic life, it rises as an appeal to the final decisive battle, as the beginning of resurrection.

March 19, 1943

Ilya Ehrenburg

OBSTINATE EUROPE

An article by a certain Michel Herbert entitled "Great Europe" has been published in the *Deutsche Allgemeine Zeitung*. In this article a German wants to prove to the Germans that they are not highwaymen, but the guardians of European culture. Michel even insists that he is not Michel, but some synthetic European, and he states "Greater Germany" has been replaced by "Great Europe." An explanation has been found why the Germans have dirtied Paris, mutilated London, and drenched the Ukraine in blood: they are "defending the great European space."

Only recently the Germans were talking about living space for themselves. Now the epithet "European" is added to this. What are the German defenses?—they are the "European Rampart." What are the forty hectares in the Kiev district on which Fritz makes money?—they are "European space."

ILYA EHRENBURG

There is no word more disgusting and blasphemous on the lips of a German Fascist than the beautiful name of Europe. A small continent, converted by the genius and labor of man into a flourishing garden, into one unusual city, the cradle of culture, Europe has been dishonored and bled white by the Germans. Only recently they were insolently mocking the prisoner. Only recently the same Michels were writing: "To the vague and meaningless concept of Europe we are counterposing the only valuable one—Great Germany" (*Das Reich*, 1942). At present the jailers insist that it is they who are the saviors of the prisoners. The thief who entered someone else's house babbles sweetly, "I am the night watchman."

An attempt on the life of Europe—this is how the indictment will read when the gang who are the leaders of present-day Germany finds itself at last in the defendant's dock. The ruin of cities, laying waste to the land, turning schools into barracks or torture chambers, the lowering of morals into savagery, spreading of ignorance, hunger, and death—this is what Germany has brought to Europe.

The German jesters try to convince the world that the Germans are defending Europe from England and Russia. It is hard not to smile: Goebbels, who protects European culture from the heirs of Shakespeare; Himmler, who is saving the freedom of Europe from the nation which has created the Magna Carta. Who will dare to deny England's extremely rich contribution to the treasurehouse of European culture? Who will forget the names of Watt, Byron, and Dickens? The attempts to counterpose Russia to Europe are just as ridiculous. The bigger the nation, the more independent its destiny, but the big son does not become a stranger because he is big. We saved the great-great-grandfathers of Europeans from the invasion of nomadic hosts. We saved the grandfathers of the foolish Michel from the "Great Europe" of Napoleon. We are saving and shall save our contemporaries—the children of multinational Europe—from the boot of the German sergeant-major. How poor would Europe be without the Russian heart, without Russian conscience, without Russian genius!

In vain do the Germans attempt to include into the concept of "Great Europe" the countries enslaved by them. The Hitlerites assert that the French, the Czechs, and the Dutch cannot manage without German guardianship. Finding himself in this or that country which has come under the wing of the German robber eagle, Fritz is at a loss: why don't the plundered nations thank him? Why don't the widows of those he has tortured to death welcome him?

The German Georg writes from France to Lieutenant Franz Herold: "France is still asleep, it will take great efforts to wake her. Last week three attacks took place in Paris, two near the 'Soldiers' Cinéma,' and the wounded German soldiers are now in infirmaries . . ." Unless one were aware of German dull-wittedness it would be hard to guess the meaning of Fritz's complaint about France, which is "still asleep"; the blockhead considers the struggle against the aggressors to be the absence of consciousness, sleep. He is surprised that "sleeping" Frenchmen kill German soldiers. Another Fritz writes in a letter from Holland: "For some reason we are still considered aggressors here . . ." A third one reports from Prague: "A strange people these Czechs, they are prepared to tear us apart . . ." The Germans make a helpless gesture of incomprehension: what strange prisoners are these who hate their jailers?

"Great Europe" under German leadership exists only in the editorial offices of the Berlin papers. In reality there exists the old suffering in a live Europe which lives for one thing now—the fight against the Germans.

It has been two years now that the Fuehrer's "Great

Europe" has been unable to cope with the partisans of Yugoslavia. They will say: mountains, forests, nature sanctuaries. But is it not remarkable that in France, where a park is the forest, where it is only a stone's throw from the most remote village to the town where every small village is connected to the world by a magnificent road, the struggle of the Franc-tireurs is evolving? And in Africa there are half-a-million Frenchmen who are ready to enter their native soil under the banner of the République. This is how Europe answers the tender lisping of the German butchers.

On the third of May Berlin Radio broadcast a survey of international events. The reporter announced, "The basic functions belong to the stomach. The part of the stomach in relation to Europe falls to Germany. We have been repeatedly accused of robbing other countries, but we are serving the whole of Europe as a stomach. We do not want domination. We only want the stomach to work properly, for shocks to the stomach reflect badly on the other parts of the organism."

It is difficult to say whether there is more stupidity in this than there is insolence. The Germans really have robbed everybody: the stomach turned out to be bottomless. But what did they bring to the conquered nations other than gallows, shameful tallies, and endless sorrow? Everybody knows that the Germans took fish and lumber from the Norwegians, butter and fat from the Danes, factories and mines, silk and wine from the French, coal from the Belgians, cheese from the Dutch. But what did they give in return? A Swiss who has returned from Paris writes in the newspaper *Neue Zuericher Zeitung*: "In the shops one will seek in vain for even trinkets imported from Germany. The French can get only German newspapers . . ."

Even Germany's friends—the Italians, the Hungarians, the Rumanians—have found out about the capacity of the German maw. But Berlin sighs hypocritically; Berlin, it says, eats only French bread so that the French would be in good health. Germany is really a gigantic maw, but she is the maw of a peculiar insect, of a parasite on the body of Europe, of a colossal bloodsucking bug.

Hitler's hopes for help from Europe are in vain. The captive nations await that wonderful hour when they will be able to punish the oppressors not only within the walls of an international tribunal but also in the squares of the long-suffering cities. It is not as a result of the good life that the Germans have started to talk about "European solidarity." Only a year ago they were priding themselves on their German essence, Aryan skulls, domineering bearing. Now they are even flirting with Monaco. Now they try to pass themselves off as "Europeans."

A prisoner-of-war told me how the fleeing Germans on the Don were dreaming of being able to change into Italian or Rumanian uniforms. Thus Hitlerite Germany dreams of changing clothes, she hopes to repaint herself, to become "Great Europe." But German loneliness has never been so striking. The Germans have shouted for ten months: "We are the only ones!" Now they begin to understand the true significance of these words.

They are forced to keep their garrisons in the "allied" countries. Their married life with Italy is a daily rape: "Great Rome" depends on a gang of SS men. There is much talk about the cowardice of the Italians who obstinately, carefully, surrender everywhere into captivity. But were Garibaldi's "Red Shirts" not Italians? Would it not be better to speak about the comprehension of the Italians for whom it is distasteful to fight for the triumph of the German stomach? The latest events in Tunis did not startle only Rome but also Budapest and Bucharest. Hitler's vassals have begun to whimper like the captured Fritzes: "We were sent . . . it is not our fault . . ." Neutral states which only recently were afraid of taking a breath under the gaze of the German constrictor have become heartened. Now the Germans know that they are alone, that no one will be saving them from the reckoning, that even the hangers-on, who in their time have been robbing Nizza or Odessa, Korotoyak or Petrozavodsk, are in search of an alibi; protesting that they were really not present at the feast. . . .

How do the Germans console themselves? With the "European Rampart." They drove suspiciously "neutral" journalists along the Atlantic seaboard and obligingly showed them concrete pillboxes. They wanted to convince, if not others then themselves that the European coastlines were protected by an insuperable wall. Perhaps they had forgotten their own sneers at the "impregnable Maginot Line?"

On the third of May General Dittmar assured the Germans that "two bridgehead fortifications on the Kuban and in Tunis are safeguarding Europe." One of these fortifications ceased to exist five days ago. The Germans will soon become convinced that different "impassable lines" and "European Ramparts" exist mainly for the purpose of being bypassed by the opponent. We can still remember the November talks about the "European Rampart." According to the German design this rampart bordered on the Volga. One wonders if General Paulus remembers it?

Berliner Boersen Zeitung says that "Europe is waging a defensive war on many fronts. She is not waging it as a besieged fortress, no; she is using weapons of attack to the fullest extent." Europe, the genuine Europe, is waging an offensive war against Germany. These are the robbers who have to defend themselves now. They are still defending themselves far from their lair. But it is not a matter of miles. Within several weeks the Germans have proceeded for many hundreds of miles from Aachen to Bordeaux, from Eydtkunen to Luga. But they could not advance for five hundred yards over the ruins of Stalingrad. In one month the Red Army advances from Voronezh to Lvov. In contemporary warfare armies mark time

OBSTINATE EUROPE

for years and complete the longest march within several weeks.

Germany is a besieged fortress. Of course, its force is still great. The defenders of the fortress are of course still able to carry out sorties. Germany will still attempt to advance. But these desperate attempts to save herself must not be confused with the strategy of an offensive. If Fritz will now crawl forward, then it is only because he has no way to retreat. Russia, the great European power, in defending her fields, her treasures, her freedom, is thereby going to the rescue of a Europe mutilated by the Germans. We shall say at the edge of a Russian village occupied by the Germans: "There shall be no Hitler." At the gate of the first town of Western or Southern Europe our Allies will say, "There shall be no Hitler." At the border of robber Germany we shall say, "There shall be no Hitler." It will be necessary for the stomach to shrink. The great, unequalled Europe will again take the sickle, the compasses, and the paint brush into her own hands.

May 14, 1943

Konstantin Simonov

IN THE DISTRICT OF PONYRY

Here on the Kursk Highway in the district of Ponyry Station, famous in peacetime for its apples, fighting has been going on for the sixth day now. The German Air Force was particularly vicious here all evening yesterday and all morning today. Everything along both sides of the main communication route leading to the Front lines has been burned and destroyed. Buildings on both sides of the road are in the last stage of smoldering. Their walls have collapsed into shapeless heaps of brick and timber, and the low south wind spreads a blanket of bitter smoke over the ground that smells of ashes, charred timber, scorched iron. On the ground, among the still-not-cleared-away corpses of horses, there are scattered about opened and crumpled German "suitcases": this is what the metal boxes which the Germans drop from aircraft are called here—when they open, dozens of small bombs pour out of them in flight. Here or there one comes across mutilated motor vehicles which had been damaged by the bombing. The sun hides, then reappears, sending a bright yellow strip of light across the tree trunks which seem to have been broken by a gigantic hand. There where a bomb has spared some building, its windows have nevertheless been pulled out along with the frames by bomb blasts, and inside the building there is black emptiness.

Silence. Presently it is broken by brief shots like the sounds of a popping cork from howitzers, then by the prolonged roll of the heavy German batteries covering this highway with harassing fire in two or three places. And for several minutes it seems that there is nothing in the world today other than these sounds.

The Staff Headquarters of the tank brigade has taken up quarters next to the headquarters of the infantry regiment, within two miles of the Germans, in a narrow gully near the road. The earth round about has been dug up to such an extent by bomb craters from heavy 250-millimeter shells and bombs that the unexpected entrance into the dugout appears at first glance to be one of the craters. It is spacious and cool in the dugout. The tank men have decided to stay put, cost what it may, and since this was the case they were not stingy with labor; six heavy layers of logs interspersed with earth cover the dugout.

But one works in the dugout only during bombardment. A few more paces along the communication passage and a second Staff Hdq. room appears next to the dugout, a square space dug deep into the ground, with niches and benches along the walls and a table in the center. This room is not covered by anything above; only thin planks laid crosswise, interlaced with greenery, hide the Staff room from the eyes of German aerial observers. If you look upwards the sky is visible between the greenery, and all this taken together suddenly recalls a southern Crimean or central-Asian small inner courtyard.

IN THE DISTRICT OF PONYRY

We talk to the tank men, and our conversation takes place alternately in this small yard and in the dugout, depending on the energy of the German artillerists. During the artillery raid Colonel Petrushin, the brigade commander, showed us the additional shelters he had constructed, just in case, in the dugout. A narrow slot was excavated in the earth floor and was covered with two wooden shields. Major Babushkin, the Chief of Staff, jumps into it and closes the shields above his head. Then he climbs back, laughing. "This is in case the two-hundred-millimeter pieces should become too exasperating. The dugout may not stand up to such a shell, for while a shell may not pierce it, you may be hit on the head with flying logs. Thus we have put shields down below and overhead. We've changed all Front-line terms from the horizontal to the vertical here. Now, these plank-beds we call the Front line—we call the dugout proper, insofar as it's deeper, the command post, and this slot is called the deep Rear. And this is how we live."

The sixth day of battle. The war does not appear to any military unit as something uniform and uninterrupted, especially not to a tank unit. The tank brigade has been at the Front for two years now, but when the tank men recall their fighting path, they recall only the most outstanding moments, those days of battle when life hung by a thread and the fate of the brigade was staked on a card. For the first time they fought at Przemysl, then at Nezhin, then they went into the German rear at Belaya Tserkov, then they covered the evacuation of Dniepropetrovsk. In the winter of 1941 they took Yelets and Livny, and there too, at Livny, they took on themselves the first blow in the days of last year's German summer offensive, securing the Army's flank. In the winter of 1943 the tank brigade, together with other units, captured Kastornoye, and from Kastornoye they proceeded here, fighting along the way to this same line where four months later they eventually came to encounter the Germans again.

These four months have not been quiet, they passed in continuous tension. Although there had been a prolonged stabilization of the Front, everyone in the Army or the tank brigade knew that this could not last indefinitely, and they knew that the Germans would attempt a revenge for Kastornoye. Day after day, week after week, all possible variants of the fighting which would take place right here, and methods of cooperation with the infantry, artillery, and self-propelled artillery, were being elaborated. Five different possible combat actions had been worked out, and for each possibility it had been determined exactly where and with which infantry division the tank brigade would come out, and where its command posts would be.

When the German offensive actually started, it took place in accordance with the second variant. It had been foreseen, and the offensive itself had been both expected and not-expected at the same time. It was known that it would take place, and it had been assumed where it would approximately take place, but the precise day and hour was decided, of course, by the Germans. The second variant proposed that the tank brigade should come out on the previously prepared defense line in support of the second echelon division in the event of a German attempt to break through along the Orel-Kursk railroad.

As they express it in the brigade, all defense lines had been prepared in advance. This preparation consisted in the first place of all commanders, up to and including the tank commanders, taking part in a reconnaissance of the locality. Apart from this, a survey by sight and a registration of the firing range of the line were carried out. But this was not all. During the days of the lull the tank brigade was moved to the nearest position in the Rear, so as to be able to maneuver in the event all five variants were to be used. In order to join the battle it was necessary first to complete a march, and all aspects of this march had

IN THE DISTRICT OF PONYRY

been prepared in advance. The routes of the march and of the secret approach to the defense line had been reconnoitered, the carrying capacity of all bridges and the practicality of all fords had been determined along the path of movement. Signals and agreed codes had been fixed upon, and a twofold-contact established with the division with whom cooperation was to take place.

During the spring the tanks came out several times upon a sudden alarm to the lines marked out for combat in accordance with all five variants. Finally, intelligence reports indicated during the first days of July that there was a complete likelihood of a German offensive between the third and the sixth of the month. At exactly midnight between the fourth and fifth of July scouts who had gone on a mission to the left bank came upon a group of German sappers removing mines for a passage through mine fields. They numbered seventeen men. Fourteen were killed, two escaped, and the seventeenth was captured. Sensing something evil, the scouts began to interrogate the prisoner in broken German while escorting him to Staff Headquarters. He said that everything was ready for the offensive, that infantry and tanks had already come up to and were concentrated at the forward positions, and that everything would start at exactly two a.m. When the scouts had brought the prisoner as far as the first telephone, it was five minutes to one. The Commander of the Army was informed of the above, and by five minutes past one the Commander of the Front knew about it. A decision was adopted: to carry out an artillery counterpreparation with every available heavy battery which the Army had five minutes before the German offensive was to begin. At five minutes to two, when the German tanks were standing at the starting lines and the German infantry had concentrated in the Front-line trenches, thousands of Russian artillery barrels began to talk along the whole front of the Army. The artillery counterpreparation lasted for a quarter of an hour. The earth right and left shook for miles from the uninterrupted rumble, and although the night was comparatively dark, the countless flare-ups of bursts along the whole line of the Front could be seen even deep in the Rear. The Germans were silent. Aside from the smashing of dozens of their artillery batteries which had been aimed at in advance, they were perplexed as to what this could mean, and they were waiting. At four o'clock in the morning when the Germans managed to get themselves in order and to prepare again for attack, they began their artillery preparation along the whole front of the Army.

As for the tank brigade—everyone had already been raised at two a.m. by the battle alarm, and they could see the distant red reflections of the explosions within the German positions. Then it became quiet for a long time, until the thundering was renewed at four o'clock. The brigade was in the reserve of the Army Commander. The direction of the enemy's thrust had not been established yet, and there was nothing to do but sit and wait. A tough battle with the divisions of the first echelon was going on ahead, and the tank men, after checking for the hundredth time to see if everything was in readiness, were nervously awaiting their turn to join the battle. By twelve o'clock noon the situation finally had established itself when the Germans burst with major forces into the position of the first echelon division, exerted pressure on it, and moved on to the Orel-Kursk Highway. The fighting sprang up in accordance with the second variant. At twelve-thirty p.m. the tank brigade was ordered to come out at the battle line in the area of the railroad with the aim of supporting with all its forces the second echelon division which was situated here, and not permitting any further German advance.

The German Air Force which, as always, was very active, operated only above the Front-line, in contrast with

IN THE DISTRICT OF PONYRY

the offensive fighting of the previous period. This time the Germans did not possess enough forces in the air to attempt to paralyze the whole strip of the proposed breakthrough for fifteen to thirty miles in depth, as had been their habit up till now. The tank brigade reached the district of its battle line without losses within two-and-a-half hours; fighter aircraft covered it from the air. Besides, the conditions of the locality were favorable to it; there were many villages along its route situated along wooded creeks and often almost linking up on their outskirts. By three o'clock all battle vehicles, plus the Rear organizations with repair facilities, tractors, and fuel, which moved under cover through the inhabited points, were in place.

At this moment the German tanks which had burst through the first echelon's defense had bypassed one of the echelon's regiments on both sides and were endeavoring to annihilate it by not allowing it to retreat to the next line. The tank brigade was then ordered to render urgent assistance when the commander of the infantry division to which the brigade was subordinated ordered the tank men to launch a counterattack immediately in order to rescue the encircled regiment. The brigade in its full complement launched the counterattack at exactly six p.m.

The tank battalion was followed by a battalion of motorized infantry—its own tank infantry—which was to come to the rescue of the tanks during a difficult moment and to assure firm success. Before the brigade there stretched the very familiar undulating plain with its frequent small hollows and hillocks overgrown with small shrubbery. The weather was clear, but the low evening sun shone straight into our tanks' observation slots. The tanks had hardly deployed when the Germans opened a violent artillery and mortar fire at them. Our tanks moved forward for two or three miles under this uninterrupted fire. The commanders went ahead of the battalions—Major

Loboda on the right, Solyukov on the left. Colonel Petrushin, along with the Chief of Staff himself, took up positions in their tanks behind the ridge of the nearest small elevation, and lifted their hatches to watch the fighting. After two miles the right-flank battalion of Major Loboda reached a chain of small hills beyond the ridge where the battle was raging with the German infantry which had broken out of the encirclement, and it was attacked on the flank by the enemy's tanks. It was simultaneously attacked by fifteen T-6 (Tiger) tanks and several self-propelled Ferdinand artillery pieces, and then German infantry, closely massed, followed the tanks. Loboda's battalion deployed with its front towards the left in order to beat off the attack, and our tanks began to strike at the Germans from the spot.

In its first moments the battle shaped up unfavorably for us. The Germans burst into our flank and immediately knocked out three K.V. tanks and set them alight. Part of our motorized infantry was turned right to support our right flank, and a battery of our heavy self-propelled 122-millimeter guns under Captain Yakovlev was transferred from the left flank. Colonel Petrushin, who observed the battle from his commander's tank, directed these maneuvers by radio. All orders were passed on by open command in accordance with a map which had been coded in advance. Inhabited places, hollows, hills—all arteries of the locality—had been marked with coded numbers, and the Germans could not understand anything.

The battle lasted for one-and-a-half hours. On encountering the fire of our tanks, which had come to a halt, the Germans also stopped and began to strike from stationary positions, and then gradually began a retreat. During this hour and a half another of our tanks was damaged, adding up to four disabled tanks, but the Germans on their part lost six tanks, one after another, and it was precisely this which caused their retreat. The prin-

IN THE DISTRICT OF PONYRY

cipal battle was taking place at a distance of 900 to 1,000 yards. When it seemed to Colonel Petrushin that his commands were not sufficiently rapidly understood and carried out, he sent liaison officers on light communication vehicles to the battalion to clarify the radio orders.

In the meantime, while Loboda's battalion was carrying the main brunt of the battle, Solyukov's left flank battalion advanced another mile and met up with violent enemy fire from dominating heights. The battalion tucked itself into the folds of the earth and answered with furious fire. The German tanks' attempts to surround the infantry regiment which was fighting in front were repulsed. The main fire of the German artillery came down on the tank brigade as it was brought into battle. Making use of this the infantry regiment, after bursting out and annihilating a detachment of German sub-machine gunners in its rear, retreated behind the fighting units of the tank brigade. The tank men did not allow the Germans to pursue it and assured the consolidation of the regiment on the next line by a prolonged battle which went on into the night.

After the infantry had consolidated itself by nighttime, Colonel Petrushin received an order from the division commander to retreat behind the infantry and to take up its own defense line, prepared a month earlier. From there the tank brigade had a view of the locality far ahead, and by fire from the flank it could block any possible attempts by the Germans to break through along the railroad.

The first day brought losses to the tank brigade which were sharply felt. Three heavy tanks had been disabled, one of the best officers of the brigade, Lieutenant Andrianov, had died in the fire of his K.V. tank, and the commander of the administration section, Lieutenant Shumsky, had perished. There were several more killed and wounded, and as it usually happens, there were more killed than wounded.

It became dark. The tanks occupied the deep trenches prepared for them from which only their turrets projected. Dinner was brought up from the rear. As usual food had been forgotten in the heat of the battle, and now the men felt famished and tackled their meals avidly. The tank men began to carry out some minor repairs together with the repair men: turrets which had become wedged were made good, caterpillar tracks that had been put out of action were restored. Fuel tankers, alerted by a code signal over the radio, came from the Rear right up to the tanks under cover of darkness and disappeared half an hour later after refueling the tanks. In the meantime the foot reconnaissance patrols of the tank brigade, who are as always destined to do the main part of their work at night, made for the German lines in three groups, under the command of Captain Stukalov. Long before dawn the reconnaissance men found out that the Germans had been impetuously pulling up tanks to the Front line. The reconnaissance men determined accurately in what places this concentration was proceeding, but not only they but everyone in the brigade could hear the distant rumble and roaring of caterpillar tracks going on all night long and everyone understood that the battle could not be avoided, that the Germans would renew the attacks at daybreak.

Sitting in the dugout Colonel Petrushin gave the necessary orders for the morning. It had not begun to get light yet but everything had already been prepared, and while sitting there alone he involuntarily remembered with what haste he and the others had done everything in the beginning of the war when there was no time to do anything, and how now, even in the heat of battle, it so happened that he had half an hour free time, thanks to experience, habit, and the know-how acquired after long torments in learning how to organize everything. He concentrated the tanks in the most convenient positions, and he foresaw that the Germans would come off with more than six burnt tanks tomorrow. He knew this with a quiet sense of assurance, and this pleased him. The war had not come easily to him. In the beginning he had experienced all the bitterness of the retreat. He had retreated along with the others, had fought to the last ditch in the forests of the Pridnieprovye and had set fire with his own hands to the tanks for which there was no fuel left, but which could not be allowed to fall into German hands. He had lost much during this war. On June 25, 1941, German aircraft had divebombed a train at Sarny station filled with women and children and had wreaked irreparable damage; a splinter of a German bomb had torn off his wife's arm and leg, and his five-year-old son, who was with her, had vanished into the unknown. The Colonel's brother, a village schoolteacher who became a commander in the course of the war, had disappeared without a trace, and his wife had been hanged by the Fascists. From his mother he had had no news of any kind for more than a year and a half, from the time that she had remained behind in Yartsev, not having managed to get away. When he remembered all this—then no matter how used he was to the depths of loneliness and to the thoughts of his destroyed home, his heart invariably contracted, and when he thought of the Germans that cold tranquility arose in him of a man who has been hating for a long time, without limits, a man who hates without loud words, without excitement, without hysteria, and therefore hates particularly strongly and terribly.

He had been with the tank brigade for a year and a half now, and for him, who had lost so much, the brigade had become everything in that time; his love, his own offspring, his home. He suffered over its setbacks and rejoiced over its victories, never separating himself from the brigade either in thought or in feeling. And when, after the Kastornoye operation he had become a bearer of the Order of Suvorov, he was proud, not so much for himself but for the brigade—he was proud that the commander of the brigade was a bearer of the Order of Suvorov. He was pleased to see how his commanders had acquired experience and calm, how they were becoming cured of the "infantile disorders" which had tormented them during the first months of the war, he was pleased at how communications had improved, and how the repair of tanks had been speeded up, how timid ones were re-educated and cowards were disappearing, how the brigade was becoming an obedient instrument in his hands—obedient and mighty to such an extent that he sometimes felt it to be an extension of his own hand; it was a strong hand which could deal a heavy blow. Shutting his eyes and remaining sunk in his thoughts, he imagined how he would deal that blow tomorrow.

Information was received from the Army in the morning that the Germans were preparing a major attack, and an order was given to hold the positions at all costs. At dawn German infantry moved immediately towards our infantry, followed by tanks. Colonel Petrushin's tank brigade attacked them on the move; and a heavy tank battle began. Forty tanks operated on the German side, of these one half were Tigers. After a massed artillery and aerial preparation when the earth all around shook from the boom of explosions, the German tanks launched a resolute attack. The Russian positions which had been previously prepared and advantageously occupied, assured Petrushin's success. Our tanks, which were under cover, shot up the German tanks which were advancing on them. Besides, the Germans had incorrectly determined the location of the brigade, and instead of coming out on its flank, they found themselves to be under its flanking fire themselves. The battle continued, with brief spaces of lull, for about ten hours. During this time the Russian tank men succeeded in setting fire to eight Tigers which had moved in front of the other tanks, and to three heavy anti-

IN THE DISTRICT OF PONYRY

tank guns. By the end of the day the Germans retreated, not having achieved any result. The earth, dug up with shell craters, smoked quietly. In some places columns of smoke rose from the still not completely burnt-out Tigers. It was clear by the end of the day that the Germans had not thrown in everything that they could throw in, that they had over-estimated their forces and had withdrawn, not wanting to undertake hopeless attacks today, so as to attack decisively tomorrow, after bringing up fresh tanks. This could be felt in the air of the battle.

German aircraft dropped bombs all day, and when it became dark several German planes bombed the brigade position at random, not allowing the tank men to have a quiet dinner and sleep. Incidentally, the majority were not sleepy in spite of terrible tiredness; the tension was so great that sleep did not come. The din of motors could be heard incessantly behind the German positions, and the brief summer night passed before one knew it, for by the time one had eaten, refuelled the engines, brought out the shells, and replenished the battle supplies, it was dawn. Foot reconnaissance patrols set out again in three directions and marked out the concentrations of German tanks on all three. By morning it was clear to everyone that a strong blow was impending during the day.

The morning dawned exceptionally clear. At exactly seven o'clock the Germans unleashed a hurricane of artillery fire on our infantry and tanks. The explosions came down in a continuous wall of fire, which continued until nine o'clock. Two Russian tanks were disabled by this fire, and they had to be towed away for repairs. Immediately, without any break after the artillery preparations, forty German tanks and two infantry regiments launched an attack on the Ponyry railroad station which was situated to the left of the tank brigade, and endeavored to pass along a convenient hollow between the railroad embankment and the ravine behind which the left flank of the brigade was stationed. There, on the left flank, in the first echelon, twenty-two Tigers were moving simultaneously. At the same time, in an attempt to distract the tank men's attention from the direction of the main thrust, fifteen more German tanks advanced on the brigade's right flank. Colonel Petrushin ordered the brigade to fire at the German tanks from the spot without leaving their previous lines in order to prevent a breakthrough to the south, and then, at the first opportunity, to launch an attack with part of their forces on the German infantry who came immediately behind the tanks.

When the Tigers had approached to within shooting range the tank men opened a hurricane of fire on them. A number of Tigers were burnt and disabled on the spot, others, moving backwards, began to retreat, but three or four passed through our infantry ranks and broke through to the southern outskirts of Ponyry station. Taking advantage of the moment when several German tanks had burst forward while others were retreating, Lieutenant Baklanov's company, on the Colonel's orders, launched an attack on the German infantry which was attempting to break through to the station following the tanks. Until then our tanks had concentrated their fire on the German tanks, and when they turned their fire on the German infantry the latter was taken by surprise. The fire from guns and machine guns inflicted heavy losses on the Germans, and all their sub-machine gunners who remained alive were forced to lie down and then crawl back to the rear singly, under machine-gun fire. After they had bypassed Ponyry station and saw that they had no infantry behind them, the German tanks which had broken through were also forced to retreat.

The battle lasted from seven in the morning to three in the afternoon. Two of our tanks and eight German tanks went up in flames in this battle. Then a sudden lull ensued at three o'clock which lasted until six in the eve-

IN THE DISTRICT OF PONYRY

ning. At eight o'clock, after a strong artillery cannonade, sixteen German tanks with infantry following close behind advanced straight at the brigade's position. The Germans immediately spread a smokescreen from their forward tanks which the wind, as if out of spite, blew straight to our side. It was almost impossible to discern anything, and the German tanks burst into the junctions between the battalions, half-encircling Solyukov's left battalion. A violent tank battle then began. At this serious juncture Colonel Petrushin called up the brigade reserve on his left flank and threw in the heavy-self-propelled battery against the tanks and the mechanized infantry against the advancing German infantry.

The latter had already gone past the battle units of our tanks under cover of the smokescreen and had come through to our rear. Our motorized battalion immediately launched a counterattack with a rush from the depths, and this decisive support by all reserves assured victory for us. Our tanks continued to fire at the advancing German tanks, while our motorized battalions took on the fight with the German infantry. Several times skirmishes went over into hand-to-hand fighting. Fighting with hand grenades went on when it was dark, and flashes of explosions flared up over the entire battlefield. At midnight the Germans were thrown back, suffering heavy losses. The soldiers of our motorized battalion, together with our tank men, searched until dawn for wounded on the field of battle and took the dead to the rear to bury them.

On the eighth of July the day's fighting started at eight-thirty. Again, as usual, it began with aerial and artillery preparation, and immediately after that the Germans once again launched a tank attack, supported by an infantry regiment. They were now striving to break through along the railroad, and feeling that it was not possible to knock our tank brigade from its position either by frontal blows or by a blow to the flank, they endeavored to penetrate further southwest, feeling for a weak spot. But while trying to bypass our brigade from the flank the Germans thereby exposed their own flank to a blow.

During the night our reconnaissance had already established the whereabouts of a concentration of German tanks and at the same time Colonel Petrushin correctly foresaw the direction of the German thrust. The self-propelled guns and a portion of the heavy tanks were transferred by morning from the right to the left flank. This time the Germans did not succeed in advancing, and a fierce shooting battle went on until midday, when it was broken off, and then it flared up with renewed violence before darkness fell. During that day the Germans launched five attacks, each time unsuccessfully. Although the enemy had been beaten back, everyone in the brigade was tired to death. When night came the men dropped asleep in their tracks—in driver's seats, in tank turrets—wherever they were.

All that night before the ninth of July the movement of tanks could be heard behind the German lines. It could be felt that the Germans were bringing up some new unit for tomorrow's launching of a decisive general attack. At nine a.m. on the ninth, the Germans launched a decisive attack straight at the front of our brigade with the objective of seizing the heights and ravines situated around a burnt-down village; that is, precisely at the spot where we are now sitting in the dugout and talking to the brigade commander.

After directing their medium tanks against our right-flank K.V. battalion, and thus tying up our chances of maneuvering with all the brigade's available forces, the Germans directed their main thrust towards bypassing our left-flank battalion. A large number of Tigers, ignoring the cruel fire and suffering heavy losses, bypassed our left-flank battalion, came out at its rear, and burst through the positions of our motorized infantry battalion which occupied the defense line, and moved on. They were followed by German infantry, massed closer together than ever. Our position was becoming critical and the outcome of the battle would be decided, depending on whether the infantry of our mechanized battalion would sit it out in the trenches, or would let the tanks pass through their ranks, or would be unable to bear it and would start retreating. But it was not in vain that our infantry had been run into by tanks, convincing the men by actual practice that if you are well entrenched and dug into the ground the tank will have no terror for you. During those days of training our own tanks had thundered past dozens of times above the heads of our infantry, they had stopped above the trenches and had turned around above them. The men felt that this could be endured and that one could fight against it, and now when there were actual enemy tanks going through our motorized battalion our soldiers fought to the last man: they set fire to seven Tigers, and it turned out that, the same as with any other tanks, their caterpillar tracks were torn by accurately thrown antitank grenades, and that they burned just as well and not any less if a bottle with "KS" was accurately thrown at them.

But not to leave the trenches while German tanks thundered overhead was only half the job. This time the German infantry, heartened by their initial success, followed closely behind the tanks, and after the tanks had gone past, the soldiers of our motorized battalion had to almost immediately engage in hand-to-hand fighting with the Germans. A lengthy battle with hand grenades broke out in the trenches and communication passages. With German tanks in its rear our mechanized infantry repulsed the German infantry in hand-to-hand fighting. In the meantime, however, the German tanks were penetrating deeper and deeper into our rear. Then by the Colonel's order, our left-flank battalion which had been bypassed by the Germans carried out a fast and bold maneuver.

Leaving its previous positions with the speed of lightning it moved to the right and back and, unexpectedly for the Germans, met up face to face with German tanks within the rear of its own positions. We suffered heavy losses in this encounter, but the Germans, who did not expect a thrust in the depth of the defense line, suffered even heavier losses. Five Tigers were burnt and the remainder began to retreat.

In the meantime the German infantry, which had been partly stopped by our mechanized battalion, managed to infiltrate deeply in front to the left of it, almost to our tank brigade's command post. The commander of our tank brigade appraised the situation and at this moment threw in his last reserve—four trucks with four antiaircraft machine guns set up on each of them. From these trucks, which leaped out into the open area where the Germans who had broken through were moving with impunity, a hurricane of fire was spewed out at them, and after wiping out with its first bursts up to two hundred of the Germans who had not managed to lie down, they forced the remaining ones to begin a retreat. By six o'clock this last decisive German attack had finally been repulsed in all sectors. But half an hour later, apparently as a revenge for the frustrated attack, 150 Junkers simultaneously fell upon our tank brigade's positions. The bombing was very intensive, creating a dense smoke pall within which nothing could be seen. However, our brigade was well concealed, and as the men had not been too lazy to carry out all the trenchwork in advance, our losses were limited to one disabled tank and some ten men killed and wounded.

Night fell, and the fifth day of the uninterrupted battle came to an end. The best commander of the company, Lieutenant Kostyrin, had been burned to death in a tank, and there were many more in the brigade ranks who were missing along with him. But if during the previous night

IN THE DISTRICT OF PONYRY

everyone had fallen over from weariness, now the nervous tension among the men had reached a limit which made going to sleep impossible. When the battle had finished and it became dark everyone felt what had not yet been spelled out: that the Germans had been stopped. There was no doubt about it. It was here, on this site where the tank brigade had decided to stay firm at any price, at the price of its blood, that it had actually stayed firm and had stopped the Germans. It was the Germans who earlier, in the days of their breakthroughs, used to cover twenty-five to forty miles a day, and who became worn out only by the end of the first and sometimes of the second month, were now being bled white and enfeebled by the end of the fifth day, having traversed on the first day some four miles through the battle units of our first echelon's divisions, but during the following four days they had not moved up by even one mile.

This was victory. He who today can stand his ground will be able to advance tomorrow. This was the feeling which one gathered from conversations with the tank men, participants in the current heavy fighting in this sector. They had learned calmness and perseverance—and this was a great deal. Before, it often happened that in the days of the cruellest retreats, some Russian units did not retreat until the end but continued fighting where they were, but these were units which had decided not to surrender and not to retreat—but to perish. They had confidence in themselves and no confidence in their neighbors. Now the men who say before the battle: "To stand firm unto death, to fight to the last drop of blood," do not feel that they are special people. This is not the bravery of despair, no—they who stand fast unto death count on surviving and do not leave their battle stations at the critical minute; they have faith not only in their own steadfastness, but they have faith in the same measure of steadfastness in their neighbors. This mutual and just, well-informed faith is precisely the cement which presently binds the Army, and with whose availability the most serious minutes do not become critical, and separate failures do not grow into a catastrophe.

Today there is a lull among the tank men. All tanks remaining in service have been re-fueled and supplied with a battle compliment of shells, and they are ready for battle. The tank men are getting ready for tomorrow. But they call tomorrow not that day which will begin today, after twenty-four hours, but that day when we shall go over to the attack, since a steadfast defense unto death was today's day for them, and the attack will be tomorrow's day. In this lies their future, and whether it will arrive tomorrow, the day after tomorrow, or after a week or a month it will come, for without a future one cannot imagine life, and the future for the Army—is Victory.

July 22, 1943

Ilya Ehrenburg

AUGUST 13, 1943

A writer may underestimate or overestimate the effectiveness of antitank guns, but he can see the heart of a soldier. On the other hand, a journalist's reports may include a profound and significant text, but they do not contain the undercurrent, and while a journalist's pen may be as sensitive as a weather vane, it cannot be as sensitive as a seismograph.

Unfortunately, books come late. Remarque's novel, *All Quiet on the Western Front*, allowed us to understand the deterioration of Hohenzollern Germany. Alas, it appeared many years after the dénouement. How much would the leaders of the Allied nations have given for that book in the summer of 1918? Perhaps, these notes will help our Western friends to understand the Russian soul and Russian resistance.

Before me is an article published on August 4, 1943,

on the front page of the English newspaper the *Daily Mail*. It tells about a parade which took place in one of the German camps where the British prisoners-of-war are held. Lieutenant Beatty, who had commanded the landing operation at St. Nazaire and had been taken prisoner by the Germans, was subsequently awarded the Victoria Cross in absentia by the British Command. The German commandant of the POW camp lined up the captured officers and made an announcement of Beatty's award. According to the words of the newspaper, the commandant "cordially applauded" the British officer. The description of the ceremony finishes with these concluding words: "The German commandant congratulated Beatty, which was a gentlemanly act."

The Fascists feed the Russian prisoners-of-war with offal, they force them to collect excreta with their hands, they subject them to refined tortures. The Hitlerites turned the captured Poles, Frenchmen, and Serbs into serfs. If the Germans treat the British prisoners-of-war in a "gentlemanly" manner, then this is of course not because the Germans are gentlemen, but because Hitler still has not lost hope of finding people who yearn to be deceived. The Germans are not adept at understanding the psychology of other nations. Hitler has apparently decided that one evening in Munich has crossed out centuries of British history, and that the descendents of Pitt have turned into naïve maidens who can be charmed. The commandant of the camp who congratulated Beatty was one of the disciples of the ill-fated Hess.

I am sincerely pleased that the British prisoners-of-war do not share the sufferings which are the lot of other Allied soldiers who have fallen into German paws. Nevertheless, the *Daily Mail* article seems sad to me. One could remind the journalist who wrote about the camp commandant's "gentlemanly" act that the Germans had tortured to death and shot thousands of defenseless

AUGUST 13, 1943

Frenchmen after the St. Nazaire raid. For some—applause; for others—the torture chamber. But I am at present interested not in the tactlessness of the journalist, but in the peculiar concept of the war which has left its mark, both on the above-mentioned article, and on many other articles.

I belong to the generation which has experienced Verdun, the Somme, Galicia. After the First World War we came to hate war. We, the writers who experienced the years 1914–1918, have written books permeated by hatred or sorrow—from Barbusse to Remarque, from Oldington to Hemingway. At the time we welcomed everything that seemed to us to counteract a new war. Some found hope in the Russian Revolution, others in the messages of Wilson and the League of Nations. How did it happen that yesterday's pacifists blessed war?

The title of Hemingway's novel *A Farewell to Arms* became the vow of a generation. Ten years later Hemingway glorified arms in the hands of Spaniards defending their freedom against Hitler and Mussolini. Something new had appeared in the world: Fascism, or Hitlerism, or Nazism, representing an absolute threat to the lives of nations and people, to human dignity, to freedom.

We rejected and are rejecting war as a natural phenomenon, as a knightly duel, as a bloody sword. We are convinced that tanks are not suitable for the organization of world economy and that fragmentation bombs do not resolve ideological arguments.

Had I considered the Hitlerites to be "gentlemen," I would consider this war to be immoral. There is only one justification for the war: the inhumanity of Hitlerite Germany, her decline into savagery, her will for annihilation, for the seizure of others' lands. To me, the *Daily Mail* article presents itself as immoral. If the reader is sympathetic to the appreciation of the German commandant's behavior he should condemn the war: a gentleman can play cricket or have a bet with a gentleman, but they do not fight.

It has been said more than once that the approach to war as if it were a sports match is harmful to the conduct of military operations. I must add that such an approach is immoral and inhuman. To the Britishers who have experienced London and Coventry a feeling of hatred for the low enemy is an understandable feeling. They know, as all Russians know, that only a hatred which is as strong as love justifies the war. For such hatred one must become mature, one must arrive at it by suffering. But a war without hatred is something shameful, like cohabitation without passion.

Our nation lives outside of the fog of national or racial intolerance. The Russians have had respect for foreign culture since olden times, they have favored and loved foreigners. Perhaps our sympathy towards Germany's misfortune after the First World War could be called excessive, but it is not unjust to recall now the bread which Russia, who was far from rich, had sent to German women. Yesterday I received a letter from a Ukrainian, Lieutenant Suprunenko, who writes, "I did not know before that one could hate someone like this. I am an artillerist, and I am only sorry that I cannot kill a Fascist with a bayonet, or with a rifle butt, or strangle him with my own hands." A sacred sentiment! It was born out of the blood of Russian women and children tortured to death by the Hitlerites, it was born out of the smoldering ruins of our cities.

In England children under sixteen were prohibited from viewing the film *The German Rout at Moscow*; the spectacle of gallows erected by the Hitlerites and the corpses of those tortured to death by the Germans was considered immoral for juveniles. I know a fifteen-year-old Russian, he fights as a partisan. His mother was killed, his sister was raped.

AUGUST 13, 1943

Some Englishmen and Americans consider that the descriptions of Fascist atrocities in Russia constitute immoral reading. In my opinion, reports of the bombing of Cologne and Luebeck are immoral. Why bomb German cities? the naïve person will ask. For one does not want to show him who is being bombed and for what reason. If it is a sin to hurt Gretchen, it is not a sin to kill that Gretchen who asks her dear one to send her a local costume from Russia, adding, "It doesn't matter if it is soiled with blood—one can wash it off." We are conducting a war against the microbes of Fascism, and this is much more humane than a neoknightly duel.

A Czech will instantly identify with the sufferings of Kiev and Kerch; he knows what happened to Lidice. The Norwegian will share the fury of every Russian; the Norwegian saw Himmler not only on the newsreel screen, but in nature. The Frenchman remembers the shooting of hostages, and he will say about Suprunenko's letter, "My brother wrote this." May the Channel remain impassable for Hitler's hordes, but may the fury and the hatred of all Europe step across this narrow strip of water. Only a living, beneficent hatred towards Fascism can inspire the Britishers and the Americans to a genuine, all-national war; only hatred can save England from the fate of France, Norway, and the Ukraine.

Ilya Ehrenburg

DRIVING OUT THE ENEMY

In these solemn hours one wants to concentrate, to look back.

September, 'Forty-one—German columns march along the Kreshchatik. Berlin Radio reports daily on the capture of cities, accompanying the communiqués with the beating of drums, whistling, clicking, Hitler's bark, and the howling of a hundred commentators. Russian peasant women accompany the retreating Red Army men with dry, hard eyes. Fieldmarshal von Reichenau gets himself photographed with Kharkov in the background, and the Germans accompany the photograph with the brief title, "The Conqueror." Dust billows above country roads: Guderian's tanks race from Putivl, from Konotop, to Orel. Women with infants in arms plod along eastward and German airmen shoot them down, and after returning to the airfield they drink a toast "to victory." Trains with

Ukrainian wheat roll westward to Germany. Hitler shouts, "There is no more Red Army." Hitler gets himself photographed with Mussolini in the ruins of Smolensk. An esteemed professor delivers a lecture in Heidelberg: "Russia is a colossus with feet of clay," and the young students who have not been called up yet to the army guffaw, "Of clay, ha, ha! . . ." The Germans burst into the Don Basin. The autumn wind rocks the bodies of hanged miners. Berlin clucks anxiously, "We have not enough commandants and policemen." It seems to them that they have won the game. And even the American newspaper *The New York Times* writes, "With the loss of the Don Basin an organized resistance of Russia seems almost unthinkable . . ."

This was two years ago, and it is worth while recalling this today; today when the colossus Russia marches west on steel legs; when there are many abroad who cannot find enough epithets to praise the Red Army; when, drenched in tears of relief, the peasant women embrace the dust-covered soldiers; when nobody even remembers Mussolini who got himself photographed in Smolensk; and when Hitler is silent—he has nothing more to say; when every day we hear about the liberation of a dozen cities; when the driving out of the enemy has begun. Yes, what is happening now is not just another battle, this is truly the driving out of the enemy. For the first time we feel the beginning of the end with our whole being.

The Germans have been writing for two years about the significance of the Don Basin. Multicolored maps of the Don Basin hung in the German consulates under the portrait of Hitler—in Argentina, Sweden, Portugal; the riches of the seized region were indicated by triangles, diamonds, and squares. Economists published works about the past, present, and future of the Don Basin. Military observers, speaking condescendingly about the "incomprehensible stubbornness of the Russians" were

DRIVING OUT THE ENEMY

demonstrating that, having lost the Don Basin, the Soviet Union could not resist for a long time. "A country without coal," this is how the *National Zeitung* entitled its editorial in December, 1942.

We know well what the loss of the Don Basin meant for us. We did not conceal our wounds from ourselves; we endured what seemed unendurable. We lost the coal of the Don Basin; the ore and grain of the Ukraine, the Kuban, and the Don; we lost the factories of Dnieprepetrovsk, Kharkov, Vorohezh, and Stalingrad; the oil of Maikop; we lost very much. In a recent battle the machine gunner Sytin was wounded, but he continued firing. In the hospital the surgeon, on seeing how much blood the wounded man had lost, asked him, "How could you endure?" Sytin replied, "I wanted to drive them away . . ." An immense inner force sustained Russia for two terrible years, a force which helped both the soldiers and the Siberian miners and the women to endure all losses.

Now the Red Army has won back the Don Basin. It has won back that great workers' ant hill, the heat and light of our Motherland. We of the workers' land love the Don Basin. It is dear to us by its traditions, the proud custom of the miners, their adherence to freedom. These are not simply two regions, not so many square miles, but the solar plexus of the Soviet Union, and the love of the young, proud new Russia.

We have a right to celebrate the liberation of the Don Basin, but even the Don Basin is only a chapter now. Something greater is happening; the driving out of the enemy. The "Konotop Sector" lasted for three days in the communiqués, and now Konotop is already in the rear. We understand what Bakhmach means—how the eyes of the Ukrainians are burning in Leningrad as well as in distant Karelia and in the Smolensk region! Kiev is waiting, Kiev can already hear a dull rumble during the night; freedom is approaching.

ILYA EHRENBURG

Only two weeks ago the Germans wrote, "The Russians succeeded in capturing one town, Orel, and a small territory, nowhere exceeding thirty miles in depth. They could not take possession of the Don Basin and knock us out of the Ukraine." The boasters, they pretended to be brave to the last: until they ran. Perhaps Kharkov, Sumy, Konotop are not the Ukraine? Perhaps it is the Germans and not us who are in Stalino? The liars, whom are they deceiving? We have stopped arguing with them a long time ago; we refute their lies with artillery fire. May they wail, after catching their breath for a minute: "We have lost more than a hundred cities. We have run for more than 150 miles . . ." and without even finishing talking they'll have to take off again.

We know that the enemy has not been finished off yet. The Germans are driving hundreds of thousands of Ukrainian and Russian women westward. The women are to build new fortifications. The Germans shout about some "Eastern Rampart." They want to hang onto hills, rivers, swamps; they are not broken yet; they still obey their superiors. Fritz, after being knocked out of the Don Basin, will fight at Zaporozhye. Fritz, who survived in Konotop, will bare his teeth at Bakhmach. We do not belittle the enemy's forces. He has still not lost his powerful equipment, he can still throw his reserves into battle. But the German losses are beyond repair; the enemies have not only lost territory, they have lost their faith in victory.

It is not easy for the Red Army to forge forward. Military specialists can lay this amazing advance to increased battle experience, to greater discipline, better order, powerful equipment, to cooperation between infantry and artillery, to the role of the tank corps. They will be thrice correct. As a writer, I would like to speak of something else, I would like to talk about that force that has turned staid and peaceful peasants of the Volga region and Siberia into fierce soldiers, that force that allows the

DRIVING OUT THE ENEMY

infantryman to march twenty-five miles a day without being afraid of a threat from the flanks, that makes him smile ironically at the sight of German bombers, and makes him march, march, and march. During these days of victory I would like to remind us again that there is something different in our war which distinguishes it from other wars; it is not only the nation's reason which conducts the war now or its ardent attachment to its land; the war is also conducted by the nation's revolted conscience. Justice and Russia march arm in arm; they are inspired by one purpose.

While it advances the Red Army can again see the aggressor's black deeds: the smoldering ruins of the cities, the desert he has made of the land, the bodies of those tortured to death. Wherever the Germans can do so they drive away the whole population. Before me is the order of the German Command regarding the "evacuation" of the Navlinsk district: "Everybody is to proceed immediately with his family, cattle, and movable possessions in a westerly direction. Whoever proceeds in an easterly direction will be fired at." The dying snake bites. In perishing, Hitlerite Germany wants to bring the whole world in ruins. Thus mined buildings fly apart and Russian children die on the roads. And if one listens to the tales of those left behind, if one should gaze into their eyes dulled by fear and degradation, a new "desert zone" will be revealed in the hearts of people devastated by two years of lawlessness. Our soldiers see how the Germans have introduced enforced labor for the peasants, how they flog the disobedient ones, how they lure, intimidate, and infect young girls. They shall answer for all this—it is with this feeling that the army of justice marches west.

One of our battalions was formed from natives of the Kursk region. The commanders and soldiers waited eagerly for news from their people. And then some terrible news arrived. Lieutenant Kolesnichenko learned that his father had been hanged in the village of Medvinka. The Germans had shot Captain Gunderov's mother. Red Army man Borodin read that the Germans had tortured his mother to death and had shot his two brothers. Lieutenant Bogachev—his wife killed, father shot. Red Army man Lukhanin—wife shot. Red Army man Karnaukhov—two children and sister killed. Red Army man Baryshek—father shot; an uncle who could not bear German mockeries laid hands on himself. Red Army man Orekhov—wife condemned to hanging. Red Army man Yesin—uncle, his wife and daughter shot. Red Army man Bridin—his nephew, a five-year-old, killed. Red Army man Rybalko—son-in-law shot. Nine had their families driven into Germany. Thirty-two had their houses burned down. All this was in one battalion. What will hold back such a battalion? Men from Siberia, the Ural Mountains, Caucasians, seeing such misfortune, such evil deeds, march forward as messengers of justice.

Germany trembles: the sword of justice has flashed across the skies. The Fritzes are confused. Only two months ago Hitler was promising them a victorious advance; now Hitler is silent and Russian artillery talks. Siegfried Mantzke, a German officer, having been captured, mutters: "A continuation of the war makes no sense." Yes, the war had sense for them when they were hellbent on a great robbery. At that time the war was fat and oil; now the war has lost its sense for them. But it is full of significance for us; we shall wean them from fighting. We shall discourage them from going after someone else's goods every quarter of a century. They will find out the cost of one pound of fat and one ton of oil.

The advance of the Red Army has changed the climate of the world within two months. Hitler's hangers-on have become dejected: indomitable France has raised her head. The most peaceloving people in the world, the gentle Danes, they, too, have risen against the aggressors. Re-

DRIVING OUT THE ENEMY

cently, in Athens, the Germans tried a young Greek who had set fire to German ships. "You have set fire to two transports?" the German asked. The Greek corrected, "No, to three." Amazed by the youth's insolence, the German colonel said, "Do you understand what fate awaits you?" And the Greek answered, "I know what fate awaits me. But I also know what fate awaits you." In these words are the thoughts and feelings of the world: in the spring Germany could still appear the victor to some, now all see that she is doomed.

And the Red Army, proud that it is marching at the head of humanity, continues its path. Before it is the Dnieper. Before it is life. There was the retreat, the counteroffensive, the defense, the offensive. And now? Now comes the driving out of the enemy.

September 9, 1943

Ilya Ehrenburg

THE LABORERS OF VICTORY

There are soldiers whose exploits are little noted. Their bravery is devoid of glamour, their valor wears camouflage. The sappers are the soldier-workers, they are the laborers of victory.

When a new building goes up everyone knows the name of the architect, and the workers are visible to everyone on their high scaffoldings. But there are men who split the stone in far-off quarries. Without them there would be no fine building; without the sappers of the army there would be no offensive.

The sapper crawls among weeds and rushes, over clay and sand. He fights death one against one. The enemy is invisible, the enemy is in the thinnest wire, in the unnoticeable peg. The sapper crawls along under fire, amidst explosions. He has no right to listen in. He must watch, intently, strenuously, for like the gold prospector who seeks grains of gold, the sapper seeks mines. He must not only be bold, he must be calculating and resourceful. One careless movement, one minute of absent-mindedness, and he will no longer see those weeks, the Dnieper sand, the bright autumn sky. "The sapper makes only one mistake in his life," has become a soldier's saying.

The sapper sees what another man would not notice. Why is the grass slightly crushed here? Why has a miniscule hillock grown up there? The sapper senses something evil with his third eye, his sixth sense. It is easy to go into battle if you have weapons in your hands. The sapper has only a mine detector, a short probe, and a spade. He must be more cunning than the most cunning. There are many mines, and they are as diverse as the snakes in the tropics. There are aerial ones, there are jumping ones; it is not easy to recognize the death-carrying antennae of the detonator. But the sapper has studied all species, and he coolly tears out the fangs of the viper.

The sappers are in front. Sometimes they join an uneven battle. A wireless operator transmitted the message: "Six sappers, headed by Lance Corporal Zamorev, fought back with spades after cartridges ran out. Died, but did not retreat."

There is an old sapper from the Novgorod-Seversky brigade. He has completed the stretch from Orel to Sozha, discovering hundreds of mines. He did not count them. He says modestly, "There is plenty of work . . ."

The war has entered the kingdom of rivers. Behind are the Desna, Sozh, Dnieper Rivers. Ahead are the Pripyat, Beresina, Bug, Dniester, and the Neman Rivers. Without the sappers our army would not be here on the right bank of the Dnieper.

The engineering reconnaissance patrols safeguard the crossing. The sappers seek to find where it would be better to cross the river, then the wireless operator transmits from the enemy bank: "Hollow. Four hundred yards. Building landing stage."

THE LABORERS OF VICTORY

When crossing the Desna River the sappers transported oak beams by hand. It was necessary to go across an open field which the Germans kept under continuous fire. Eight hundred yards is not much, but what does every foot mean if there is a heavy load on you, and the six-barrel mortars never fall silent?

On the Desna River the sappers discovered a loophole. The right bank is steep, but under the hill there is a small strip of bank which the Germans cannot subject to fire. This is a dead zone. Lieutenant Dolgikh swam across the river and immediately started to construct a mooring pier in the dead zone. Then Lieutenant Yefimov swam across the river and pulled through the first line. By the third year of the war we had ceased to notice bravery. Still: to be the first one, and all alone on the other bank. . . .

The sappers carried cargo from a distance. They were collecting "for the Dnieper." They carried ropes, wires, cramp-irons. They were preparing themselves for bridge building. They were also building rafts.

The rafts on the Sozha were constructed from telephone poles, with room on each raft for one 45-mm gun and two horses. When several rafts were wrecked by enemy mines the sappers immediately turned into divers; they dragged up the guns from the river and finished ferrying them across by hand. When I was at the river crossing of the Sizh the Germans bombed the bridge, scoring six direct hits. But the sappers did not cease working, and several hours later the artillery crossed over the bridge.

October nights on the Dnieper are cold. The sappers stand in the icy water: they drive piles into the river bottom and erect trestles, working for twelve hours on end. The medical orderlies carry away the wounded while the sappers work without stopping. They have not slept now for six days. Before that they carried logs on their backs for two miles with their legs sinking into deep sand. The sapper knows that one cubic meter of wood supports a load of three hundred kilograms on water. But who will work out what a sapper can stand, an ordinary person who, before the war, wrote papers, or sowed oats?

Now it is necessary to take the artillery across. There is no bridge so a raft has been built. How to bring it up to the shore? It will take twenty men—the Germans will notice them. So the raft was taken apart, it was carried in sections and then quickly put together again. One cannot make a noise with a hammer? One ties up the logs with rope. When the bombing started Senior Lieutenant Lolebanov blocked the gash in his arm with his tunic. The sappers have built the longest of bridges in one night or in one day. Cunning is also required: the sappers will construct sham crossings to distract the enemy's attention.

The heavy ferry has sunk but the surviving pontoons must be saved. Gas masks to which small pipes are affixed are used for breathing underwater. Chekmessov and Osipov are underwater wearing the improvised breathing masks. They work for three hours on the bottom dismembering the ferry and dragging up the surviving pontoons. Steam rose from their clothing when they resurfaced. They were silent, then Osipov said, "We did it." Not a word more.

On the right bank the tank men are crushing the enemy's Rear. Their path is illuminated by the lofty light of glory. But how did they find themselves on the right bank? The sappers know about this. I traveled over the bridge. A quarter of an hour later the bridge was mutilated by bombs. It was repaired during the night. In the morning the bridge was smashed again, but at midday trucks were traveling over it again. One cannot say: it has been built—it is being built. It is being reconstructed day and night. Both shells and bombs are powerless here, the sappers' will conquer everything—with the hammer, with the

THE LABORERS OF VICTORY

axe, with the saw, with the spade. Bombs and mines explode, bullets hail down in streams. What does the sapper counterpose to the enemy? The sapper has one weapon: courage. He builds a bridge. Others will pass over the bridge. Victory will pass over the bridge. And the sapper will be in front then with a probe. With a spade. With scissors. With a mine detector. He is always in front. And glory? . . . Happiness does not lie in glory, but in the profound consciousness that you did everything you could, and more than you could.

Laborers. Perhaps, in a different world, this word sounds offensive. We are a land of labor, and there is no greater honor here than to be a worker. Miners, pontoon builders, perhaps one writes little about them, but one lives by them. Now they lead Russia westward.

October 28, 1943

Ilya Ehrenburg

THE NEW BROTHERHOOD

I met a Czech in Kozelsk. A Ukrainian partisan said with pride: "This is Anton." Anton Kutil, before the war, was a peaceful tailor. The Germans drafted him and sent him to the Ukraine. He was to fight for Germany as a soldier of the Ninth Tank Division. But Anton Kutil went to the Partisans and fought for the liberation of the Ukraine. He told me: "A Czech cannot be against Russia." In these words lies a profound historical meaning. There are alliances which are not born in diplomats' drawing rooms, but in the depth of the people's soul.

In a Ukrainian village a peasant woman showed me a letter from her daughter, eighteen-year-old Nadya. This letter reached her by a lucky chance. In early spring Nadya was deported west. She writes to her mother: "I live in a foreign country, far from my relations, in cursed Germany, in the town of Storkow near Berlin. We live in a barracks built of plywood. We eat scraps from boiled potatoes. The German women do not believe us when we tell them that this is how we are kept. The cursed ones do not know how our people fare. Never mind, the time will come when the sun will rise above our gates. I wish that they would get it like we did, then people will believe, the young ones in particular do not realize, but then they are all tarred with the same brush . . .

"Two miles from here our prisoners-of-war are kept—fourteen men. They tell me that they were captured in the beginning of the war at Smolensk. They were sent to a camp in Germany where they were beaten, mocked, starved. That camp was situated within sixty miles of Storkow. Few have stayed alive. These fourteen have been lucky, they were taken from there to work in the field. On Sundays they are not allowed to go anywhere. You go past and can hear them singing, 'They kept us long in chains.' It makes you cry.

"Within five hundred yards from us, in the forest, is the camp where the French prisoners are kept. They have been here for three years now. They all work for outside employers, but they have to spend the night in the camp. They're dressed in their military uniforms. They are very cultured people, not at all like the Germans. In spite of everything they wash and mend their clothes and bear themselves well. There are many middle-aged ones among them—forty, forty-five years old—and while they work at their jobs from five o'clock in the morning to nine at night, they still manage to look after themselves. They are all sympathetic towards us, they call us comrades and say: 'You are our sisters, and we are your brothers, since we have been deported.' When the Russians were approaching Sumy a French electrician came to the camp to repair the electricity. He told us everything that was going on. And the next time that we met on Sunday he brought us a map on which the line of the Front was marked out.

THE NEW BROTHERHOOD

They were all pleased that our side is advancing. This Frenchman is called Roger. . . ."

Repeating the name of the distant town of Sumy, until then unknown to him, Roger probably thought of the fate of Tours or Dijon. Everything has blended now into one lump. What brought the Czech Anton to the partisans has brought together two prisoners—Roger and Nadya: common misfortune, common hope. In the days of the terrible spiritual blackout which Fascism brought to the world, millions upon millions of people—Russians, French, Czechs, Norwegians, Belgians, Serbs—have learned of the new human closeness. In this lies the pledge of that better future of which we dare not dream at present while the Germans still burn Ukrainian towns and shoot French hostages.

Kiev is waiting. Paris is waiting. Roger and Nadya are waiting. The Czechs are waiting. Thus the battle for the Ukraine becomes the battle for humanity. Thus the Russian infantry becomes the hope of the world.

November 3, 1943

Ilya Ehrenburg

THE SOUL OF RUSSIA

Two years ago I wrote: "Let us grit our teeth harder. The Germans are in Kiev—this thought nourishes our hatred. We shall liberate Kiev. The enemy's blood will wash away the enemy's traces. Kiev will arise from the ashes like the Phoenix of the ancients."

Long and bitter months went by. The Germans were moving into the heart of Russia. They reached Nalchik and Stalingrad. Military observers in different countries made conjectures as to where the conquerors would move: to Iraq or to India. The owner of a hotel at Bad Kissingen made an application to have the sanatoria at Borzhom granted to him. Courses at Cassel were preparing *Sonderfuehrers* for Bashkiriya. In the financial sections of German newspapers it was pointed out that the "Azov factories of F. Krupp" would recover by 1945, and would make the shareholders happy. A great civic sorrow lay like a stone on the breast of every one of us. Among the victory salutes we do not forget what we have gone through, and we shall not forget it; to us it is misfortune and wisdom and the key for alertness of the spirit.

Radio waves—long, medium, short, rush across the world at night. They have long ago left off the twitter of peaceful days. Now they scream, they still contain the same words: counterattacks, centers of resistance, roads, crossings. Now they talk in forty languages about one thing: the Germans are retreating. Military observers no longer remember about Iraq. They look at the Dniester, the Bug, the Dvina. The *Sonderfuehrers*, trained for the instruction of the Bashkirs, are included in the draft battalions. The Mariupol shares have become worthless paper. The owner of the hotel at Bad Kissingen, gone mad, shouts to his wife, "You will see—the Russians will come here . . ." German divisions rush about in the southern steppe. Phoenix Kiev has risen from the ashes.

How did this happen? asks the astonished world. We were in the very thick of events, we lived from communiqué to communiqué, we fought and we worked, we had no time to reflect. Now we know how the Sixth German Army had been surrounded. We know how the German offensive at Kursk has finished. We know that we are pursuing the recent conquerors. But we too did not stop to consider how all this happened, we only know that we have come to the surface and that before us is the green shore of victory. But let us step aside for a minute and look at ourselves with the eye of history.

We often talk and write about the weakening of the German Army. We know that Hitler's reserves are drying up, that Allied aerial bombardments are destroying his home front, that two years of fierce fighting in Russia have broken down his infantry. We also know that an army of bagmen and chicken-eaters cannot have any genuine ideals, that discipline alone cannot replace the fire of the spirit

THE SOUL OF RUSSIA

in difficult times, that the Hitlerite soldier was weakened internally and was ripe for downfall. But is it only a case of Hitlerites? Let us think of something else: let us think about the increased strength of our Army.

War is complex, obscure, and dense, like an impenetrable forest. It does not resemble its descriptions, it is both more simple and more complicated. It is felt, but not always understood by its participants, and it is understood but not felt by later investigators. Perhaps the historian, after correctly evaluating the significance of the crossing of the Dnieper, will represent this crossing differently: he will bring it involuntarily into order, he will dress up the unkempt soldiers, shave the sergeants tired from the marches, brush the dust off the officers' tunics. He will scarcely see the people around the bonfire who are thinking of their family cottages and who say that the cook has prepared the gruel, and that it would be good to bake some potatoes. Their descendants will least of all imagine that these were precisely the people who, without pontoons, crossed to the right bank of one of the widest rivers in Europe. As for the participants of the war, they know what the war looks like. They know that a 250-mile march with battles is not a parade, they know that not only companies, battalions, and regiments fight, but that it comes down to individuals, to people with a separate life history which is warm like a bundle of wool and that every soldier is attached to the Motherland with his own special thread. But it is difficult for the participants of the war to appreciate the historical significance of what was taking place: the great excitements of the present day are enough for them.

Foreigners often ponder the question of how our State was able to stand fast during the tragic days of 'Forty-one and 'Forty-two. Everyone now knows how powerful the German Army was and how carefully Germany prepared for its robber campaigns. The fate of France, with her fighting traditions and the incontestable courage of her freedom-loving, bellicose people, is in everybody's memory. Hitler has subdued Europe. I do not speak about the British Isles. But we were not separated from Germany by the sea, neither did we have mountains. We stopped the aggressors by our might and main, and there the foreigners argue: in what lies the clue? Some say that it lies in the nature of Russian courage, in the traditional staying power of the Russian soldier, in the magnitude and natural resources of Russia, in the fact that no one has ever conquered Russia. Others object, saying that times have changed. The bayonet, even the Russian bayonet, is powerless against the Tigers. In the industrial age space alone cannot save a nation. They say: if Russia has stood fast then the answer lies in the merit of her structure, in the special patriotism of her peoples, and in the vital interest of every citizen in the fate of the State. They add to the word "Russia" another word: "Soviet."

Both they and the others are correct. During the war the past arose before us to combine with the present and the future, bringing into vivid life the organic connection between Russia and the October Revolution. We understood that the Revolution had saved Russia on two occasions: in 1917 and in 1941. If there had been no revolution Russia might have lost her national independence and have betrayed her historical mission. But the October Revolution was not born accidentally in Russia, it arose from all the strivings of the Russian people. Its significance has grown beyond its national boundaries; it is not for nothing called the greatest event of the twentieth century, for its roots go back into Russian history and it cannot be divorced from the Russian character, or even from the Russian landscape.

The soldiers at the bonfire on the right bank of the Dnieper are, of course, the sons of the soldiers of ancient times, who carry within them the same love for their na-

THE SOUL OF RUSSIA

tive land, along with the valor, the knowhow, and the staying power of their forebears. But there is something new in them, born of the Revolution; they are not only soldiers, they are citizens.

In front of me is a secret report of Lieutenant-General Dettling, commander of the Sudeten Division, on "The Mood of the Local Population." This is what the German general writes: "The overwhelming majority of the population does not believe in a German victory. . . . In some inhabited places many local people have made attempts to establish contact with the remaining adherents of the Soviet system. . . . The youth of both sexes which has received an education is almost exclusively pro-Soviet-minded, and regards our propaganda with distrust. After the lectures these young people with a seven-year or a tertiary education ask questions which reveal their high mental standard. Usually, however, they pretend to be simpletons for camouflage reasons, and it is very difficult to exert an influence on them. They still read Soviet literature, which has survived. This youth loves Russia stronger than anything, and is fearful that Germany will turn their motherland into a German colony. . . . From the beginning of the German occupation young people felt themselves deprived of their future. They are always pointing out that youth was very well off in the Soviet Union, since everything possible was being done for it, and a great future was assured to it."

Lieutenant-General Dettling would hardly have composed such a memo in 1916. There was patriotism before, too. There has also been valor before, but the young men and girls, the peasants of the Smolensk province in the times of the Tsar and of estates and castes could not dream about a "great future." A Napoleonic officer had called the partisans of 1812 the "vague spirit of the Russian soil." It was not reason but the heart which suggested the correct path to the serfs of that time, and they marched with pitchforks against the aggressors. Their exploits have been justified by history, the grandchildren of these serfs have become the masters of the greatest State on earth. But the heroes of the "Young Guard" were guided by reason. They looked down on the German officers. Oleg Koshevoy knew that he was the representative of a superior human society which was fighting against armed barbarians. Such was the role of the October Revolution.

The Soviet Union is fighting not only as an immense State, it is also fighting as a genuine democracy: the war is conducted by the nation for whom the State is its own backyard. I saw many German generals. I think that they can be recognized even in the bath: this is a breed, as the industrialist Krupp or the landowner from East Prussia are a breed. Such generals are bred, they are a race within the Aryan race. And who beats them? General Dettling was beaten at Kiev by Lieutenant General Chernyakhovsky. Thirty-six years old, the son of a railroad clerk from Uman, Chernyakhovsky has gnawed science like a stone since childhood. He is a man of great culture, he stands out by mind, knowledge, and talent, but not by breed. He is one of the many generals of a free and democratic State. I can remember fighting colonels who, at the beginning of the war, were lieutenants, teachers, agronomists, mechanics, on whose chests I saw orders of Suvorov. We can say that the German Army is now pursued by an army enriched by battle experience, led by skillful officers, and we can also say that the enemy is pursued by a nation which had taken the reins of government into its hands twenty years ago.

The outstanding performance by our military industry remains, as everybody knows, one of the explanations of our victory. Let us recall the difficulties: Stalingrad, Kharkov, Dniepropetrovsk, Voronezh, Rostov, and the Don Basin had been occupied by the enemy, but the factories were moved eastward to rise again among vacant fields.

THE SOUL OF RUSSIA

The steppes of Eastern Russia are not Detroit, our workers endured all kinds of privations, they did not eat enough or sleep enough, but they gave the Army tanks, planes, and weapons. The factories were born yesterday, but the workers were not born yesterday; they were people created by the Soviet State, they are not Krupp's slaves, they are creators, and the creative spirit helped them throughout the terrible months.

Why could the Armenian Petrosian, captured by the Germans, find strength while covered with blood, to escape the executioners and reach his own people? What helped the Georgian Gakhokidse to annihilate the enemies on the last patch of Sevastopol land? Why did the Uzbek Kayum Rakhmanov not spare his life in defending Leningrad? Why did the Jew Papernik perish on the approaches to Moscow? Because of the October Revolution. In its purifying storm a new Russia was born, the mother of all nationalities. Yesterday's "aliens" have become citizens, builders of the nation, and when their Motherland was attacked by the Germans they went into battle, they spoke different tongues and had different faces, but they had the same feeling in their hearts.

I do not want to say that we had achieved everything before the war; a quarter of a century is a brief hour for history. There is much that we have not managed to achieve. In our society there were not only our best intentions, there were also our shortcomings. During the war years we made many changes on the move. We saw that we often lacked discipline, organization, personal initiative, feelings of responsibility. We understood that our children required firmer moral foundations, that human dignity, patriotism, faithfulness, feelings of chivalry, respect for age and care for the weak had to be more deeply instilled in them. But having understood our shortcomings, we saw in the fire of trials how exalted our life was, built as it was on equality and labor. The war has not only ravaged our country, it has tempered and spiritually uplifted our people. After returning to peaceful work they will not forget about these things to which they have given a great deal of thought and feeling. They will bring into their everyday existence the wisdom and heroism of the war years, they will help to create that society which will be the expression of the thoughts and feelings of the much-tried Soviet nation.

Our effort will be made lighter by the historical perspective which has now become everybody's property. Without foregoing the ideals of the future, we have learned to derive our strength from the past. We have realized the full significance of the heritage left us by our forebears. We do not want to indiscriminately deny the past, neither do we want to accept it as something faultless. We have learned from the military genius of Suvorov, but not from the stupid willfulness of Emperor Paul I in government. The German Fascists love to speak of traditions, but what did they take from the past of the German people? Schiller's love of freedom? Goethe's reason? No. They have taken the tortures by the executioners of Nuremberg, the superstitious, cock-and-bull stories of the alchemists, the atrocities of the savage Teutons, and the military drill of Frederick the Great's sergeants-major. Every nation takes from its past that which corresponds to its spiritual level, to its life, to its ideals. For us the past is Pushkin and not Benkendorf; Kutusov and not Arakcheyev; the Decembrists and not Saltychikha; Plekhanov and Gorky, not Purishkevich and the shopkeepers of Okhotny Ryad. The October Revolution has helped us to appreciate Russia, to use the past as a source of inspiration.

The victories of the Red Army are now allowing us to discern in the vague, predawn mists that great victory celebration of which the head of our State has spoken to us during our gravest hours.

What will the world be like after the war? This thought

THE SOUL OF RUSSIA

is now beginning to come to us in those rare breathing spells between battles, marches, and military labor. The Fascists have brought so much evil to us and to all of Europe, so much destruction, so much suffering that the heart is often gripped by gloomy sorrow. We see that the schools, the day nurseries, the museums, and the spacious bright buildings erected with so much difficulty by our generation have been burned down. We see how cows have replaced the tractors the Hitlerites stole from us. We see that the ideals dear to us of brotherhood, human dignity, and freedom have been trampled on. We see the letters of the women-slaves from Germany, photographs of Fascist fanaticism, we see savagery, we see the eclipse of the entire century. The imagination easily continues on with the picture: one sees the desert zone spreading to Paris, to the vineyards of Greece, to elegant Danish villages, and to the factories of Belgium until the same ashes which now cover our earth—weeds, called "German crops" by our peasants—cover all of Europe; one sees the spread everywhere of the torture and degradation of man, the violation of reason, of justice and of humaneness. How can the earth arise again from the dead? one wonders. And at times faint-heartedness overcomes one: has not humanity been thrown too far back to primitive times by Fascist barbarism?

I do not want to gloss over anything. I know how difficult it will be to rebuild both the destroyed cities and the psychological balance of a people who have spent years under the sway of fanatics. And yet I gaze cheerfully into the future: truth wins on the battlefield; it will win on the scaffolding of human reconstruction. We have learned to value freedom even more after the despotism of the Hitlerites, after the Gestapo, the "burgomasters," the denunciations, and the flouting of human principles brought about by the Fascists. The only limits of freedom are the freedom of others, and the happiness of the Motherland. In the self-restraint of the warrior lies the guarantee of the triumph of freedom.

We have always understood the magic power of labor, it is not for nothing that we swore by it in our most sacred vows. The labor of a free citizen is not a curse, not a yoke, it is exalted creation. It will not be easy to raise cities and villages from the rubble but the people who did not spare their blood in order to defend the Motherland will not spare their sweat, either. In burnt-down villages I saw old men who helped soldiers' wives rebuild their houses. Here lies the guarantee of our future happiness. We shall be able to put self-love to shame: there is no room for it next to the heroes' graves.

It would seem that the ideas of brotherhood have been burned to ashes, but no, they will arise with a new force. I dare to say this now, at a time when the Fascist hordes are still performing their black work. The Hitlerites have proclaimed themselves to be a "nation of masters." The national dignity of all nations of the world has risen up in response. It must not ruin the idea of brotherhood, but revive it to give it substance. The Siberian understands the misfortune of Greece, the Ukrainian knows what France is experiencing, the torments of the Norwegian fisherman are close to the Belorussian peasant. The idea of brotherhood has become more tangible, more palpable. The Red Army has become the army of freedom in the eyes of all nations. One speaks with hope about its exploits both in enslaved France and in distant America. Having parried the blows of predatory Germany, it has not only saved the freedom of our Motherland, it has saved the freedom of the world. In this lies the guarantee of the triumph of the ideas of brotherhood and humaneness, and I can see in the distance a world, clarified by misfortune, in which the good will radiate. Our nation has demonstrated its military virtues, and now all nations know that the Soviet Union and her Army bring peace to the tortured world. We say this amidst the smoldering ruins of the Ukraine and Belorussia, with a heart covered with wounds: who has not lost a brother, a son, or a friend? We say this uplifted by the consciousness of our strength and our rightness.

November 11, 1943

1944

There was little grace in life—
Much blood, ashes, and misfortune.
I am not complaining about my lot.
I only wanted to see
A day, an ordinary day,
When the dense shadow of a tree
Meant nothing ominous
Only summer, silence, and sleep.

I. Ehrenburg

Ilya Ehrenburg

FEBRUARY 21, 1944

Recently an American asked me: "What do the Russians think about the future?" I answered him, "We have no time to think about that—we are too busy fighting." During the First World War there was an abyss between the Front and the Home Front. The Front fought, the Home Front philosophized and diverted itself. Bloody fighting took place in the Carpathian Mountains, in Petersburg one argued about anthroposophy, futurism, and Tibetan medicine. The earth at Verdun was drenched in blood; in Paris one was excited about whether the Viviani Cabinet would fall and whether Picasso's stage decorations for the ballet "Parade" were any good. We have no Home Front now; all of Russia is the Front. Millions of refugees are living for yet a third year in outdoor camps. Factory workers in the Urals and in Siberia work themselves to exhaustion. Engine-drivers go without sleep for three days on end, driving long, heavy freight trains through the storm. Young girls lay five thousand bricks a day to rebuild the ruins of Stalingrad. Don Basin miners restore damaged mines. In the villages women, old men, and children struggle to care for the crops. There is neither rest nor contentment in the country. Russia clenched her teeth; she fights. She wants to make an end to the war as quickly as possible. Our soil yearns for fields of wheat, and our hearts yearn for meadows of cornflowers. A peaceful people, we fight with so much fury because we hate war.

It would be very sad if a division between the Front and the Home Front and a lack of understanding should form between nations. There are no neutral countries now, but there are Front-line countries and Home Front countries. I can see a city in one of the average states of America. At night the people, when meeting, discuss world problems. They argue whether one must hate the enemy. They discuss the virtues and the sins of distant Europe. One of them, the respected owner of a drugstore, or the representative of an insurance company, says that the Finns always paid their creditors, that General Franco has saved Spain from anarchy, that the French have degenerated, that the Benedictine Abbey must not be destroyed, that Germany is still a cultured country while the Bolsheviks are still suspicious experimenters. He talks about this without particular seriousness or particular conviction; he talks about this as if he were talking about the spots on the moon or about stellar mists. Of course, he remains a good patriot, he is pleased about both the successful Allied raids on Berlin and the victories of the Red Army. He wants the United Nations to smash Hitler. He loves goodness and justice, but he argues like a man in the deep Rear. I would like to tell him and his fellow-citizens what the Russians think about the future, because the Russians, it must be understood, do think about the

FEBRUARY 21, 1944

future; they think about it during those brief hours when they happen to have some leisure. They talk about it in the dugouts and in shelters, in trains during a long journey, and after work.

They believe, first of all, that it is necessary to win as quickly as possible. The future of Russia, the future of Europe, the future of the world depend not only on how the victory will be won, but also on when it will be won. What is the future? It is children. Every day thousands of children die from hunger in lands seized by the Germans: in Belorussia, Poland, Greece, France. Millions of children who had fallen into German slavery are becoming savages: they have no schools, no moral standards or kindness. They grow up in market places, they see gallows, their hearts are unmoved. What is the future? It is living people. They perish under the Germans. Would it not be better, instead of deliberating about the degeneration of France, to give some thought to her winegrowers and gardeners, her workers, her professors, artists, and writers who are dying—some in concentration camps, others in Germany, still others in dark, unheated buildings? What is the future? It is also the past. It is, of course, a pity that the Benedictine Abbey has been turned by the Germans into a fort, although I do not understand why the world's attention is concentrated on this particular vandalism of the Hitlerites—have the Germans not destroyed a multitude of wonderful monuments? I would like to assure our American friends that Novgorod, which has been destroyed by the Germans, is worthy of greater attention than Monte Cassino. Novgorod—this is Ravenna, this is Chartres, this is Sofia. But would it not be better, instead of crying over destroyed treasures, to think about saving those which have survived? There is only one method of saving a church, a museum, a city—and that is to double the force of our attacks.

A few days ago I heard a radio survey by Mr.

Ewer—the rather informed BBC commentator. He said, "The Russians are teaching us not to strike a blow before we are completely prepared." Of course, every military operation must be prepared—our Allies know this themselves. I believe that if the Russians are teaching their friends anything, then it is something different: war is not a book of arithmetic problems. He who is preparing himself also gives his opponent time to get prepared. The Germans placed immense hope on the Dnieper. This is a very wide river, its western bank is steep and unapproachable. I was at the Dnieper when the Russians were forcing its crossing, and I can assure you that our troops crossed this river not because they had themselves well-prepared for the crossing, but because they did not give the enemy enough time to consolidate himself properly. The Russian infantry crossed on boards, on barrels, even on waterproof cape-tents filled with straw, without waiting for pontoons.

The Red Army offensive began on July 12th of last year, and it is continuing: 225 days of uninterrupted fighting, covering a distance equal to that from Calais to Berlin. The offensive takes place along a very long front equal to the front between Oslo and Biarritz. This is how Russia fights and she fights like this because she really thinks about the future, because she really wants peace.

The victories of the Red Army infuriate the Germans. For they thought they could seize Russia within a few weeks; they expected to bury the Red Army long ago. Now they are not only embittered, they are confused: they cannot understand how the profoundly democratic people's Army of the Soviet Republic can beat the professionals of warfare, the specialists in military campaigns, the famous *Reichswehr*. The German soldiery is an artificially-produced breed. I am convinced that Generals von Reichenau or von Rundstedt did not play hide-and-seek, but their outflanking maneuvers were nevertheless child-

FEBRUARY 21, 1944

ish. They have been brought up on magic words: Clausewitz—Schlieffen—Cannae—pincers movement—and now the notorious "pincers movement" has fallen into Russian hands; the favorite of the *Reichswehr*, the "cauldron," turned out to be in our kitchen, and some ten German divisions have just boiled away in such a cauldron. Who will deny the military qualities of a young German soldier? The Germans have lived from childhood on for one thing: preparation for war. They were not civilians during peacetime, but were only released on leave to temporarily carry out the duties of workers, shop assistants, cattle breeders, brewers, or philosophers. The world had not seen such an army, ideal for conquest, like the one that crossed our borders on June 22, 1941.

And it is this army that the Russians are beating.

I can understand the indignation and confusion of the Germans. I cannot understand the embarrassment of certain friends. Sometimes it seems to me that the owner of the drugstore whom I have mentioned loved us much more when he thought that we were weak. But there is nothing more pleasant in an ally than his strength. The Germans whisper: "The conqueror's instincts have awakened in the Russians, who are inebriated by their victories." This is a low slander. The Russian people never loved war. Although bold, they remained peaceful. Only when the enemy broke into Russian soil, when the enemy spat upon a lump of bread and upset the sleep of a child did the Russian nation give its soul to the war. This is how it was in the days of the Tartar invasion and of the Polish and French invasions, and this is how it is now: a nation of ploughmen, builders, and singers became a nation of warriors. We did not stop loving the sickle over the sword. We learned to fight in order to destroy the carriers of war, but we have not turned into conquerors or campaign professionals. Between battles Russian soldiers talk about land or flax or buckwheat, about bees or apples, seeds, weddings and children, the peaceful past and the peaceful future.

Strength and the love of peace supplement each other well. Twenty-six years ago the bayonets of the first Red Army men defended the young Republic from the Kaiser's troops. At that time the words of brotherhood were taken by many as a weakness, as a renunciation by Russia. Our country appeared to some as goods without an owner. Even Rumanian boyars tore off a large lump of our land on the sly. Now, when the Red Army has demonstrated its strength, the robbers are naturally alarmed. But why is the owner of the drugstore embarrassed? Russia is not a conqueror. Russia only wants what is rightfully hers.

Loving peace, the Russians want to finish once and for all with the eternal threat of the German plunderers. These thoughts are connected with anxiety for our children and for the future of the world.

There are the defeated, from whom the victors have learned much. The nations of Europe hated the aggressor Napoleon, but behind Napoleon there was visible, though mutilated, the shadow of the French Revolution, of progress, of the "Declaration of the Rights of Man and of the Citizen." Russian officers fought bravely against Napoleon. They returned from Paris inspired by the idea of freedom, and ten years later the Decembrists' uprising broke out in Petersburg. The Spaniard Riego fought against Napoleon's soldiers, but after driving out the French he entered into battle with the Spanish tyrants, inspired by the ideas which had come from France.

What does lie behind Hitler's soldiers? A poverty of ideas, savagery, Prussian soldiery, the obscurantism of the "Race Theory," amorality, and cruelty. We must bury this corpse lest it infect the earth with its miasma. We are far from the desire to force our ideas, our tastes, and our order onto others. People and nations arrive at justice by different paths. When we think about the necessity of

FEBRUARY 21, 1944

annihilating Fascism, we are not guided by fanaticism, but by purity of heart and concern for the fate of future generations.

It is a little over ten years since the day of the Fascist revolt in Paris. February 6, 1934, was the prelude to June 14, 1940, when the Hitlerites marched into Paris, betrayed by the French Fascists and semi-Fascists. I was in that city on February 6th and on June 14th; I know what the germs of Fascism are. Does the carefree owner of the drugstore know them?

Superstitions spread much faster than knowledge. Medicines must be invented, prepared, and conveyed, but microbes do not require either licenses or steamships. Racial and national intolerance, anti-Sovietism, the fear of progress, criminality, the cult of brute force penetrate from Germany into other countries. There is one method of finishing with the disgusting epidemic: to smash Fascism. Perhaps most dangerous is the Fascist who is ashamed of that appellation, the Hitlerite made up as a humanist, the poison administered in a milk bottle. In Spain Fascism is called Falangism, in Germany National Socialism, in Croatia *Ustashism*, in France Doriotism. But semi-Fascism, or more correctly, camouflaged Fascism looked even more surprising. Thus, in Serbia the Fascists call themselves Chetniks and make believe that they are fighting against the Fascists. Thus, in Finland Tanner calls himself a Social Democrat, although in fact he is an ordinary henchman of German Fascism. It is necessary to destroy the essence of the disease without paying any attention to the little labels.

We can see how Europe is fighting against ptomaine poisoning. The servitors of Pétain are being tried at present in Algiers. In Bari the Italians have denounced the high society masquerade of yesterday's friends of Hitler. The Yugoslav patriots are unmasking Mihailovich. This is not a Party struggle, or a collision of ideas, this is the resistance of the living organism to ptomaine poisoning.

ILYA EHRENBURG

It is easy to guess what the Germans will do when the Red Army approaches the borders of the Reich. For even now many German officers talk about 1960 and 1965—foreseeing a military rout, they are already dreaming about revenge. It will be easier for them to betray Hitler than their dream of world domination. They are specialists in substitutes: they will arrange an ersatz-repentance, an ersatz-purification, and an ersatz democracy, only in order to save the military inventory, the heavy industry, and the clandestine *Reichswehr*. Herr Schultz will call up Herr Mueller and say, "Tomorrow you will be a crazy anarchist, you will set fire to a church and kill Frau Quatschke." And then Herr Schultz will begin to shout over the radio: "Anarchy is threatening Germany! A firm power is necessary! Our police must not be weakened!" He will also appeal to the owner of the drugstore. He will endeavor to deceive the world once more.

The Russians believe that there must be no new war in 1960 and 1965. Fascism must be buried. The world must be cleansed from infection. The German aggressors must be weaned from periodic raids on Europe. The graves of the dead demand this, the cradles of the children demand it. The future of the twentieth century depends on the boldness and honesty of the United Nations. We want the second half of the century to be more humane and beneficial than the first.

Konstantin Simonov

DELAYED IN DELIVERY . . .

This time your correspondent will have to start his telegram with an explanation. Some of the events which will be dealt with in this and the following articles took place several days ago, and others happened a month ago. However, I was unable to contact you by telegraph from where I was because of the roads. I shall start with the roads.

I maintain that a person who has not seen the roads here in the South this spring could not fully understand what it is like. Imagine an old highway, formed of huge cobblestones joined one against the other, which has been overtaken somewhere in the very midst of repairwork after the workers had wrenched out the stones one after the other and left them lying about without either removing or resetting them. That's the first thing.

Secondly, imagine that two feet of liquid mud has

been poured over these wrenched-out stones and that it cannot drain away anywhere because there is deeper mud lying on both sides of the highway at the same level with it.

Thirdly, imagine that, after crawling along such a highway in a Land Rover after having grown rabid from dismounting and pushing the car and placing logs, straw—anything at all to hand—under its skidding wheels, you would want to get out onto the adjoining ground and ride over the fields, you will be prevented from such an ill-advised act by the following sight: within fifteen yards from the highway, sticking straight out of the mud, is the turret of a tank which on closer inspection turns out to be a whole, undamaged tank that has simply sunk nearly out of sight into the mud. I shall add to this that when I finally walked—I repeat walked, and not drove—up to General Gola of Khalkhin fame whom I was attempting to reach, he merely burst out laughing in response to my swearing at the roads, the slush, and the need to abandon my car and walk on foot, and he replied that I was simply following his example, for in order not to fall back from his advance units he, too, had been walking for the last two days after abandoning his motor car.

And finally, as strange as it may sound, there is a circumstance pleasing to the eye which is connected with the disgusting state of the roads: the roads are all cluttered up with the traces of a German retreat. It has been hard to impress me by similar sights for quite a long time now, and yet, having got here, I am amazed day after day by the quantity of machines, both fighting and transport, of all types and of all branches of the military services, abandoned by the Germans. Here are the notorious Tigers and Panthers, burnt and whole, and tanks of older types, and self-propelled guns, and huge armored carriers, and small carriers with one driving wheel looking like motorcycles, and huge, snub-nosed Renault trucks stolen from France,

DELAYED IN DELIVERY...

and numberless Mercedes and Opel staff cars, wireless units, field kitchens, antiaircraft installations, disinfection-chambervans—briefly everything that the Germans had thought up and utilized in their past impetuous advances. And all that is now smashed, burned, or simply abandoned, stuck in the mud of these roads.

In places it is almost impossible to drive past all this. Mountains of smashed metal which once constituted machines are lying about at bridges and steep drops. It has been necessary to push them to both sides of the road in order to walk and drive past, for they sometimes stood four rows deep after becoming stuck on the roads. Along one of these roads, near the border, I experienced a feeling of vindictiveness. It was along this road that one of our light tank divisions had been retreating in 'Forty-one. The Germans had locked it into a ring then, had thrown all their aircraft and heavy tanks at it, and that division which we had not been able to re-equip at the beginning of the war and which consisted in its entirety of out-of-date light tanks, had perished in its entirety on this road.

At that time, in 'Forty-one, after removing their own smashed and burnt machines from the road, the Germans had left our destroyed tanks in full view for our edification, and in some places they had even, for greater effect, dragged these small, mutilated green tanks closer to each other and placed them in whole strings in the most visible places, on hilltops and on the curve of roads. There they had remained until this spring, but now, when you drive past all this and see right here, in proximity to those small green tanks which had grown rusty from three years of snow and rain, all this smashed and abandoned German equipment of which I have spoken, it is hard not to give in to a feeling of vindictiveness!

I don't know—perhaps at the time, in 'Forty-one, no one had sworn here above the graves of our killed tank men to avenge them. Our soldiers are not generally disposed toward vows and big words. But I am sure that many people had, in 'Forty-one, made themselves silent promises of settling the score with the Germans. And now these promises are being fulfilled here, before my eyes. And not even in accordance with the Biblical law—an eye for an eye, a tooth for a tooth—but in a much more shattering proportion.

A small detail. Between the highway and the village there stands, partly submerged in mud, a giant German carrier intended for the transport of especially heavy loads of many tons. A small boy, about ten years old, is sitting on the carrier looking like a small insect on the huge machine. With a spanner in his hands he is looking intently at something in the machine. The driver, with whom we are slowly crawling and skidding along the highway past the young boy, had noticed him and says without a smile: "Now a mechanic has turned up there. He is already engaged in reconstruction work."

There is, of course, nothing special in this small detail. But I am driving past this small boy and I'm thinking involuntarily how many thousands of rumbling German machines must have raced past this child of a border village during the past three years! How many German tanks have thundered past him, and how many planes have howled past above his head! And now he is sitting there with a spanner on the huge machine, which is no longer powerful and frightening, and is wondering what bolt should he unscrew to use in making a catapult? It must be what he's up to, for small boys of that age are wreckers by vocation.

All that I have written to you about roads are, of course, merely fragmentary observations, for that's not the main thing I wanted to talk to you about. The main thing is the man who marches along on these roads: the infantryman, the Russian soldier.

As much as your correspondent had to get drenched,

DELAYED IN DELIVERY...

had to be jolted and shaken and to swear at these roads, all his complaints about having to push his car more than he rode in it are in the end simply ridiculous in the face of what the most ordinary rank-and-file infantryman is currently doing, one of the millions marching along these roads, sometimes carrying out marches of twenty-five miles per day under the conditions I have already described to you. Around his neck he carries a sub-machine gun, behind his back there is a full kit. He carries on him everything a soldier needs on the way. The man passes there where machines cannot pass, and in addition to what he carries on his back he also carries what should go by truck. He marches under conditions approaching those in the life of a caveman, sometimes forgetting for days on end what a fire was. His greatcoat has not fully dried out on him for a month now, and he can continuously feel its dampness on his shoulders. During the march he cannot sit down for hours to have a rest, for he is surrounded by such mud that he can only sink knee-deep into it. Sometimes he does not see hot food for days, for at times not only motor vehicles but even horses pulling the kitchen wagons cannot get through to him. He has no tobacco because the tobacco supplies have also been held up somewhere. Every day so many experiences befall him in a concentrated form that they would not be the lot of another man over an entire lifetime. And of course—so far, I have not even mentioned this—aside from all this and in the first place, he fights daily and fiercely, subjecting himself to mortal danger. Such is the life of a soldier in this, our spring offensive.

I believe that if any one of us had been asked to endure these trials on his own we would not only have answered in the negative, but would really not be able to endure them either physically or psychologically. However, millions of our people endure these trials at present, and they endure them precisely because there are millions of them. The feeling of the immensity and universality of the trials imbues the hearts of the most diverse people with an indestructible collective force, unheard of before, which can arise within an entire nation only in the course of such an immense, real war, a war which has not for a long time now resembled the battle pictures of painters or heroic movies, or even what we have written about it ourselves, no matter how we may have striven to write the whole truth.

I am returning to what I started with: please accept the foregoing as a sufficient explanation as to why this dispatch and possibly the following as well has been, so to speak, delayed in delivery over the telegraph.

April 1944

Konstantin Simonov

THE SIEGE OF TERNOPOL

As on all crossings at the Front there stands on this crossroads a signpost, with one signboard pointing left to an "Automobile Base," and the other pointing straight ahead to "Ternopol—2 mi." At the signpost there is a traffic controller, and trucks and tanks and motor cars turn to the left or proceed straight ahead to where, behind the hills, Ternopol lies. The signboard looks quite peaceful, as if it stood on the Home Front, but fighting goes on in the town.

At first our motor car climbs along the rise to the highest hill, which is furrowed with rows of deep trenches, crumbled from explosions. This is the so-called quarry district, the spot where particularly fierce fighting took place at the approaches to the town. Actually, when one stops on the ridge of the hill and looks back to where our troops had begun their assault on Ternopol, it is not difficult to imagine the effort it had cost to gain possession of the approaches to the town. A wide valley, open from all sides, stretches beneath the hills; our troops had to attack along this completely open site to capture the quarries. The complication of the assault was exacerbated by the fact that apart from the usual trenches, numerous galleries for stone quarrying had been excavated in the hills, burrowing so deeply into the ground that only an endless barrage of heavy artillery shells could smash and bury these hills.

If one looks from the hill in the opposite direction, Ternopol will be revealed to the eye. A picturesque town, descending like an amphitheater to the reservoir located west of it.

Greyish smokepuffs whirl now here, now there, above the center of the town at this hour of the morning, and the clatter of sub-machine guns is carried to us on the wind. Our car descends to the street at whose opposite end the Germans are still entrenched. In the dirty gutters along the sides of the road one now and then sees corpses which have not yet been cleared away. And there is the town itself: crooked lanes along its eastern outskirts, low, small buildings whose roofs are covered with tiles gone dark and with bright galvanized metal sheets. The imprint of the war which has taken place here without sparing a single building is visible everywhere. Some buildings have their roofs completely blown off, but almost next door, only two buildings further on, the glass has remained intact in the windows, and one can see the interior of abandoned apartments with pots of dried-up flowers still on the window sills, and cupboards with open doors.

We cross the small town park which has been half mowed down by shells, and enter the street where, in a comparatively undamaged building the Staff headquarters of one of the two divisions which are storming the town has accommodated itself. In a small room which still pre-

THE SIEGE OF TERNOPOL

serves traces of its former life there are field telephones, and infantry and artillery commanders are leaning over a table on which is spread a map of the town. On the wall there is a Madonna, and next to her a small, roughly-made crucifix. Heaps of German magazines are spread about near the couch on which lies a thick volume of the *History of Polish Art*, bound in red leather. Equestrians wearing helmets or *confederatkas* gallop in the book, while indifferent beauties sit immobile in magnificent ancient costumes.

On the map on the table in the middle of the room, or more correctly on the plan of the town of Ternopol, all the blocks have been numbered: ours—they are in the majority—have been outlined in red, while the German-held ones, squeezed into the center of the town, are marked with a blue pencil.

A decisive assault on several blocks through the day and night has been proposed for today, whose seizure would guarantee the possibility of a general and final assault. The main factor which determines the character of the fighting here is our proximity to the enemy. Along the entire line of the Front which runs through the town, nowhere does the distance between us and the Germans exceed fifty yards, it becomes reduced to fifteen yards in places, and here and there it is measured only by the thickness of a wall or a ceiling in situations where both our troops and the Germans occupy different parts of the same building. This proximity to the enemy has both its good and its difficult aspects. We find ourselves everywhere at a distance which permits a direct rush into attack but, at the same time, we are deprived of the possibility of bombing the Germans from the air, and we are also deprived of the possibility of destroying by artillery a series of buildings immediately adjoining our Front-line, and even the artillery fire on buildings in the interior is concentrated on such a "five-cent piece" that all artillerists' calculations must be exceptionally careful. The German Ternopol garrison which is currently comprised of the remainder of an SS security division, the remainder of an infantry division, of several artillery regiments and of several special units, and of the penal officers' battalion, is entrenched in the center of town. This part of town consists mainly of ancient, solid buildings whose walls at places are two-, or even two-and-a-half-yards thick, whose brick bonding is indestructible, and on which a direct hit by the shell of a 76-mm. field gun leaves no more than a small patch of crumbled plaster torn from its walls. These buildings are the jail, the Dominican Monastery, the officers' school, and the castle. Hundreds of heavy shells are needed for the destruction of each one. However, the streets where these buildings stand are so narrow and winding that to shoot point-blank, which would have achieved the greatest result, is almost impossible. In short, the task of taking this small part of town still held by the Germans constitutes an exceptionally difficult task.

It is enough to spend one or two hours with the Staff officers and hear the series of instructions, orders, and reports in order to understand how complicated was the strategy which took place here yesterday, and the day before, and how complicated it will be today. At present the immediate tasks of the day are being defined in accordance with the plan lying on the table. Today the entire artillery will conduct firing from 1500 hours to 1700 hours, fifty-five minutes. But this is not a general random firing at all the area occupied by the Germans. Definite objectives have been defined for each battery and each division; the destruction of which will be particularly important for the success of the forthcoming assault. At 1700 hours, fifty-five minutes, when firing for the purposes of destruction will cease, the entire artillery will undertake a simultaneous five-minute fiery bombardment, and the infantry will go into attack.

THE SIEGE OF TERNOPOL

Under conditions of street battles, the fighting unit was no longer to be the battalion or the company but the assault group, comprised of fifteen to twenty men armed with sub-machine guns, rifles, hand grenades, and incendiary bombs. Each such group was allocated several artillery pieces which would fire as instructed by the commander of the assault group at gunports, windows, and machine gunners who had ensconced themselves in buildings, thus clearing the path for the infantry. The task set for these groups was also not that of advancing generally; no, for each of them a building had already been designated, which their assault group was to burst into during the attack.

Painstaking work is going on. The artillerymen make sure of their instructions and then leave one after the other. They proceed into the very heart of the fighting some fifty yards away from the Germans; from there, finding themselves together with the infantry commanders, they observe each explosion by direct sight, and correct the fire of their guns.

Fourteen hours, forty-five minutes. Fifteen minutes are left until the opening of the fire. Colonel K. orders the telephone operator to call the commanders in turn. He checks by phone the readiness of the infantry and urges them to hurry. The commanders in turn report to him on their state of preparedness. They are already sitting at their observation posts, and the breath of the approaching battle rushing along the wires is felt more and more acutely in the Staff room.

Five minutes are left before the battle begins. We are coming out from the Staff room and begin to ascend the creaking stairs with the broken-down balustrade to the third floor when the deafening crash of the artillery salvoes is heard at the back, followed by the dull explosions of the heavy shells, with a double and triple echo rolling over the town.

KONSTANTIN SIMONOV

On the third floor several men have crowded together at the stereoscopic telescope which has been put out directly from the window. Major Kozlov, a still very young, beardless youth, watches the explosions through the stereoscopic telescope. Others watch impatiently through binoculars. Black columns of smoke begin to rise up more and more often above the center of the town. It is crowded in the room. The major sits in front of the stereoscopic telescope in an elegant woven chair. In the room there are the usual traditional Madonna and crucifix and broken window glass, and at the same time carpets hanging peacefully on the wall, bookcases, a couch heaped with embroidered cushions, and a table in the corner on which, for God knows how long, a dinner has been left uneaten by the owners. I approach the bookcase and select several books. It is interesting to conjecture who lived here. There is a history of Ancient Greece in the Polish language, a whole shelf of books by Mickiewicz in leather bindings, heaps of Lvov newspapers. I enquire as to how long the inhabitants have disappeared from here. "They haven't left at all," I am told. "This evening the old lady owner—the wife of a professor—has come around. They are camping out in the village."

"And what did she come for?"

"Well, just like that—she looked at the broken windows and frames, cried a bit, and then asked if she could save what was left. So we said, 'If the German doesn't lob a shell in here, it will stay whole.' She went back to the village again."

Not wanting to be in the way we first climbed up to the attic and then onto the roof. There was no stereoscopic telescope up there, to be sure, but everything could be seen directly and perhaps even better than from below. My guide points to a building where the Germans are entrenched. They are at present being fired at. Fountains of earth rise up all around, and it can even be clearly seen

THE SIEGE OF TERNOPOL

how fragments of the walls fly up into the sky and come down again in a fan shape. In two or three places I can see some red spots on the roofs of buildings.

"What's that?" I asked. My guide passes the binoculars to me. I look through them and still do not understand. Large red lumps, looking like crumpled sheets, lie directly on the roofs. "Those are their parachutes," my guide says. "There!" He takes a piece of red cloth from his pocket. "This is what they're made of. I have torn this off a parachute. Every night they drop parachutes with shells and cartridges tied to them, but during the last few days the circle has narrowed down so much that only three quarters drop our way, and one quarter drop on their own men, and some get stuck on the roofs. Try getting one of them—under our fire!"

The artillery bombardment continues. Now the German artillery replies, but its bursts are drowned among the solid boom of our guns. I ask whether we could find one of the local inhabitants.

"Well, of course, we will find some," my guide says. "There, they live in that building."

We come down from the roof. Only one room in the building opposite has remained whole—in it two Red Army men of the quartermaster's platoon have settled there at the window, one of whom, after sitting down comfortably in the corner of the window, is repairing someone's boots. A still-young woman with traces of fading beauty is washing children's linen in a large basin. A decrepit old man, shrinking from cold, is sitting near the cold stove while a small boy on the couch is gnawing a bread crust, dipping it into granulated sugar, a gift from the soldiers.

The woman replies to my questions. Her name is Magdalina Zadoraiko. Her husband was killed by a German shell a week ago, but she did not leave here, she only moved from the room where her husband was killed to this one, someone else's room. Her husband's name was Dmitri. He worked on the railroad. The son's name is Liubomir. He is two-and-a-half years old. The woman falls silent and wipes her eyes with the corner of her apron while Liubomir Dmitrievich, who fortunately still has little understanding of life, sits quietly on the couch, chews bread and melancholically passes his small fingers over the strings of a mandolin lying next to him on the ottoman. The mandolin twangs plaintively.

I ask the old man sitting near the stove, "Is this your grandson?" But the old man says that he is a stranger, he is Semyon Chubaty. His house was smashed, the Germans killed both his sons, and he is eighty-four years old and has nowhere to go, so he went to his neighbors —Zadoraiko—and sits at their place.

The glass panes begin to shake in the room, and the thunder of heavy explosions is heard. The woman starts, is petrified for a moment, then rushes to the child.

"They have come in planes to drop bombs again," one of the soldiers says quietly, leaning out of the window.

"Perhaps one should go to the basement?" the woman says, still not letting Liubomir out of her arms.

During this time, having apparently made a second run, the German planes drop a second series of bombs. The building shakes as the bombs explode somewhere close by. The woman runs to the basement, clutching the child to her breast. Old Chubaty limps after her.

We come out into the street and watch, standing under cover of a wall. The planes make a third run, this time dropping the bombs far from us, and then they leave. The drone of their engines has scarcely faded away when the woman with Liubomir in her arms reappears from the basement. "Have they gone away?" she asks.

"They have."

"I shall go back to the room," she says, "otherwise the child will catch cold. He has already become sick in the basement."

THE SIEGE OF TERNOPOL

"Would you like to see what the basements here are like?" the guide asks me. We descend to the basement and inspect it. The stairs leading down to it have at least fifteen steps and I discover that the basement is very deep and is partitioned off into separate compartments. "There, you see, the building is small and not much to look at, but what a basement! And it's like this everywhere in town. You may have already taken the building, but then the basement is a whole other matter. You can smash all the upper stories of a building but the Germans will still be sitting safe and sound in the basement."

We return to the Staff room. The Colonel questions the infantry commanders regarding the results of the work of the artillery. Almost all give the same answer: "The artillery is hitting wonderfully."

"Wonderfully?" the colonel repeats, and smiles at Lieutenant-Colonel Burnasian. "Well, if the artillerymen work wonderfully for you, then you must be ready to do likewise so that they can also say 'wonderful!' about you."

The Colonel makes haste to question everybody. The time for the assault is approaching.

"There, there," he growls caressingly into the mouthpiece to the telephone operator. "Girl, why are you taking so long? Come on, come on, connect faster!"

There are eight minutes to go. In three minutes there will be a common salvo by the entire artillery. "We shall tighten all the strings at once and fire a salvo," says Burnasian. "We shall report on the completion of the task with fire."

I hurry to the observation post again, reaching the roof at the very moment when the fiery onslaught begins. Dozens of gun barrels roar at the back. There is a solid sea of smoke above the town, and although the buildings at which the artillery is presently firing are only within 600 to 700 yards, they cannot be seen. A solid blanket of smoke hangs above them, and only the long tongues of flames from the newly started fires pierce it at five or six places. And then suddenly two white flocks of frightened domestic pigeons fly up above the roofs of the nearest buildings.

The artillery onslaught falls silent after five or six minutes, and fierce machine gun fire breaks out over the whole town, accompanied here and there by artillery shots. But the shells no longer fly above our heads, the artillery now fires pointblank from sixty, forty, twenty yards. The artillerists bring the guns up by hand and strike at the targets. The assault begins.

We return to the Staff room again. Reports of the course of the assault now begin to come in every half hour. Soon it is reported that another building—this time a large substantial one—a school, has been captured.

"Every soldier knows his building now," says the Colonel, tearing himself away from the telephone. "His building is not the one where he was before the assault, his building is now the one which he has to take."

It begins to get dark. One more building has been taken. The Colonel telephones the commanders who are directly in the field of battle, and demands that every effort be made to proceed more decisively. There is a telephone call from the colonel's immediate superior. He reports that matters are proceeding much more successfully in the neighborhood of K., Colonel Dergachov, who has already taken some ten buildings by this time.

"All right!" the colonel says. "All right!" and he repeats again, "All right!" He puts down the receiver and immediately asks the telephone operator to call all commanders in turn. Telephone calls and reports from the commanders begin again. After fifty minutes a report arrives that the Germans have retaken one of the captured buildings. The Colonel sends a Staff officer to ascertain the facts and to reestablish the position in the building. After a few minutes there is a new report. It turns out that the first report was false. A rare conjuncture has come

THE SIEGE OF TERNOPOL

about: the building has not been ceded to the Germans, but they are still in it. On the first floor are our sub-machine gunners and signallers who, in the very beginning had reported over the telephone that we had captured the building, our men are also on the third floor, having rushed up there in the force of the attack. But the Germans still remained on the second, the central floor. Now, however, they are being flushed out under a shower of grenades. After a few more minutes it is reported that the building has finally been captured. It is dark now and self-propelled guns rumble along the streets past us on their way to support the assault groups which are attacking one of the main points of German entrenchment—the jail.

Several minutes pass, and we hear the dull explosions of the shells from the self-propelled guns which signifies the beginning of the storming of the jail.

Night falls. The battle continues. Nineteen buildings have now been taken by the storming divisions. Obviously a few more should fall during the night. Machine-gun fire merges with the bursting of grenades and the firing from guns, and above all this din is the even drone of German aircraft above the town. The entire sky is filled with multi-colored bursts from anti-aircraft machine guns and the yellow flashes of explosions.

Day one of this latest attack is coming to an end. The next day will begin within a few hours, but the battle for Ternopol continues. It goes on without interruption from day into night and from night into day, but the ring around the Germans is continuously contracting slowly and surely, in spite of the desperate resistance of the enemy. And I believe that by the time this dispatch reaches Moscow the battle will conclude with the capture of Ternopol, and that one of the most difficult and at the same time heroic pages in the history of the war will be turned over and will recede into the past.

April 16, 1944

Ilya Ehrenburg

JULY 23, 1944

I have spent two weeks with the advancing troops in Belorussia and Lithuania. The time is past when episodes described in haste by war correspondents will satisfy us, but the time for the epic tale when artistic details will create something whole has not yet arrived. I would like to tell about the main thing. The whole world asks itself: what has happened during the last few weeks? For only recently the Germans were halfway between Orsha and Smolensk, while now the Red Army is beyond the Neman, and inspired by sorrow, anger, and hope, it hurries on to the very borders of Germany.

In a suburb of Vilnius the Cemetery of Roses was an assembly point for prisoners-of-war. It was raining and the excessively splendid red roses had shed their petals. Partisans stood at the gates—a light-haired Lithuanian peasant and a dark-skinned young girl, a Jewess, a student of Vilnyus University. Every ten minutes new German prisoners were brought in, gazing about them with dull uncomprehending eyes. The battle did not fall silent: the fight was still going on for buildings and for streets in the center of the city. The German prisoners-of-war sat on old graves among marble tombstones and unruly tall grass. One of them, Captain Mueller, was speaking dejectedly to me: "What happened? Three years ago we were marching east as if you did not exist. We did not want to notice you, and we won victories. Now we have changed parts: you are marching west not noticing us. And I ask myself: do we exist? . ." He muttered something to himself for a long time in the rain. Suddenly a sharp, unbearable sound was heard: a crow which had been wounded somewhere in a nearby street and which had managed to fly as far as the Cemetery of Roses, fell dying at the feet of the conqueror.

The next day the summer rain gave way to autumn rain. It was very good. I walked through the city to the western outskirts. Mortar bombs were still exploding near the Skrev infirmary: the last groups of Germans were endeavoring to defend themselves in a small forest. Buildings were on fire. The bodies of slain inhabitants were lying about on the sidewalks. I can remember a dead old man, he had his hand clutched around a stick. Then we saw corpses of Germans, abandoned motor vehicles with goods and chattels, champagne and delicacies, revolvers and moustache bands, iron crosses and jars of cold cream for softening the skin.

We proceeded to the center of the city and its unusual beauty amazed me: the ancient castle, churches in the baroque style, hills, and old shade trees; old women praying at the Ostra Brama and young partisans with grenades; narrow medieval streets, reminiscent of Cracow, Vienna, and Paris, streets of writers, and the house where Mickiewicz was born; the bent, mincing saints of the churches

JULY 23, 1944

of Kasimir and Anna and the memorial tablet on the Russian Orthodox cathedral, reminding one that here, in the city of Vilynus, the emperor Peter the Great had attended service in 1705 celebrating the victory over Karl XII; the inns where Napoleon's grenadiers stayed; the beauty of the women and the melodious language—the extreme west of our State.

Now the soldiers went into attack. I saw bronze medals with green ribbons on soldiers' chests: these were Stalingraders. They had performed the march from the Volga to the Dnieper, and they had now reached the Vilia and each one of them knew that he was going across the Neman to the Spree. This is not an episode, this is not even a chapter; this is the solemn beginning of the epilogue.

I shall tell about yet another meeting so that the mightiness of the events which are taking place will become clearer. Wishing to justify himself, Hitler tells the Germans that Normandy interests him far more than Belorussia or Lithuania. But then German paratroopers began to pour down into a forest near Vilnyus. The spectacle is reminiscent of a caricature of the summer of 1941. I do not know whether Hitler had hoped to hold the city with the help of these soldiers? Something else is of interest: the paratroopers who were soldiers of the 2nd Aerial Landing Division flew to Vilnyus on J-52's on July 8th from Normandy. I talked with captured paratrooper Albert Martins of the 6th Regiment of the above-mentioned division. Six days before his unfortunate landing he had been in Abbéville guarding the launching platforms of the notorious V-2 flying bombs aimed at London. If Hitler is forced to send soldiers from Normandy to Lithuania then this means that our offensive occupies him very, very much.

What was it, then, that happened on the central sector of our Front? It is a mistake to think that victory came easily to us, that in opposition to us were morally sapped

Germans. We not only encountered powerful defense structures but the enemy's elite troops. The Hitlerites had been discouraged by a series of defeats in the south. The German at the Donets remembered with terror the Don, at the Dnieper he remembered the Donets, and having reached the Bug burdened with somber memories he became easy to shift. But the Hitlerite soldiers defending Vitebsk and Orsha looked different: they succeeded repeatedly in beating off our attacks, and the myth of German invincibility, buried in the Ukraine a long time ago, still lived in Belorussia. On July 21st, two days before the offensive, Sergeant-Major Johann Stoltz wrote in his diary: "The Russians are obviously getting ready for something. Let them poke their nose in—it will be a beautiful extermination of all Soviet forces . . . ."

Everybody who has seen the German defense lines knows that Hitler has not been let down by the art of fortification construction: the Germans had enough time to construct their defense lines, and the Germans were not asleep. The German defense line went into depth for fifteen miles. These defense lines were defended by such strong units as, for example, the 78th Storm Division which has a reputation among the Germans of being insuperable.

The Germans expected a blow, but they did not know precisely when and where it would be struck. They thought that the offensive would start in southern Belorussia, and when the Germans began to transfer troops from the Pripyat to the Geresina, the First Belorussian Front moved. A reconnaissance by combat preceded the artillery preparation. The enemy moved all his forces to the Front line. The beast ran at the hunter, and the hunter did not miss—the force of the artillery fire was at the rate of 200–200 barrels per mile.

If the German Command had made haste after the first defeats to withdraw its troops west it could perhaps

JULY 23, 1944

have succeeded in saving part of its manpower. But the Hitlerites were once more undone by their arrogance and their lack of appreciation of our strength. They clung to the ground, and the ground swallowed them. Prisoner-of-war Lieutenant General Ochsner, commander of the 31st Panzer Division, told me with indignation that his division had not faltered under pressure—"its neighbors faltered." A friend of General Ochsner, General Drescher, commander of the 267th Panzer Division, told his Staff officers, "We have been let down by the other divisions." Hans nods at Karl, and Karl nods at Fritz. In the meantime our units rapidly advanced west. When all German defense lines had been overcome, cavalry and major tank formations were put into action through the neat breach. The tank men of General Rodmistrov, General Budeny, and General Obukhov came out into the open space and rushed west.

One can defeat the enemy and pursue the enemy but, beaten and retreating, he can still gather his forces and fight back. Something different happened in Belorussia; the enemy was annihilated. The Hitlerites who were defending Vitebsk, Orsha, and Mohilev did not leave for the west: they remained on the ground or they sat in hundreds of prisoner camps near the Front, or they marched in anything but a triumphal manner through the streets of Moscow. Army General Chernyakhovsky, one of the youngest and most brilliant generals of the Red Army, a man who fights with inspiration, told me with justice: "This time we did not limit ourselves to liberating the territory and wiping out the enemy's equipment, we destroyed his entire manpower." I would like to remind you that General Chernyakhovsky beat the Germans both at Voronezh and at the Dnieper; he has a basis for comparisons. In vain do Hitler's communiqués speak about withdrawal and the clearing of cities—the German divisions which fought on the Central Front no longer exist. The troops which tried to offer resistance in Vilnyus had never been in Belorussia—Hitler could see those troops from Belorussia only in his dreams. A few days after the beginning of the offensive the Germans lost command of their troops: dozens of crack divisions deteriorated into tens of thousands of roaming soldier who no longer defended this or that line, but only their own skin.

Ilya Ehrenburg

AUGUST 10, 1944

A correspondent of the Reuters News Agency reports from Granville of disorders in Saint-Père-sur-Mer; on August first a battle broke out there between supporters of collaboration and supporters of the Resistance. By evening the patriots gained the upper hand and arrested twenty-five collaborators. But then the Americans came and liberated eighteen of those arrested.

This small incident is of great interest: it makes one ponder the future of France. And who in the world can imagine the future, not knowing what France will be like?

None of the countries seized by Hitler has known such profound and organized treachery. Quisling and Mussert are vagabonds. In Poland the Hitlerites could not even find a Quisling. But in France the German Gauleiters are people who are well known to everyone. It was not a petty thief who stood at the head of the Vichy enterprise, but a marshal of France. If in other countries we can speak about individual betrayal, about the dark past of this or that rogue, then in France we must acknowledge the existence of group betrayal. The ruling circles of France's prewar society turned out to be partly rotten. The Germans found traitors available wholesale among smart dealers, generals, journalists, and politicians. In Norway it is possible to hand over a case of treason to an ordinary criminal prosecutor. In France it will be necessary for the nation to deal with treason: the difference is not a quantitative one. If the Duchess of Luxembourg turned out to be more implacable than the President of the French Republic, if Vichy has become a common noun to designate legalized treason, then we have the right to speak of gangrene. Pétain is more dangerous than Laval, and the "peacemakers" in Algiers, New York, or London are more dangerous than Pétain. Vichy is not only in Vichy. Vichy is tolerance toward treason and intolerance toward the nation, it is a return to the period of the "drôle de guerre," an attempt to cover up all traces and to burn the evidence.

For even the German generals who are rebelling against Hitler endeavor to come out dry from the river. These are people of the same breed as the Vichy rats who try to insure themselves by friendship with the niece of a cousin of a Gaullist or with some American tourist.

It is not possible to clean up Europe without cleaning up one's own house. People who want to hinder the clean-up in France display an inhuman indulgence in respect of the German child-killers. This is logical: he who shows mercy to the hangman's lackey will not hurt the hangman himself.

Unparalleled suffering fell to the lot of the French nation. It was forced to fight unarmed or badly armed, it was forced to argue every hour for its right to exist. It proved itself to be a hero. The partisans' exploits have overshadowed in the consciousness of mankind the black

AUGUST 10, 1944

summer of 1940, the blood of the hostages, the heroism of young men and girls, the bravery of the workers, priests, professors, housewives, peasants, the heroism of the whole nation. The traitors and half-traitors do not only blacken the name of France, they contribute towards a disparagement of her national independence. Saint-Père-sur-Mer without twenty-five local Lavals is the Commune of a free and irreconcilable France. The same Saint-Père-sur-Mer with twenty-five Lavals is something like a miniature Rome, in the best case a colony for those undergoing correction, an evidence of lack of moral and political independence.

In order for France to regain her greatness anew, she must finish with the traitors and with those who, under the mask of tolerance, endeavor to save a living corpse—with the people of collaboration, with the friends of Vichy. As strange as it may seem, Pétain is evidently more stable than the Fuehrer: Hitler has already been overthrown morally, soon he will also be physically destroyed. But one still argues about Pétain and the spirit of Pétain.

A few days ago two major "death factories" have been discovered in which the Germans have annihilated millions of condemned: in Beljec near Rava-Russkaya, and in Lublin. Among those destroyed in these death factories were quite a number of Frenchman. Some of them were brought in as "Communists"—supporters and participants of the Resistance—others were brought in as Jews. French workers from Lille, students from Nancy, young girls from Paris and Lyons, Jews from the Provence; after living there for many centuries and not being different from other Frenchmen either by appearance or accent, or even by their thoughts and feelings, they had been brought to Beljec or to Lublin. In Beljec the killing was done by electric current, in Lublin by gas. The dead were burned...

ILYA EHRENBURG

When the liberation of France is achieved we will find out how many defenseless people the Fascists have tortured to death. Let us say in advance that not only Hitler killed them, but the Hitlerites. Let us say that not only the Fascists but all the supporters of collaboration are involved in the death of innocents. The manufacturer who supplied rifles, cloth, and preserves to the Germans is a lackey of the executioner and his hands are steeped in French blood. France has a conscience, and this conscience is revolted. In Europe it was once said that one could see a beacon—the Torch of Liberty—when entering the Port of New York. Let the Americans now see that in the night of France a bright light is burning—hatred and anger have made the heart of France red hot. The land of liberty, the land of 'Ninety-Three—this is not only what they think. This is not only the bright sky of the Île de France, the verdure of the Limousin and the bonnets of the Bretons, and this is least of all the perfumery of Grasse or the night establishments of Montmartre. It is the Phrygian cap, it is the thirst for justice, and it is those furrows of cracked earth, resembling the lips of the parched, which demand the blood of the traitors.

Konstantin Simonov

EXTERMINATION CAMP

That which I am about to write of is too immense and too frightening to be comprehended in its entirety. There is no doubt that jurists, physicians, historians, and politicians will be examining this frightening case for a long time. In future, as a result of the most detailed investigations, the full scope and myriad details of the crime against humanity committed by the Germans will become clear. At present I am far from knowing all the facts and figures; I talked perhaps only with a hundredth part of the witnesses, and saw perhaps only one-tenth of the full traces of the crime. But a man who has seen this is not in a position to be silent, not in a position to wait. I would like to tell precisely now, today, about the first uncovered traces of the crime, about what I heard in these days, and about what I saw with my own eyes.

1. At the end of 1940 several officers of the SS forces and

surveyors with tape measures appeared on an immense vacant site extending to the right of the Chelm Highway within two miles of Lublin. Within a few days a huge area which took up almost the whole of the vacant site of twenty-five square kilometers had been measured out. Sixteen huge squares had been marked out on the plans prepared at the Gestapo of this area of land, and in each of these squares there were twenty equal rectangles. The rectangles represented barracks, the squares represented so-called fields or sectors surrounded on all sides with barbed wire. At the top on the first plan was the title, which later disappeared: Camp Dachau No. 2. The Gestapo undertook the construction of a concentration camp on an unheard-of scale, representing an exact copy of the infamous Dachau camp in Germany, but exceeding it several times in size.

Construction began in the winter of 1941. In the beginning a number of Polish civil engineers and workers were engaged in it, these were soon joined, as the main labor force, by Polish and Jewish prisoners-of-war captured during the German-Polish war of 1939; and from about August, 1941, the first thousand Russian prisoners-of-war and civilians were settled as labor force in the camp under construction. By this time the first field, or as the Germans called it, the first "block," had been half covered with buildings in the camp, and ten barracks had already been built. The construction continued throughout all of the autumn of 1941 and the winter of 1942.

The number of persons engaged in construction gradually increased. The Russians were soon followed by large groups of political prisoners, Czechs and Poles, and of those transferred from other camps where they had been imprisoned since 1933. In the autumn of 1941 the first 2,000 Jews were transferred here from the Lublin ghetto. Following them, 700 Poles arrived in December, 1941, from the Lublin castle. Then 400 Polish peasants who had

EXTERMINATION CAMP

not paid taxes to the German Government on time found themselves in the camp. In April, 1942, transports with 12,000 persons arrived at the camp from Slovakia—these were Jews and political prisoners. New transports from Czechoslovakia, Austria, and Germany arrived throughout the whole of May. The construction of the camp proceeded at the most intensive tempo, and by May they had completed the first, second, third, and fourth barracks, calculated for about forty thousand places.

May, 1942, can be considered as the end of the first stage in the history of the camp. This was the period of feverish building activity. Now that barracks for 40,000 persons had been completed, and principal, subsidiary, and special premises had been built, and now that all had been surrounded by two rows of largely barbed wire, the Gestapo considered that the camp was ready to come into operation. It continued to expand and would have continued to expand *ad infinitum* if it had not been for our troops capturing Lublin, but the construction tempo was already different. From May, 1942 on, finishing work took place in the camp, and gradually, without haste, all kinds of improvements were added. In May, 1942, this camp, which was named in official papers the "Lublin Concentration Camp of SS Forces," began to be called in unofficial documents, letters, notes, and verbally the *Vernichtungs Lager*, which in Russian means "Extermination Camp."

The Germans had built within three miles of Lublin on a vacant site along the Chelm Highway the greatest death complex in Europe, whose main and single purpose was the simplest, most utilitarian and fastest extermination of the largest number of prisoners-of-war and political prisoners. The organization of the camp was original in all respects, and if in other German institutions of death one could find separately all the elements comprised within the Lublin extermination camp, then these terrible products of German barbarism have nowhere appeared before our eyes in such complete and, so to speak, complex form. We know of such places as Sobibor and Beljec, where trains brought people condemned to death along narrow-gauge tracks to an empty field located in a remote corner, where they were shot and burned. We know of such camps as Dachau, Oswiecim, or the *Grosslazarett* in Slavut, where the civilian prisoners and prisoners-of-war were gradually killed off by beatings, starvation, and disease. But in the Lublin extermination camp there was a combination of all these things. Here in the barracks lived tens of thousands of prisoners who continuously built and carried out additions and alterations to their prison. Here there were thousands of prisoners-of-war who, beginning with the autumn of 1942, were not admitted to the work, and since they were receiving rations which were meager even compared with those of the civilian prisoners, they died with terrible speed from hunger and disease.

Here there were fields of death with bonfires and crematorium ovens, where thousands and tens of thousands of persons were exterminated after being held in the camp for only a few hours or days, depending on the size of the team required for searching and complete undressing. Here there were the ordinary type "murder buses," mobile gas chambers on motor vehicles, as well as solidly constructed casemates for asphyxiation by means of "cyclon" gas. Here the burning was carried out by the Indian method in the most primitive manner: a row of logs, a row of corpses, a row of logs, a row of corpses. Here the burning was carried out in cremation ovens of a primitive type, made in the form of large iron kettles, and here the burning was also done in a specially constructed crematorium perfected for blitz-cremation. Here one gunned down people in ditches and killed them by blows of iron bars, fracturing the jugular vertebrae, or one caused people to be drowned in a pool, or one carried out hangings by various methods, beginning with ordinary

EXTERMINATION CAMP

gallows with a crossbar, to perfected portable gallows with a pulley system and a fly-wheel. This was a factory of death in which the number of daily deaths was regulated by two circumstances: firstly, by the number of persons received in the camp, and secondly, by the required labor force at this or the other stage of the endlessly continuing construction.

Final figures will be ascertained later. But some preliminary figures are already beginning to be revealed at present. The camp has been functioning for more than three years altogether. When the Red Army came to Lublin it found only several hundred Russians there. When we approached Kovel in the spring, the Germans, according to the testimony of witnesses, had evacuated from 12,000 to 16,000 prisoners. Even if the figure of 16,000 is adopted, there were less than 17,000 persons left in the camp at the end of its existence. Yet, the average number of prisoners present, according to the daily communiqués of the camp commandant's office, amounted in 1943 to 40,000 persons, fluctuating by several thousand one way or another. However, if one takes the total number of persons who had been received at the camp during somewhat more than three years, then it will become clear that between the last figure of 17,000 and the number of those brought to the camp, there will be a difference of many hundreds of thousands of persons. And this will correspond approximately to the number of persons exterminated in the camp, not counting those who went through it directly to their death without even being registered as prisoners. All these figures have been taken from the official books of the camp commandant's office throughout each year of the camp's existence.

In describing the reception of prisoners during the original construction of the camp, I had stopped at May, 1942. During April and May, 1942, mass batches of Jews from the Lublin and neighboring ghettos began to arrive at the camp. During the summer another 18,000 persons came from Czechoslovakia. In July, 1942, there arrived the first batch of Poles accused of partisan activity, consisting of 1,500 persons. Another large batch of political prisoners arrived during the same month from Germany. In December, 1942, several thousand Jews and Greeks arrived from the Oswiecim camp near Cracow. On January 17, 1943, 1,500 male and 400 female Poles were brought from Warsaw; on February 2nd, 950 Poles arrived from Lvov, on February 4th, 4,000 Poles and Ukrainians arrived from Taloma and Ternopol. In May, 1943, a batch of 60,000 arrived from the Warsaw ghetto. The whole of the summer and autumn of 1943 transports from all the main German camps—Sachsenhausen, Dachau, Flossenberg, Nuengamme, Grossenrosen, and Buchenwald—arrived within intervals of a few days. None of these batches contained less than a thousand persons. The place the newcomers arrived from could be discerned immediately, not only by their speech but also by their external appearance: each camp had its own imprint. For example, it was the custom in Oswiecim to shave all prisoners' hair close to the skin, including the women, and not to hang numbers on their necks as they did everywhere else, but to brand them on the arm. From Buchenwald came people who could hardly bear the sunlight: in a department of that camp, named Dora, there existed beneath the rocks an underground factory in which the notorious German flying rockets "V-1" were produced. Those working there were without exception Slavs, mainly Poles and Russians. They worked without ever coming out into the daylight, and after half a year of underground work their sight deteriorated so much that they were immediately sent in batches to the extermination camp in Lublin.

I have mentioned only some figures and some camps, not in order to present a real computation of the figures of those who perished, but so that one could have an idea

EXTERMINATION CAMP

of at least part of the picture. A few words must also be said regarding the national composition of the persons who found themselves in the camp. A large number of those who perished were Poles. Here were the hostages, real and alleged partisans, and the relatives of partisans, and a huge number of peasants, in particular those who had been evicted from the districts where German colonization was taking place. Following the Poles came a huge number of exterminated Russians and Ukrainians. Just as large was the number of the exterminated Jews brought to the camp practically from all countries of Europe, beginning with Poland and finishing with Holland. Further on there are impressive figures, each exceeding several thousand. These comprise the French, Italians, Dutch, and Greek. Smaller, but nevertheless impressive, figures fall to the Belgians, Serbs, Croats, Hungarians, Spaniards (the last-mentioned, evidently from among the Republicans apprehended in France). In addition, among the documents of those who perished there were found those which belonged to different people of the most diverse nations—Norwegians, Swiss, Turks, and even Chinese. In one of the rooms of the camp office, the floor of which was completely buried under documents, passports, and certificates of those killed, I found within ten minutes, by picking up these papers at random, documents of representatives of almost every European nation. There was the passport of Sofya Yakovlevna Dusevich from the village of Konstantinovka of the Kiev region, a Ukrainian, a worker born in 1917. There was a document with the stamp "République Française" of Eugène Duramé, a Frenchman, a metalworker, born in Le Havre on the 22nd of September, 1888. There was a certificate issued by the Public School of Banja-Luke to Ralo Junic, who finished school in 1937, of Moslem faith, with marks *dobar*, i.e., "good" for "morale, natural science, and history." There was a passport issued in Croatia to Yatiranovic, who was born in Zagreb and who had received this document on January 2, 1941. There was the passport of Jakob Borgardt, who was born in Rotterdam on November 10, 1918. There was a document of Eduard Alfred Sack, born in Milan in 1914 at 29 Via Plimo "height 175c., solidly built, no special features." There was Certificate No. 8544 issued to Savaranti, a Greek from the island of Crete. There was the German passport of Ferdimand Litmann, a civil engineer from Berlin, born on August 19, 1872. There was the workbook with the stamp of the "Polish General-Governorship," belonging to Zigmund Remak, a Pole, a worker, born on March 20, 1924, in Cracow. There was a Chinese document, with a photograph and hieroglyphs which I could not decipher. There were documents here drenched in blood and washed out by water, torn in two and trampled on. This terrible mountain of documents was a sepulchral mound of the whole of Europe, narrowed down to the confines of one room.

It is hard to even envisage what nightmarish details will be revealed by the detailed examination of these documents and the questioning of countless witnesses. And how many terrible revelations, pertaining to the fate of the most diverse persons from the most diverse nooks of Europe will come to light after all the material has been dug up and all witnesses questioned.

2. If you proceed along the Chelm Highway the outline of a whole town will appear to the right of it within only some three hundred yards: hundreds of low grey roofs, arranged in regular rows and divided by wire. This is a large town in which tens of thousands of people can live. You swing off the highway and drive through the gates past the barbed wire. Rows of neat houses with neat little front gardens, with seats and benches knocked together from birch sticks. These are the dwellings of the SS guard and the administration. Here is also the *Soldatenheim*, a specially constructed small building in which the brothel

serving the guard is situated. The women for it were taken solely from among the prisoners, and as soon as one of them became pregnant she was exterminated.

Further on are the chambers where the clothing removed from the prisoners was disinfected. Pipes had been built into the ceiling through which the disinfecting agent was poured. Then the pipes were sealed, the doors were hermetically closed and the disinfecting carried out. And this is really like that: the walls of the building, put together out of boards, and the doors which were not lined with iron—all this was built far too insubstantially for carrying out anything else here than the disinfecting of clothing.

But now we open the next door and we come into the second disinfection chamber, which is built according to quite a different principle. This is a square room, slightly more than six feet high and about 18 x 18 feet in area. The walls, the ceiling, the floor—everything—consists of solid grey concrete. There is not even a trace of the shelves for clothing which we saw in the previous room, everything here is bare and empty. A single large steel door hermetically closes the entrance to this room, which is locked from the outside by impressive steel shackles. There are three openings within the walls of this concrete crypt; two of these are for pipes coming from outside and taken through to the inside. The third opening is a peep-hole consisting of a small square window, screened by a thick, close-knit steel grille, built from inside into the concrete. Thick glazing is built in from the outside in such a manner that it cannot be reached through the grille.

From where does one look in through the peep-hole? To answer this question let us open the door and go from the chamber to the outside. Another small concrete chamber into which the peep-hole gives has been built to adjoin the former. There is electric light in this small chamber, and a switch has been provided here. From here the whole interior of the large chamber can be seen through the peep-hole. Also here on the floor are several round, hermetically sealed cans, on which is written "Cyclon," and further on, in small type: "for special use in eastern regions." It was the contents of these cans which were poured through a pipe into that adjoining chamber when it was filled with people.

The people were naked, they were placed close together, and they did not take up too much room. More than 250 persons were squeezed into 40 square yards. They were pushed in there, the steel door was closed behind them, the edges of the door were coated with clay to effect a greater hermetic seal, and a special crew, having donned gas masks, poured Cyclon from these round cans into the chamber through the pipes. These were small, blue, innocent-looking crystals which, when combined with oxygen, began immediately to give off poisonous substances which acted simultaneously on all nerve centers of the human body. Cyclon was poured through the pipes, the SS man in charge of asphyxiation operated the switch, the chamber was lit up, and through the peep-hole he watched the process of asphyxiation which lasted from two to ten minutes. He could see everything through the peep-hole, the terrible faces of the dying and the gradual action of the gas. The peep-hole had been arranged exactly at the level of the human body, so that when people died the observer did not have to look down; the dying did not fall, for the chamber was so packed that the dead still remained standing.

Let us walk on for a few more hundred paces. We came next to an empty site. Judging by various indications there had previously been a structure here. Yes, until last autumn the crematorium had stood here. In autumn the construction of another one was completed, a perfected one, to which we shall proceed, and the first mentioned one which had been primatively constructed, was demol-

EXTERMINATION CAMP

ished. It had an inadequate capacity, being much smaller than the well-thought-out, newly perfected gas chamber. That crematorium was simply a large structure with a cement floor in which two huge iron kettles had been installed on brick footings laid lengthwise. The burning in these ovens took place too slowly. It is true that one did not expect a complete transformation of the corpses into ashes here, but even the disintegration of the corpse into bones reduced to ashes, took at least two hours. Fourteen corpses were stacked simultaneously into both furnaces. Thus the capacity of the crematorium was not greater than 150 persons a day, while the gas chamber had a capacity of 300 persons a day, even, as it was expressed here, with one "gassing." Before the building of the new crematorium it was thus necessary on days of major exterminations to cart away a considerable number of corpses by truck from here to a field, situated behind the camp, and bury them there.

The fence consists of two rows of four-yard-high posts with wire, which is also curved down at the top in the form of a canopy. Both rows of posts are separated by a space of two yards within which a third row of wire runs diagonally from the top of one row of posts to the bottom of the other row. That row of wire has been installed on insulators and has been electrified; a current of lethal tension was conducted through it, excluding all possibility of escape.

Such an electrification system was not installed immediately. Originally there had been the same wire barriers in the camp, but they were not electrified. The transition to the electric system was the result of the following episode:

In May, 1942, a batch of Russian prisoners-of-war who had been dispatched near the camp to bury those shot in the Krembec forest, slaughtered seven German guards with their spades and escaped. Two of them were recaptured, the other fifteen hid. The 130 prisoners-of-war remaining in the camp (of 1,000 accommodated here in August, 1941, only 130 had remained alive), were then transferred to the block where the civilian prisoners were kept. One evening at the end of July, on seeing that they would perish here in any case, the Russian prisoners decided to escape. Several dozen prisoners stayed behind. After collecting all the blankets and placing five of them one on top of the other the prisoners formed bridges across the barbed wire with these blankets and escaped. The night was dark, only four of them were shot, the others succeeded in hiding. The fifty remaining persons were led into the yard immediately after the escape—those who had been afraid to try to escape—they were laid on the ground and shot with sub-machine guns. But the Germans did not limit themselves to this retribution. The fact of a successful escape remained a fact, and the Germans immediately carried out the electrification of four out of five blocks. Only one block remained unelectrified; women were kept in it, and it was difficult to expect an escape from them.

Before us is a new subsidiary block. It is less painstakingly enclosed than the residential blocks. Incidentally, there is nothing surprising in this: the dead or half dead, or those intended for killing, arrived here under a reinforced guard. Here, behind this wire, no one except the SS men and the crematorium crew ever survived for longer than one hour. In the middle of an empty field we see a tall, square chimney with a long, low brick rectangle adjoining it. This is the crematorium. It has survived in all its original completeness.

Somewhat further on are the remains of a large brick structure. During the few hours which the command of the camp had between the news about the break in the defense line and the arrival of our units, the Germans attempted to wipe out all traces of the concentration camp.

EXTERMINATION CAMP

They did not manage to blow up the crematorium, but they set fire to the subsidiary premises. In spite of that, the traces did not become any less evident. The terrible smell of corpses still fills the air.

The subsidiary premises of the crematorium consist of three main chambers. One chamber is packed with the half-burnt remains of clothing. This is the clothing from the last batch of those who perished, and which has not been removed from here yet. Only part of the wall has survived in the adjacent chamber. Several pipes of a smaller diameter than in the gas chamber which we had seen earlier have been cemented into this wall. This is also a gas chamber, for asphyxiation was also carried out here (it has not been ascertained yet whether by Cyclon or by some other gas). When a particularly large number were to be exterminated, too large a number to fit into the principal gas chamber, some of the victims were brought here and "gassed" immediately next to the crematorium. The third, the largest chamber, was evidently intended for the stacking of corpses awaiting their turn to be burned to ashes. The whole floor is covered with skeletons, skulls and bones half turned to ashes. This is not from regular cremation, but the result of the Germans' setting fire to the premises to hide the evidence of what went on here. There are many skeletons—possibly dozens, possibly hundreds—it is hard to say, for it is impossible to make a count of this mash of bones half turned to ashes, with scraps of half-burnt flesh still clinging to them.

Now we have to walk only a few paces in order to get across to the crematorium proper. This consists of a large rectangle, constructed of bricks of the highest fire-resistant material. Five large furnaces which can be hermetically closed by small, cast-iron doors, are situated one next to the other in this brick wall. The small round doors are at present open. The deep furnaces are partly filled with half-burnt vertebrae and human ashes. In front of the furnaces in the area in front of each fire box lie skeletons half-consumed by fire which had been prepared by the Germans for cremation. In front of three furnaces the skeletons are mostly those of men and women, in front of the other two furnaces the skeletons are those of children, about ten to twelve years old, judging from the size. There are five or six skeletons in front of each furnace. This corresponds to its capacity; six corpses should be stacked simultaneously into each furnace. If the sixth corpse could not be packed in, the crematorium crew chopped off the part of the body which could not be packed in—an arm, a leg, a head—and then the small doors were hermetically closed.

There are altogether five furnaces, as I said, and their capacity was very great. The crematorium was designed for the burning of corpses within forty-five minutes. But the Germans gradually learned to speed up this work and doubled the capacity by increasing the temperature: they strove to achieve cremation within twenty-five minutes or even less. Experts have already inspected the lining of which the fire boxes of the crematorium had been built, and by its deformation and regeneration have discovered that the temperature within them must have been higher than 1,500 degrees. The cast-iron sliders, which had also undergone deformation and melting, serve as additional proof. If one assumes that each batch of corpses took an average of half an hour to cremate, and if one adds to this the general testimony that, beginning from the autumn of 1943, the chimneys of the crematorium smoked day and night, and that the crematorium, like a blast furnace, did not stop for a single minute—then the figure for the crematorium's capacity emerges as approximately 1,400 corpses per day.

The necessity for building the crematorium was to a large extent provoked by the story of the Katyn affair. Afraid of further disclosures in the course of opening the

EXTERMINATION CAMP

pits where they had been burying the corpses of those killed, the Germans undertook, beginning with the autumn of 1943, colossal excavations in the territory of the Lublin camp. They were exhuming from an immense number of pits around the camp the half-decayed corpses of those who had been shot to death, and burned them in the crematorium in order to finally cover up the traces. The ashes and the decomposed bones from the furnaces of the crematorium were then poured back into the same pits from which the corpses had been exhumed. One such pit has already been excavated. An almost one-yard-thick layer of ashes has been discovered in it.

Behind the camp there is one more unfinished block. Here there are only brick foundations behind the barbed wire. The walls have not been put up yet; only one building has been completed in which no plank beds have been installed. No people lived in that barracks, but it has nevertheless become perhaps the most terrible witness of what was happening here, for this barracks, some hundred feet wide and hundred feet long, is filled for its entire length and width, from floor to ceiling, with the footwear of those who had been executed here in the course of three years. It is hard to say how many pairs of footwear there are here. Perhaps a million, perhaps even more. There is not enough room in the barracks for the shoes, they spill out from windows and doors. In one place their weight has fractured the wall, and part of it has collapsed under the mountains of footwear.

Everything is here: Russian soldiers' boots, Polish soldiers' shoes, men's boots, women's slippers, rubber galoshes, and what is the most terrible sight of all—tens of thousands of pairs of children's footwear: sandals, small slippers and shoes from ten-year-olds, from eight-year-olds, six-year-olds, one-year-olds. It is hard to imagine anything more terrible than this spectacle, this horrible silent testimony of the death of hundreds of thousands of men, women, and children. If one should pick one's way over the mountains of footwear and enter the right corner of the shed, one can immediately find the explanation for the existence of this monstrous store. Stocked separately here are thousands, tens of thousands of soles, vamps, and separately stored leather offcuts, for it is here where they took apart in one piece the soles, vamps, and heels which were still good. As everything else in the death camp, this store had been set up with a utilitarian purpose: nothing from those killed must be lost—neither the clothing, nor the footwear, nor the bones, nor the ashes.

The last department of the camp is in one of the large city buildings in Lublin, where in dozens of suites, dozens of large and small rooms, a huge, sorted stockpile of everything taken from those executed has been established. In one room we can see tens of thousands of women's dresses, in another tens of thousands of trousers, in a third tens of thousands of sets of underwear, in a fourth, thousands of women's handbags, in a fifth tens of thousands of sets of children's wear, in a sixth shaving gear, in a seventh caps and hats.

I talked to captured Germans who were made to file past the crematorium, past the pits with the corpses in them. They denied their part in all this. They said that it was not they who did that, but the SS. But when, later on, I was questioning one of the SS men who had been working in the camp, he maintained when speaking of the mass executions that this was not done by the SS but by the SD—that is, the Gestapo. The Gestapo men said that this was done by the SS men. I do not know which one of them did the burning, which one of them was simply killing, which one was removing shoes, and which one sorted out women's underwear and children's dresses—I do not know. But when I look at this store of clothing I think that the nation which has given birth to

EXTERMINATION CAMP

those who have done this will have to bear the responsibility and the curses for what has been done by its representatives.

3. I have related the history of the Lublin extermination camp, I have described its present appearance. Let us now dwell on the testimony of the various witnesses with whom I have spoken. Their testimony will comprise possibly only one-hundredth of the testimony which will in future become the material for a commission of investigation. I had occasion to speak to the Russian doctor Barychev, a prisoner-of-war—the chief doctor of the camp infirmary, and also with the doctor's assistant at the same infirmary, with civil engineers and workers who had been engaged in constructing the camp, with persons who had been in the camp as civilian prisoners and as prisoners-of-war as well as with SS men who had served in the camp's guard. Out of all these conversations the picture of the "extermination camp" arose before me.

The first premise from which the SS men who ruled over the camp set out was the following: all persons who found themselves in the camp, be they prisoners-of-war or civilian prisoners, be they Russians, Ukrainians, Poles, Belorussians, or Jews, Frenchman, Greeks, etc.—would, in any case, be exterminated sooner or later, they would never during their lifetime leave the precincts of this camp, and therefore they could not tell about what was going on there. This basic premise determined both the behavior of the guard and the methods of extermination used in the camp. The dead are silent and cannot talk, they cannot communicate any details, or confirm these details by documents. Consequently, there will be no proof in anybody's hands, and this, according to the Germans' reasoning, was the main thing.

Rumors about the camp as a whole, as an extermination camp could, of course, reach the surrounding population, but this did not worry the Germans. In Poland they felt as if they were at home; the "Polish General-Governorship" was for them a land conquered for good. Those who remained alive within its boundaries had to be in fear of the Germans in the first place, and the terrible rumors about the Lublin camp which circulated all over Poland even appeared desirable to the Germans. The cadaver odor which on days of particularly large exterminations penetrated into the environs and forced people even in Lublin to cover their faces with handkerchiefs only served to intimidate the local inhabitants. This gave to all of Poland an impression of the strength of German domination and of the terrors to which all those who risked resistance would be condemned. The column of smoke, standing for weeks and months above the tall chimney of the main crematorium, was visible from afar, and this did not embarrass the Germans. This frightening smoke was used for intimidation, just like the cadaver odor. Columns of thousands of people marched for all to see along the Chelm Highway, and after pouring into the gates of the Lublin camp never returned from there anymore—and this was to be a testimony of the strength of the Germans who could permit themselves everything they wished, and who would not have to be responsible to anybody.

I wish to begin my story with the most "humane" institution of the camp—the infirmary. Before being dispatched to the barracks, all those received at the camp were sent for twenty-one days to the quarantine and to the infirmary, in accordance with the strictest medical rules. This corresponded, without doubt, to medical requirements. Only one detail is left to be added to this: all prisoners-of-war who arrived here at quarantine were accommodated, by order of the camp Command, exclusively in barracks where persons with an overt form of tuberculosis were located. In each such barracks where there were up to two hundred patients with overt tuberculosis, up to two hundred more persons undergoing quarantine

EXTERMINATION CAMP

were also placed there under conditions of monstrous overcrowding. If one takes account of this small detail, then it will not be surprising that of the people who died in the camp from so-called "natural causes," from 70 to 80 percent died from tuberculosis.

The infirmary was essentially only part of the extermination camp. Within it the Germans had their methods of bringing about death, sometimes even faster than in the ordinary barracks. However, if one should speak about methods of bringing about death generally, then these were rather varied, and increased progressively as the camp became larger.

When the camp was first built the first place of mass extermination was a cabin built of boards, standing between two rows of barbed wire. A long squared beam passed underneath the ceiling of this cabin and on it there always hung eight belt loops from which all those who had become enfeebled were hanged. In the beginning there was not enough labor force in the camp and the SS men did not amuse themselves just in that way. They did not annihilate the healthy ones, they only hanged those who through hunger or sickness had become too weak to work. But prisoners-of-war were privileged—only civilian prisoners were hanged in this cabin built of boards. Batches of prisoners-of-war who had become enfeebled and unfit for work were taken beyond the bounds of the camp where they were shot. Prisoners-of-war were hanged only when a whole batch could not be collected and it was unprofitable to take one or two men into the forest. Then one or two prisoners-of-war were hanged together with civilian prisoners.

Soon the original primitive crematorium consisting of two furnaces, which has been mentioned earlier, was built. The gas chamber lagged behind, it was not finished as yet. During this period the following method became the main way of exterminating the sick and enfeebled! A small room with a very narrow and low entrance was added to the crematorium; the entrance was so low that a person squeezing through it had to bow his head. Two SS men stood on either side of the door, each holding a short, heavy rod. When the person stooped trying to go through the door, one SS man struck at the person's jugular vertebra with the iron rod. If the first one missed, the second one stood in for him. If, as a result of these blows the person was not dead but fell down in an unconscious state, then this was of no significance. The one who fell was considered dead and was put into the furnace of the crematorium. It must be said that the camp followed the general rule that anyone who fell to the ground and could not rise was considered dead. Emaciated persons were sometimes left for many hours in the cold to bring about death. To this should be added the so-called evening physical culture exercises, which consisted of forcing persons who were generally emaciated and exhausted by the day's work to run after the evening check-up in mud that came up to their knees, or in winter in snow, or in the summer's heat, around their residential block, the circumference of which was considerably more than a mile. The corpses lying along the whole length of the fence around the block were collected in the morning.

These were, so to speak, the ordinary, everyday methods of killing. But the beasts, who had already tasted human blood, were not content with ordinary methods. The death of their victims was not only a job to them, but also an amusement. We are not going to speak about the "amusements" customary to all German camps; that is, shooting at random among the prisoners from guard towers, or beating to death hundreds of starved persons who were hurling themselves at bones thrown to them. Let us mention only some of the amusements peculiar to the Lublin camp.

The first "witty jest" consisted in the following: one

of the SS men would pick on one of the prisoners, declaring that the prisoner was guilty of not observing camp rules and was therefore liable to be shot. The prisoner would be stood against a wall and the SS man would place his pistol against the prisoner's forehead. Expecting the shot, the latter would instinctively shut his eyes. Then the SS man would shoot into the air while another SS man who had approached the prisoner without being seen by him would hit him over the head with a thick club, causing the prisoner to fall down unconscious. When he came to after a few minutes and opened his eyes, the SS men would say to him, laughing: "You are in the Other World. You see, in the Other World there are also Germans! You cannot get away from them anywhere!" Since the prisoner, who would usually be covered with blood, would not have the strength to rise, he was considered condemned to death and, in the end, after being the object of some fun, he would be shot.

"Jest" No. 2 was connected with a large pool situated in one of the barracks of the camp. The prisoner, who would be accused of committing an offense, would be undressed and pushed into this pool. When he came to the surface and tried to climb out of the water, the SS men would boot him back into the pool. If he could dodge the blows he would be granted the right to climb out. Now he would have to observe only one condition—he would have to get fully dressed in three seconds while the SS men timed him with a watch. Nobody, of course, could manage to get dressed within three seconds, so he would be pushed back into the water and tormented until he drowned.

"Amusement" No. 3 was connected with the obligatory death of the one who was the object of the amusement. Before killing the offender he would be taken to a resplendent white machine used for wringing out washing, and forced to insert his fingertips between two heavy rubber rollers, where the washing was wrung out. Then one of the SS men or one of the prisoners ordered to do so would turn the handle of the machine. The person's arm would roll into the machine up to the elbow or shoulder. The screams of the tortured person would be the basis of the entertainment. It was clear that a person with a smashed arm, the same as anyone else who could not work, would be subjected to extermination following the torture.

The enumerated "amusements" were, so to speak, generally accepted. Different SS men amused themselves each in their own way. Let us cite only one example, confirmed by two witnesses. One of the SS men, who guarded the workers engaged in building the perfected crematorium, a lad of nineteen, approached without cause the most healthy and handsome man among the workers, ordered him to bow his head, and struck him with all his force on the back of his neck with a club. When the prisoner fell the SS man ordered two other prisoners to take him by the legs and drag him face down in a circle in order to bring him around. However, after he had been dragged for a hundred yards or so over the frozen ground he did not regain consciousness and lay there motionless. Then the SS man seized a hollow cement pipe, intended for canalization, lifted it, and threw it on the back of the prostrate man. Then he picked it up and dropped it again, up to five times. After the first blow with the pipe the prostrate man twitched in agony, after the second blow he again became immobile. After the fifth blow the SS man ordered him turned face upwards and with a stick he opened the prisoner's eyelids. Seeing that the prostrate man was dead the SS man spat, lit up a cigarette, and walked away as if nothing had happened. By the way, this was not the result of only his personal monstrous inclinations: during the autumn and winter months of 1943 each of the SS men considered it his duty to boast

EXTERMINATION CAMP

that he had killed not fewer than five prisoners within twenty-four hours.

I would like to tell also about the women. During different months there were up to 10,000 of them in the camp. They were kept the same as the men, with the only difference that they were guarded by SS women. I shall tell about one of these furies who held the rank of non-commissioned officer and was the most senior of the supervisors in the women's barracks. Unfortunately, it has not been possible, so far, to establish her name, since everybody called her the *Lagerseyerka*, having modified the German designation of *Lageraufseher* (camp supervisor). The *Lagerseyerka* never appeared without a *peitsche*—a two-yard-long flexible whip consisting of thick wire covered with rubber, and with leather above the rubber. The *Lagerseyerka*, an ugly and skinny shrew, was distinguished by sadism, linked with sexual abnormalities, and was half-crazy. At the morning or evening check-up she would pick out from among the emaciated and exhausted women the one who was the most beautiful, and who had more or less retained a human appearance, and without any cause, swinging her whip she would hit the woman across the breasts. When the victim, felled by the blow, would fall to the ground, the *Lagerseyerka* would deal her a second blow with the whip between the legs and a third blow to the same place with her metal-shod boot. Usually the woman would no longer be capable of rising, and before getting up would crawl for a long time, leaving a bloody trail. After one or two such executions the women would turn into cripples and soon die. It is difficult to talk about this. One can only nourish the hope that this terrible creature and thousands of those like her will be called by name, found, and executed; that is, will bear at least a one-hundredth part of the deserved punishment.

Until now we have been speaking about the suffering and deaths of those who spent a more or less lengthy period in the camp. But the Lublin camp was truly a death factory and many persons perished immediately upon arriving there. Over three years hundreds of thousands of such persons came to the camp. They came through to the fields of death almost every day. During the night, specially provided tractors roared within the camp boundaries in order to muffle the crash of sub-machine gun firing and the cries of those who were being shot. When a tractor began to thunder everybody in the camp kenw that the hour of death had struck for thousands of people. Let us say only a few words about one such shooting, the biggest of these which place on November 3, 1943.

Early in the morning the guard was aroused by an alarm and the camp was cordonned off by a double ring of Gestapo men. From the Chelm Highway there moved an endless column of people through the camp who went with linked arms, five persons to a row. Altogether 18,000 of them passed during this day. One-half consisted of men, the other of women and children. Children under eight years of age went with the women, and those who were older formed a separate column. They, too, went five in a row with their arms linked. Two hours after the column had passed into the camp music began to play all over the camp and surroundings. Deafening fox-trots and tangos blared forth from several dozen speakers. The radio played all morning, all day, all through the evening and all night long.

These 18,000 were shot in an open field next to the crematorium. Several pits, two yards wide and several hundred yards long, had been excavated. All those to be executed were undressed to the skin and laid prone into these pits. As soon as one row of people was laid into the pit, they were shot from above with sub-machine guns. Then the second row was laid down, and the shooting carried out again, and so on, until the pit had been filled. Then those who remained alive covered the pit with earth and went over to the next pit where they were shot in turn. The last row of those shot in the last pit were buried by the Gestapo men, who buried them only to the extent of shoveling earth over them. From the next day on, the burning of the corpses of those killed by the machine guns was undertaken with unprecedented intensity in the furnaces of the new crematorium. Thus the Germans killed 18,000 people in one day.

In conclusion, it is necessary to mention two Germans, or rather, one German man and one German woman who have been taken prisoner by us. The man had a direct and the woman an indirect relation to what had been happening in the death camp.

The man is called Theodor Scholen. He has not undergone the deserved punishment yet, he is still alive. He is forty-one years old. He was born in Dusseldorf. He joined the National Socialist Party in 1937, going into the SS detachment. In 1942 he arrived at the Lublin camp and became an SS company commander. He is a butcher by profession from the Berlin slaughterhouse, and he carried out the duty of storeman at the camp. His duties consisted in undressing the prisoners who arrived at the camp, then he was to search them and to remove from them the clothing in which they arrived before sending them to the gas chamber. He calls himself a storeman, he says that he joined the SS troops by mistake, in a drunken state; he says that his attitude to the prisoners has been exceptionally humane, and he weeps when witnesses who had fallen into his hands remind him during confrontation how he used to extract people's teeth with locksmith's pliers in search of diamonds which could have been concealed in cavities, and pulled golden crowns from teeth which, according to the nomenclature, did not come under the official inventory of property and could be appropriated by him personally. He swears that he is all-in-all a noncommissioned officer of the SS, while it was the SD, that is, the Gestapo, who was killing people. After being unmasked he lies and weeps such big tears that a naive person could believe him from the first minute.

Such is the man. And here is the woman. Her name is Edit Schostek. She is twenty-one years old, she is from central Germany. She arrived in Lublin two years ago, following the law, in accordance with which German girls who had reached the age of nineteen had to work for the benefit of the State. She came for one year, but stayed for two. She did not kill and did not beat women with the whip across the breasts. She was only a stenographer with the German director of the Lublin electric power station, and her hands are not stained with blood. But when we begin to interrogate her minutely, one small circumstance is revealed: she and her sister, who also worked here in Lublin, were receiving as an additional compensation clothing from the same store of clothes of those executed about which I was speaking. She and her sister received lace and slippers from the Lublin storerooms. Others, perhaps, received underwear and dresses. Still others, who had children, received children's singlets and slippers removed from murdered children.

Thus closes the chain which embraces the whole of Germany. At one end of this chain is the executioner Theodor Scholen, extracting golden teeth from people and pushing them into murder buses, at the other end of the chain is Edit Schostek, who only received the clothing of those killed as payment for her work. They are at different ends of the chain, but there is only one chain. Some will have to answer for more, others for less, but they will all have to answer. Let them not put the blame on each other. Let them understand once and for all: they will all have to answer.

August 10 –12, 1944

Konstantin Simonov

SERGEANT-MAJOR YERESHCHENKO

This was right here, in Belgrade. On the fourth day. It was comparatively close to the end. Our company was in the theater. The structure had been badly wrecked, and due to the continual firing there was no access from the street—one had to make one's way through courtyards, across the roof of an adjoining building, over the fire stairs, and down again.

In the morning a soldier and I went out for something to eat. As soon as we returned there was an order: we were to attack another block. We began the attack.

Two large-caliber machine guns are firing along the street, and when the two of us, Abdulayev and I, ran across the street, we were both wounded in the legs, he seriously, and I lightly. I also received a scratch over the head. When we tried to enter the building we found the gates to the yard were locked, so we leaped down into the basement. It was dark there. I lit a lantern. It was eight a.m.

Abdulayev could not go any further as his leg was completely smashed. I dragged him deeper into the basement and when I saw that he was wounded above the knee, I removed his belt and mine and used them to tie up his thigh in a tourniquet. "Don't shout, be quiet, there are Germans here," I told him. "They'll kill us."

I went upstairs. From there I could see light shining outside on a door to the yard. And a machine gun stands there directed straight at the closed gates, and there are two Germans at the machine gun. Here I have a thought—that if I do not kill them they will kill me. I killed them with the sub-machine gun from a distance of some five yards and went back to the basement. And there Abdulayev asks for a drink.

"Where can I get some for you? Wait, rest for a while, I'll find the entrance to the building and will bring you some water."

I went to search. Apparently this must have been a factory; a narrow-gauge track went down into the basement. And there were stairs leading upwards. Clean, empty stairs leading to a corridor that turns right, and two rooms open off it on the left. I entered these, and when I heard someone walking along the corridor I hid behind a wall, holding my sub-machine gun in readiness. A woman comes up, she says, "There are no Germans here." She is an old woman, a cleaner.

"And where are the Germans?"

"Follow me." We went along the corridor, and she led me up to a window where three Germans were lying there outside in front of the window, screened by stones. And again a machine gun. The old woman pointed them out and went away from sin.

I threw a grenade through the window and blew up the machine gun, killing two of them, but the third one crawled away. I was about to leave the room when suddenly a German appeared on the stairs and threw a grenade down from the second floor to the corridor, but it did not hurt me. I stood behind a projection and the grenade rolled along the steps past me, exploding lower down. Everything along the corridor was shrouded in smoke.

I quickly ran across the corridor and lifted the hook on the gates. When I opened them I saw that our men were visible across the street. Senior Lieutenant Kiselev was in command. I called out to them, "Lend a hand. I'm left on my own here, and there are Germans all around!"

A machine gunner, number two, ran over to me along with an infantryman, but he was wounded. He ran up to me and then fell down. We lifted him and carried him up to the first floor. As soon as the two of them had run across the street the violent firing started again and no one else could follow them. We went along the corridor into those rooms which looked out on the building from which the Germans were keeping the whole street under fire. We could see that an iron curtain had been raised on a window on the third floor and that a machine gun was firing from there.

We fired two short bursts at them and they fell silent, but at that moment a grenade was thrown from the street below into our other window. In our room there were plank beds with mattresses. The grenade exploded on the mattresses, but nevertheless the machine gunner was wounded in the shoulder. I tied him up with a bandage without removing his shirt. Then I came down again to Abdulayev.

"Abdulayev!" I called.

"Give me some water!" he begged.

"I shall carry you upstairs now. Grab my shoulders."

He grabbed my shoulders, put his arms around me from the back, but could not hold on and fell.

"I'm dying," he said.

I ran upstairs and told the machine gunner, "A man is dying down there. Let's go. Give me a hand."

"But I'm wounded, too," he said.

"It doesn't matter. We're all wounded here. Let's go!"

He and I took a mattress and went downstairs again for Abdulayev. And this is how we carried him upstairs on the mattress. We told him that we would bring him some water now, and I went off to make a search. There was quiet everywhere. When we reached the last window they fired at us with a machine gun from the building opposite. We hid behind a partition and I pulled out the ring from a grenade and hurled it, but it did not reach the window opposite and exploded at the foot of the building. I hurled a second one. This one flew through the window, and after it exploded we heard no more from the machine gun. Now we could go freely past the window into the kitchen where some haricot beans were being cooked on the stove. There was also tea being warmed, and there was a bucket of water.

I said to my comrade, "Keep watch while I have a drink of water and fill the bottle."

He had a drink, too, and we went back to Abdulayev and at last I gave him some water.

It began to get dark. An engine was heard in the street—either a tank or a motor car was coming. We looked out to see that a German self-propelled gun had come up and had stopped in front of our window—and we had no anti-tank grenades. I said to the machine gunner, "I shall run across the street for grenades now."

But now the self-propelled gun has begun to fire along the street, and the machine gun was also striking along the street, and when I got to the gates I saw that it was impossible to to pass. I shouted to our men across the street, "Give me a grenade!"

But they couldn't hear me for the thunder of the guns.

SERGEANT-MAJOR YERESHCHENKO

Then, as it fell silent for a moment between two shots I shouted again, "Throw me a grenade!"

"All right, we'll throw it," they shouted, "But make sure you catch it. First we'll throw you a fuse." They wrapped the fuse in a piece of paper and threw it to me. It fell two yards short. I crawled out flat against the ground, seized it, and then crawled away. Then they threw the grenade, without the fuse, straight through the gates.

I caught it and rushed back along the corridor into the room in front of which the German self-propelled gun was standing, put the fuse in, pulled the ring, hurled the grenade at the front caterpillar treads, and lay down under the window myself. The explosion came in about three seconds. I got up immediately, and saw two Germans jump off the gun. I fired and killed one, the other crawled behind the gun. The gun stopped. I posted our machine gunner at the window for observation and went back downstairs and gave water to my two wounded comrades. Then I ran out across the yard to the gate. A machine gun was still firing along the street but it had become dark now, and the machine gun would fire a burst and then be silent for a while. It was easier now, but although our men were on the other side of the street in the main entrance of the building, they couldn't come over to me. And I had three wounded men, since the machine gunner has also lain himself down in a state of exhaustion, having lost too much blood from his shoulder.

But then I had an idea, and I went upstairs again and carried three mattresses out into the yard to the gates from the room where the plank beds were. Then I carried down Abdulayev and the other wounded man and laid them on the mattresses. The machine gunner, it's true, managed to come down by himself and lay himself down on the mattress.

From the kitchen I took some rope—there was a lot

of rope there, fortunately—and a heavy metal soup ladle. The machine gunner asked me, "What are you doing?" But I didn't say anything, there was no time to talk. I took a knife, pierced Abdulayev's mattress in two places, pulled the rope through, and made two knots to make it firm. Then I tied the ladle to the other end of the rope and threw it across the street to the main entrance where our men were sitting. At first they were frightened, thinking it was a grenade, but then they understood and they grabbed the ladle and with it the end of the rope.

"Pull it quickly now!" I shouted to them. And I said to Abdulayev, "Grab the mattress with your teeth, for if your hands can't hold on you'll fall off and you'll be done for."

They drew in the rope and pulled the mattress across the street in one second, as rapidly as if it were a sledge. Then they detached the rope and threw it back to me, together with the ladle. Thus I transferred all the three wounded men while I remained alone in the whole building, like the landlord. After it became very dark I received some reinforcements from across the street, and we went to occupy another building. But as for effecting a crossing on a rope across the street—this wasn't the first time we've done that. We did the same thing before—we transferred both ammunition and provisions in vacuum flasks. . . .

Here the story of Yereshchenko breaks off. It remains to be said how and where I met Yereshchenko in person.

It was early morning. During the night our units and the Yugoslav units, after clearing the station district, finally broke through across the Sava River, and the fighting still went on on the other side, in Zemun in the last suburb of Belgrade which had not as yet been taken.

In spite of the early hour the smashed, blackened and, in some places, the still smoking streets of Belgrade were full of people. People walked along the sidewalks and the driveways, stepping on crunching glass splinters,

SERGEANT-MAJOR YERESHCHENKO

stepping over torn-down wires. And yet the city had a festive appearance with all the red-white-and-blue Yugoslav flags and our red flags hanging down from all the roofs, windows, and balconies.

My attention was suddenly attracted by a picture which was unexpected in its combination of the sad and the amusing. A cart was moving slowly along the driveway, loaded to the top with a pile of domestic goods and chattels that were covered with dust and plaster. In the front of the cart, cowering awkwardly next to an indifferent, sullen-faced driver, sat a white-haired general in the uniform of the old Yugoslav Army, with a round general's cap of French pattern. His costume was as discolored and dusty as his belongings piled up on the cart behind him—the worn cap and the uniform with the transverse creases and the faded braid on the trousers had apparently just been taken out of camphor and hurriedly put on. Where the general was going, why he was driving with his belongings in a cart I did not know. But one thing was clear from his appearance: one knew for certain that all these years he must have sat in his corner, indifferent to everything except the maintenance of his own life and comfort. And now he was driving just as indifferently through liberated Belgrade with his belongings on some business of his own.

All those who passed him paid him back with the same indifference, casting brief, contemptuous or ironically-sympathetic glances at him as they encountered him. He did not exist for them. Only some partisan, meeting up with the cart, suddenly saluted the general. The latter awkwardly and hurriedly responded to the greeting and with a chilly motion he pushed his cap over his ears, shrinking even more, as if from cold, on his seat on the front of the cart.

In that same moment I saw a sergeant-major walking along the sidewalk, limping heavily on his wounded leg.

He wore a tunic which had been bleached to whiteness, with two decorations, on his chest, broken-down tarpaulin boots, and a soiled forage cap which had served its time, and from underneath which bandages showed up white and clean. Two partisans, who were gazing admiringly at him, walked next to him. Those coming toward him lifted their caps before him, patted him on the shoulders, and said something joyful to him in their own way, shaking his hand for a long time before releasing it. The sergeant-major had a handsome, still quite youthful face. He was embarrassed, and yet at the same time he was proud of the attention that was accorded him, smiling modestly at the people. Soon he caught up with the cart carrying the general, and without a glance at it he overtook it with his swift, limping gait.

1945

Not as we found her in fairy tales, not
    as we knew her from the cradle,
Nor as we learned about her from textbooks.
But as she burns with inflamed eyes,
Weeping—have I remembered the Motherland.
I see her on the eve of victory,
Not in stone, or bronze, crowned with glory,
But as a Russian woman who has cried her eyes out,
    who has suffered misfortune,
Who has endured everything, withstood everything.

K. Simonov

Ilya Ehrenburg

JANUARY 24, 1945

It is difficult to talk about the battle in the midst of the battle. The future historian will study the liberation of Poland and the battle for East Prussia, and if our children are lucky a future Tolstoy will lay bare the soul of a young Soviet officer who is at this moment dying under the winter stars. Events evolve so rapidly that not only transports but also war communiqués fall behind the advance units. Even the Moscow antiaircraft crews have not known such hard work as this: five salvoes a day. People on the Home Front listen enthusiastically to the names of German cities, which the Russian announcers pronounce with difficulty, while those at the Front, without pondering over names or how to overcome tiredness, go ahead with that impetuosity peculiar to a person who is nearing home after a long journey. This may appear paradoxical, but to every soldier "Berlin" sounds like "going home."

ILYA EHRENBURG

When the Red Army inflicted a heavy defeat on the Germans in Belorussia last summer some American observers explained the Russian victory by the weakness of the Germans. These observers will hardly return to the old melodies after the intermezzo in the Ardennes. But they will think up something. Before speaking about the character of our offensive I must dwell on the character of our former ill-wishers. It is said that the Americans are realists. I begin to doubt this when I read the articles in some American newspapers about the Red Army. Have American readers forgotten that we are a "colossus with feet of clay?" If they have not forgotten, let them ask their observers why German Tigers are powerless when confronted with "clay," and how Russia has marched up from the Volga to the Oder on feet of clay. It is quite likely that American readers also remember that Moscow was to fall in the autumn of 1941. How did it happen that the observers who used to write about the inevitable fall of Moscow began to write about the inevitable fall of Berlin without even changing their signatures for the sake of decency? Why, when speaking about the Russian victory in Belorussia did these observers try to make believe that the German Army had disintegrated while, when speaking about the negligible advance of the Germans in Belgium, these same observers tried to pretend that the German Army was fairly efficient? Why, when the Allies took three years to prepare themselves for a landing in Europe, did the observers explain this exclusively by military circumstances while when the Red Army, after three-and-a-half years of bitter fighting, took three months to prepare itself for a breakthrough of the powerful German defense, then this was "politics," according to the words of the observers? Why do the observers who tried to make believe in 1939 that we allegedly wanted to conquer the world, try to make believe that we shall not cross our State boundaries owing to evil intentions? Why do they feel

JANUARY 24, 1945

hurt when we advance, feel hurt when we stop, and feel hurt when we advance again? One could believe that the Red Army is not engaged in smashing Germany, but in insulting some American observers. In reality, this interests the Red Army very little. No newspaper article will help us take Koenigsberg a day sooner, nor will it hinder us from arriving in Berlin precisely when we shall arrive there. If I dwelled on American observers, then this was in the interest of American readers: we don't need a new Tolstoy in order to understand the absurdity of many claims about the Red Army; a grain of common sense is sufficient.

The Germans claim that we are advancing only due to numerical superiority. This is not true. We are now superior to the enemy both in the fighting qualities of our soldiers and in the skill of our Command and our equipment. At present we fight better than the Germans, and if one were to put one Russian division against one German division, we would beat the Germans. And since in many places we have two divisions against one German division, we are beating them with rare speed.

Everyone knows what role our artillery played and continues to play in this offensive. Much has been written about the qualities of the Russian artillerymen. I wish only to emphasize once more our sober understanding of the war. The Germans rely on psychological effects, on theatrical acts, they bluff. What are all those different V Rockets if not a desperate attempt at a psychological attack? We do not want to overwhelm Berlin housewives, we prefer to annihilate the aggressors. We have applied energy, force, and invention towards the creation of a powerful artillery, new excellent tanks, and high-quality aviation. Neither do we thirst after effects in the sky, our modest attack aircraft is remarkably good in the offensive. The Germans had a strong defense. They knew that our offensive was inevitable, and if we deceived their watchfulness on this or another sector, then the German Command still did everything in order not to let us pass.

Yet, we passed.

Some Americans are interested in the "degree of decomposition" of the German Army. An idle pursuit. In America one can obtain polls from the Institute of Public Opinion on everything, from what to do with Hitler to which wives are more faithful, brunettes or blondes? Even the most stupid question requires some thought before answering it, but German soldiers do not think. They shout unanimously "Heil Hitler!", and after being captured they shout just as unanimously "Hitler Kaput!" It is much more useful to storm German cities than the illusory German soul. The German Army, it stands to reason, is not the same as in 1942, nowadays among German prisoners we often see elderly men and juveniles. But the Germans defend themselves desperately. It is necessary to finish them off.

I hope that the Americans, with the inquisitiveness peculiar to them, will study our country. It is time to drop the kind of talk that says the Russians are winning only because the Russian soldier has always been brave. We have now occupied places in East Prussia where the Tsarist Army had suffered defeat. It had also been claimed previously that the Russians can fight only on their own land. Perhaps this was true even for the soldiers of Tsarist Russia, but we are now fighting excellently miles and miles away from our native forests, in the Carpathians, in the cities of Silesia, in East Prussia. The Red Army is not only well equipped, it is a modern army enriched by experience, with soldiers and commanders who have initiative, with a sensible discipline which preserves it equally from laxity and from Fascist mechanical cretinism. Our generals have become great military leaders who have preserved democratic ways and an organic link with the people. The American reader will ask: "Why are you praising your-

JANUARY 24, 1945

selves?" It stands to reason that we have many shortcomings, and we are trying to correct them. If I speak about the virtues of the Red Army to our American friends, then this is only for the sake of love for them: I want them to understand the legitimacy of our victories. The sooner Americans learn that we are a strong and completely modern country, that our victories are not accidental gains but the fruit of striving and of toil, the better will it be for us and for America and for the world.

There is no doubt that the Germans have strong defense lines. They also have reserves. Thus, sitting in New York, there is no point in calculating how many miles the Russians have to march to reach Berlin: this is not a walk. One can say, however, that the offensive is evolving sufficiently well. I do not know what the Gauleiter of East Prussia, the former vice-regent of the Ukraine, Eric Koch is doing now, but I think that he is blown about by the draft from General Chernyakhovsky and General Rokossovsky. The incursion of tanks and infantry into German Silesia worries Hitler possibly even more. Here Germany is hit in her most sensitive spot: these are not extremities, but intestines. I have saved to the end the advance of General Zhukov, of his tank men and cavalry. Perhaps this advance alarms the German people less, insofar as Zhukov's troops have not invaded Germany, but it must particularly alarm the German generals.

It is the fourth year of the war—it is exactly the fourth year—and I wrote with all frankness in one of my last articles that we are fed up with the Nazis. This is exactly why our soldiers are in a good mood: tiredness gives them energy. I saw officers who begged to be discharged from hospital on the eve of the offensive. Americans must understand that for us the war is not a sports contest; we have suffered much sorrow from the Fascists, and cannot take an attitude toward them like Dorothy Thompson's. We are marching on Berlin with the firm resolve to punish the villains. Be it in Silesia, in East Prussia, or in Czechoslovakia—everywhere we are driven west by an injured conscience. This is what makes our artillerymen advance fighting twenty miles a day.

Hitler is transferring troops from the West. It is necessary to take this into account. Hitler announced to his troops, "You must fight only in the East, there will be no offensive in the West—we have called it off." This must also be taken into account. Of course, it is not my business to discuss questions which should be discussed by the leaders of the Allies armies, but since I am writing this for an American newspaper, and since military questions are discussed in American newspapers by persons who are just as uninformed as myself, I would therefore like to express my simple opinion: if a blow from the West will supplement a blow from the East, the war will finish far sooner than is contemplated by various respectable commissions. And I believe that American women and men will have no objections to this.

Konstantin Simonov

IN THE HIGH TATRA MOUNTAINS

During this year's winter I had occasion to be at the Polish-Slovak border, in the district where partisan detachments and groups crossed through the Front one after another, after the Slovak uprising. I wanted to write a book about the uprising, and every person coming from there, from beyond the Front line, interested me very much. Partisans, both Russians and Slovaks, mentioned a certain Dr. Bernard several times in conversations with me, and said that he could give me information about something very interesting—more interesting, they said, than what they had told me.

"And what can he tell me?" I asked.

"He has been saving our seriously wounded for two months, in the mountains, in a small cabin . . . when you meet him he'll tell you all about it."

Fate finally brought me together with the doctor. It

was a frosty day. We were sitting around a clean scrubbed wooden table in a Slovak peasant hut: Doctor Yuri Bernard, two Slovak girls—Bozhena and Katerina—who worked with him as nurses, and myself. The girls were sisters, both pale, skinny, with big eyes in their emaciated faces. It is obvious that they have not quite recuperated from all that they have been experiencing.

Yuri Bernard is some thirty years old according to his looks, perhaps younger. He is fairly tall, spare, rather narrow-shouldered, with a head of dark chestnut, almost black hair, a lean energetic face, and a shy, slightly ironic smile. We sat with him around the table for five or six hours in a row while he told me his whole story from beginning to end. I wrote down all that he told me, word for word, and what you are going to read is simply an exact record of the tale of Doctor Yuri Bernard, which I heard in February, 1945, at the border of Poland and Slovakia in the village of Krempakhy:

I was born in 1916 in a village, or more correctly, in the small town of Chop, in the Trans-Carpathian Ukraine, on the very border of Hungary. I studied at the secondary school in Uzhgorod, and later at the Medical Institute: first I completed the courses in the pharmaceutical Department, since I wanted to become a chemist like my father, but then I enrolled in the medical faculty.

When the German occupation began the Germans sent my father, mother, sister, and fiancée to the concentration camp. They died there. My brother who, like myself, was a doctor, and I were arrested and sent to the concentration camp in Elshava. We spent quite a long time there, but in the beginning of 1944 we were lucky enough to escape to Slovakia, to the small town of Revuzy. There we obtained illegal documents in which our names had been slightly altered: we were called Ivan and Yuri Bernat, of Slovak nationality.

We soon established contact with the partisans and

IN THE HIGH TATRA MOUNTAINS

left with them for the mountains: they needed physicians very urgently. First we were in the detachment which was under the command of the former Russian prisoner-of-war Vassily, and later we transferred to the partisan detachment of Belic. My brother and I stayed there during the entire period of the uprising, and at the end of October we left with a transport of wounded partisans for the district of Tridub, where we delivered the wounded to the airfield to be flown behind the lines. After dispatching the wounded we went back to the mountains to look for our detachment, but it was no longer where we had left it. This was on October 28, 1944.

After having despaired of finding our detachment we met Peter Velichko on Prosheva Mountain. He was the commander of the partisan brigade called after Stephanic. He asked us, "Who are you boys?" We replied that we were partisans from the Belic detachment. Velichko told us that Belic's group had left the area quite some time ago, and he asked us, "What can you do, what are you good at?"

We told him that we were physicians.

"Well, then, this is what we need, too," said Velichko. "Come to us."

And so my brother and I worked over a month in Velichko's brigade.

During this time the Germans were organizing punitive expeditions everywhere against the partisan detachments. Fighting took place every day. We crossed from the High Tatra to the Low Tatra Mountains and back; we kept moving around the mountains, but the ring around us kept on tightening.

Up to December sixth the wounded stayed with us in the partisan hospital in the valley near the village of Zverovka. But on December seventh the situation became so acute that the seriously wounded were transferred by order of the brigade commander from the village to a hunting cabin which stood in the deep forest in the mountains. One of the two of us—my brother or I—had to go with the brigade, and the other was to stay to give medical attention to the wounded in the cabin. In all our life until that time my brother and I had never been parted, but this time parting was unavoidable. We sat together in silence for a while and had a smoke, putting off as long as we could the decision as to who was going to stay in that cabin and who would leave with the brigade. But before we did anything else we had to go to the cabin and give the wounded a proper examination. We decided then that the one who arrived first at the cabin would stay there. We went to the cabin along different paths. I got there first, and so I was the one who had to stay there.

I had, of course, seen such hunting cabins before, but I had never had to live in them for more than one or two days, but now I had to stay in this one for what would be more than two months, and not by myself but with the sick and wounded.

What was the cabin like? It was very small, about five yards long and three yards wide. At my height I could not stand upright. There were no walls, only a foundation which had been laid from stones and earth, and a roof that started directly from the ground. There was one tiny window, and a brick stove with an iron flue coming to the outside through a hole in the roof.

Fifteen people were accommodated in this tiny space: myself, the two Slovak sisters Katerina and Bozhena, the Slovak partisan Jan Holesa who had been left behind for our security, and eleven wounded and sick partisans. There were two plank beds along one side of the cabin; two of the seriously wounded lay there. They were in splints and could not move. A narrow passage separated the other plank beds, and on these all the other wounded lay crosswise. We, the attending staff—four persons—slept on the ground in the passage between the plank beds. We used to get nearly frozen at night when it was particularly draughty through the cracks. It is true that in the beginning we attempted to block some of the cracks with moss, but then the wounded used to pull out all the dry moss for smokes.

The partisans had left in the cabin all the supplies which they could spare, calculating that there would be enough for ten days. After ten days the supplies were to be replenished. I also expected that there would be better times ahead, and that the situation regarding medicaments would improve; but in the meantime the only medicine I had on hand was hot water and fifteen grams of manganese, which I cherished like the apple of my eye. It is true that on the way to the cabin I spied some more medicine: several oaks stood within the coniferous forest, and I thought that if the wounded had stomach complaints it would be possible to grind some oak bark and prepare powders with tannin. This, incidentally, had to be done later.

Generally, however, oaks were a rarity so high up in the mountains. Everything all around was covered with coniferous forests, and the cabin itself stood in such a dense fir grove that one could pass within five feet of it and not notice it. Not far from the cabin a small spring, which never froze, gushed out between stones from under the snow. Sometimes it flowed strong, sometimes it flowed drop by drop, but later on we made a hollow in the ice and enough water collected there during twenty-four hours to provide for all our needs.

Among the wounded we had three Slovaks, one Czech, and seven Russians. With one or two exceptions they all had either been badly wounded in the legs, or were seriously frostbitten; they had a long treatment in prospect, and there could be no thought of a rapid move.

The first week went by. On the ninth day we heard the sound of heavy fighting in the morning, and by nightfall fifty men came to the cabin—all those who had survived from Stephanic's brigade. The brigade had been engaged in heavy fighting with the Germans all the previous day and all of this day and had barely escaped from encirclement by coming this way through the remote mountains.

In order to continue the struggle the partisans would have to immediately cross the Tatra Mountains, reach new places, and assemble detachments and groups which were disorganized after the defeat of the uprising—in brief, everything had to begin again from the beginning. To drag seriously wounded men across the pass was out of the question. It would have meant their death.

I shall never forget that night when everybody stayed in our cabin. A lot of work fell upon my brother, who had arrived with the partisans, and upon myself, and we worked half the night bandaging many fresh wounds. The partisans were gloomy. They could not get the heavy fighting, in which very many of their comrades had perished, out of their mind. The wounded on their part were nervous, for they had previously thought that the brigade would remain somewhere nearby: They did not expect that it would move beyond the Tatra Mountains. As a matter of fact, those who were leaving did not spend even one entire night at the cabin. The snow storm began to abate by morning, and in order not to leave any traces and bring about the doom of the wounded, the commander decided to leave at sunrise while it was still possible for snow to cover their tracks.

It is difficult to say at present how another fifty persons besides us could have been accommodated in the cabin, but somehow we all squeezed in. The men lay one on top of the other in such a way that they could not immediately get up in the morning; that is how many arms and legs had become numb. There were few conversations. The wounded did not sleep at all and looked

IN THE HIGH TATRA MOUNTAINS

questioningly at those who were about to leave. The commander of the brigade lay underneath the window and chain-smoked one cigarette after another. Everybody began to rise at daybreak. Two of the partisans who had wounds—one in the chest, the other in the shoulder—pulled on their greatcoats.

"What are you getting dressed for?" the commander asked.

"We shall go with you," they replied. And they actually left with the detachment. The other wounded who could not go in any way had doleful expressions on their faces and deep despair in their eyes that seemed to plead: take us with you.

The commander pressed the hand of each of them and said to me, "Doctor, please listen to what I say—even if it should cost the life of some of our comrades you'll receive provisions from us wherever we might be!"

My brother left with the detachment. I was making a bandage at that time, and since my hands were covered with blood and pus, we could not press each other's hand, but only bowed in silence, and he left. The snowstorm had not stopped yet and it rapidly covered up the detachment's tracks. We remained completely alone.

Now this day was really terrible. Loneliness! We all had a depressed feeling; it took hold of me, too. There was an unimaginable stench from purulent wounds in the cabin. I saw that only the seriously wounded were left with me; it was almost impossible to help them, given the absence of medicaments. I was prepared to do everything for them, but where could I obtain medicaments? Besides, my brother, a more experienced physician than I, was absent. In short, my heart was very heavy, but there was no other way out. It was necessary to fight for the life of these people.

In addition, the situation regarding provisions did not augur well. After the fighting, which the regiment had carried out in the environs, the Germans had blockaded all surrounding villages—Zuberec, Gabovka, Guty, Bely Potok—and in the Zverovka Valley, lying beneath us, they had formed a shooting range which was hard to pass through.

"How shall I feed the wounded?" I thought.

All our provisions were contained in one tightly filled kit bag. It is true that the partisans who had stayed the night had not only not eaten from our provisions, but some had given the last they had—some a pinch of snuff, some a crust of bread. However, this was still not much.

Towards the evening of that day when it was not yet dark two German detachments passed close to the cabin, one on the left, the other on the right. They were obviously searching for traces of the brigade. I am to this day amazed at our luck, because one of the German detachments passed only within a hundred and fifty yards above the cabin. We could clearly hear the voices of the Germans, and they could hear our voices, since they had appeared unexpectedly.

From that day on I introduced the rule that we were to speak aloud at night only. During the day we must speak in an undertone or in whispers. Besides, this incident taught me that I could not remain a physician only, I must also become the commander of the garrison, and we accordingly organized an observation post where I, Bozhena, Katerina, and Jan Holesa took turns being on duty.

This is how our life began. During the mornings we heard the Germans practicing on the shooting range below. Distant sounds of shooting reached us during the day and sometimes during the night. This meant that partisan groups which the Germans were hunting were still roaming somewhere around.

We encountered many difficulties. The wounded needed warmth, but the stove could not be heated during

IN THE HIGH TATRA MOUNTAINS

the day since even the lightest smoke could be detected by the Germans. The stove was heated at night only, but during the day the cabin froze up. Firewood was needed. We could not saw trees, for in the frosty mountain air the sound of a saw resounded for over a mile, and a German sentry was constantly on guard not far from us. It was necessary to collect windfallen branches and dry logs, but the cutting up had to be done inside the cabin; to do so and to prevent the saw from squealing, it was not taken by the handles but by the blade, and two persons had to guide it slowly while two others were firmly holding onto the log. If windfallen branches could not be found and we had to haul up a fallen pine tree, we could not drag the whole tree inside the cabin, but dragged in only the end, sawed a bit off, and dragged in some more, sawed off more—and thus to the finish, while everyone in the cabin froze because of the open door.

Early morning was fixed as meal time, since the stove was lit all night and we could heat our food before the sun rose. Some of the wounded fell sound asleep only by dawn and it was difficult to get them to wake up, but it was necessary to wake them every morning at daybreak for a hot meal.

It was the same thing with the bandaging. My main means of disinfection were manganese and boiling water, and all bandaging was therefore done at night and right before morning. I woke the seriously wounded earlier in order to feed them first, and then after they had had some nourishment, I bandaged them. I was worried most of all, of course, by the absence of medicaments. This was the most complicated and difficult matter. Sometimes one would lose heart, and feel that one was powerless, but one wanted to save these people without fail. I felt sad, looking at them, knowing the torment I had to put them through every morning. I had no healing ointments of any kind which usually would make it possible for a doctor to apply bandages every two to three days. In order to prevent the wounds from suppurating I had to wash out and bandage them every day, while inflicting against my will a hellish pain on the wounded, since for deep wounds which suppurated and had to be cleaned every day, I had nothing apart from a long, narrow piece of rubber. I used to push this rubber through the continuous wound, pull it taut, and effect the drainage thereby.

Almost all my patients had leg wounds. Many were lying in splints and braces, but it was not possible to accommodate a motionlessly stretched-out leg on the short plank beds. Legs in splints were therefore tied around with cords and held suspended from the ceiling. The wounded sometimes brushed against each other when getting up in the terribly crowded cabin, and it happened that the nurses, who were tired due to lack of sleep, sometimes inadvertently brushed against them when trying to make their way between them. And it is better not to speak about what pain even a light touch would cause in such cases.

I had fifteen grams of manganese. I kept this manganese in a small bag under my shirt against my chest so as not to spill it or lose it under any circumstances. I used to dissolve it in boiling water and proceed with the bathing of wounds. I treated those with frostbite according to the old method, applying alternately cold and hot baths.

On the fifth or sixth day when our meager provisions began to run low some of the wounded became afflicted with dysentery. I did not know what to do, but put on a cheerful air and told them that I had some concealed medicaments in the forest. Medicaments in the forest I had none, but I remembered about the oaks, and I decided to pound some bark and to prepare a powder for use against dysentery. I did so secretly, it was important for me that the wounded should have faith in those powders. I tore off several pieces of bark and pounded these during

IN THE HIGH TATRA MOUNTAINS

the night when everybody was asleep. Some wrappers for powders happened to have been accidentally saved in my kit bag, and I accurately poured the pounded bark into these wrappers, turning out proper pharmaceutical packets which I gave to the wounded in this form. It was my luck that this helped: within one week the dysentery died away. During this time the Germans around us were hunting down partisans, even chasing after individuals. They were not only hunting for people, they were also searching for lodges and hunting cabins in the mountains—in brief, for any dwelling where partisans could hide during this bitter winter. After finding such a dwelling they would immediately burn it down. The reflection of fire could always be seen at night above the tops of the pine trees; there was always something burning somewhere.

Apart from this the Germans used to fire from mortars during the day and particularly during the night, without taking aim, at areas within a square grid, in order to create panic among the partisans.

On one such day Seleznev, the Chief of Staff of the Suvorov Detachment, came to us. Although I had seen him before, I did not recognize him when I met him; he was so completely ragged, frozen, and terrible-looking. A week before when the Germans had surrounded his detachment he had happened to be in a different place with a duty detail; he had lost his men and no matter how much he searched for them he could not find them. He wandered over the mountains for six days without eating anything. Wherever he went he could see peasant huts burning, and it seemed to him that all the mountains were enveloped in flames. And when he approached our "hospital" and saw that there were people coming towards him—myself and Bozhena—he fell unconscious into the snow.

Seleznev stayed with us for seven days. He helped organize an observation post in a better place than we had put it, and after recovering a little, he began to go out on reconnaissance. During the second or third reconnaissance he came upon scouts from Captain Tikhonov's detachment. Although he was still very ill he nevertheless decided to go with the scouts since he knew that we had only a minimal quantity of provisions left which were indispensable for the wounded. He handed a note to Jan Holesa, who was with him. It said, "Doctor: I am ashamed to stay any longer and to eat the wounded out of house and home. I met some partisans and I am leaving with them. Goodbye."

Thus we parted with Seleznev.

During the following few days it seemed to quiet down somewhat: the fires abated and the Germans began to do less shooting. My brother, on leaving, had given me a note in which he described the Zverovka Valley where he had buried a small amount of medicaments under one of the pines, making a notch on that pine. It had not been possible to reach that place before because the German shooting range was precisely there, but the Germans had gone from there for the time being and were about a mile or so away.

I decided to go there and find those medicaments, whatever the cost. But a great disappointment awaited me. My brother had made the notch at the very roots of the tree so that it would not be noticed, but during these last two weeks nearly four feet of snow had drifted everywhere in the Tatra Mountains, and unfortunately my brother had made no other special distinctive marks on the tree, hoping that the notch would be visible.

I walked for three nights and dug up the snow at a guess at dozens of trees, but I did not find the tree with the notch. And there were thousands of trees in the valley. . . . And even though I knew that somewhere close by there were medicaments which I needed desperately, I was forced to abandon the dream of finding them.

IN THE HIGH TATRA MOUNTAINS

On the third morning, on returning from this fruitless search, I met a Slovak in the Zverovka Valley who turned out to be our partisan scout from the village of Gabovka. I learned from him that we had almost been done for during these past three days. It seems that the cabin in which we lived had been recommended to us for occupation by the forester Ludwig Maier, who had given much help to the partisans during the uprising. After the fighting in the Zverovka Valley when the Germans were burning all the lodges and houses for miles around, they burned down the forester's small house. Maier left for Gabovka with his wife. There traitors pointed out to the Germans that this was the same Maier in whose place partisans had once lived. Just at that time the Germans had captured one of the fighters from our brigade—we never did succeed in finding out who he was—and after being beaten he said at the questioning that somewhere in the nearby mountains there was a partisan hospital. The Germans sent for the forester and said, "You must know where their hospital is and you must lead us to it."

They spoke to him through a Czech interpreter; this interpreter, after translating their words, added in the same tone of voice so the Germans would not be suspicious, "If you are the only one who knows, and you tell them where the hospital is, I will kill you."

Maier only looked at him and smiled, and giving him a wink, he asked him to tell the Germans that he knew where the hospital was. The Germans got ready at once for the journey, and Maier led them to the entrance to the Zverovka Valley. Our hospital was situated on the right side at the top, but the forester led them to the left, downwards. He knew that there was a peasant hut there in which some Jews in hiding from the Gestapo had once lived. He led the Germans to that hut and said, "This is the hut where the partisan hospital was located." The hut was, of course, vacant.

"How can you prove that there was a hospital here?" the Germans demanded.

"I shall prove it by the existence of traces of habitation and the remains of provisions."

"And where are the wounded?"

Maier replied that the partisans had most likely taken them with them.

The Germans searched around the hut and on finding remains of provisions they were convinced that there had been a partisan hospital there and they accordingly released Maier. Thus we were saved from what would appear to be inevitable doom.

Gradually one of the wounded, the Slovak Anton Huta, began to recover, and I was able to leave Jan Holesa to guard the hospital and go on reconnaissance with Huta. We were attempting to reach a village, any village, in order to obtain provisions, but all the villages were still blockaded by the Germans, who had posted sentries around them. Yet there was absolutely nothing left to eat. I was becoming desperate by now. But on one of our reconnaissances we met a partisan from Tikhonov's detachment who told us that he had seen an abandoned horse in the Rogachevka Valley. On hearing this we went straight to the Rogachevka Valley without returning to the hospital. It took all night to walk the fifteen miles over deep snow to get there and we did not arrive until morning. In the valley hollow we found traces of an abandoned partisan camp and scraps of tents; we also found a sack of lentils, half spilled, but the sight of the old boney horse that was wandering about was the best sight I had ever seen in my life.

We were a long time collecting the spilt lentils, grain by grain—there was about ten kilograms, as it turned out later. We loaded the bag on the horse and made for home, arriving there by evening. There was no limit to the joy of the wounded when they learned that we had brought the horse and the lentils. We tied the horse with lines from an old parachute to a tree next to the cabin and decided to slaughter it in the morning. Until midnight I kept busy with calculations as to how long this horse would suffice for us if everyone were issued 150 grams a day. Desperately tired, I finally fell dead asleep, resting on the knowledge that, thank God, we would not be threatened by hunger for twenty-five to thirty days.

Morning came. One of the wounded, Sergeant Major Ivan Reshetnev, had worked in a slaughterhouse in his youth. Now he had frostbitten legs and was almost unable to walk, but we wrapped his legs in rags and tied them up with cords so that he could get up and do his job. He took our only axe, I picked up a bucket, and we went outside, followed by two or three of the patients who were able to move about in some manner or other. To our horror we saw that the horse was not there. During the night it had torn loose from the lines and had run away. Someone among us found the strength to joke and say, "This is a strange story! Perhaps this horse was a German spy!"

But nobody smiled at the jest. The disappearance of the horse signified death for us by starvation.

I went to search for the horse with the wounded Slovak, Jan Kovacz, who was on the road to recovery. It was our luck that the horse's footprints were clearly visible. They led straight to the Zverovka Valley. But as we got closer we heard shots from that direction and realized that the Germans must have reestablished a shooting range there. We felt better, however, when we saw that the horse had not liked the sound of shooting either, for his footprints abruptly veered to the right.

We tracked him for a whole day until finally the footprints led us to the same valley where we had found the horse in the first place. We saw it standing with its head lowered in almost the same spot. The feelings we experienced in that moment could only be understood by a person who knew that fifteen hungry mouths were waiting for him.

We took the horse and went back home as fast as we could. Some three miles from the cabin we saw a man in the forest crawling on all fours over the snow. As we came close we saw that he was a Russian partisan, Maksim Oleynikov, from the Suvorov Detachment. He could only give his name and surname, being in an almost unconscious state, and was unable to tell us anything more.

As it became clear later on, he had gone on reconnaissance several days earlier. The Germans had spotted the scouts and had opened fire from machine guns, killing all his comrades. He had crashed through the ice in attempting to cross a small river, but had managed to crawl out and make his way to the village of Zuberec where there were more Germans. The peasants hid him and surreptitiously gave him several lumps of bread and some domestic slippers, *papushi*, for his feet; no other footwear would any longer fit his frostbitten feet. There was no possibility of remaining in the village, however, for there were Germans in almost every house. He went into the mountains, lost his way, and froze over completely. We laid him on the horse, and supporting him from both sides we brought him to our cabin.

After slaughtering the horse we cooked ourselves meat for the first time in many days. The meat appeared tasty to us, like goose meat. We dug deep burrows in the snow near the cabin and buried the meat there so that it would not be spoilt.

Sergeant Major Ivan Reshetnev, who could turn his hand to anything, cut uppers for slippers out of our blankets and soles out of the horse's hide, making footwear for us: by this time we had become almost barefoot. Now we began to go out on reconnaissance in these slippers; incidentally, they had the added advantage that the footprints they left were of such a strange shape that they could be taken for the prints of some unknown animal rather than of a human. In brief, everything was put to use.

But after two to three days the salt ran out. We endured for several days and then decided to obtain at least a little salt however we could, so Anton Huta, another wounded, and I descended into the Zverovka Valley and went on further to the village of Zuberec. But literally within fifty feet of the last hut we heard German speech. There were German patrols in the village, as before. Meanwhile, the night was quiet without even a hint of a snowstorm, and we had come so close to the village that our footprints would be noticed in the morning. We decided to return to our cabin separately, in roundabout ways, so as to confuse the Germans. We wanted to leave the impression that many people had passed here, and we therefore walked dragging our feet, leaving an almost solid track.

Thus, by different paths we reached the agreed-upon meeting place where a spring, which was not frozen, flowed along the incline. We entered the course of the spring, walking uphill for a long time in the freezing water, and came out into the snow again much higher up in the mountain. Our feet were unbearably frozen and we barely got them warm again in the cabin.

A new worry arose for me during these days. Maksim Oleynikov was in a far more serious condition than all my other wounded. I had only to look at his legs to see that his feet were almost dead, frozen to the extent that it was extremely problematical that they could be saved. I did everything I could: cold baths, hot baths, and bathing them with manganese, but the flesh was already putrefying and decomposing, and I felt that he must have an operation, otherwise the man would die. But I wanted to save him under all circumstances, for although I had already seen much by now, never in my life had I seen such a patient and grateful man. Many of the wounded were nervous and moaned and groaned, but he, whenever I bathed his feet, never uttered a single groan. He even soothed me, saying, "Never mind, never mind, doctor."

I was always ready to bow before this man and take off my hat to him. I wanted very much to save him but there was nothing with which to carry out the operation. And the necrosis of his legs kept advancing day by day. His temperature was 40 degrees (Celsius). I understood that if he was not given an operation he would die of blood poisoning, but I had absolutely nothing, not even the most primitive instrument.

And now we received our first news from our partisan brigade. It came near morning when I was bandaging the wounded. Jan Holesa was asleep after guard duty, Katerina was helping me with the wounded, and Bozhena stood guard with the sub-machine gun. The door opened and Bozhena entered the hut. I was just about to say to her, "Why did you leave your post?" when she cried without letting me say a word, "They have arrived!" Even then I didn't understand who had arrived, but the next moment there appeared behind her the familiar face of the Trans-Carpathian Ukrainian, Misha—I cannot remember his surname.—who used to be in our brigade. He removed a small kit bag from his shoulders and put it at my feet. All the wounded men began to shout in a chorus: "Misha! Misha!" and began to ask what he had brought, and whether there was something to smoke.

A blanket was spread out on the floor and Misha began to lay out everything that he had brought in the bag. He did not bring anything to smoke, but he gave us six of his cigarettes. We spread them over six days: one cigarette a day among the lot of us. Each of the wounded had a draw and passed the cigarette to the next man.

Misha brought a kilogram-and-a-half of salt, some rice groats, a little lard, and three blocks of chocolate. He had to walk for more than sixty miles across two mountain ridges. He could not carry more than fifteen kilograms on account of the difficult path, five kilograms for himself for both ways of the journey, and ten kilograms for us. His journey took five days coming and five days for the return. And all this for ten kilograms of provisions.

The wounded men questioned Misha during this night: who in the brigade was alive, who had been killed?—and he answered all questions as well as he could. In general, the news he brought was good: the brigade had been reinforced in its composition, although its position remained grave, and the fighting went on without interruption.

From that time Misha made four such runs during the existence of our hospital. These runs took forty days, and he hurried every time to such an extent that he never had enough sleep, for after arriving during the night he would rest for only an hour or two before leaving at daybreak.

After seeing Misha I made the decision to operate on Oleynikov, and I gave Misha a note to the commander of the brigade asking him to send me a scissors, a knife, a saw, and if possible, some narcotic means. I explained to Misha how important it was to receive all this as soon as possible—they were even more important than the provisions.

I waited for him for twelve days. During all this time Sergeant Major Oleynikov hovered between life and death. With my cleaning and bathing I apparently only tormented this man. He had become completely weak and only an iron will stopped him from screaming and moaning and worrying the other patients. On the thirteenth day Misha returned and brought what could be found at the brigade: an ordinary large penknife, ordinary scissors, a cabinetmaker's saw, and tweezers. My brother sent a note to say he was sharing everything he had, but he had given away the only tweezers he possessed.

In order to feel stronger I had more sleep than usual before the operation—almost half a day. As soon as it became dark and the water had been boiled, I began the operation. Katerina, who as medical nurse was to help me, opened her eyes in surprise; it was clear that my decision to operate was totally unexpected by her. But ignoring her amazement I did not let her say a word, for it was hard enough for me to make the decision. She boiled the knife, the saw, the tweezers, and the scraps of parachute with which our so-called operating table was lined—strictly speaking, it was not a table, but a section of the plank beds, cleared of blankets.

Several of the wounded men who were feeling better gathered around in order to assist me. They cut some wood splinters to provide light, and Bozhena held the splinters lighting the "operating table." Anton Huta tightly tied up Oleynikov's legs above the knees with parachute lines. He held his legs while Katerina was passing me the instruments.

The plank beds were low, and it was necessary for me to get down on my knees in order to operate, and there was not enough light for me to see by. The instruments were not suitable, either, but what worried me above all else was, of course, not the physical difficulties, but the moral seriousness of the lack of certainty as to whether I would really be able to save the man, rather than simply inflict unnecessary suffering on him before his death. But there was no other way out—it was necessary to operate.

I began to operate on the left leg. I sawed off Oleynikov's toes, after which a violent hemorrhage began, and I searched for the blood vessels which had to be tied up in order to stop the flow of blood. I tried not to think of Oleynikov, but he was trying to help me as much as he could; now he was lying quietly, now he was humming some Russian songs in a barely audible voice. I do not dare to imagine what he must have felt during those minutes.

The operation on his left leg took two-and-a-half hours. When I finished I carried out a general bandaging, and the hemorrhage stopped. But then I had to stop for a while, too, having been on my knees for two-and-a-half hours without a break. I lay down on the floor and stretched out my legs, which had gone numb. It was twenty minutes before the numbness subsided.

After my own circulation was restored I got down on my knees again and began on Oleynikov's right leg. It was frostbitten even more than the left leg. When I had sawed off the toes I saw that the blood vessels and the flesh had disintegrated to such an extent that it was difficult to find a place to tie up the vessels to stop the bleeding. Finally I succeeded in doing so, and the operation was completed. When it was over I was oppressed by the thought that I may have done all this in vain, that it was possible that the operation would not be successful.

I emerged from the hut into the cold mountain air. Perspiration was running down my face in streams, but I didn't notice the cold. Katerina, who had been helping me all the time, came out behind me and sat down in the snow and promptly dissolved into tears.

"There, there, don't cry," I soothed her. "Don't cry, do you hear?"

"But I did not cry in there, during the operation," she sobbed.

"If you had started crying in there I would have hit you," I told her, and after returning to the cabin I went over to Oleynikov. He was lying on his back, his eyes closed, and was singing something, but so quietly and in such a weakened voice that the words were almost inaudible.

For the next two days, until his temperature returned to normal, I could find peace neither day nor night. Then he started to feel better, his temperature stabilized, and I understood then that he was most likely saved.

The days dragged on. The horse had deceived our expectations; it contained far less meat than we had assumed. It turned out that we could give our people only one hundred grams per day of horsemeat. The daily menu consisted of soup, cooked from horseflesh, with lentils. It was apportioned in the following manner: at first a piece of meat was issued to everybody, then everyone was issued in turn his portion of broth in our only tin plate, and finally, when nothing was left in the bottom of the pan besides the lentils, Bozhena, who played the part of our chief cook, counted out ten lentils each. There could be no mistake here, since the lentils were poured into the pan not by weight, but by count.

As always happens with very hungry people, this meager food occupied a large place in our life, it was talked about, and it was eagerly awaited. But I would say that in the end we had even become used to this hard ration; the absence of something to smoke was much more painful. It is true that later on Misha used to bring us not six, but ten, and even fifteen cigarettes; this was all that his comrades could apportion us from their supplies, but what are fifteen cigarettes among fifteen people for ten days!

During one of the painful evenings when Misha had not been here for a particularly long time—fourteen or fifteen days—and everybody had an infinite desire to smoke, one of the wounded, I think it was Vassily Tkachenko, suddenly said: "Can you remember, boys, when the commander of the brigade spent the night here?" (This was over one-and-a-half months ago.) "As I recall he was smoking cigarettes. What do you say?"

"Yes, we seem to remember that he smoked," the others agreed. "He smoked three or four self-rolled cigarettes. Where was he sitting?"

They began to remember where the commander of

IN THE HIGH TATRA MOUNTAINS

the brigade had lay down, recalling by way of common effort that it was over near the window. Vassily Tkachenko climbed out of the plank bed with some difficulty, dragged himself up to the spot where the commander of the brigade once had lain, and began to search among the stones with which the gaps between the lower logs and the floor had been filled. It is true that he did not find four cigarette butts, but he did come up with two.

The commander had been excited that night before he left and had not smoked the cigarettes to the end, so there was a little tobacco left in both butts. Tkachenko carefully poured out that tobacco, collected it in his palm, then added some moss, and all this was rolled into a fairly heavy self-rolled cigarette. Drawing on it with delight, everybody smoked the homemade cigarette in turn. It was sufficient for exactly two draws each, going around twice in a circle, without missing me either.

To tell the truth, with every day it became more and more difficult to exist. Apart from the difficulties with food and smokes, the fact that this was now the second month that we had been here was beginning to take its toll on our morale, but although the majority of the wounded felt better and were even ambulatory, there was still no possibility at all of our undertaking a major independent march.

The winter was severe. Imagine our ordinary winter day towards the end of the second month: a scant light struggles through the tiny frost-coated window, illuminating the unattractive picture of our life: the ceiling is completely covered with hoar frost, water runs continuously down from the walls when the stove is alight, the wind rattles at the little window, hurling snowflakes against it. And we are sitting there, conversing from time to time, and brooding about what else could be used for bandages, since it is still necessary to apply bandages to the patients every day, and there is nothing left from which bandages can be made. In the beginning there was a small quantity of bandages, but they had long since been laundered into rags.

We had scraps of a parachute which we had cut up for bandages, but these, too, had been used up. Then I had ordered all patients to remove their underwear and to lie in their outer garments, or simply wrapped up in blankets, since we had to use their underwear for bandages.

Our complete ignorance of what was happening in the world weighed on us. Often towards evening, being unable to fall asleep due to cold as well as to hunger, we talked at length about what, for example, Moscow would now be broadcasting if we had a radio, and wondering what events could have occurred during this time. And everybody let their imagination loose on that subject.

We never heard any news, not even when Misha came. It is true that he used to give us news of the brigade, but their radio receiver had been smashed by a mortar bomb during the recent fighting, and news from the outside world did not reach even the brigade.

Hygiene took up a good deal of time. We all felt that we could not let ourselves go in this grave situation. Therefore when we succeeded in lighting a more intense fire in the stove and in heating more water, we not only dressed wounds and laundered bandages, but if possible we washed ourselves.

One of the wounded, Jan Krepisczak, had once been a hairdresser, and those scissors which Misha had brought—and with whose aid I had operated on Oleynikov—were now being put to their proper use—all of us were shorn, gradually, and without haste—without haste, since there was no hurry to go anywhere.

At the very end of the second month an event occurred in the cabin which almost destroyed us. I completely forgot to mention that an old man, a Slovak—a cook who had fallen behind one of our detachments—had come to us during the first month. He had been neither wounded nor was he sick, he was simply old, and it was difficult for him to cross the mountain ranges with the other partisans. We gave him shelter. He did not distinguish himself in any way either by anything bad or anything good, and he lived as we all lived, trying to help in whatever way he could.

In the beginning of February when matters stood very badly in respect to food, the cook volunteered to go down the mountain, and taking advantage of being an old man and of hardly being suspected by anybody, to make his way to the village and to bring back some provisions. I did not feel like letting him go, but he insisted, and since the food was running out completely, I finally let him go.

As I was told later on, he had safely reached the village, and after collecting some provisions, had loaded them on his shoulders and begun the return journey. But the Germans had seen him arrive and had purposely let him collect his provisions and then followed him when he set out on the return trip. It would have ended with our doom if one of the Germans had not become nervous, and catching up with the cook, called out to him. Hearing a German shout, the cook started running. The Germans began shooting at him and a bullet pierced his lung. He fell. When the Germans ran up to him he asked them to carry him somewhere and give him aid, and then he would tell them everything.

We will never know whether it was a ruse on his part to gain time and save us, or whether he did really get scared and would have told about our cabin. Nobody will ever be able to find this out, for he died before the Germans carried him down to the village.

This incident did us a disservice. The Germans suspected that there was still someone hiding and began to search again through the mountains. One day I was on guard duty some 150 yards from the hut when I suddenly heard someone below shouting and calling for aid in the Slovak language. My first involuntary urge was to run below and find out who was calling for help: I thought that this was most likely a wounded or freezing partisan. Fortunately for me, Sergeant Major Reshetnev who was with me and who always distinguished himself for circumspection, told me: "Wait, doctor, perhaps it's a German trap. Let's wait."

We kept quiet and waited. From below there came several more shouts in Slovakian, and then I clearly heard German speech. Someone said in German, "No, let's go on, there's nobody here." Then the Germans went on for some 300 yards or so, and again we heard them shouting in Slovakian, "Help! Help!" Sergeant Major Reshetnev had proved to be correct; this was indeed a German trap.

And yet, after the next day two of our wounded men who were out on reconnaissance went down to the Zverovka Valley and there they met peasants from the nearest village who told them that a big Russian offensive had begun and that the German detachment which had been staying in the village had left. The wounded men descended with the peasants to the village, took some provisions (they were in such a hurry to tell us the good news that they didn't even try to take much back with them) and returned to the cabin. This was in the evening.

The next morning I took three wounded men with me, all those who could walk, and went down to the valley to bring back more provisions, and to find out more accurately what was happening. But as we were approaching the Zverovka Valley we were alarmed by the sight of smoke coming from there. On descending further we saw bonfires burning in the Zverovka Valley and we could see from behind the trees how the Germans were busying themselves sawing down trees. They were building something like a block house. There was no possibility at all of stealing into the village. It turned out that the Russian offensive had really begun, but while the German rear-guard detachment had gone, the front-line units had arrived in its stead.

Those two wounded men who had been in such a hurry to bring us the good news that they had not bothered to bring back enough provisions cursed themselves bitterly, but it was too late to correct anything. Of food, we had only half the horse's head left. It was impossible to stay here any longer.

In general I knew the locality fairly well and could visualize how to make our way across the mountains to the Russians. According to the fragmentary information from our scouts and from Mischa's stories, it could be assumed that to the northeast of us the Front lay within only twenty-five to thirty miles from the Polish border health-resort town of Zakopane, which was already in Russian hands. I decided to make my way there in order to get help and to transfer the wounded to Soviet-occupied territory. I had neither a map nor a compass and the journey ahead was difficult. I could not take a single gram of provisions with me, and I had nothing warm to wear, I had only trousers and a threadbare jacket and the slippers Reshetnev had sewn from the horse's hide.

I decided to go through the Rogachevka Valley, then through another valley, across the High Tatra Mountains, and from there make my way to Zakopane. This was the most remote and indirect route, but I felt it offered the best possibility of by-passing German barriers and posts. I shall not tell how the journey went. I can scarcely remember it now. All I know is that I did it, spurred on by the thought that I had to get there, and that if I died it would not only be my death, but the death of all those waiting in the cabin. It took me sixty hours to get to Zakopane, and I never encountered a single German. Only once did I hear distant shots to the left and to the right: possibly when I crossed the Front line.

KONSTANTIN SIMONOV

Zakopane is a well-known Polish health resort which I had had occasion to visit before. It is a beautiful town, with hotels and good-quality buildings, and it turned out that it had been almost untouched by the war. I was in such a hurry to reach the Soviet commandant that at first I did not even notice how people in the street were looking at me. My appearance, as I think of it now, must have been really strange: ragged clothes worn over bare skin, disheveled hair, a sub-machine gun slung over my shoulder, almost bare feet.

I sat at the commandant's desk and ate as I told my story. As I can remember now, I was fearful of falling asleep: such warmth was flowing over my body that sleep could overcome me any second.

"How can I help you?" the commandant asked me, after telling me that there were no military units in the town; they had all gone ahead and only a small commandant's detachment was left.

I asked him for a guide who could help me find the people in the town that I needed. I told him that I had once done some mountaineering and knew several Polish alpinists in Zakopane who could help me more than anyone. I must say to the honor of the Polish sportsmen who lived in Zakopane that within two hours I had collected some fourteen men. All those whom I approached agreed to go with me to save the wounded. Among these people I would like to mention the brothers Voitekh; Jakob and Stanislaus Vovridko; Simon Zaritsky; Stanislaus Marusesh; the brothers Stanislaus and Jacob Gasyanits; the rest followed their example.

On the fifth day after I had left my wounded, we arrived back at the cabin. It was hard to describe our joy. We all wept, but I do not know the details of the meeting, for after I reached the hut and told the wounded men to get ready to leave I immediately fell asleep. When I was shaken out of my slumber they were all ready to set out on the road.

IN THE HIGH TATRA MOUNTAINS

The experienced mountaineers had taken spare skis with them. For those wounded men who could in no way proceed by themselves they fastened together several pairs of skis, secured boards to them, and spread fir branches on top. The wounded were tightly bound to these self-made sledges. The deep snow was collapsing in places, and it was often necessary to drag the sledges through underneath the snow. The weakened girls, who went on foot, got stuck in the snow and had to be carried several times.

There was no warm footwear. Everybody's feet were wrapped in rags. Sometimes I fell asleep while walking, other times I was gripped by anxiety lest someone get frostbitten feet, and I walked along the column begging them to take care of their feet.

It was particularly difficult on the crossings where strong winds had blown away the snow, and only icy crests remained which still had to be crossed. We had attached eight-yard-long cables to our mountaineer sledges. The alpinists went ahead, crawling on all fours to hack away the ice, then they pulled up the sledges, drove in a stake, and tied a cable around it so that the sledges would not slide back; then they climbed again, once again hacked out a step, once more drove in a stake, and pulled a cable from one stake to another and proceeded forward again.

Thus we achieved the crossing of the mountains in twenty-six hours, got across the Front line unnoticed by the Germans, and reached the Kokholovka Valley where there was a territory already liberated by Russian troops, and where previously prepared sledges were awaiting us, as I had arranged with the Zakopane commandant.

Here all the wounded men were loaded onto sledges and sent to the Zakopane hospital. The girls and I also went to the hospital. At its gates I thanked the Polish alpinists on behalf of the wounded. The wounded themselves were half-dead from fatigue, and none of them had even enough strength left to move their lips as a sign of gratitude and farewell.

I cannot remember how we entered the hospital or how I got undressed and washed myself. I was laid down somewhere and did not wake up till forty-eight hours later.

Now this is the whole story. Two weeks later I was told about the fate of our cabin. It was as if some instinct had told us that it was time to save ourselves, for one day after we had left the Germans happened upon our cabin and burned it down. Two days later the area was occupied by Soviet troops, and the partisans from our brigade who had joined up with them found only smoldering brands and were horrified at the thought of our fate. It was some time later that they found out we were alive and well, and that this whole story, which had dragged on for more than two months, had finished happily.

December 27–30, 1945

Ilya Ehrenburg

APRIL 27, 1945

It is easy to write now, easier than in October of '41; for if misfortune is silent, joy is not stingy with words. And in our hearts there is great joy—the tragedy of the twentieth century is nearing its end: we are in Berlin!

It started in a small way: the Reichstag burned, set on fire by the Fascists. Now the saga is finishing in the same place—with the fire of Berlin.

Justice marches slowly, its paths are torturous. Years of cruel trials were needed, the ashes of Warsaw, Rotterdam, Smolensk, so that the arsonists would finally come to know retribution.

There is something dull and disgusting to the end of the Third Reich: swaggering inscriptions on walls and white rags of surrender, heart-rending howls of the Gauleiters and servile smiles, werewolves with knives and wolves in sheep's clothing. In vain did the gangsters who recently ruled over almost the whole of Europe call themselves "ministers" or "field marshals;" they remained and will always remain gangsters. They do not think about saving German cities, but only of their own skin: every hour of their lives is paid for by the lives of thousands of their compatriots. But nothing now has the power to delay the dénouement. Hitlerite Germany is disintegrating like a rotten tissue. The Allies are swiftly moving through Bavaria to Berchtesgaden, to the eyrie of the hermit-cannibal. In the meantime the Red Army is annihilating the last armies of Hitler in Saxony and in the streets of Berlin. If Germany is not capitulating, then this is only because there is no one to do the capitulating: the leaders are preoccupied with saving themselves, and the citizens, left to the mercy of fate, are only able to hand over their buildings, or at best their cellar or alleyway.

It is just, legitimate, humane, that it is precisely the Red Army which is subduing Berlin: we began the crushing of Hitlerite Germany and we are finishing it. We began at the Volga, and we finish at the Spree. Perhaps when battles were fought in places unknown to foreigners—in Kastornoye or in Korsun, or in Sinyavino—the world still did not understand what it owed to the Red Army. But now even the blind can see whose feet have marched from the Salskiye Steppes to the Elba, whose hands have smashed Germany's armor.

To the streets of Berlin came soldiers who have been through much. Some had already shed their blood on their native soil; they have risen like Anteus and have come to Berlin. The shadows of the fallen heroes have come with them. Let us remember everything; the heat of the first summer, the clank of the enemy tanks and the creak of the peasant carts. Let us remember the steppes of '42, the bitter odor of wormwood, and the clenched teeth of the defenders. Let us remember the oath of those years: to hold out! We have come to Berlin because staunch Soviet

APRIL 27, 1945

people died but did not surrender when fate tempted them with faint-hearted salvation. The world now sees the shining face of victory, but let the world remember how this victory was born: in Russian blood, on Russian soil.

The Red Army is marching through the streets of Berlin. It is not far now from the Brandenberg Gate and from the "Avenue of Victories." Let us rise for a minute above the events of the hour, let us meditate over the significance of what is happening. Since the time when Berlin had become the capital of a predatory empire not a single foreign soldier had passed through its streets. The reckoning was simple: the Germans fought on foreign land: they constricted the throat of tiny Denmark; they felled Austria-Hungary; then they started the First World War, and having lost it but not having paid for their loss, they began to get ready for the Second. If in Nuremberg, in Weimar, and in Dresden there are old memorials to the genuine greatness of the German spirit, then Berlin is the monument to the arrogance of the Prussian generals.

We are in Berlin: an end to Prussian militarism, an end to robber raids! If all freedom-loving nations can now talk at a long table at San Francisco about international security under conditions of safety, then this is because the Russian infantryman, who had tasted sorrow somewhere at the Don or at Velikiye Luki, has scribbled with charcoal beneath the subdued Valkyrie: "I am in Berlin. Sidorov."

We are in Berlin: an end to Fascism! I remember how many long years ago young cannibals were practicing shooting in the streets around the Alexanderplatz: then they began shooting at obstinate fellow citizens. Then they marched through Prague, through Paris, through Kiev. Now they are shooting off their last cartridges in the same streets. A British journalist writes: "When we were told about German atrocities, we considered this an exaggeration. In Buchenwald and Oradour we understood what the Nazis were capable of . . ." What can be added to this? Yes, perhaps one thing: that Buchenwald and Oradour are miniature models of Maidanek, Treblinka, and Oswiecim. I know that sorrow cannot be measured in figures, and yet I shall cite one figure—the film-producers have filmed a storeroom in Oswiecim: six tons of women's hair, shorn from those tortured to death. The world sees from what fate we have saved the women of all lands, our distant sisters from the Gascogne, from Scotland, and Ohio.

What a terrible chain! Peaceful Berlin was enjoying harmless pastimes: a citizen buying shoes demanded that they should first be inspected with the aid of radioscopy to see whether they fitted him well. Then he went to a restaurant and before swallowing a steak enquired how many calories it contained—four hundred or five hundred. But in a neighboring building specialists were drawing up plans for the ovens of Maidanek, Oswiecim, and Buchenwald. And now there is the dreadful figure: six tons of women's hair . . . What would have happened to the children of the Canadian farmer and the Australian shepherd if Comrade Sidorov had not reached Berlin?

We have never been racists. The leader of our State told the world: the wolf is beaten not because he is grey, but because he ate the sheep. As victors we do not talk about the breed of the wolf. But we talk about the sheep and we shall talk about them: this is longer than life, this is the sorrow of us all.

I would like to recall once more that I have never even thought of low revenge. During the most terrible days when the enemy was trampling our soil I knew that our soldier would not lower himself to reprisals. "We do not dream of vengeance . . . for Soviet people will never become like the Fascists, they will not torture children and torment the wounded. We seek something else; only justice can soften our pain . . . We have decided to annihilate

APRIL 27, 1945

the Fascists; justice demands this . . . If a German soldier will drop his weapon and surrender into captivity we shall not lay a finger on him—he will live. Perhaps a future Germany will reeducate him: will make a toiler and a man out of a dumb killer. Let the German pedagogues think about this. We think of something else: of our land, our toil, our families. We have learned to hate because we know how to love."

When I wrote this the Germans were in Rzhev. I shall repeat it now when we are in Berlin. There was much talk about the keys to this terrible city. We entered it without keys. Or perhaps each soldier had a key in his heart: a great love and a great hatred. It is said of old that victors are magnanimous. If our nation can be reproached for anything it is not for a lack of magnanimity. We do not fight those who are unarmed, we do not take revenge on those who are not submissive. But we remember everything, and our hatred of the executioners of Maidanek, of the hangmen and arsonists, has not cooled down and will not cool down. I shall sooner chop off my hand than write about pardoning the evil-doers who buried children alive in the ground, and I know that this is how all citizens of our Motherland, all honest people of the world, think and feel.

We are in Berlin: to put an end to the darkening of the century, to the darkening of countries, of conscience, of consciousness. Berlin was the symbol of evil, the nest of death, the hothouse of violence. It was from Berlin that the predators raided Guernica, Madrid, and Barcelona. It was from Berlin that the columns came which trampled the gardens of France, mutilated the antiquities of Greece, tormented Norway and Yugoslavia, Poland, and Holland. Coming to Berlin we saved not only our country, we saved culture. If Britain is destined to beget another Shakespeare, if there will be another Delacroix in France, if the dreams of a golden age of the best brains of humanity will come true, then this is because Sidorov is striding now through the streets of Berlin past beerhouses and barracks, past torture chambers, past those workshops where improved hammocks were woven from the hair of the women martyrs.

Listening to the thunder of the guns which fills the streets of our capital every evening, let us remember the silence of an arduous June morning. Even when we were retreating among the burning villages of Byelorussia and the Smolensk region we knew that we shall be in Berlin one day. How much can one talk about this—but perhaps words are not even needed here except one word: Berlin! Berlin! This was the darkest word, and now it is for us the one most beautiful of all: there, among the ruins and fires of the city whence war had come there is born the happiness—of the Motherland, of the child, of the world.

Ilya Ehrenburg

JUNE 16, 1945

France recently commemorated by a day of mourning the anniversary of the destruction of Oradour-sur-Glan. In Czechoslovakia President Benes drove out to the ashen ruins of Lidice. I think about our own Oradours and Lidices: how many are there? If you proceed west from Moscow to Minsk, or south to Poltava, or north to Leningrad, you will see everywhere ruins, ashes, graves, and after removing your cap you will not put it back on again. And everywhere the surviving inhabitants will tell how men swung from the gallows, how mothers attempted to save babes-in-arms from the executioners, how houses with live people in them were burned to the ground.

I don't want to forget anything, memory is not a trinket or ballast, memory is a great gift. If there were no memory, human life would be easy but meaningless. After the First World War Western Europe yearned for one thing: oblivion. This was the epoch of the fox-trot, Paul Morand, and nightingale trills on the shores of Lake Geneva. The Duce was already getting ready for the seizure of Rome. Schlagetter and the German *putschists* had already made an appearance, Krupp and Schneider, Deterding and Zaharov were already calculating how much they could earn on each ton of human flesh, and the people, who yearned to be deceived, exclaimed between dances, "There will be no more war!" No, they said, we shall not allow the voice of the dead to be drowned either by saxophones or by windbag orators. We don't want our children to suffer through another war in twenty years' time.

Not only wicked fairies, but idiot fairies stood at the cradle of Fascism. They wanted to teach good manners to the newborn cannibals. During those years one could see sketched on the walls of Paris a "man with a knife between his teeth," depicting a Communist, for at that time the Russians were considered barbarians thirsting to destroy civilization, while the Fascists were seen as frolicsome but noble youngsters who were simply undergoing growing pains. I recall this not because I have a bad character, but because in order to save the future one must remember the children of Madrid—after them came the children of Paris and London. Horrified, the world press tells about the Oswiecim extermination camp, about the tons of women's hair found there because the Nazis shaved the women before asphyxiating them, and their hair was used to stuff mattresses. But does the world press remember that the road to Oswiecim passed through Munich?

What will our descendants say after reading that the most terrible war, which inflicted tens of millions of deaths on the world, was in the beginning christened by half-Fascist-half-idiots a "strange war"—a "drôle de guerre?" What will our descendants say after reading that these

JUNE 16, 1945

half-Fascist-half-idiots, having survived until victory, declare that this is their victory?

It is not enough to annihilate Fascism on the battlefield, it must be annihilated in the consciousness, in the semi-consciousness, in that underground of the soul which is more terrible than the underground of the wreckers. One cannot wipe out an epidemic by being lenient to microbes. I do not expect years of remorse from the witches, although all witches have already provided themselves with handkerchiefs in the fashion of 1945 and the post-war camouflage. But why do the idiot fairies sob? We don't want the Fascist poison diluted with their tears . . .

The nations look with hope to our country. Peace is only a month old; this long-expected child does not walk or talk yet. The nations ask themselves in alarm; mightn't the careless nursemaids smother the baby in their sleep?

I remember a sentence on a sun-dial: "All things wound, only one kills." If one should inspect the corpse of Fascism one will find many wounds on it—from scratches to serious wounds. But one wound was mortal, and it was dealt to Fascism by the Red Army. In the autumn of 1941 the Germans were at the very gates of Leningrad and Moscow. The witches smirked: "We have always foretold this." As for the idiot fairies, they were blessing Neptune and were trying to find good bomb shelters. Fascism was at its zenith but it turned out to be the beginning of its decline. Two worlds collided: the world of arrogance and the world of human dignity, the world of brigandage and the world of creative labor, the world of Fascism and the world of Socialism.

May the idiot fairies know that a peaceful nation which loves books, compasses, and the globe, saved humanity.

I shall permit myself to quote here an extract from my article, published in 1932 and which has been incorporated, in French, in the book, *Through the Eyes of a Soviet*

ILYA EHRENBURG

Writer (Gallimar, 1934): "When I was in Moscow I received a letter from a Soviet teacher in a small town in the Ural region. This unknown correspondent told me about his doubts and his beliefs. 'By the way,' he wrote, 'ask the French writer Drieux la Rochelle which evil spirit whispers in his ear various absurdities like the following: "That which is life presents absolutely no interest. Consciousness is no longer possible, for there is nothing to be conscious of." Tell him also that in the opinion of his opponent from the distant Urals, human consciousness is only getting ready for the implementation of that great role assigned to it by history; the role of the literate translater of the great language of feelings, consisting of love, hate, courage, daring, readiness to sacrifice, etc., into its own new language, liberating humankind from the fetters of dogma for the new life.'

"I showed this letter to Drieux la Rochelle. This letter contains all that we are rightfully proud of: our profound interest in the destiny of universal human culture. It is not we who destroy coffee plantations, not we who wreck machines. It is not we who melancholically spit at 'that which is life.' Who, then, is going to defend everything that was best in this old world—such things as Balzac, as well as the cathedral of Notre Dame de Paris, and the great joviality of the French people—the Frenchmen of letters, or the Ural teachers?"

History has answered this question. Everybody knows the shameful biography of Drieux la Rochelle. Everybody knows the exploits of the Soviet people.

Some foreign men of letters still call our victory a "miracle." They cannot understand how the Red Army could beat the *Wehrmacht*. For in the beginning the Germans had more military experience and equipment. Some foreigners add: "With this, the Germans had more culture." An old and sad delusion! Among the stokers of Maidanek and Oswiecim there were bibliophiles and nu-

JUNE 16, 1945

mismatists. One may sit behind a wonderful microscope studying the life of the infusoria and be more worthless than an infusorian. One can obtain a scientific degree, acquire a refrigerator and a vacuum cleaner, and remain a savage. Culture is not only technology. Neither is culture an annuity, nor ready formulae, nor rules of good behavior. Culture is an uninterrupted creative process, one cannot live off culture, culture must be created. And in the growth of this new consciousness, new feelings, we turned out to be ahead of the others.

In the summer of 1941 I was astonished by one of the first German diaries. The author, an intellectual, on coming up against the resistance of the Russians, immediately passed from enthusiastic exclamations to melancholy in the spirit of Remarque's novel, to the mournful, eternal "why?" Did the heroes standing to the last man at Leningrad ask "why?" Did the women, old men, and the children of the long-suffering city ask "why?"

The greatness of our nation proved itself at its most brilliant in the years of terrible tribulation: stoutness of heart is not tested by roses, but by iron. The solution to our victory rose out of the suffering of the years 1941 and 1942. There are moments when a person resolves the question of life and death alone in the depth of his own soul. The Germans were advancing rapidly. Our cities were burning. Our divisions were being surrounded. But our people did not lose heart, they did not submit. Everything that had preceded the trials now manifested themselves: the birth of a new world, equal to a shift of geological layers, workers' faculties, and day nurseries on collective farms, the blast furnaces of Kuznetsk, and Shakespeare on the stage of a remote village, and multi-million editions of books. One of the clever Germans, General Dettling, prepared a report during the days of the German victories about the attitude of the Russian population toward the invaders: "The overwhelming majority of the population does not believe in a German victory . . . The youth of both sexes . . . is . . . pro-Soviet-minded. It regards our propaganda with distrust. . . . These young people ask questions which allow one to judge their high mental standard . . . They read the Soviet literature which has survived."

There were teachers and writers, people of the mind and of the heart who had been sowing seeds for a quarter of a century, not knowing whether they would see the fruit. In 1942 the world was amazed at Russia's spiritual strength. This was the fruit of these long years. Should one recall how a radio operator broadcast "Fire at me!"; how, after heaving a sigh, a Red Army man crawled with a grenade under an enemy tank; how young girls died without uttering a word in the torture chambers of the Gestapo? Should one recall the courage of the Home Front, of the workers who saved factories, of the women who worked in the fields in place of their husbands?

One wrote about exploits, that is, about those episodes which arrested attention by their unusualness; then even the exploits became humdrum, for heroism was in the very air itself—it was there to breathe, and it was not noticed.

We are happy that we have not only defended our own home, but we have also defended that sun which shines for everyone. We are happy that we have helped the French to liberate Paris, the British to save London. During the years of the war we felt more acutely that brotherhood which binds people of toil, all friends of freedom. We know what the nations who fell into the claws of the Fascists have experienced, and our soldiers will understand a Frenchman or a Norwegian without spoken words. . . .

Now it is not bright midday, but sunrise. Europe has experienced too much to abandon herself to uproarious joy, there are too many empty seats at the table. And yet

JUNE 16, 1945

a new day is beginning. Paris and Milan, Rotterdam and Athens and Warsaw yearn for renewal. The ship of Lutèce has set sail and all who know the history of France believe that she will reach the new shore.

We have known victory when she marched in our battle formations, and when she warmed herself at the bonfire with our soldiers. Now victory is among our banners on parade. Soon she will enter every home, she will become tangible, warm and close; victory will cut the bread and taste the wine. And then the people will feel the taste of victory, the taste of happiness achieved through suffering.

Konstantin Simonov

LESSONS FOR THE FUTURE
Address at a United Nations Meeting in San Francisco

I have not been in this country for a long time, a whole thirty years—this is exactly as many years as I am old. And when you talk to people once in thirty years, you will always want to say too much, and you do not know where to start.

I would like to talk about our friendship—past, present, and future—for this is, in the end, the most important thing in the world. In Russia we have an Eastern proverb about a bad friend and a good friend. This is what it says: a bad friend is like a shadow, on a sunny day he is always nearby, but on an overcast day you will not find him. A good friend is the opposite: on a sunny day he does not walk behind you, but on an overcast day he is next to you.

KONSTANTIN SIMONOV

Friendship is a broad and loose concept, but I would like to believe that those who have assembled here in this hall are good friends of my country precisely in the sense illustrated by our Eastern proverb. I know that we had friends in America not only during the clear days after Stalingrad, but also during the overcast days before it. At present the weather of the world is not completely overcast, but it is, in any case, fairly gloomy. In such weather good friends are particularly dear.

By the way, an interesting question: what does it mean now to be a friend of Russia, a friend of the Soviet Union? Every person is a patriot of his or her own country. An American is a patriot of America, how can this rule be brought in line with friendship with the Soviet Union these days when all kinds of diplomatic quarrels are floating to the surface, when in the morning papers you most frequently read three bad words about Russia for each good word? Did you ever happen to watch a river on a cold spring day when the wind blows against the current? It raises small waves, sometimes even small whitecaps, and if you look at the river in such weather it will seem to you at first glance that it is not flowing in the direction in which, in fact, it does flow. But the wind is fitful, it springs up and disappears, while the river flows as before the way it always flows.

The things that a considerable part of your press has been writing about us recently reminds me of these small whitecaps caused by the opposing wind. But look more intently—the river still flows under them in the same direction, while the day, although cold and windy, is nevertheless not an autumn day, but a spring day. I believe profoundly in this, for not to believe in this is to think that our friendship-in-arms was in vain, that our soldiers shed their blood in vain on the shores of the Volga and on the shores of Normandy, in the mountains of Sevastopol and on the rocks of Okinawa. It seems to me that there is no

LESSONS FOR THE FUTURE

conflict whatever in being simultaneously an American patriot and a friend of Russia.

Moreover, it seems to me that to be a good American in these difficult times means to be a good friend of the Russian people, and to be a good Russian means to be a good friend of the American people. And even more than that, I would like to put it this way: in these difficult times to be a good friend of Russia, and in Russia to be a good friend of America—means to be a good father to one's children, and even more than that, it is the only possibility of being a good father to one's children, for hostility between the fathers turns into war between the children, and friendship between fathers turns into brotherhood between the children.

Sometimes people say: yes, we, the generation which has experienced the war, do not want and shall not want a new war, but what will our children, the new generation, say: perhaps it will decide differently. This is not correct. The children will not decide differently, if we do not decide differently. Now when you go home from here—ask your five- or six- or ten-year-old children how they look at the possibility of a new war, whether they want it. You will say that it is ridiculous to ask children such a question; and I shall answer yes, of course, it is ridiculous to ask children such a question because their answer, not now, of course, but in fifteen years, will depend on your answer, and only on your answer, the answer of the fathers!

During three weeks of living in America it has fallen to me several times now to address meetings; but wherever and to whatever number of listeners I have been speaking, I have always spoken in exactly the same manner about three things: firstly, about the necessity for friendship between our nations; secondly, about the necessity for friendship between our nations, and; thirdly, about the necessity for friendship between our nations. I shall never tire and shall never cease to repeat this, because this is the most important question in the life of our children and, in the end, the question of the life of mankind.

Meanwhile, I think that far from enough people here in America understand the importance of this problem. And in the first place, this must be said, unfortunately, about many people and about many American journalists. There are different categories of people, and there are different categories of journalists. Freedom of conscience is a fine thing but, unfortunately, some American journalists understand this freedom of conscience as the freedom to not have a conscience. May God be their judge, I do not want to talk about them, nor about their masters.

I would like to talk about another category of journalists, about people who are subjectively honest, but who unfortunately do not always understand their responsibility for their words. In Russia there is a proverb: a word is not a sparrow, it will fly away, and you will not catch it. . . . And how many of these uncaught, rude, unjust, cruel words do fly around the world now by the grace of journalists?

One often objects to my saying that we have freedom of the press; we have no censorship, every person writes all that he or she may think of. All this is possibly very good, and I think that any writer in the world may agree or disagree with the need for censorship in this or in any other time; I think that there is not a single writer who would say that he loves censorship, and I do not constitute an exception in this sense.

But I think that there is a different kind of censorship of which I am an advocate always and everywhere: this is the inner censorship, the censorship by oneself over oneself. And it is this inner censorship which many people often lack here, and consciously and subconsciously cause harm to our friendship, and therefore to our nations.

Recently an American friend who was in Russia a

year ago asked me in alarm: do ordinary Russian people still regard America and the Americans with such an open heart, with such a friendly interest as they did before? I was pleased to reply to him: yes!

Yes, I said, yes, because the majority of these people, fortunately for their feelings and fortunately for our friendship, do not read your papers. And I think that I was right, because a nation which has lost so much, which has suffered so much, which has been so exhausted by the war as the Russian people have, reacts very painfully to ill-will and slander, to a gloating attitude towards its misfortunes.

They often say here that we Russians don't want foreign journalists to write the whole truth about us. This is wrong! I don't know anything in our life that I could be ashamed of, that I would not want and could not show to any of our American friends.

What do certain journalists write about Russia who have been there only a month or two, and who have already managed to establish for themselves a most categoric impression? They write that the majority of Russian families in Moscow live in one room. Is this true? Yes, it is true. They write that people in Russia are badly dressed, that one rarely sees a well-dressed person, that one often sees darned trousers on an adult, and a faded, outsize grown-up's overcoat on a child; is that true? Yes, it is true. They write that in certain villages one seldom meets a man, that cows are used to plough the soil, that whole families live in dugouts because they have no houses; is that true? Yes, it is true!

And we cannot and do not want to be either hurt or annoyed over the fact that journalists write about this. Yes, it is like this, yes, this is the bitter truth! But tell me, why in these books and articles on Russia do I too often discern in the lines and between the lines some malicious joy, incomprehensible to a normal person? What are you rejoicing about, Messrs. White? About families crowding in one room because half of Russia was burnt down by the Germans? Are you rejoicing about this? Why are you rejoicing that children walk around in their mothers' torn and altered overcoats? Because we were not rich enough to simultaneously produce new overcoats and new guns, and we preferred to produce guns? Why are you rejoicing that women have eyes red with weeping, and that you will rarely see a man in a village, because these men fell on the bloodstained streets of every town and city from Stalingrad to Berlin? Why are you rejoicing over this, I ask you? If such misfortunes as have befallen our nation had befallen the American people, we would not be rejoicing, we would be weeping with you. We, the Russian intellectuals. And we would be subjecting those people who would dare to gloat over your misfortune to such a harsh moral judgment that no freedom of the press would help them!

My dear friends! Every nation has a heart, you know that no less than I do, and every nation feels it very painfully if one wounds its heart. We have the same kind of heart that you have, it is not covered with a buffalo hide, and it's not shackled into irons. It feels pain, and above all, the heart of a nation is not a ball with which one can play. Therefore, do not allow anyone to do so, in spite of your freedom of the press, for the heart is easy to wound, but difficult to cure.

I am very pleased to talk with you in this hall, I am pleased that I am in America. After a six month's journey to Japan I returned to Vladivostok and was looking forward to being home within a few days when I suddenly received a telegram saying that the American Association of Editors was inviting me to America. I immediately agreed, although in order to reach America in time for the opening of the editors' congress I had to fly across the whole of Siberia within two days, and had only fourteen

LESSONS FOR THE FUTURE

hours—the time between two flights—left to meet with my family. But I agreed because I did not want to postpone to an indefinite time the meeting with a country which, since my youth, has interested me profoundly and seriously. And, although I am talking here about myself, I talk to you not only about myself but generally about the people of my generation.

The profound interest regarding America has been increasing in our country with every year, and there are several different and sufficiently serious reasons for this. Let us begin with literature. In the region of literature, perhaps our strongest impressions during childhood and adolescence were those which came to us from American literature. At first Mark Twain and Bret Harte, then Jack London, then Longfellow with his Song of Hiawatha, which, during our school years, we all read in Bunin's excellent translation. When we grew a bit older we were carried away by Edgar Allen Poe, and I read Mark Twain all over again, seeing him now from a new, serious side. I think that there is not one person among my generation who has not read from cover to cover the amusing and touching, sad and noble stories of O. Henry. Over the last two decades it was the great, contemporary American literature which influenced us most among all foreign literatures. I would even say that it was in this sense simply without competition. Firstly, Upton Sinclair and Dreiser, whose books were published in our country as complete collections of works. Then Sinclair Lewis, Woodward, Eugene O'Neill, and finally during the last decade Hemingway, who has become the favorite writer of a considerable section of our intelligentsia. It is difficult to find a person among my generation who has not read Hemingway's *A Farewell to Arms*, or Steinbeck's *Grapes of Wrath*.

But America has come to us not only through literature, she came to us through the cinema; our childhood is indissolubly connected with memories of American silent comedies and adventure films. Not everything was clever in them, not everything was artistic, but they breathed joy, health, and energy, and this was close and dear to the people of my generation. When we grew older we were amazed and shaken by Chaplin. He amazed us once and for all, and has remained for us the beloved, the one who reached the greatest peak of film art.

But America became close to the people of my generation not only through her literature and her art, but also through her technology, the talent of her engineers, the sweep of her organizers.

The people of my generation began to build the first Five-Year Plan as youths. We carried on our shoulders the second Five-Year Plan, and began the third when the war made us into soldiers. And we introduced much that was new, much that was our own into both construction and industry. But if one speaks of external industrial-technical influences, then the lion's share of these influences falls to America. Remembering my youth I remember the building that housed the Stalingrad Tractor Works, that same one in whose workshops I had to fight thirteen years later. Then in 1929 we were carried away by American industrial methods, we were good and excited students, and I am pleased to say here now that recollections about the initiation of the Five-Year Plans are connected for me with a profound respect for the technical genius of the American nation from whom—I do not want to make little of it—we learned much—very much.

I am saying all this because I am deeply convinced that the friendship between our nations is founded not on temporary political combinations, but on the profound basis of respect, of understanding and, in many things, of similarity of character. Persistence, independence, ability to work without let-up, ability not to halt in the face of difficulties, respect for the work of others and the opinions of others; I believe that all these qualities are peculiar in equal measure to both our nations.

LESSONS FOR THE FUTURE

And if one should still add to this that genuine democratism, which in everyday life is so peculiar both to the Russian and to the American, the feeling of one's own dignity, the absence of obsequiousness and flattery and the firm feeling that every person can "make himself or herself,"—if one should add this great and important resemblance, then one must say that our nations have more than sufficient reasons for friendship, perhaps the most reasonable and firm friendship in the world.

And permit me, as a writer, to talk about one thing more that joins us—about feelings. Both Russians and Americans—we are people who like to laugh in a full-throated way when we are amused, without being ashamed to weep when we are sad, and are prepared to firmly press a hand when we are grateful. I can remember now how we met a year ago at the Elba, near the small town of Torgau.

I crossed the Elba with an interpreter and met an American tank colonel on the other bank. He was a cheerful, energetic little man with a red scarf around his neck which made him look like a cowboy. He hailed from Kentucky; I think his name was Williams; by the way—both Americans and Russians always scandalously muddle up each other's names, and if I have it wrong then may the colonel forgive me.

In any case, even if I do not remember his surname correctly, I nevertheless remember the man vividly. His first words when we met were, "Listen, let's drive up to Leipzig right away, there's a big camp there of your prisoners-of-war, and they sure want to see someone of their own people fast, so let's go quickly, I'll drive you straight there." He said it so ardently and he was in such a hurry to drive me there that I saw at once what a big, kind heart that man had. He drove the jeep very fast all the way, as if our lives depended upon getting there at once.

I shall not describe the events that passed once we

arrived at the camp. You will understand it yourselves if I tell you that there were 7,000 men there who had been taken prisoner in the first year of the war, none of whom had seen anyone from the homeland for three years. I climbed on a barrel and began to talk to the men. I do not remember whether I talked for a long time or what I said, I even suspect that from the point of view of oratory I did not say anything remarkable; in brief, I don't remember what I said, but the joy of meeting was so great that everybody around listened and wept while I spoke, and I also wept. Then I climbed off the barrel and suddenly remembered that I was an officer, a lieutenant colonel, and that it was somehow embarrassing for me to have such a tear-stained appearance in front of an American colonel, but when I looked at him I saw that he himself was wiping his own tear-stained eyes with his red scarf. As you will easily guess, I did not credit this to my oratory, especially since the colonel did not know a single word of Russian; he was shedding tears simply because, without knowing the language, he understood what was going on within the men's souls, and also because he had a big, kind heart.

Redwoods grow in America, birches grow in Russia, but thank God, kind hearts grow equally in both countries, and it seems to me as a writer that this is a reason for friendship that is not less but may be more important than all logical categories.

I have spoken much here about our common friendship and love; these unite us, but allow me to tell you that it is not only mutual love which unites people, but also common hatred.

On May 9, 1945, I had the personal pleasure of seeing with my own eyes how Field Marshal Keitel came up to the table of the Allied Command and signed the capitulation document of Fascist Germany. But sad as it is to think about this, the capitulation of Fascist Germany is,

LESSONS FOR THE FUTURE

unfortunately, still not the capitulation of Fascism, and I think that the common hatred of Fascism which has forced us together with you, to fight shoulder to shoulder in this war, that this hatred must even now be preserved in the arsenal of our feelings.

Fascism is hatred of mankind.

Fascism is contempt for other nations.

Fascism is the cult of brute force.

Fascism is the destruction of human personality.

Fascism is the ideology, with the help of which one man wants to put his foot on the neck of another man and make this man a slave.

Surely no one thinks that the whole of that ideology has been crossed out on a world scale by a single stroke of a general's pen signing the capitulation document of the German Army. Fascism still lives; it lives in open and in hidden forms, for this is not one of those diseases which is cured simply by the sun and fresh air. And in vain do some people—those who are inclined to let as large a number of repentant and non-repentant Fascists go free—in vain do these people think that these Fascists will be cured of Fascism with the help of the sun and the fresh air. Fascism is not a head cold! Fascism is gangrene. Gangrene is not cured with fresh air, gangrene is fought by means of surgical interference.

During the last years the word "Fascist" was most frequently connected throughout the world with the word "German." But I must tell you that if there is talk about the struggle against Fascism, we Russians have no national bias, and I cannot see why I should love the Spanish Fascist Franco more, or the Greek Fascist Zervos, or the British Fascist Mosley; why should I love them more than the German Fascist Goebbels?

I shall not talk any more on this subject, but I wanted to share my point of view with you on this question.

May 1946